EMILY DICKINSON

EMILY DICKINSON

Monarch of Perception

Domhnall Mitchell

University of Massachusetts Press Amherst

Copyright 2000 by
The University of Massachusetts Press
All rights reserved
Printed in the United States of America
Designed by Kristina Kachele
Printed and bound by Sheridan Books, Inc.
Typeset in Janson Text, display type in Engravers
Roman BT by Graphic Composition, Inc.
ISBN 1-55849-226-7
LC 99-33651

Library of Congress Cataloging-in-Publication Data

Mitchell, Domhnall, 1962–
    Emily Dickinson : monarch of perception / Domhnall
Mitchell.
        p.   cm.
    Includes bibliographical references (p.   ) and index.
    ISBN 1-55849-226-7 (cloth : alk. paper)
    1. Dickinson, Emily, 1830–1886 — Criticism and inter-
pretation. 2. Literature and society — Massachusetts —
Amherst — History — 19th century. 3. Women and literature — United States — History — 19th century. 4. Dickinson, Emily, 1830–1886 — Political and social views.
    5. Manuscripts, American — Massachusetts — Amherst.
    6. Dickinson, Emily, 1830–1886 — Manuscripts. 7. Com-
munity life in literature. I. Title.
PS1541.Z5M58 2000
811'.4 — dc21   99-33651
                                                    CIP

British Library Cataloguing in Publication data are available.

Dó Seosamh agus Caitlín Misteáil
Til Lise Utne og Patrick Mitchell Utne

One should make a sacrament of the mundane.
One should arrange experience in noncausal patterns
that point to no action. At best, one may remain a
monarch of perception, safe in a world one controls,
and insulated from historical process.

—RICHARD OHMANN, *Politics of Letters*

CONTENTS

ACKNOWLEDGMENTS

FIRST versions of this book were written during a year's paid leave spent in Amherst, Massachusetts, from summer 1996 to spring 1997. I am grateful to my employer, the Norwegian University of Science and Technology at Trondheim, for granting my leave and for the additional financial allowances that enabled me to make several research trips to Harvard University, the Boston Public Library, and Brown University. I would like to thank the secretary of the Department of English at NTNU, Aashild Malm, for her administrative support during this period. I am grateful to the staff of the Houghton Reading Room at Harvard University, and to Leslie Morris in particular; Giuseppe Bisaccia, Eugene Zepp, Roberta Zonghi, and the staff at the Galatea Room of the Boston Public Library, Rare Books and Manuscripts Division; Mark Brown at the John Hay Library, Brown University; Jessica Teters and the staff of the Jones Library in Amherst; John Lancaster and the staff of the Special Collections Room of the Frost Library at Amherst College; the staff at the University of Massachusetts Library; Betty Bernhard, Dossie Kissam, Ruth Owen Jones, and the wonderful guides at the Dickinson Homestead.

My wife, Lise Utne, and son, Patrick Mitchell Utne, generously accompanied me to America and made the transition from Norway much easier. Lise kept me well fed, paid bills, organized a new domestic and social environment, and helped me to enjoy Claudia's Café, the Raw Carrot, Nancy Jane's, Antonio's, the Back Bay in Boston, Cape Cod, and Providence, Rhode Island; Patrick decorated walls and learned to walk, an achievement that put everything I tried to do into proper perspective. The few bouts of sanity I experienced during that time were due entirely to their efforts. Stephen Clingman of the Department of English at the University of Massachusetts, Amherst, invited me to spend a year in Amherst and was a conscientious host. David Porter took the trouble of contacting me at an early stage and introducing me to Amherst; conversations with him were a source of inspiration. Peggy O'Brien, who began my interest in Dickinson, offered my family and me the use of her house and car when we first arrived in Amherst; she and Wynn Abranovic did so much in making Lise, Patrick, and me feel at home. So too did Marcy Tanter, her husband, Alex, and their children, Laura and Robyn. Suzanne LeManto and Stephen Frasier drove us regularly to the supermarket after we made the mistake of not purchasing an automobile in America. Claudia Lewis, Zack, and Nadia also generously offered cars, accommodation, and a wonderful parting meal. Stefann Müller and Heike Müller-Sedlaczek regularly drove us to the laundromat, cooked food, and took us on day trips.

A number of friends alerted me to relevant material and read and commented on parts of the book. Jeremy Hawthorne deserves particular credit for drawing my attention to useful articles and writers, and for his constant willingness to read and respond to each chapter of the text in depth and at short notice. I am also indebted to Daniel Lombardo for his humor, intellectual generosity, and his many suggestions, as well as for his and Karen Banta's extraordinary hospitality at their cottage on Cape Cod. Cristanne Miller and Jonathan Morse are thanked for their insights, advice, and criticisms. Cindy Dickinson supplied valuable information and encouragement, a personal guided tour of the Homestead, and a picnic in the Dickinson garden; Greg Farmer showed me around the Evergreens and answered questions about the house. Tim Morris, Martha Nell Smith, and Gary Lee Stonum offered encouragement and criticism at various stages, as did Al Habegger, who read later versions of the text and made many valuable comments. My thanks also to Bruce Wilcox and Pamela Wilkinson of the University of Massachusetts Press for their work with this book.

The author and publisher wish to thank the following for permission to reproduce copyright material. Transcribed letters and poems from the Thomas Wentworth Higginson Collection by courtesy of the Trustees of Boston Public Library. Quotations from photographic reproductions of Emily Dickinson's manuscripts are used by permission of the Houghton Library, Harvard University, © The President and Fellows of Harvard College. Letters are reprinted by permission of the publishers from *The Letters of Emily Dickinson*, edited by Thomas H. Johnson, Cambridge, Mass.: The Belknap Press of Harvard University Press, copyright © 1958, 1986 by the President and Fellows of Harvard College. Poems are reprinted by permission of the publishers and the Trustees of Amherst College from *The Poems of Emily Dickinson*, edited by Thomas H. Johnson, Cambridge, Mass.: The Belknap Press of Harvard University Press, copyright © 1951, 1955, 1979, 1983 by the President and Fellows of Harvard

College; from *The Complete Poems of Emily Dickinson*, edited by Thomas H. Johnson, copyright 1929, 1935 by Martha Dickinson Bianchi; copyright © renewed 1957, 1963 by Mary L. Hampson: Little, Brown and Company, Boston; and from *The Poems of Emily Dickinson*, edited by Ralph W. Franklin, Cambridge, Mass.: The Belknap Press of Harvard University Press, copyright © 1998 by the President and Fellows of Harvard College; copyright 1951, 1955, 1979 by the President and Fellows of Harvard College.

A previous version of chapter one, "The Train, the Father, His Daughter, and Her Poem: A Reading of Emily Dickinson's 'I Like to see it lap the miles,' " appeared in *Emily Dickinson Journal* 7, no. 1 (1998): 1–26, and is used here by permission of Johns Hopkins University Press. A previous version of chapter seven, "Revising the Script: Emily Dickinson's Manuscripts," appeared in *American Literature* 70, no. 4 (1998) and is used here by permission of Duke University Press.

A NOTE ON THE TEXT

QUOTATIONS from Emily Dickinson's poetry, unless otherwise stated, are taken from the three-volume variorum edition of *The Poems of Emily Dickinson* (Cambridge: Harvard University Press, Belknap Press, 1998), edited by Ralph W. Franklin. In all references to the poems, I cite the number assigned by Franklin prefixed with a capital P and a number sign (P#), followed by the variant chosen (A). For the sake of convenience, I have also provided the number assigned to the poem in both Thomas H. Johnson's three-volume edition of *The Poems of Emily Dickinson: Including Variant Readings Critically Compared with All Known Manuscripts* (Cambridge: Harvard University Press, Belknap Press, 1955), and his one-volume *The Complete Poems of Emily Dickinson* (Boston: Little, Brown and Co., 1960), which until now have been the standard editions for Dickinson's works: these citations are prefixed by the capital J and a number sign (J#). References to the letters are from the three-volume *Letters of Emily Dickinson*, edited by Thomas H. Johnson and Theodora Ward (Cambridge: Harvard University Press, Belknap Press, 1958).

Poems quoted in full are accompanied by Franklin's textual notes immediately after the final line. These notes usually indicate the presence of word variants in the manuscript original: for example, immediately after P#320A (J#258), "There's a certain Slant of light / Winter Afternoons," the note "2 Winter] on winter" indicates that Dickinson had written down a variant phrase for the word "Winter" in the second line. In these notes, Franklin also records features such as word, line, and stanza division in the original, as well as cancellations and emendations, in order to reproduce the autograph poem as fully as print will allow. As a matter of procedure, all discussions of the poems are based on a close consideration of as many textual versions as possible, and to that end, wherever possible I have compared Franklin's print editions with photograph facsimiles in his two-volume *Manuscript Books of Emily Dickinson* (Cambridge: Harvard University Press, Belknap Press, 1981), as well as looked at facsimiles of the poems and letters at Amherst College, Harvard University, and the Boston Public Library. (Although they were requested, actual Dickinson manuscripts were not made available to me by either Harvard or Boston Public Library.) In the majority of cases, I am satisfied that Franklin's print translations of Dickinson's handwritten lyrics accurately and splendidly reflect her practices. I am also convinced that Johnson's interpretations of Dickinson's epistolary procedures are much more dependable than has been suggested in recent times.

INTRODUCTION

EMILY DICKINSON was long thought of as a sensitive but historically isolated poet: not only was she a mythic recluse who allegedly published next to nothing in her own lifetime, she also wrote lyrics, commonly viewed as the kind of poems most removed from social and political realities.[1] True to the myth, the makers of Largely Literary T-shirts portray her as a woman squeezed into a room the size of a box, with nothing beyond this blocked-out square of seclusion but blank space: like an advertisement for New Critical poetics, she represents literary genius without external contexts.[2] Although this view has begun to be modified in the 1980s and 1990s, even those who claim that Dickinson was not a private poet tend to re-privatize her writerly practice by concentrating on its cultural, religious, or textual-biographical aspects.[3] One wonders then if the popular image of Emily Dickinson may not exist as a response to a reclusive stance *in her writings:* Is the ahistorical approach a reflex prompted by the way in which her texts were written and transmitted and by the subjects they address? Is there evidence of a poetics of segregation, a quarantining of language from the contamination of social and political actualities, or is this perhaps a side effect of their subsequent presentation in print, where at least some of them are removed from their historical and epistolary contexts? *Emily Dickinson: Monarch of Perception* seeks to answer these questions. For although the poems often do appear to separate themselves from actualities, or to take the possibility of separation as a perspective to write from and on, they employ a vocabulary that inevitably reveals the presence of those actualities as pressures operating within the text and sometimes governing and undermining its premises. This book aims to amend the tendency to privatize Dickinson's literary documents and to look instead at how and why her poetry relates to the social spaces and languages that surrounded it in nineteenth-century Amherst.

For many readers, "The Soul selects her own Society" is the classic formulation of Dickinsonian reclusiveness: it not only describes privacy; it seems to enact it. The speaker records her relation to society only in order to reject it, and the visual appearance of the printed text seems to reinforce that refusal, for what lies outside the poem has been erased: all that remains of any defining context is silent, invisible, blank. It is as if the speaker takes revenge on society by evicting all but a few of its symbolic ambassadors from within the frame of her writing. Nevertheless, the vocabulary she uses has an emphatically social nexus, and even refusal can be thought of as a form of relation, a social stance. The problem is how to recover the historical context that can help us better to appreciate the possible significance of that negation. For instance, in the final line of the poem it is easy to take the word "Stone" for granted: we proceed from the assumption that the definitions we carry with us are sufficient to a proper understanding of the contribution the word makes. But for a nineteenth-century audience, which also included the writer living and working in Amherst, Massachusetts, at that time, what were the social nuances of that closing word? And how, if at all, do those nuances connect with what the speaker tries to keep out *in* the poem and with what the writer may or may not try to exclude *from* it?

The Soul selects her own Society –
Then – shuts the Door –
To her divine Majority –
Present no more –

Unmoved – she notes the Chariots – pausing –
At her low Gate –
Unmoved – an Emperor be kneeling
Opon her Mat –

I've known her – from an ample nation –
Choose One –

Then – close the Valves of her attention –
Like Stone –

3 To] On 4 Present] obtrude 8] On [her] Rush mat 11 Valves] lids –

Division 9 ample | 11 of |
P#409A (J#303)

Even apparently transparent and relatively timeless concepts or words can take on added meanings when placed in their latent historical perspective. Large stones were and continue to be a common feature of the New England landscape and in Dickinson's time slabs were frequently used to cover wells and to seal smoking and drying chambers. The growth of the garden cemetery movement in the 1840s saw the rise of family vaults in many communities, and these were most frequently made of stone. Some towns, including Amherst, also erected town vaults of brick or stone to store bodies during the severest months of winter, when the ground was too hard for burial.[4] In 1826, the Granite Railway in Massachusetts moved eight-ton blocks of granite for the first time from Quincy to Charlestown for the Bunker Hill Monument, which was completed eighteen years and 6,600 tons later. Boston itself, financier Thomas Handasyd Perkins remarked, "would be changed from Brick to Stone as it was from Wood to Brick."[5] Nineteenth-century America was a country still in the process of constructing its legal, political, and social institutions, and it embarked on a massive program of building to house and to represent these institutions symbolically. The United States Capitol was completed in 1826, but then extended and recompleted in 1850–1851: Dickinson visited Washington, where her father was a member of Congress, in April 1854 and February and March 1855.[6] During the same period, Amherst too had its own campaign of creating pragmatic and visually expressive structures: from as early as the 1820s and on, scarcely a year went by without some architectural project for the college being completed and another one begun. In May 1858, for instance, Williston Hall was dedicated on the Amherst campus. On the third floor an art gallery held eighty-five plaster casts of classical and Renaissance statuary.[7] New residences and public edifices were commissioned from necessity but also for the purpose of representing social, cultural, religious, and political values through symbolic space. Amherst and America were gradually fabricating images of their own importance for themselves and for the world.[8] Building projects provided a set of symbolic coordinates by which to measure historical achievement, civic eminence, and future ambition.

In Dickinson's poems and letters, there are occasional records of her responses to such commemorative architecture, as in 1855:

> if you haven't been to the sweet Mount Vernon, then I *will* tell you how on one soft spring day we glided down the Potomac in a painted boat, and jumped upon the shore – how hand in hand we stole along up a tangled pathway till we reached the tomb of General George Washington, how we paused beside it, and no one spoke a word, then hand in hand, walked on again, not less wise or sad for that marble story.[9]

If shrines and monuments are marble stories, what do they say? In this instance, what the tomb says is what it does, how it affects the people who view it. The reverential posture that the Dickinson companions exhibit is a *sociopolitical* response conditioned by the values encoded in and by the monument. Their behavior is exemplary, for bound together in respectful humility, they perform on the personal level the kind of effect which these buildings were meant to have on the political—uniting the viewers in recognizing the heroic grandeur of the founding fathers.[10] The silent pause and the walking hand in hand form part of a display that is both aesthetic and ideological. There is a case for saying that the reference to "Stone" in the closing line of "The Soul selects her own Society" traces the contours of a similar desire for elevation, consequence, and permanence: if the low gate and mat are seen as the surrounding railings and enclosed surface of the grave, then the speaker can be understood as seeking from others in life (and in poetry) the kind of mute deference occasioned by the inscribed gravestone or posthumous commemoration (the emperor is both a suitor and an enforced pilgrim). Such stones were not cheap and they were not within the economic reach of much of the population, however: the form of the speaker's desire for memorializing and perpetuating the self places her in a fairly definite social alignment. In many of the poems, indeed, the expression of excellence takes as its frame of reference the positions and titles of older European political systems, in order to suggest a cultural meritocracy: the terms are the same, and the sense of hierarchy is still seen as necessary, but the definitions are different.

When Dickinson incorporated a poem (P#1636B [J#1620], "Circumference, thou Bride of Awe") in a message sent to the sculptor Daniel

Chester French to commemorate the unveiling of his statue of John Harvard, she focused on the sculpture's capacity to generate wonder and veneration, to persuade the viewer of her or his inadequacy and therefore to reinforce a sense of hierarchy that corresponds to the stratification of classes within society. What the speaker arguably pursues in this poem is a similar monumentalization of the self amid an array of destabilizing factors. Knowing that America and Amherst were also in the process of announcing their own importance, or that the construction of the Dickinson mansion on Main Street involved a similar process of aggrandizement during a period of shifting class definitions and relations, helps the reader to understand some aspects of the poem's search for status and durability. In the light of this information, it is probably a mistake to take literally the speaker's rhetorical identification of herself as "low" (through her association with the gate): it is rather that she is *lower than* an emperor (though her subsequent negation of the emperor is a sleight of hand, which complicates that), but also *higher than* the majority. In this context, the invocation of the stone may be seen as an attempt at fixing the speaker's position along a sliding scale of rank: if the stone is additionally thought of as *precious*, then one detects here an alliance of class privilege and culture, for the speaker's difference is not only or even inherited or externally assigned, it is also an attitude of the mind, an act of attention, an intellectual proclivity.

Dickinson's assignation of primacy to the mind and its choices is a way of distinguishing her speaker from the society around her, but it is also an attitude that united her as a writer with several generations of male Dickinsons. Her grandfather, father, and brother were all lawyers, provincial members of the professional middle classes, whose value resided in their knowledge rather than in what they possessed or manufactured. Like many men in Amherst, they generated capital through their extensive dealings in shares and property, but as justices of the peace (with the honorary title of squire) they also administered and witnessed the legal documents that recorded such dealings. Their value was thus crucially linked with their ability to transfer the authority of their educational and social background onto works of legal currency. The Dickinson women were also involved in this process: Betsy Fay Norcross, Lucretia Gunn Dickinson, Emily Norcross, Emily, Lavinia, and Susan Dickinson all functioned as additional witnesses for such documents, in individual cases sometimes signing away their right of dowry in certain buildings or tracts of land if the deed involved a husband, father, brother, or son.[11] The men additionally possessed considerable economic and political influence, of course, but for their dependents the act of observation was one of the public spheres in which they could exercise power and display authority (the cultivation and preservation of cultural values and knowledge was another). It is interesting that the Old Testament associates stone with witnessing in several places, including Joshua 24. 27. In Exodus, the names of the children of Israel are recorded in stone (Exod. 28. 11). By extension, the process of diminution, which the poem describes and performs, can be understood as acknowledging a limited sociopolitical realm in which exclusion and exclusivity are two sides of the same coin, and where the speaker can only achieve and sustain excellence by protecting the intellectual or spiritual property at her disposal. The writing of the poetry can be seen in this light as a formal declaration of excellence, an identification of culture as a kind of stock, a form of capital. James Guthrie, speaking of a different poem, has interesting things to say in this connection: "A poem was a rock of stability for Dickinson, a perch from which she could assess events in their eternal contexts. Yet being a poet also helped her by giving her an elevated or 'aristocratic' stature, a dignity that helped her to maintain a sense of self."[12]

Of course, the "aristocratic" stature of the poem is already hinted at by the phrase "divine Majority": it is primarily kings and queens who deploy the plural about themselves, the royal "we" instead of the common "I." Guthrie's comments are therefore perceptive, but I am not otherwise persuaded that the only kinds of context for Dickinson's poetry are eternal. Though this is clearly a poem about the relations of renunciation, integrity, and vision, I take issue with the fact that the slow and selective disengagement practiced by the spectral and spectatorial self has always previously been understood in strictly personal, religious, or literary terms. Every act of enclosure has a potentially *political* aspect to it: the poem's preoccupation with *exclusion* (and exclusiveness) may, for instance, be understood as embodying a middle-class anxiety about *intrusion* from, respectively, below and above. The phrase "divine Majority" inevitably echoes and recoils from its secular or democratic equivalent, the masses, while the reference to an "Emperor" rejects the rights of that minority of the population who possess sufficient wealth and power to impose those rights on others (in the shape of laws, appointed representatives, social practices, and institutions). More precisely still, the poem defines the process by which the soul comes to make a choice in terms that simultaneously invoke and revoke the American electoral system. Instead of voting for one man to govern the body politic, the soul chooses "One" to rule the body.

Like the elected representative, an individual appointed to his post by the wishes of a democratic majority, the soul is both one and many: unlike him, it or she is self-appointed. The speaker adopts the literary posture of indifference to the world because the world seeks to appropriate and disfranchise her: in creating the image of the soul, she seeks to fashion herself in such a way that she remains impervious to interference. There is an interesting dynamic at work here, for Dickinson is drawing on an emphatically public and political store of images but converting them into private references; although it is proper to describe this as a kind of denial, it is also important to keep in mind that the two spheres are congruent. In other words, flight from the social sphere is in itself a sign that there are developments within that sphere that require a protective response: even if the trajectory described is from society to self, that emphasis still has a clearly social dimension. In this case, the rejection of external power as it was situated both in the democratic majority and in the president shows that Dickinson was concerned about the increasing significance and extent of that power and its implications for the social field that she inhabited.[13] At a time when the ideology of social mobility was gathering strength, when effort and talent could help one join the ranks of a new meritocracy, Dickinson's speaker goes nowhere, does and says nothing. Or to put it another way, doing and saying nothing is what she has to say. Like the speaker of P#519A (J#441), "This is my Letter to the World," this speaker records the process by which she distinguishes herself from others, rather than the basis of her superiority. Her identity is conferred through this sense of distinction—being select rather than elected. Saying and doing nothing is the guarantee of this distinction, for to reveal information about oneself is to compromise not only the sense of one's difference, but one's social and personal integrity as well.

The speaker's imagery is consistent with a negative reaction to mobility: it is all barriers, closed doors, and gates, the very opposite of a political inclusiveness or egalitarianism. The stone at the end of the poem aligns itself with the past, with tradition, with what has been rather than with what is coming to be: its purpose is to bestow grandeur on the environment of the self, to mark it off as a mysterious and wholly private space. If the name "Soul" is a title, an honor, which the self confers upon itself, part of its effectiveness as a badge of distinction involves its not having to be defined any further: saying what it exists in opposition to reproduces verbally the physical height and weight with which a statue or shrine embodies its distance from, and superiority to, the ranks of the undistinguished. For the speaker of "The Soul selects her own Society," the consolidation of power finds its expression in the right to withdraw and witness, to observe but not to participate, to attract devotion but not to have to return it. This is not a poem about aspiration: it argues from a position of accomplishment, weight, and worth (the soul is a soul already at the beginning of the poem). Nevertheless, although there is privilege in privacy, there is also the recognition of a threat to the boundaries of both the home and the head, domestic and mental interiors, partitions of self and social class.

The vocabulary of this poem links the speaker's and/or the writer's search for exclusivity with similar efforts at the civic and national level, and at the domestic level too. The first four chapters of this book are all concerned with the ways in which Dickinson negotiated with the historical, even when the historical appears to be absent from the writing, or invisible within it only as a set of unspoken assumptions, as the blank and silent space that surrounds the printed poem on the page. These chapters are case studies that attempt to chart the interaction between the writer and a range of institutions, ideologies, and practices represented by the railway, domesticity, and horticulture. The first begins with a poem (P#383A [J#585], "I like to see it lap the Miles") in which there appears to be an almost direct attempt at understanding a contemporary phenomenon, and it is therefore useful to see how Dickinson seeks to naturalize and to displace the sense of danger which technology and the new order of industrial capitalism can be seen as posing to the self. The next two chapters (the book's second and third) deal with Dickinson's ideas of home as a physical place, as a site of refuge, and as a location within culture. Her *real* home was first started by her grandfather in 1813 and built with brick and stone quarried (among other places) in nearby Pelham. Brick houses were generally more expensive than the more common frame houses, and stone as a building material was not widely used for residential construction in the Amherst area (the one notable exception is the so-called Stone House in Belchertown, Massachusetts, built by the Dwight family in the 1820s). Most other houses, including the Dickinson mansion, used stone in limited quantities, for fieldstone foundations, granite steps and walkways, window lintels, and slate roofs.[14] Perhaps more important, nineteenth-century architecture for the middle and upper classes saw an increasing emphasis on closing the home off from the world outside: architecturally, interior space was organized in such a way that, for instance, the hall served as a barrier and intermediate point between public and private spaces and agents, while the house was further divided so that front rooms were used for receiving guests, while the family gathered and worked (or had its work carried out) in the rooms at the rear, at one farther remove from the street. Upstairs bedrooms provided additional privacy *within* the family, and there were gates, hedges, and fences outside. As long as one owned one's own property, the right to privacy was protected by law. But if the home was mortgaged, then that right became compromised. The newspapers in Amherst were full of advertisements for the enforced sale of property which had been seized by local authorities: as a lawyer, Edward Dickinson was sometimes asked to administer the resultant auctions. "The Soul selects her own Society" seems effortlessly to rehearse the speaker's autonomy, but its emphasis on closure and consolidation can be understood as deriving from a perceived *economic* threat to the traditional class privileges that partly underwrite the mask of self-confidence, and as a flight to culture. The poem works to prevent intrusion, fluctuation, and instability and to deny the self's vulnerability, but it also fears those things: stone may seem hard and impenetrable, but as *Webster's Dictionary* would have reminded her, it was also "brittle and fusible."

The sanctity of the home can be haunted by what happens outside it. What happens *inside* the house includes, for Dickinson almost exclusively, the writing of poems and letters and the tending of flowers, and this can be seen as an extension of housekeeping as Marilyn Chambers defines it, "as a kind of autobiographical enterprise—a visible and concrete means of defining and articulating the self."[15] But Dickinson's interest in flowers and her writing about them is to some extent a conditioned one, which is to say that it does not originate entirely from within the sphere of her own consciousness, but is determined in part by the accidents of her gender, education, and class. As a young girl, she studied botany at Amherst Academy. As a woman, arranging and displaying flowers were supposed to be parts of her accomplishments, and having her own stove in the bedroom helped her to produce plants and poems. As a member of a prominent Amherst family, growing and tending flowers was an important way of distinguishing between her own activities and those of the agricultural, capitalist, ethnic, and proletarian cultures around her. Flowers were items of luxury: they were not grown for reasons of utility or profit. Indeed, their vulnerability was part of their attraction for a social class looking for images of its own importance: it was necessary to preserve such beauty, not only literally in the form of herbariums, but also figuratively in the shape of a culture that increasingly promoted the appreciation of the beautiful as a way of distancing itself from adjacent and alien populations. This is a valuable reminder that nature is not some neutral zone that is free of ideological pressures and impulses: horticulture, like culture itself, is a human construct. By using flowers as a thematic device with which to investigate aspects of her poetry as a whole, we can learn a lot, not only about Dickinson but also about the complexity of her engagement with the times in which she lived and about her conception of her *social* roles as a writer. And the more we know about the times she lived in, the better we will be able to understand the range and also the limitations of her achievement.

"The Soul selects her own Society" attempts to keep its own secrets: it is not only an emperor, but the reader as well, who is barred from the interior of this chamber of consciousness. The speaker's identity and motives remain hidden: creative materials become an intellectual property over which the writer attempts to secure an exclusive right of ownership, one based in principle on her position as a member of a privileged class that regarded privacy as a right. It is interesting that the Dickinson property on Main Street had a fence: according to Martha Dickinson Bianchi, the house rules stated that the gates were always to remained locked. The Dickinsons themselves were preoccupied with preserving this distance between themselves and others: in the following quotation, Bianchi provides a gloss both on the poem and on Dickinson's attitudes to publicity (and by extension to the public and to publication):

> Of the three [Dickinson children], Aunt Emily herself would have been the most extreme in her aversion for having her romance a subject of public remark. It would have filled her with horror to have realized the idle curiosity about her and her private affairs, and her will, though unexpressed, emphasized their instinctive reserve. Her uncompromising conviction, that her life was sacred and of no legitimate concern to the public, constrained them; for with her gentleness, sensitiveness, and the shyness so popularly associated with her, went a tacit and coercive will and an unconscious power of personality that imposed its own terms.[16]

The hatred of gossip described by Bianchi on her aunt's behalf is the same hatred of disclosure, exposure, lawful and unlawful entry that we find in the poem. There were reasons for this: the sanctity of the home was under pressure from more than government, social unrest, banks, and individual mortgage-holders. Improvements in the technology of the printing press and in methods of distribution increased the number of newspapers that reported on activities within the town, across the country—and within the household. Domestic fiction emerged as the dominant literary form and reflected a public obsession with events in the home. Dickinson's choice of genre and the private collation and selective distribution of her texts may be understood as a rejection of the published or serialized novel, which was not only *the* social form, but which also brought additional publicity for the writer and speculative attention to the details of her life and that of her family. For any writer, the act of publication necessarily infringed on and compromised privacy by making one's feelings and thoughts the property of others, though of course any form of inscription carries with it the threat of exposure to unauthorized eyes. In the fifth, sixth, and seventh chapters of this book, I attend to some of the various historical contexts that can help us attempt a partial understanding of Dickinson's nonpublication. In these three linked chapters, I argue that Dickinson's attitude to publication was not consistent, a fact that is partly borne out by the diverse ways in which she distributed and even performed her poems. Although only a few poems were published in the conventional sense, many were sent in letters, others were gathered in little booklets discovered only after her death, and still others were recited: my point is that, separately, none of these habits is necessarily paradigmatic for the reading of the poems. In this connection, I examine (in the book's sixth and seventh chapters) related but distinct claims made about Dickinson's private collections of manuscript poems (the fascicles or manuscript miscellanies) as well as about *individual* manuscripts. Beginning with the sixth chapter (the middle of this sequence of three), I look at one of Dickinson's fascicles and test out the thesis that poems placed within a fascicle should be understood as contributing toward an overall structure of meaning, and also toward the narrative that fascicles as a whole enact. In the seventh chapter, I examine the view of current scholarship that Dickinson's manuscripts demonstrate a consistent, conscious manipulation of handwriting as a factor in the construction of meaning: the shape of a letter reflects the significance of the word it is a component of. But by looking closely at details such as line arrangement, word splitting, and the relationship between end words and the right edge of the paper (in both poems and letters), I query these findings and suggest instead that the visual presentation of the poems is less important than has been claimed, and is more likely to be an accidental side effect of an informal and home-based literary production. The cumulative effect of these chapters is to suggest that Dickinson wrote not for one audience but several; that the medium of print itself was not what made her most anxious about publication; and that the fascicles provide us with one paradigm of reading but not necessarily the only one. It is the recovery of a contextual mode of critical intervention sensitive both to biographical details and to contemporaneous ambiguity about women's appearance in public fora that, together with textual evidence from both letters and poems, makes such an interpretation possible.

Filling in the blanks on the page, recovering the cultural, economic, political, and social nuances that provide the supporting matrix for any work of art, is what this book attempts. The eighth chapter takes Bakhtin's allegations of an absence of dialogue in poetry as a methodological framework for a discussion that seeks to summarize my conclusions about Dickinson's relations with other societal discourses. "The Soul selects her own Society" is exemplary in this instance: it may appear to reject specific aspects of social practice but it complies at the personal level with a search for images of grandeur and permanence that was conducted simultaneously at familial, local, and national levels. (Samuel Fowler Dickinson and Edward Dickinson employed some of the same materials and men that were being used in the ongoing process of building Amherst College, while Emily sought to display her taste and proficiency in poetic stanzas). In short, what it represents is not simply a flight from some vaguely articulated threat to some private sphere of the imagination, some monarchy of perception, but also a negotiation between one pattern of belief and another. Any act of exclusion has a clearly social dimension that can be recovered in part through attention to historical particularities, and Dickinson's emphasis on fixity, stasis, and noninvolvement dramatizes a very precise response to social unrest, conflict, and tension at that period. It seems to me that an investigation of Dickinson's greatness as a writer necessarily involves our going beyond the premises of the poem, situating Dickinson in the details of her nineteenth-century background, and attempting to see how those coordinates oppose or converge with her rhetorical strategies and habits of textual production and transmission. For the focus on removal and closure is more than a conservative or reactionary gesture of dismissal: it is a *moving* act of alignment with an embattled way of life, and its verbalization also reinforces the insistence and strength of those external attitudes, actions, and opinions that exist as pressures outside it. No matter how much the poem may actively work to deny external agents and agencies the right to intervene in its affairs, the vocabulary it employs leaves open a space in which the insistent presence of those forces continues to be felt. Dickinson's poem is more than a private act of expression: it speaks to and defends a certain system of values where refinement, culture, and detached contemplation are identified as marks of caste, badges of honor. The poem therefore serves as a complex interface between an urgent and personal formulation of what are essentially social allegiances and priorities (the desire for distinction, permanence, privacy), and other views that were still in the process of defining themselves at that time (the ideas of equality and democracy, mobility, public opportunity, and achievement).

I have said that this is a poem that seeks to define itself in opposition to forces above and below it, but so far most of my attention has been focused on the speaker's efforts to distinguish herself from the common mass of American humanity. Nevertheless, it has to be allowed that the desire for fixity, which the poem appears to express, does not necessarily make the poem itself static. It is always possible, for example, that a nineteenth-century reader would have been alert to other kinds of latent meanings in the final word: Lucy Stone (1818–93), a pioneer in the women's rights movement and a lecturer for the Massachusetts Anti-Slavery Society, was instrumental in organizing conventions on women's rights in the 1850s. Though she married (Henry Blackwell in 1855), she retained her own sur-name as a matter of principle and was known as Mrs. Stone.[17] If such an echo is indeed allowed, then it opens the poem up further, for Stone might have provided a model for a poem in which choosing "One" might be understood as a future option rather than as an action completed in the past. Emperors will be refused (the poem might be construed as saying), but not necessarily every other individual as well. In ideological terms, too, it might be noted that a woman like Dickinson, the disfranchised daughter of a member of the professional middle class whose prosperity depended on the patronage and stability of those around him, may well have felt herself to be just as excluded from sites of economic and political power as the laboring classes, even if she could not bring herself to identify with them in any obvious way. In making a point that might have implica-tions for Dickinson, Paul Foot argues that being an aristocrat gave Shelley a political understanding that was not available to poets with an uncompli-cated relationship to contemporaneous systems of power.[18] Indeed, if one looks closer, one sees in Dickinson's poem a possible alliance between the speaker and the slave, partly because Lucy Stone was an abolitionist but also because the aggregate of references to emperors, chariots, and low gate together might recreate verbally the system of underground passages by which political and religious prisoners as well as captives and slaves entered the Roman Colosseum to be killed in ritual games. In a nineteenth-century America that measured its importance in terms of great imperialist civilizations of the past, Dickinson's speaker seems to find the most appropriate analogue for the complex coordinates of her social position to be African American rather than nativist. However one chooses to interpret this, I hope it is clear by now that recontextualizing Dickinson within a network of missing discourses and practices is not a way of closing down the possibilities of the poem or simplistically recording a reactionary insulation from the economic, political, and social disputes of the historical moment. Instead, one must see that her poetry functions as a kind of antechamber where foreign ambassadors are admitted in order to meet with the lyric representatives of the monarch's consciousness. Even alleged recluses can be shown to have windows, entrances, paths leading to and from other houses. The doors may appear closed, but they are certainly not locked.

CHAPTER ONE

The Train, the Father
His Daughter, and Her Poem

"I like to see it lap the Miles"

There is to me an idea of energy and strength of will connected
with traveling by railroad . . . [You] are ushered into a long cage
full of people, and with a puff from the engine and a shock you are
off, through hill and over valley, as swift as an arrow and in almost
as straight a course. It harmonizes well with the spirit of the age.
— WILLIAM GARDINER HAMMOND, *Remembrance of Amherst*
(1846)

> I like to see it lap the Miles. . . .
> Then – prompter than a Star
> Stop – docile and omnipotent
> At it's own stable door –
> — EMILY DICKINSON

IN 1838 Ralph Waldo Emerson complained testily (to himself in
a journal) about "This invasion of Nature by Trade with its Money,
its Steam, [and] its Railroad, [which] threatens to upset the balance of man,
and establish a new Universal Monarchy more tyrannical than Babylon or
Rome."[1] The association of trains, trade, and profits was an increasingly
obvious one to make in nineteenth-century America, and it was one of the
reasons why members of the economic elite of Amherst, including Edward
Dickinson, the poet's father, were anxious that the town whose interests
they represented should be connected with the railway network then being

developed and with the national market it would eventually make possible. At the middle of the century, Amherst had a small number of established industries and manufacturers, many of which were in decline. The production of palm-leaf hats and "Shaker Hoods," carriages, wagons, and sleds, paper, machinery, metal tools, and textiles gave the town a limited but fairly secure economic base; although industries came and went (and between 1850 and 1870, there were more going than coming),[2] those that remained expanded (Hills Company was America's largest hat factory through the 1870s, for instance). Nevertheless, historian Daniel Lombardo has written that by 1855 "the value of Amherst's manufactures was only slightly above what it had been in 1837" and Amherst's population was not growing at the pace of other (competing) towns in the region.[3]

Amherst, in other words, was static at a time of regional and national growth, and its town leaders decided "to advance Amherst into the prosperous industrial age by placing the town on a major north-south railroad route."[4] Already, two earlier attempts to have the railroad come to Amherst had failed (perhaps as a result of political maneuvering on the part of neighboring towns);[5] but in 1851, House Act 137 of the General Court of Massachusetts incorporated "the Amherst and Belchertown Railroad Company" with Edward Hitchcock (president of Amherst College from 1845 until 1854), Edward Dickinson, Ithamar Conkey (lawyer, county commissioner, judge of the Probate Court of Hampshire County, and representative to the General Court), and Luke Sweetser (a leading merchant, justice of the peace, and a relative and lifelong neighbor of the Dickinsons) named among the trustees. On 6 February 1852, Edward wrote to his son (William) Austin:

You will see by the Editor's glorification in to-day's "Express," that the Am. & Bel. r.road is "a fixed fact." The contract is made—the workingmen will be digging, in "Logtown," next week—& we shall soon see those animating shanties, smoking through an old flour barrel, for a chimney, before many days. The boys fired a few guns—old folks looked on approvingly—and the whole thing seems so much like a dream. . . .
The two great eras of the history of Amherst, are
    1. The founding of the College.
    2. The building of the railroad.
We here "set up our Ebeneezer."
HaHa!!![6]

On 3 May 1853 the first locomotive ran from Palmer to Amherst, followed by the first passenger train on 14 May.[7] On June (at the invitation of luminaries from Amherst), a trainload of enthusiasts came from New London to celebrate the connection between the towns, and a march was held, with Edward Dickinson at its head. His daughter did not participate in all of this but still observed it (appropriately enough, as I hope to demonstrate) from the woods. Here then are some of the coordinates of this chapter: an alleged refugee from nineteenth-century history witnesses the arrival and celebration of the steam engine (built of iron, the raw material of the new industrial order) while situating herself within an oppositional and residual matrix of nature, personal property, and the organic base of much of the local manufacturing economy:

> The New London Day passed off grandly – so all the people said – it was pretty hot and dusty, but nobody cared for that. Father was as usual, Chief Marshall of the day, and went marching around the town with New London at his heels like some old Roman General, upon a Triumph Day. . . . Carriages flew like sparks, hither, and thither and yon, and they all said t'was fine. I spose it was – I sat in Prof Tyler's woods and saw the train move off, and then ran home again for fear someone would see me, or ask me how I did.[8]

The comic tone of this passage, with its bemused description of her father's triumph, is also (it might be thought) the tone of Dickinson's most celebrated poem on trains, P#383A (J#585), "I like to see it lap the Miles." The sense of ironic distance is clearly signposted in the little asides ("so all the people said"; "they all said"; "I spose it was") and in the comparison of Edward Dickinson with an old Roman general, but Dickinson is astute and informed enough to know that the transcontinental progress of the railroad was integral to how Americans generally compared their territorial, industrial, and political expansions to the achievements of great civilizations of the past.[9] It is typical of Dickinson's technique simultaneously to use details that are accurate and alienated; the grandeur and scope of Rome is manipulated (somewhat gently, by her standards) to make relative or deflate Amherst's (and her father's) achievement, but there is nonetheless a sneaking sense of admiration—the reported speech might distance her from what it witnessed, but it also serves to objectify her father's very real significance in the community as a dominant political and civic figure. Finally, there is also the (much commented on) final sentence of the passage quoted, where Dickinson flees before the possibility of exposure to public scrutiny and interrogation. Whatever the psychological implications (and the last words suggest that the poet herself was aware that some aspects of her health and behavior might have been issues for larger discussion), the description neatly encapsulates Dickinson's flight from the potential for publicity, for the increased traffic and commerce (with people, with centers of population, as well as with centers of trade and industry) that the train represents, to the privacy of the imagination.

There is, in my view, a similar dynamic of sight and flight in the following poem, though it is not explicit either as a theme or as a statement: instead the language of the description represents an attempt (however conscious, I do not know) on the part of Dickinson's speaker to neutralize and privatize what the train represents by employing a language drawn from nature and from the writer's own familial mythology.[10]

> I like to see it lap the Miles –
> And lick the Valleys up –
> And stop to feed itself at Tanks –
> And then – prodigious step
>
> Around a Pile of Mountains –
> And supercilious peer
> In Shanties – by the sides of Roads –
> And then a Quarry pare
>
> To fits it's sides
> And crawl between
> Complaining all the while
> In horrid – hooting stanza –
> Then chase itself down Hill –
>
> And neigh like Boanerges –
> Then – prompter than a Star
> Stop – docile and omnipotent
> At it's own stable door –

1 see it] hear it – 9 sides] Ribs – 14 And] And, ˙ then – (*written*, And, or then –) 15 prompter than] punctual as –

Division 3 at |
P#383A (J#585)

There are two main impressions I take from my first reading of the poem. One is the animation of an inanimate object, the assignment of personality and purpose to a mechanical device, and the other is the combined sense of noise, speed, and power, which must have impressed Dickinson and which she (like many before her and since) tries to impart in her writing. The route itself has its own historical and aesthetic fascination, of course, for American railroads differed from British (and Irish) railways; where the latter described a straight line through the landscape—leveling climbs, creating embankments, cutting tunnels and paths, and building bridges— the former proceeded often by curves, which is why Dickinson's train does not go *through* the mountain, but steps *around* it. The reasons for these different modes of construction were less geographic than technical and economic: as Wolfgang Schivelbusch writes, the "the rigid axles of the English rolling stock required a line that was straight as possible [—] English rolling-stock would inevitably derail in the attempt to take a sharp curve."[11] And whereas in Britain, labor was cheap and land expensive, in America the opposite was the case. But labor is not present in the poem: there is no direct reference to the human beings who constructed and helped to maintain the railroad, or to those who work or travel on it. Indeed, the attribution of will to the machine she describes (which feeds itself at water tanks by the tracks) reinforces this feeling of an industry without human labor or freight. There are no drivers, no firemen, no conductors, no passengers, and no stationmasters or porters anywhere to be seen (or heard).[12] And yet they existed. Why then, one might ask, have they disappeared from all but the margins of the poem (where there is a reference to shanties, but not to the laborers who inhabit them)?

A number of possible answers suggest themselves. One potentially radical interpretation is that Dickinson is situating this blindness to the working class not just in the machine but also in the Age of the Machine: it is what the train symbolizes (industrial capitalism) that ignores or undervalues the work of those who carry out its tasks and whose conditions of employment contributed to the enormous profits made by a small percentage of the population at that time. Of course, in *On Literature and Art* Karl Marx himself wrote about the eradication of labor's specific characteristics under capitalism, both for the worker and for the capitalist, and distinguished this from the special work carried out by the guild member and craftsperson.[13] Dickinson's poem can be seen as the poetic equivalent of the Marxist view that art is an ideal site of labor that does not have to be contaminated by capitalist relations and market demands. The poem (especially if it is circulated or published privately) is free in ways in which other kinds of products can never be. Like the speaker of Donne's "Canonization," the speaker of Dickinson's "I like to see it lap the Miles" finds space in stanzas for a form of enterprise that is not compromised or defined by the demands of society, or—in the case of "I like to see it lap the Miles"—by nineteenth-century literary production and consumption. Marx, however, would not set the writer, artist, or craftsperson apart from other workers: he would instead say that creative activity is (or should be) the universal mode of unalienated practical occupation. It is not clear (from this poem at least) that its speaker, or its writer, would subscribe to that position: here, literary competence functions as a kind of class marker, differentiating the "I" from the strata of the industrial machine and minions that he or she describes.

Another approach would be to say that the blindness (or indifference) is located in Dickinson herself, and one can react to this either by saying that critical understanding of her poetry can be advanced little (if at all) by imposing the standards of social (or socialist) realism on her work (or by berating her for not employing a more politically correct poetics herself), or by pointing out that such indifference is consistent with a woman whose recorded opinions on the laboring classes (when they occur) are almost completely in keeping with the opinions of her class and time. In the poem, the engine's supercilious peering at shanties (echoed in Edward's rather patronizing description of the shanties in his letter to Austin) is superseded in turn by the equally aristocratic gaze of the writer who trivializes the squalid and crowded housing conditions of the (mainly immigrant) workers who were the real force that cleared a road for the train to go through. There may well be an *economic* or class-related opposition here between the physical labor of the men laying the tracks and the mental labor of the upper-middle-class poet who records the progress of the crude machine in sophisticated and ludic language (and as a riddle, which the reader must in turn labor to decipher). I also sense an element of competition between the poet and her subject: the sounds made by the train symbolize its physical progress across the landscape but also the achievements and values of nineteenth-century mercantile and industrial society as against the private values and achievements of the poet (who measures the locomotive against a set of aesthetic criteria and finds it wanting).[14] Even the speed of the engine is matched (at the very least) by what David Porter describes as this "satirically breathless" poem: as Charles Anderson records, it is easy to overlook the fact that this is an eighteen line but one sentence text, and that it has only one predication, but seven "ands" and four "thens," which (together with the run-on of lines and enjambment of stanzas) has the cumulative effect of a "breathless chase."[15] And against the type of poetry-speech represented by the train-poet-orator-preacher (which hoots its stanzas to the world), there is the genteel sophistication of a poetry that does not publish its meanings abroad, preferring to circulate them privately—if at all (albeit in correspondence, which was sometimes carried as freight by the very transport she plays with here). Finally, at the end of the poem, there is a marked reduction in the speed of the poem, which matches and contends with that of the engine: the poet literally controls her subject language—especially through the tone of bemused condescension with which she describes the mechanical monster that her father had helped to tame.[16]

Of course Schivelbusch reminds us that, unlike the farmers' wagons, the family carriages, and the stagecoaches, that were to be seen around Amherst at that time and that were propelled by a draft animal or by a team of draft animals, the train appeared to *set itself in motion*. Its workers *were*, his argument continues, for the most part invisible: there were no sweating, straining horses *outside* the engine pulling it—they were *inside* it, present only as ghosts in the machine, as horsepower, as abstract measurements of mechanical superiority. Similarly, the train driver and fireman were concealed within the machine too, rather than (in the driver's case) perched in front or on top of it. Because the engine driver followed visual signals operated by telegraph wire, and the engine was propelled along a predetermined line, he too was a cog in the machine.[17] Michael T. Gilmore (paraphrasing Lukács) writes that in "modern industrial civilization, objects are no longer produced by hand and their link to human labor is concealed. These commodified objects appear to lead an independent existence. In contemplating them, the writer can find no trace of their human origins, and he is compelled to construct a fictive meaning to compensate for the apparent emptiness or muteness of its meanings."[18] It seems to me that Dickinson's creative transformation of the train is governed by precisely this need: she writes about the journey, and about its completion, but not about the beginning, not about how the engine sets off or even how it is made. In a sense, starting the poem with the train already in motion reproduces both its perceived essence (speed, movement) and this sense of "independent existence." But by describing it as an animal, she attempts to give it a *natural* origin (either a birth, or a rebirth). And by reattaching it to nature, she makes it subject to the laws of the natural world, which is governed by God and man. Dickinson's anxiety about the origins and consequences of the industrial machine lead her in the end to seek solace of a kind in the ultimate Judeo-Christian myth of origin: the birth of Christ at the stable in Bethlehem.

I want to postpone further discussion of these issues for the moment by shifting focus back again to the issue of animation, for it seems clear that Dickinson likens the power of the machine to some kind of beast, though exactly which one is difficult to say. Indeed, it is possible that this difficulty represents a degree of indecision or uncertainty on the writer's part: the locomotive appears to be like many animals, rather than one, because Dickinson's attitude to the railroad is not a fixed one. It begins (to my mind at least) like a cat, though subsequent readings might suggest that the verb lap refers not only to the activity by which a cat takes in liquids with its tongue but also to the process of completing parts of a journey (taken together, of course, these actions suggest both mobility and consumption, the identifying characteristics of entrepreneurial capitalism). Nevertheless, the licking, complaining, self-chasing, and superciliousness are all consistent with some of the particular moods and actions that domestic cats are capable of displaying (I speak as one who looked after a colleague's cat for a year).[19] Of course, the horse is (or can be) an equally aristocratic, temperamental, and playful animal: certainly, the phrase "docile and omnipotent" echoes W. B. Adams's 1837 description of the horse as "powerful yet docile."[20] Again, "neigh[ing]" in the final stanza would suggest that the poet is comparing the noise made by the whistle of an approaching locomotive to that made by a horse, and an additional point of correspondence would be the speed of both (the phrase "iron horse" already had currency by the time this poem was written). Though the public image of the train-as-horse carries with it the recognition that one replaced many of the functions of the other (as a carrier of freight, the train undercut the costs of transport by a team of horses by as much as a quarter), Dickinson's poem erases any sense of economic competition by using imagery (in the latter stanzas of the poem) that effectively collapses the differences between them (or in other words, remakes the train in the image of something familiar, alive, and therefore less threatening).[21]

But what is interesting is that Dickinson shifts imagery from a domestic animal she was ambivalent about (no one who liked birds as much as she did could be consistently fond of cats)[22] to one that her family (and, more important perhaps, her father) admired and prized. The shifting terms of the comparison record a similar uncertainty in the poet's attitude to the object she describes and the phenomenon it represents. But the cumulative effect of the comparison (as I interpret it) is to naturalize (and to neutralize) the effects of industrial technology and the opening of the railroad system. One is reminded of J. M. W. Turner's painting *Rain, Steam and Speed*, 1844, the title of which not only describes the painting's subject (a train traveling through rain and over a bridge, itself symbolic) but also defines Turner's artistic and ideological technique of fusing nature and technology: water is a common element in both rain and steam, and the train's speed is a harnessing of the potential within nature. Industrial capitalism is therefore not seen as acting outside and beyond the realm of nature, but as being at some level ultimately subject to the same processes and laws. Similarly, the pace generated by the train in Dickinson's poem, and the slowing down at the end, can be seen as an extension of the speed that is directed and controlled by the rider of a horse: in this context, it is perhaps useful to note that the poet's father, according to George Whicher, "drove the fastest horse in town." According to his granddaughter, Martha, Edward liked horses that were "fleet" (a remark repeated by Cynthia Griffin Wolff in her biography of the poet, where she claims that Edward owned "the sleekest, fastest horses in Hampshire County").[23] It is possible to argue that Dickinson's imagery reflects not only the popular or *public* parallel between the new machine and the domesticated animal, but also a *private* parallel, which asserts Edward Dickinson as the agent of domestication, the man of property whose ownership of fine horses and equestrian skills extended to the sphere of business. Dickinson's father owned shares in the company that operated the Amherst, Belchertown and Palmer route (to the value of 5,400 in 1862) and, as we have already seen, he was instrumental in getting the railroad to come to Amherst in the first place—to a depot [stable] door where (according to the tax returns of 1856 and 1859) he also had property.

Edward Dickinson was known in Amherst for his keen and competitive interest in horses, which he occasionally exhibited at the annual cattle shows:

The exhibition of horses included the entire space of the common and down the Main Street. Deacon Luke Sweetser, Seth Nims, and Emily's father, Squire Dickinson, were invariably owners of fine horses, and they drove about on these occasions sitting very straight in the backless open buggies, reins taut, and the high showy heads of their steeds refusing the senseless check. . . . [24]

According to the records kept in the secretary's book of the East Hampshire Agricultural Society (vol. 1, 1850—81), there were prizes for horses at shows from 1850 to 1856, although Edward's name is not mentioned among the winners.[25] It seems possible that the competition was not open to the kinds of horses he kept until sometime after 1856, when the following note appears among the minutes of the annual meeting for that year: "It is the duty of an Agricultural Society, to encourage horses, adapted to farm, or agricultural uses. But it has been suggested, that, if the funds of the Society will admit, premiums might well be offered, in future, on carriage horses."[26]

Carriage horses are mentioned in connection with competition at the eighth annual cattle show of 1858, which took place on 12–13 October, though the list of prize winners in the equestrian categories (published in the *Hampshire and Franklin Express*), does not include Edward's name. That the Dickinsons were known as good judges of fine horses, however, is attested to by Austin's election as chairman of the judging panel on carriage horses in 1862 (the conjectured year of composition for "I like to see it lap the Miles," and the year Edward was awarded next best premium in the—separate—category of single carriage horses),[27] and Edward's election as chairman in 1863, and again in 1867, as well as his being a committee member in 1866. Austin was a member of the committee on equestrianism in both 1863 and 1864 (and, according to his daughter, "liked to drive down the Main Street from his law office with his horse going at racing speed . . . and never slackening the pace till the flaring nostrils of the proud animal hit the carriage house door").[28] Dickinson interest in such animals proceeds not from necessity (the passage quoted from the agricultural society records acknowledges differing standards of usefulness and excellence) but derives from a culture of luxury where horses are gracious but explicit symbols of status, leisure, and success.[29] (According to Adam Smith, the upkeep of a horse was equal to the cost of feeding eight laborers.)[30]

Indeed, the horse is something of a private symbol of power (or its loss) for the Dickinsons: the Amherst historian William Tyler reported that when Amherst College was being built, Samuel Fowler Dickinson's increasing financial problems were reflected in the fact that "when there was no money to pay for the teams to draw the brick or men to drive them, his own horses were sent for days and weeks till in one season two or three of them fell by the wayside. Sometimes his own laborers were sent to drive his horses, and in an emergency he went himself. . . ."[31] This was in the first half of the nineteenth century: toward the end of the second half, Susan Gilbert Dickinson (by then probably aware of her husband Austin's adulterous affair with Mabel Loomis Todd) wrote to her son about another scene involving the family horse and a male Dickinson, but this time a more problematic one.

> I was roused about half past four this morning by very strange sounds – wild snortings & hufflings and rushing to the window I saw Tom tearing over the grounds as fine a picture of the Scripture warhorse as I ever expect to see. Papa made one of his hasty toilets and joined Stephen who had already begun pursuit. They both approached him with *honeyed words* but Tom knew the situation, and lifted himself in superb disdain, making bolder plunges and swifter circuits of the Mansion till Papa [waved?] a pitchfork and he was obliged to make an ignoble retreat to the barn, and be led back to his stable where there was no beautiful morning for him to sniff. I shall never forget the picture – the moon just over the elms with one star fainting in its light – the east pink with dawn – everything a little dim and shadowy, and fresh and dewy as only early morning can be, and that great splendid animal exulting in it all, *swishing* through the wet grass with head aloft, blowing and triumphing in his freedom. For a moment it seemed enough to be Tom.[32]

I quote the passage in full partly because it illustrates Susan's own skill as a writer, partly because many of the details of her description are circumstantially similar to Emily Dickinson's poem (the strange noises; the runaway horse moving in circles within a confined space; the attempted use of language to control and domesticate a potentially dangerous animal; the barn and stable as sites of dominion; the shift of focus from the earthly to the celestial), and partly because it reveals the privatization of a natural experience. Susan's manipulation of this event is, of course, the reverse of the poet's: one identifies with the escaped animal ("I am sorry to say," Susan continued, "that he did no harm"), the other with the attempt to master it. Horses, in short, are screens onto which a variety of Dickinsons project anxiety, exasperation, or triumph.

By imagining the train as a horse Emily Dickinson attempts to define the new technology as an extension of her family property and as continuing evidence of her family's prestige in the social landscape of her town: Austin, it was said, could (normally) calm a nervous horse with just the sound of his voice, but Edward's powers of oratory could perform acts of even greater mastery, persuading the railroad to stop at Amherst when there seemed no sound economic reasons (outside of Amherst) to do so. Just as the horse returns to the resting place assigned to it by its owners, the train returns to the resting point assigned to it by the economic elite of Amherst society, and in particular by the poet's father. Indeed, it is surely possible to argue that the poet herself attempts to assert power over the train, not only by attempting to play with it in language, but by situating herself (or her speaker) off rather than on it, and watching from a nonmoving vantage point while it travels through the countryside. Her *linguistic* immobility is the equivalent of the *geographic* and *economic* immobility of her father and brother: in the end, the railroad came to them (to Amherst and to the imagistic spaces reserved for it by Emily), rather than they to it. In a sense, this reverses Emerson's demand that the "poet, by an ulterior intellectual perception, gives [symbols] a power which makes their old use forgotten, and puts eyes and a tongue into every dumb and inanimate object."[33] Dickinson sees through the new (train) to the old (horse), and however much she assigns it eyes and a tongue, it produces sounds rather than speech acts, and it becomes "dumb and inanimate" at the close of the poem.

For the Dickinsons especially, and for the people of Amherst generally, the announcement in the *Hampshire and Franklin Express* of 6 February 1852, that the stock of the Amherst and Belchertown Railroad had been fully subscribed, was an event that carried with it a certain amount of civic pride:

> Since we have written you, the grand Rail Road decision is made, and there is great rejoicing throughout this town and the neighbouring; that is Sunderland, Montague, and Belchertown. Every body is wide awake, every thing is stirring, the streets are full of people talking cheerily, and you really should be here to partake of the jubilee. The event was celebrated by D. Warner, and cannon; and the silent satisfaction in the hearts of all is it's crowning attestation.
>
> Father is realy *sober* from excessive satisfaction, and bears his honors with a most becoming air. Nobody *believes* it yet, it seems almost like a fairy tale, a most *miraculous* event in the lives of us all. The men begin working next week, only think of it Austin; why I verily believe we shall fall down and worship the first "Son of Erin" that comes, and the first sod he turns will be preserved as an emblem of the struggles of

our heroic fathers. Such old fellows as Col' Smith *and his wife*, fold their arms complacently, and say, "well, I declare, we have got it after all" – *got it*, you good for nothings! and so we *have*, in spite of sneers and pities, and insults from all around; and we will *keep* it too, in spite of earth and heaven! How I wish you were here. . . . [34]

Dickinson had good reason to be smug: as her last paragraph evinces, there was intense and even bitter competition for the railroad from other towns. Such rivalry was founded on the fear that, with the demise of the canal system and the opening of a network of iron linking provincial satellites to large urban markets, failure to be connected with this network would mean a slow slide into extinction. At the May 1851 session of the General Court of Massachusetts, three corporations (including the Amherst and Belchertown one) were chartered, with the proviso that no section of a proposed route could be started "until its due portion of the capital had been subscribed, and 20 per cent thereof paid in."[35] Intense lobbying followed, with Amherst even starting up a newspaper to promote the railroad extension. Although outside support (in the shape of goodwill and financial guarantees) was necessary, nevertheless a large proportion of the stocks was raised by the citizens of Amherst themselves, which is ultimately why their proposal was successful. The happy complacency of Dickinson's letter to Austin emerges from this newly acquired sense of economic self-confidence and promise, which was then grafted on to the town's sense of its own traditional importance—which, however jokingly, is still conveyed by the reference to the heroic fathers and to the old couple. Edward too mentioned the approval of "old folks" in his correspondence with Austin. Behind the mask of irony and the spontaneous delight, there is the self-congratulatory posture of a member of the provincial elite whose social status (it would seem) has just been renewed for at least another decade. Dickinson can even afford to be playful about the "Son of Erin" who would perform the labor of preparing a path for the train to go through (the phrase "Sons of Erin" is used regularly by the *Hampshire and Franklin Express* and is almost always negative or patronizing). Nevertheless, the ironic reversal of social positions that the squire's daughter here imagines *in her letter* reflects the historical destabilization of relationships between the established land-owning families and the working classes. *The poem*, by contrast, seeks to erase elements of conflict, as I have said, by making railroad workers invisible.

For the rest of the 1850s, Dickinson seems to have maintained this posi-

tive attitude to the train: in another letter dating from this time, it is almost as if the railway had become a kind of dialysis machine, signaling
new hope for the future: "While I write, the whistle is playing, and the
cars just coming in. It gives us all new life, every time it plays. How you
will love to hear it when you come home again!"[36] The convergence of
the moment of writing with the arrival of the train may be accidental, but
it is apt, for the letter Dickinson writes to Austin will be eventually carried
to him by this same train. In addition, the noise of the whistle symbolizes
the potential of her brother's return journey, and it therefore has a private
or personal significance for the poet that converges with the train's strictly
economic function as a carrier of freight. The increased market attrac-
tiveness betokened by the daily and regular arrival and departure of the
train signifies the hope of prosperity for the town and thus the prospect
that Austin's return will one day be permanent.

In another letter dating from this same period, Dickinson again refers
to the train, and reports: "Everybody seems pleased at the change in arrangement. It sounds so pleasantly to hear them come in twice. I hope
there will be a bell soon."[37] The note of buoyancy is again linked to the
increased volume of traffic between Amherst and Palmer, another signal
of economic improvement and ambition. At times like these, the poet's
mood seems to illustrate Marx's most famous, and most abused, remarks
in the 1859 Preface to *A Contribution to the Critique of Political Economy* that
it "is not the consciousness of men that determines their being, but, on the
contrary, their social being that determines their consciousness,"[38] though
there is just a hint that familiarity has provided her with sufficient distance
to recognize (as she does in the poem) that technological progress is not
always compatible with literary standards of excellence.

It might seem strange that a poet whose letters often express opposition
to the city appears to be so enthusiastic about the new "machinery of motion." Although there are nuances of ambivalence, I suspect that the answer lies partly in Dickinson's education (the best available to a young
woman of her class at that time) and its emphasis on science, and partly
on the historical accident of the poet's father being largely responsible
for the coming of the railroad to Amherst (when subsequent experience
suggested that there was little benefit of its being there). Rev. Elias Nason
observed in his 1874 *Gazetteer of the State of Massachusetts* that railway "cars
were not unlike several stage-coach bodies set together on a platform,"[39]
and although Noah Webster wrote that "the track of a railway cannot be

a road upon which every man may drive his own carriage," "I like to see it lap the Miles" suggests that, if this were the case, then Edward Dickinson was no ordinary man.[40] It is worth pointing out that the railway station in Amherst was (and is) situated just off Main Street, and thus not very far from the Dickinson estate (with its barn for storing the family horse[s] and carriage[s], one of which was described by Martha Dickinson Bianchi as the "Pompous family cabriolet, lined with cream color broadcloth, with high doors and oval windows at the sides and back").[41] There is a sense, in the poem, that the depot becomes figured as an extension of that property.[42] The reference to the stable door in the last line may therefore do more than reinforce the likeness between the train and the horse; it may give further force to the idea that the former is simply a newer version of the family carriage belonging to the "Squire" (as Edward was known). The proximity of barn and railway station is not only geographical but economic: both are owned by the father. And that must have appeared to have been almost literally the case in that year: on 17 February, the *Springfield Daily Republican* reported that "Edward Dickinson was re-elected President of the Amherst, Belchertown and Palmer railroad for the current year" and on 12 December the *Hampshire and Franklin Express* included the following notice: "The 'Old Amherst,' has emerged from the Machine Shop with a new face and new name, 'The Edward Dickinson'. The A. B. & P. R. R. have had a successful business season, and we believe is making money."[43]

The final line of "I like to see it lap the Miles," with its reference to stopping at "it's own stable door," may allude to the train named after her father (or to one of his horses, or to his control over the environment in which he lived, or to her brother's horse, or to all or none of these things), but it does surely reflect how the poet's father was synonymous with the railroad in Amherst. Indeed, when he died, it was after being taken ill during a "debate on a bill to appropriate $3,000,000 to finish the Troy & Greenfield railroad to the [Hoosac] tunnel," which would connect Amherst with the Massachusetts Central Railroad and, through it, with New York and the West.[44] In 1871, three years before this, Edward's daughter reported to her cousin Louise on his apparent recovery from illness, using imagery that links his single-mindedness and relentless pursuit of public goals and the impoverishment of his private life with the train: "You know he never played, and the straightest engine has its leaning hour."[45]

By 1862, however, the truth was slightly more complex than either the

Republican or the *Express* suggests. That Edward had managed to bring the railroad almost as far as his stable door was "a personal triumph," but a "financial failure" for Amherst as a community:

> The railroad cost about $290,000, practically all coming from local sources. A losing venture from the beginning, a reorganization of the road became necessary in 1857. Those who invested $195,000 in the stock of the company lost all, and the fate of the bond holders was little better. The building of the railroad was made possible by a tremendous civic effort, but its chief results were to redistribute the wealth of the community and to siphon into an unproductive venture local capital which might otherwise have been available for sounder investments.[46]

The directors' report for the year ending 1 December 1855 informed the stockholders of the Amherst and Belchertown Railroad Company that the corporation was $90,057 in debt. Edward Dickinson's name is on the report as one of the directors, but he seems not to have incurred the kind of personal debts which had led to his father's bankruptcy. In fact, it was Amherst College that lost on its investment in the railroad: it "had invested some $13,000 in the project [partly on Edward's recommendation], for which it ultimately recovered $9,640."[47] Although many of Edward's financial records were destroyed in a fire, his tax records show that in 1855 his twenty shares in the railroad were worth a total of 400 (the equivalent of his declared yearly income as a professional lawyer), but were valued at 6,480 in 1859 and at 5,400 in 1862 (the year the poem was written).[48] Shares in the Sunderland railroad bridge were worth another 1,900 in the same year. Perhaps Edward was simply lucky, but his daughter's poem (as R. E. Lowrey has proposed) suggests that she thought his success was due to his skills as an entrepreneur.[49]

Over the next several years, the Amherst and Palmer Railroad Company ran into financial problems and reorganized several times (in 1858 and 1864), so that by 1886, the year of the poet's death, it had become the New London and Northern Railroad (later the New London and Northern Division of the Central Vermont Railroad). But the "completion of just the Palmer-Amherst section of the railroad connected the town with Boston, Albany, Worcester, and Springfield (at Palmer), Hartford and Bristol (at Willimantic), Worcester and Boston (at Norwich), and New Haven and New York (at New London)."[50] In other words (as several of Dickinson's letters record), travel to and from Amherst was made quicker and cheaper—but that combination enabled people other than just her brother to come visiting more often:

> The cars continue thriving – a good many passengers seem to arrive from somewhere, tho' nobody knows from where – Father expects his new Buggy to come by the cars, every day now, and that will help a little – I expect all our Grandfathers and all their country cousins will come here to pass Commencement, and dont doubt the stock will rise several percent that week. If we children and Sue could obtain board for the week in some "vast wilderness," I think we should have good times. Our house is crowded daily with the members of this world, the high and the low, the bond and the free, the "poor in this world's goods," and "the almighty dollar,["] and "what in the world are they after" continues to be unknown – But I hope they will pass away, as insects on vegetation, and let us reap together in golden harvest time. . . . [51]

Until now, I have argued that Dickinson's response to the railroad was, for the most part, positive—at least in the sense that it brought merit to the family and confirmed her father's status in the community. The tensions apparent in the 1853 letter to Austin about the parade led by her father, however, and in the passage quoted above, taken from an 1853 letter (again to Austin), are also the tensions implicit in the imagery of the poem, with its move from the noisy cat to the horse made pliant and dumb on reaching the familiar territory of home. Here, the equanimity of Edward's immediate family is seen as being incompatible with the needs of the railroad company over which he presided: the invasion of privacy is counterbalanced (ironically) by the increase in the value of the shares. Suddenly, the worth of a visit (which could often be disruptive and long, but which was much harder to accomplish before the advent of steam) is calculated according to volume of freight, and home is invaded not only by more guests but by the marketplace. The result is an interesting reversal: since Amherst has begun to take on some of the features of the industrial metropolis, the Boston that Emily would again describe in L#293 (July 1864) as a "wilderness" is here imagined as a haven where she, Lavinia, and Susan can find the anonymity and refuge formerly associated with home. What we see here, I would argue, is that the intensification of social mobility made possible by the railroad threatens *and* strengthens the internal coherence of a worldview that had remained fairly stable since childhood: the rural retreat that was home becomes (in this letter at least) a microcosm of urban America and its class divisions, but this produces an opposite reaction, a flight to an agrarian home *of the imagination*. What accompanies this is a fairly standard questioning of the search for wealth, albeit in language that is simultaneously pastoral, scriptural, and bourgeois (the Dickinsons often express their contempt for the things of this world, but they do so from a position of inherited wealth and property, which—however unstable at times—underwrites the figurative, but ideologically saturated, vocabulary of golden harvests and ephemeral insects).

Although Dickinson is surely communicating her hope that the visit(s) will be short (or that they will become less frequent as time progresses), her imagery also acknowledges the larger changes brought about by the railroad, among them the increase in traffic to and from the town of Amherst. In her letter, both the visit and its antidote, flight, are facilitated by what Schivelbusch describes as the "annihilation of space and time," which was a characteristic of the railroad. Suddenly, people (and not just relatives) were much closer to each other (in terms of physical geography) than before, and the result is an alteration in spatial and social relations: "country cousins" are nearer to their (presumably superior) relatives in Amherst, and provincial Amherst in turn comes closer to Boston. Isolation (from other people, other places, other levels of society), which had preserved the coherence of a local identity, was gradually being eroded. New England was becoming a smaller place. There were direct connections with major points of commerce and trade, including Boston and New London, then the two most important ports of arrival for Irish immigrants. The population of Amherst had remained static not only in terms of numbers but in terms of ethnicity during the first half of the nineteenth century: the railroad changed that (though not dramatically). There were other consequences too:

> Railroads created a vastly enlarged and more complex market in which goods made in New England could be sold throughout the United States but had to compete with products from other parts of the country. Since they were protected from outside competition by slow and expensive transportation, producers in the past had been largely restricted to a noncompetitive local market, but now both protection and restrictions were lifted except for bulky or perishable goods. Cheap transportation meant each place and each producer could com-

pete with all the rest. [But] an enlarged market also allowed manufacturers to expand and to operate firms with many, sometimes several hundred, employees.[52]

The result was that, for example, the Hills Company Straw Goods Manufactory and the H. D. Fearing & Company Straw Goods Manufactury increased their workforce, so that by 1880 (the year of a massive fire when both these wooden structures burnt to the ground) there were over 200 persons working there (mainly women). These workers and transport vehicles (carrying supplies to and from the factories and the railway station) went past Dickinson's window six days a week (and the workers may have been the subject of the poet's shocked and shocking remarks to Higginson about people in the street who "live without thought").[53] The human traffic on Main Street also included passengers on the stagecoach to Northampton, Belchertown, Palmer, and Boston, as well as guests coming to or going from the Union Hotel farther down the street (or to Amherst House, at the corner of Amity Street and Pleasant Street), local inhabitants on their way to or from the First National Bank or to the store beside it, and students of Amherst College who lodged in the vicinity of Main Street (an average of around 300 students were in the town when the college was in session).[54] In addition, there would have been the blast of steam whistles sounding from the factories at 6:00, 6:50, and 7:00 in the morning, again at noon (a time Dickinson strips almost completely of its social specificity in her poems), 12:50, and finally at 5:00.[55] In an era when time was capital, and therefore regulated by strict schedules (though the Amherst railway was the butt of much newspaper humor because of its allegedly poor time-keeping),[56] Dickinson's train represents a potential conflict between new time and old time, between time as an instrument of production and the universal, essential law of the "Star."

One of the points to be made here is that if the Industrial Age is not present in the poetry of Emily Dickinson, it is because she has chosen not to include it, and not because it had not yet come to Amherst at the time she was writing. Jonathan Arac, for example, writes that a weakness in Walter Benjamin's identification of the urban qualities of Charles Baudelaire's poetry is that the "insights about Baudelaire [could be transferred] quite directly to the poetry of Emily Dickinson." "For she lacked wholly," he adds, "the urban experience so fundamental to Benjamin's argument about Baudelaire." And he continues: "Indeed, the worlds of the poets, both biographical and imaginative, seem wholly different: against the city and its crowds, the isolation, the provinciality, the sheer availability of nature; against the satanic debaucheries, the ascetic renunciations."[57]

Arac's point (in a short but brilliant account of the poet's protomodernism) is well taken, but as the excerpt from Dickinson's letter to Austin surely demonstrates, the poet *was* exposed to crowds (and knew enough about herself to avoid them)—not only in Amherst (on occasions such as New London Day, or College Commencement Day, or the East Hampshire Agricultural Show, or on the day the news of the railroad first broke, when "the streets [were] full of people talking," or between six and seven on weekday mornings) but in Washington (which she visited for three weeks in February 1855), Philadelphia (where she spent two weeks, also in 1855), New York (passed through during the same trip), and Boston (in 1844, 1846, 1851, and later from April to November in both 1864 and 1865, when she went for treatment to her eyes, by train on each occasion, at a time when the population would have been over 175,000).[58] Arac's use of the phrase "satanic debaucheries" echoes Blake's celebrated lines about the "dark Satanic mills," but again it has to be said that Dickinson knew about those too: in a photograph of the meadow in front of the Dickinson house on Main Street (and reprinted both in Sewall's biography and in Polly Longsworth's *The World of Emily Dickinson*), at least one of these factories can clearly be seen in the background (both were situated around the area of the railway depot, between Dickinson Street, College Street, and Railroad Street). Two maps of Amherst brought to my attention by Daniel Lombardo make it seem probable that from her bedroom Dickinson would have had an unobstructed view of these buildings from 1873 at the latest (though at least one was already built in 1863). The first of these maps, from *Beer's Atlas* of 1863, suggests that both would have been visible, while the second (published by L. R. Burleigh of Troy, New York) shows both factories as well as a number of smoking chimneys, which she could not have avoided noticing (even if she could avoid writing about them). In addition, there was another chimney attached to the L. E. Dickinson Planing Mill and Box Factory located at the intersection of Whitney Street and College Street, which the poet could probably not have seen directly, but whose smoke she almost certainly would have.[59]

Amherst was in fact bordered by mills (powered by water) in two directions: on the north side was Factory Hollow, and on the south Mill Valley, and the largest of these had brick chimneys (the textile mills as needed heat to bleach cotton; otherwise, the chimneys were a sign that wood and coal were the main means of keeping warm, even in factories).[60] In addition, during the early period of the urban-industrial transformation in Massachusetts, from about 1850 to 1875, the town of Holyoke (some fifteen miles from Amherst, but visible directly to the poet only from the Holyoke Range, which run from east to west on Amherst's south side) grew rapidly into an industrial site that attracted large numbers of immigrants who lived and worked in conditions that facilitated the spread of infectious disease: the death rate from typhoid fever for Holyoke for 1871–75 was the highest of all the Massachusetts cities.[61] The housing density was 10.5 persons per dwelling unit, though this increased to 14 in some of the tenements occupied by Irish and French Canadian laborers and their dependents (these figures were the third highest in the United States). A contemporary writer noted that "such was the hell-hole that industrial development created in the open countryside where twenty-five years before cattle had browsed."[62]

The writer's comment effectively opposes the urban-industrial transformation of the landscape and its accompanying demographic changes with a nostalgic vision of empty fields and grazing cows, a modern inferno with a lost rural order. Dickinson's poem attempts to reconcile these opposites by recruiting the train not as an agent of change but as a welcome confirmation of social stasis: the new machine may be powerful and strange, but it is also pliant and familiar. According to historian Rowland Berthoff (as he is paraphrased by Robert Doherty), "nineteenth-century America is best understood as embodying a struggle to maintain stability in the face of overpowering forces of instability,"[63] and it seems to me that this was what Dickinson is attempting to do in her poem. "I like to see it lap the Miles" shows her moving away (on the one hand) from the uncertainties of capital investment and the changing values of shares, stocks, and bonds (and the subsequent insecurity of social status) and (on the other hand) from the realities of immigration, industrial relations, unsatisfactory wages, and unsafe working conditions, all issues that were very much connected with the building of the railroad. These are displaced by a privatized and pastoral discourse of expensive and temperamental animals and their aristocratic owners:

And neigh like Boanerges –
Then – prompter than a Star
Stop – docile and omnipotent
At it's own stable door –

I mentioned a perceived opposition in this last stanza between industrial time and universal time and argued that the reference to the star would suggest a conception of time at odds with the regulated schedules of both the factories and the railroad companies. Dickinson's appeal to the star is crucial because, as Arac writes, "the stars, and the sun and moon, have been for almost all of human history the measure of time and therefore incapable themselves of being timed."[64] But when Arac goes on to argue that the word "punctual," which accompanies the reference to the star, suggests a post-Newtonian consciousness, he is basing his comments on Thomas Johnson's edited version of the poem (J#585) and not on Franklin's edition of the manuscript poems or indeed on Johnson's three-volume variorum, where "punctual as" is listed as a variant for "prompter than." The difference is small but important: the alternative phrase (which Johnson, not Dickinson, chooses) confirms that—despite its apparent novelty—the machine obeys the same laws that can be observed in the (stable) motions of the star, while Dickinson's own first choice dramatizes a potential conflict between post- and preindustrial time, between (as it were) Amherst before the railroad (and gas and electric lighting) and Amherst after (I should add that Arac's point about a new consciousness of the time in the poem is strengthened by the "prompter than" variant). Saying that the train is "punctual as a Star," therefore, would mean that there was no conflict between industrial and celestial time: saying that it is "prompter than a Star," however, acknowledges that the two are not necessarily consistent with each other (though is also possible that the very act of negating resemblance still confines the train within the natural sphere: it may be faster than a star, but a star is still the right thing to compare it to).

Before 1853, when travel between places was done by horse and took days rather than hours, it did not matter very much that noon (to take a favorite Dickinson state) differed in Amherst, Boston, New York, and Washington (and even within Amherst: the clock on "Grace Church which, because it had been made in Boston, ran on Boston time, [was] a full six minutes faster than Amherst time").[65] Indeed, the alternative phrase "punctual as a Star" would make sense in only this very narrow historical and geographic context: stars (and moon and sun) occupy different parts of the sky depending on the physical location of the viewer, but this is not immediately apparent or even significant unless one changes environment very quickly or often. It was only with the advent of the railroad that something of a historical crisis (or estrangement) occurred: since there was no single or national American railroad, each private company had its own time, "in most cases, the local time of the company's headquar-ters,"[66] and coordination between companies, although possible, was dis-cretionary. The different configurations of time made available by factor-ies and railroads therefore presented not only Dickinson but the federal government with a problem: standard time zones were not introduced un-til 1883 (three years before the death of the poet), and in the period before that (and after the arrival of the locomotive) local certainties were sus-pended. The result (at least in the poem) is a temporal and spatial disloca-tion: the tremendous and relentless energy with which the machine ap-pears to consume distances calls into question traditional complacencies. Alan Trachtenberg has some interesting things to say about this:

> The popular images of the "mechanical horse" manifest fear in the very act of seeming to bury it in a domesticating metaphor: fear of dis-placement of familiar nature by a fire-snorting machine with its own internal source of power. Once it appeared, the machine seemed un-relenting in its advancing dominion over the landscape—in the way it "lapped the miles," in Emily Dickinson's words. . . . [67]

The implications of the debate about the significance of the star, which are set up by the alternative readings for line 16 in the manuscript version and silenced by the Johnson edition, go beyond the local and the natural. At stake are the validity and integrity, the *genuineness* of, Christianity itself. For the reference to the star and to the stable, following so closely the allusion to the apostles James and John as they were nicknamed by Jesus (who called them Boanerges, or "sons of thunder" / "sons of rage") surely introduces a specifically Christian dimension to a poem that does not oth-erwise seem to lend itself to interpretation as a religious allegory. Of course, one cannot rule out a submerged (and strictly local) pun here: al-though there is a Bethlehem in Connecticut, and although there is no evi-dence that it was connected in any way to the Amherst and Belchertown Railroad or that it was on any of the routes Dickinson took on her travels to New York or Washington, still there was a *John* Adams who was clerk and treasurer of the corporation formed to raise the capital for the line, and a General *James* Palmer (formerly of the New London, Willimantic and Palmer Railroad) whose job it was to drum up support for the new enterprise by (among other things) making speeches. Either one or both of these names might have suggested Boanerges to Dickinson: certainly the sense of critical distance between the silent poet and the noisy engine might suggest that public oratory (or the claims being made on behalf of the locomotive by a variety of its proponents) is being cartooned here, and this impression is extended in an interesting direction when one recalls that Dr. Joseph Vaill, an early fund-raiser for Amherst College and a minister who often led the prayers during Commencement Week, was known as "the Boanerges" because of the power of his preaching.[68]

And yet, any journey carries with it an allegorical potential, and the last stanza of the poem would appear to want to activate that potential for some purpose. There was precedent for that desire. In a ground breaking ceremony that took place at Belchertown on 12, February 1852 (and that was reported in the *Hampshire and Franklin Express* the subsequent day), an enthusiastic crowd gathered to hear Edward Hitchcock of Amherst College remark that the success of the road depended upon Divine Providence. He was followed by Rev. Samuel Wolcott of Belchertown, who gave a speech that interpreted the first removal of soil as "a prophecy of the future[.] What do we not see written upon it?" he continued. "We can all read those large capital letters—'LOOK OUT FOR THE ENGINE, WHILE THE BELL RINGS.' It is a hint that it will not always be safe for us to stand where we are now; it tells us that the train is coming, and we must clear the track." He then rhapsodized about the future "thoroughfare of trade and traffic" and concluded that "in a few months hence the snorting of the Iron Horse will be heard among these valleys, and his tramp will reverberate among the hills!"

Wolcott's speech, reproduced in the *Express*, is fascinating not because of the (fairly predictable) orthodox approval that he, as a representative of an established religious denomination, gives to essentially commercial enterprises such as this one, but because of the way his discourse seems to hover between secular and scriptural meaning, or to inhabit a linguistic territory that sees religious significance in daily events. Whereas Hitchcock (after the genuinely unselfconscious piety of his gratitude to God for helping the citizens of Amherst raise enough capital to build the railroad) describes the experience of speaking before his audience on such an occasion as "very like romance" (repeating the tone of Edward Dickinson's disbelief in his letter to Austin where he writes that "the whole thing seems so much like a dream . . ."), Wolcott collapses time in the way that the train annihilates space: it is almost as if the success of the Amherst and Belchertown corporation brings America a step closer to the coming of Christ. Wolcott, in other words, moves effortlessly from the arrival of the machine to the arrival of the Messiah (as he is imagined in the Book of

Revelation). There is no opposition between the two spheres (had there been, Wolcott could not have allowed himself to speak on a platform celebrating the arrival of the train as a civic achievement): instead, one event predicts the next.

In what way does Dickinson's poem fit into this typological scheme, where the coming of the train confirms God's blessings on New England but reminds his faithful that this world is only preparation for the next? The answer, I suspect, is that (initially at least) it doesn't: Hitchcock and Wolcott merge the discourses of industrial capitalism and evangelical Christianity, but the train's journey to the stable in "I like to see it . . ." echoes the journey of the Magi (and the phrase "docile and omnipotent" surely invokes the infant Christ, at once helpless and all-powerful) only to oppose and even threaten the original narrative with a new and disquieting one. Presumably this could be read as a piece of social prophecy on Dickinson's part: the train will turn the world upside down much as the birth of Christ did. But this solemnity seems at odds with the speaker's attitude to her subject, for the train does not seem dignified enough to act as a vehicle for eternity. Rather, the tone of the poem (together with the neutralizing effect of bringing all of the restless energy of the locomotive to a stop, as well as the reference to docility) would suggest that the end is anticlimactic: the noises associated with the coming of the train (which can be taken to mean either the real sounds it produces or the interpretation of its significance by contemporary agitators on its behalf—like James Palmer, Samuel Wolcott, Edward Hitchcock, or Noah Webster) promise a cataclysmic event that does not happen. Dickinson's train is all show and no substance: it carries no messages. The final point seems almost literary critical—the train is not worthy of being a symbol. It may be "prompter than a Star," but it has less significance. The stable it stops in front of contains nothing but itself. To paraphrase Keats's description of Byron, it cuts a figure, but it is not figurative.

Looking back through the poem, one detects a submerged and parodic (because mechanical, meaningless) emblem of eternity in the train's circuit from one station to another, from the "stop" in the third line to the "stop" in the seventeenth, and especially in the image of the engine chasing itself downhill, emptily approximating that traditional New England image of immortality, the snake eating its own tail (this snake, however, is the endless capitalist cycle of consumption and production, which the train serves and symbolizes). What Arac rightly terms "the new, empty time of modernity" is opposed by (what I take to be) Dickinson's essentialist view of time as having its origins in eternity (and in the birth of Jesus Christ, from which event the church derives its calendar).[69] The train may be "prompter than a Star," but it does not have the same gravitational attraction, the same weight of significance, as *The* Star. One wonders, incidentally, if the submerged references to Christ's birth may have been inspired by Edward (Ned) Dickinson, who was born on 6, June 1861 (almost five years after Austin and Susan were married on 1, July 1856), thereby (it was thought) ensuring the succession of the family name. It has been speculated that there may have been some anxiety on the part of Edward Dickinson about the failure of his son to produce an heir, and it is possible that this anxiety and any others about the railroad's future are dramatized in the poem. It is a cruel historic irony that Edward Dickinson has no direct descendants alive today, and indeed, that the stasis, which his daughter celebrates at the end of her poem, was the very reason for the failure of the railroad company he helped to establish. The original plan was to connect with the Vermont and Massachusetts line farther north at Montague, but the railroad tracks stopped at Amherst for sixteen years, until 1867 (when it was by then out of local hands). As David Sargeant writes, "its failure to make the northern connection . . . made it a 'dead end' line."[70] In hindsight, Edward Dickinson's great achievement was in directing the line to Amherst in the first place, but he could not make it progress any farther, and in doing so he diverted useful capital away from the local economy (whatever benefits accrued from the siting of the railroad went to a small portion of the local manufacturing and merchant classes: freight became quicker and cheaper, and the production of hats was centralized at the depot, where they could be produced more quickly and in greater numbers for enlarged profits by hundreds of underpaid Hampshire County women and men).[71]

How does all of this fit together? To begin with, there are contradictions in the poem and these contradictions mirror Dickinson's own ambivalence toward the social forces she symbolizes in the poem. The speaker asserts that she *likes* to see the progress of the (unnamed train) across (and sometimes through) the landscape, but the vocabulary she employs is less positive and reveals, I would argue, something closer to disdain (at worst) and a condescending amusement (at best). Perhaps these two positions are interdependent: it is the writer's sense of her superiority that allows her to enjoy the train as a spectacle. Again the speaker focuses on the *movement* of the machine, while she herself remains hidden, observing (and listening) but *static* (an opposition also present in her watching the public world of crowds, commerce, and capital, on New London Day, from the private, pastoral world of Professor Tyler's woods). It is possible that it is the loco-motive's abrupt change from relentless motion to stasis that she finds most reassuring (because it *seems* unstoppable, but its freedom is in fact lim-ited).[72] Furthermore, the train is like a cat (a common animal she did not always care for), but it is also like a horse (an aristocratic creature she ad-mired but had little to do with, although for Dickinson having little to do with animals was often another reason to like them). In addition, although the train travels almost immeasurable distances, it is finally contained (physically and ideologically) within the space (and image) of a stable: for all its potential, it is ultimately just another piece of Dickinson property, to be bought and sold, given free rein or reined in, like a horse. And al-though the train can cover great distances, it is time-bound (it has a sched-ule to keep, and its significance is ephemeral): Christ's message, by con-trast, is for ever. There is, I suspect, a historically modified element of the Elizabethan Chain of Being idea at work in the poem: Edward Dickinson's triumph over the railroad (which Edward himself described in scriptural terms to Austin) is sanctioned by God (in nineteenth-century Protestant New England, one's worldly success is a sign of Divine favor) and shows that the prestige and influence of his class is destined to continue.

These alleged contradictions in the poem can be explained (partly) by looking again at local historical contexts. Daniel Lombardo's portrait of a mid-nineteenth-century town in economic stasis and, perhaps, even de-cline is one where there could be no overnight changeover in the estab-lished political landscape: the landed gentry of the first half of the century were still, by and large, the landed gentry of the second. But nevertheless, the number of manufacturing enterprises started before the financial panic of 1837 (and the disastrous attempt by some farmers to invest money in mulberry trees for the purpose of raising a surplus cash crop rather than for the traditional reasons of subsistence or exchange) shows a town where capitalist and entrepreneurial ideologies had begun to infiltrate the older order. In other words, agrarian and capitalist modes of production over-lapped—even the Dickinsons kept horses, hens, cows, and swine and grew their own fruit and vegetables, while Edward speculated in land and shares (in the railroad, the Sunderland Bridge, the Holyoke Water Power Com-pany, and the Hampshire Cotton Manufacturing Company, among oth-ers). The Dickinson property symbolized this encroachment: in front (or to the south) of the Homestead on Main Street was a meadow (just over nine acres in size), where the grass was mown every autumn by hired labor, and on either side of it there were residential and commercial buildings (stretching west toward the town common) and factories, depots, and railroad lines. In *Ideology and Utopia*, Karl Mannheim writes that the coexistence in rural societies of the modes of thought of an established elite and a new rising class meant that in "thinking about an object, two modes of explanation collided,"[73] and there is, I believe, evidence to support this assertion in the correspondence and poetry of Emily Dickinson and in her simultaneous attraction and contempt for the monstrous machine. One is reminded at this point of Mary Shelley's Frankenstein and Blake's tyger, two other metaphors for the engine of capitalism that begin by admiring its drive and energy but end (in the case of Blake) by questioning whether God is still directing that energy and (in the case of Shelley) by trying to erase it.[74] In a sense, Dickinson's poem does both: she erases the train by transforming it into a horse, and she draws comfort from the fact that her father has manipulated the beast of industrialism, something that suggested that Amherst (and the Dickinsons—and the locomotive) somehow figured in God's plans for America. The star, which witnesses the train's cessation, is like the "Master's eye" in Milton's seventh sonnet, "How Soon Hath Time," which sees everything and everybody from the perspective of eternity.

I began this chapter with a quotation from Emerson's journals that indicated his anxiety about a new monarchy of trade and industry symbolized by its technological advances. "I like to see it lap the Miles" would appear to refute a fear evidently shared by the upper-middle stratum of society (especially in country towns, where is was thought that not having the railroad could signal economic disaster; if there is fear in this poem, it is the fear of being left behind, which disappears as the train moves, not farther away, but closer to home). The educated voice, which cannot resist displaying its classical learning in the first line of the last stanza, distances itself simultaneously from the values of industrial society and from its victims, because to look down on a train looking down at shantytowns is to define one's own superiority successively on the grounds of culture, taste, and class. Education and imagination are the twin standards of excellence, the figurative capital, by which technological innovation and progress are measured and found wanting: riddle and satire are the weapons of that superiority. Dickinson uses imaginative discourse to play with the train, domesticating the engine and its sound effects by incorporating it into the sphere of the natural (and therefore of the familiar, the known, and —crucially—the controllable) while also distancing herself from those sounds by contrasting the "horrid – hooting stanza" with her own fluid use of alliteration and enjambment. The modern machine is made over into a nostalgic, agrarian vision of highly strung animals and their bemused but tolerant masters. This is a kind of imaginary holding operation, a playful but very profound attempt at containing the energies of nineteenth-century industrial capitalism (as represented by its contraptions) and adjusting the balance of power between established and newer- manufacturing classes (and their worldviews). If Thomas the Tank Engine can be said to be the human face of industrial technology, then this poem is a Whig forerunner to Thomas the Tank Engine: the speaker attempts to reassure herself that the new technology will not disturb the old order by essentially domesticating its components.[75] And yet, for all that, Dickinson remains scrupulously attentive to details that do not fit into her (or her speaker's) scheme of things. For the train stops at "its own stable door" (rather than at "our" stable door, or at a more neutral "a" or "the"), which might be said to problematize the apparent resolution offered by the text's ending, suggesting that Dickinson at least was aware of a potential gap between the train and her images for it. Her grandfather may once have owned the meadow on which the station was built,[76] and her father still owned property on the site of the depot at the conjectured time of the poem's writing, but a part of her may have recognized that the train represented social forces over which neither she nor her family could exercise control—except perhaps briefly, in the space and time of the poem itself.

CHAPTER TWO

"HOMELESS AT HOME"

The Politics and Poetics of Domestic Space

> The structure of social space thus manifests itself, in the most diverse contexts, in the form of spatial oppositions, inhabited (or appropriated) space functioning as a sort of spontaneous metaphor of social space. — PIERRE BOURDIEU

 THERE are three related areas of interest that I want to pursue in the opening section of this chapter, as a way of introducing its main patterns of investigation. The principal focus will be on aspects of "home" in Dickinson's work—as a place in which she lived and worked, as a trope for a site of refuge, which is linked to notions of subjectivity and culture; and as a literal and literary property over which there are changing and sometimes conflicting claims of ownership. In a later section, I look at issues of mobility (both geographical and social—the two are often linked) and travel, and the ways in which these necessarily impinge on all three aspects of Dickinson's "home" as I define them. I also look more closely at many architectural details of the Dickinson mansion, or Homestead (with the purpose of rendering the specific social implications of those details), as well as at the history of financial relations surrounding it. What emerges from this discussion is an impression of the home as a projected haven from the vagaries of historical and social change, but one progressively invaded by history through the mediation of, among other things, the market. Dickinson and her family want to use the home as a refuge from a volatile social reality, but that volatility causes her and them all, to have to keep reestablishing new homes. The values associated with "home" are in opposition to those of the market and are yet based in a physical house located right in the middle of market forces: investment, borrowing, the public advertising of status and its loss through newspaper reports on mortgage foreclosures and repurchases (all of which are tokens of one's credit and thus one's marketability) are as irrevocably linked to the home as are more intimate feelings of family relation and privacy.

There is a kind of infinite regression in Dickinson's life, letters, and literature. The economic and demographic mobility, which characterized American experience in the nineteenth century, led to a destabilization of her own family life: her grandfather and grandmother relocated to Ohio, her father spent long periods away from home pursuing his political career, and at one stage it looked as if her brother, Austin, would also move to the Midwest in order to find a niche for himself. Dickinson's reaction was perhaps predictable at first: her letters dwell on, and sentimentalize, both her family and her home in turn. Neither provides a safe haven from economic uncertainty, however, and gradually one detects an increasing tension in letters and poems between home as an actual place with verifiable historical and geographical coordinates, and home as a state free of the demands and contingencies of a life lived under the conditions of expanding capitalism. The failure of family and home to provide Dickinson with a refuge from uncertainty led her to try other means of establishing integrity, purpose, and (even) social superiority. Adrienne Rich writes of "hovering like an insect against the screens of an existence which inhabited Amherst, Massachusetts, between 1830 and 1886," and Randall Jarrell states that "after a few decades almost everybody will be able to see through Dickinson to her poems."[1] But perhaps the myth *is* the meaning: perhaps the seclusion Dickinson sought is not a sign of loss, or psychosis (which is not to demean any study that takes that approach; nor is it to suggest that these approaches and my own are necessarily exclusive), but a deliberate and solitary strategy of self-dedication to a "career" in culture, as a means of conferring distinction on herself and as a bulwark against historical forces (or, perhaps more accurately and fairly, as a source of counterresistance to them, or as a vantage point from which she could gain some purchase on reality without claiming that she had to influence or govern it: relinquishing that claim, in fact, was the source of her differential power).

In the poem that follows there are signs of a parallel struggle between traditional myths of the unified self (imagined as a home) and divisions, contradictions, and instabilities that invade this self-home and threaten to possess it. The poem does not tell us the outcome of the struggle: instead, it records a variety of attempted strategies of resistance (which, however futile, may indicate the possibility of more successful but unstated strategies, including that of the poem itself), the failure of which betray the self's vulnerability. Structuring this poem about subjective partitions is a threat to the nineteenth-century rationalization of domestic space into public and private areas: what menaces the speaker is the fear of a breakdown in normal standards of conduct and relation, and it is difficult to say where internal and external anxieties begin or end. What is clear is that the pressures described by the poem threaten to overturn the formal coherence of the social self as much as its subjective corollary. So both the self and the home are endangered areas, and poems in which the two are compared, related, or juxtaposed are to be expected. The more intimidated one's sense of home is, the less secure one's sense of self is.

One need not be a chamber – to be Haunted –
One need not be a House –
The Brain – has Corridors surpassing
Material Place –

Far safer of a Midnight – meeting
External Ghost –
Than an Interior – confronting –
That cooler – Host –

Far safer, through an Abbey – gallop –
The Stones a'chase –
Than moonless – One's A'self encounter –
In lonesome place –

Ourself – behind Ourself – Concealed –
Should startle – most –
Assassin – hid in Our Apartment –
Be Horror's least –

The Prudent – carries a Revolver –
He bolts the Door –

O'erlooking a Superior Spectre –
More near –

4 Material] Corporeal 8] That Whiter Host. 17 The Prudent] The Body 17 a] the
19–20]

A Spectre – infinite – accompanying –
He fails to fear –

•

Maintaining a superior spectre –
None saw –

Division 1 chamber – | 3 Corridors | 5 Midnight – | 9 Abbey – | 11 A'self| 12 place – ‖ 13
behind Ourself – | 15 Apartment] Apart-|ment 17 a| *alt* 19–20 accompanying] accom-
|panying *no* |
P#407A (J#670)

A number of commentators have drawn attention to the division of selves
in the poem: like a single cell that separates and multiplies, there is a
progression (or disintegration) from the opening "One" through "One's
A'self" (with its implication of a set of other selves behind this one) to
the dizzying pluralities of "Ourself – behind Ourself – concealed" and the
state of "Our Apartment," which explicitly links the segregated status of
the self with the segregated status of the domestic environment in which
the speaker lives and relies on for her similes (or in this case for her anti-
similes). Thus the "Assassin" in the room, which both derives from within
the self and exists in opposition to it (to such an extent that it can be
imagined externally), calls into question the mind's sovereignty, its alleged
capacities of self-reliance, and even ideas of free will and individual determination. Uncertainties about (and the complexities of) personal identity
are dramatized in the tensions within consciousness that threaten to compromise, overwhelm, or destroy it. The paradox of the poem is that these
encounters take place *within* the self, but that the fears or dangers they
play out derive ultimately from forces *outside* it. It is for that reason that
Dickinson's speaker deliberately draws on, and distances her- or himself
from, external images to describe an inner condition, for these experiences
betray the porousness of boundaries established to express and maintain
the separateness of those categories. The trope of the home is especially
appropriate because it provides the speaker with a means of exploring this
paradox of simultaneously inner and outer states: the home is connected

with privacy and interiority, of course, but also exists as a structure, which is subject to other, outside, forces.

Architectural interiors reflect not only the minds of those who design and commission them, but also the ways in which society organizes its own internal landscapes generally. Dickinson's poem, with its passages, doors, and private rooms reflects "a rational post-Newtonian reorganization of space into more specialized zones," where the separation of private and public spaces have their analogue in the separation of subjective and social categories of thinking.[2] These divisions are in turn a mirror of the increasingly segregated and competitive nature of economic life in the nineteenth century. But Dickinson's poem does not reflect the ideal arrangement of domestic order: instead, it looks carefully at what that order conceals—both from the world outside and from the people who live inside. Behind the layers of chambers, walls, and doors, which encode social values such as gentility and distinction, home is haunted by contradictions, guilt, anxieties, and fears—the very experiences which (in the nineteenth century) it is designed as a sanctuary against.

For Dickinson's society, which included her father, the opposite was the case: the outer did not mask, but matched, the inner. In a speech delivered at the annual agricultural fair, Edward Dickinson refers to the perfect symmetry of domestic exteriors and internal order:

> The neatness of the farms, the excellence of the fences, the absence
> of brush in the highway, all told that thrift was there . . . and a nearer
> view of the domestic arrangements, showed that the neatness which
> prevailed *without*, was but the consequence, or the accompaniment of
> the neatness, and order, and system, and comfort, and thrift that
> reigned *within*.[3]

This speech was given in 1837, four years after Edward's father had been declared bankrupt, and when Edward himself was living as a lodger in what formerly had been his father's home. There must, therefore, have been a degree of tension between the public profession of a socially approved ideal (home ownership, the security of property) and the private reality (a history of debt and financial embarrassment)—not only for Edward, but for the rest of his family. Until he repossessed the Homestead in 1855, such statements carried within them a devastatingly hypocritical or ironic potential. As Jonathan Arac writes, the "desperately earnest facades of bourgeois respectability provoked the wish to take off the roof and see what was really inside," and I am suggesting that this desire-fear is what—literally—animates Dickinson's poem.[4] Even when Edward eventually did succeed in repurchasing his father's property, the cost of maintaining the image of the Edward Dickinsons as a significant and long-standing Amherst institution sometimes must have led the family to reflect on this disjunction between social surfaces and opposite possibilities and realities.

In the poem we are never told what experiences are being described, or why and how they frighten the speaker. But we are told, albeit in a indirect way by a persona who appears to state exactly the opposite, *where* the encounter of self and self occurs—and the where leads (again by indirection) to the why. The conscious manipulation of Gothic effects to hint at a very different set of subjective correlatives creates a kind of confusion, which acts as a formal equivalent to the social disequilibrium and uncertainty that are part of the poem's base. Notice then, that the reference to the "Host" in the second stanza reverses the normal logic of haunting, which constitutes an invasion of privacy, an unwarranted intrusion by an unwanted guest: suddenly, the *self* (and not the "other") is a tenant or perhaps even an interloper in a chamber of her or his thoughts. Of course, the word "Host" suggests the use of formal codes and conditions by which one regulates the public use of private property: in the nineteenth century, guests were received in front parlors (or, in times of good weather, on the lawns) and were not given access to the inner family rooms (or to the bedrooms upstairs). Thus rooms functioned as spatial codes for the etiquette that increasingly rationalized social behavior in the nineteenth century, and in this poem those codes are flouted or turned on their head: the "Host" does not observe the rules of hospitality; the self locks the door only to find that someone has entered its inner territory—or worse, that it has entered the wrong room, or has entered the room only to find that it legitimately belongs to someone else. Surely, this part of the poem indicates (at one level) a fear of powerlessness—the revelation that the state-status of the mind in which one lives *cannot fully dispense with the material conditions of its being.*[5] What the poem dramatizes are the tensions or contradictions of its opening line, where the speaker defines herself in opposition to a "chamber" but nevertheless depends on the chamber to undertake that definition. The poem's imagery, in other words, enacts the very conflict it attempts to describe, for the switching back and forth between the subjective experience described and the terms of the description produces a defamiliarization of accepted categories, a confusing of subject-object relations.

As part of the external display of their position in the community, the Dickinsons were celebrated hosts, as Martha Dickinson Bianchi reports:

> Edward Dickinson, with his Trustee tea party, held on the Wednesday night of Commencement week for forty years, was too pronounced a feature of those days to be forgotten or omitted. Friends were received all over the house and grounds from six to eight. A supper was handed about with most remarkable tea and coffee. Here one could always find Governors and Judges, interesting missionaries, famous professors from our best colleges, editors of high repute, fair women and brave men. . . . Later on in her life Emily Dickinson forsook her usual seclusion at these times, and radiant as a flying spirit, diaphanously dressed in white, always with a flower in her hand, measured her wit and poured her wine amid much excitement and applause from those fortunate enough to get near her.[6]

Many of Bianchi's statements are written from the vantage point of someone who establishes her own importance partly by reference to an inherited status, and this is typical, but it is nonetheless a fact that Edward Dickinson did hold such parties and that they attracted political, social, and cultural dignitaries (Susan and Austin continued the family tradition after their marriage). Emily's presence at these occasions does indicate the kinds of divisions that I have been talking about, between the public performance in a highly ritualized setting and the private performances of the self in domestic and lyric seclusion. What might have impressed itself on Dickinson's mind, however, was the realization that such social significance depended on her family's having its own property: having guests in one's house and grounds relies (in different ways) on one's having a house and grounds in the first place. The house in which Dickinson lived for most of her life is therefore the guarantee of her (and her family's) social identity, but also (it shall be argued) the source of many of her (and its) fears. It encodes the aspirations but also the anxieties of occupants who did not fully own it. A house with such a troubled history becomes an excellent means of dramatizing uncertainties about personal identity.

I suggest that the constant association (and distancing) in the poem between houses and hauntings bespeaks a perceived (and troubled) relationship between private property and identity: it is primarily a fixed prosperity that guarantees ownership and control over the self. The ruined abbey, for example, may be read as a potential reference to the Dissolution of the Monasteries (1536–1540) during the reign of Henry VIII and the subsequent transference of "something like a fifth of the country's landed wealth to new hands," and it therefore functions further as an oblique or suppressed reference to Dickinson's own fear of dispossession.[7] I should add that I do not forward this as the only way in which to read the poem, or indeed as the interpretive approach that best explains the totality of the poem's imagery and preoccupations. But I am saying that a poem that employs the language of supernatural visitation to describe the process by which the mind loses control over its own thoughts may receive much of its charge from economic and political factors. This is not a poem about literally disputed property rights, but it is a poem where the possession and dispossession of inner spaces are related in very important ways to issues of title generally: indeed, as Walter Benn Michaels observes, haunted-house stories (even, or perhaps especially, those that claim they are not about haunted houses) "usually involve some form of anxiety about ownership."[8] The Gothic genre is therefore singularly appropriate as a vehicle for exploring (without fully revealing) these concerns: the dread experienced by female characters in Gothic novels is often linked to doubts surrounding the legitimacy or authenticity of the family heritage, title, and estate, as Daneen Wardrop has argued in her compelling study of Dickinson's Gothic allegiances and procedures.[9] They also necessarily reflect the ambivalence that middle-class women might have experienced toward property in the nineteenth century, since such women were often without legal entitlement at a time when social prestige was defined in relation to ownership.

In Webster's 1844 *American Dictionary of the English Language* "specter" ("an apparition; the appearance of a person who is dead; a ghost") is related by its Latin root to both of the two meanings supplied for the verb "speculate" ("To meditate; to contemplate; to consider a subject . . ." and "In *commerce*, to purchase land, goods, stock or other things, with the expectation of an advance in price. . . ."). The definition for the noun "speculation" includes the following:

In *commerce*, the act or practice of buying land or goods, &c., in expectation of a rise of price and of selling them at an advance, as distinguished from a regular trade, in which the profit expected is the difference between the retail and wholesale prices, or the difference in price in the place where the goods are purchased, and the place to which they are to be carried for market. In England, France, and America, public stock is the subject of continual *speculation*. In the United States, a few men have been enriched, but many have been ruined by *speculation*.[10]

Webster's explication implies a moral distinction between the profits that accrue from legitimate labor and the sale of one's produce in different geographical and economic environments, and the practice of appropriating the labor and produce of another and others to produce a separate and often more substantial profit for oneself. Edward Dickinson was someone who did both: as an attorney-at-law, he sold his knowledge of the legal system to anyone who could afford to pay him (and, according to Christopher Clark, he also made character assessments for credit reports, for which he was presumably paid).[11] And as a lawyer, he was supremely well positioned to take advantage of the court cases that emerged at the times of greatest financial instability. According to the records of the Hampshire County Court of Common Pleas for 1844 to 1845, "the town with the highest proportion of [debt] suits was not Northampton, the largest center, but Amherst, still dominated by farmers and small manufacturers."[12] But Edward was also a speculator, a man who bought shares in a number of railroad companies, as well as "the Sunderland bridge, the Union Bank, and Michigan land bonds," and therefore someone who was often caught up in the fluctuations of value that land, property and stock were subject to.[13] He was, finally, a man who had gotten himself into debt in order to buy back the Homestead in 1855: improvements made by him increased the value of the place from $3,000 to $10,000, but only after he had borrowed the same amount of money purchasing and renovating it. In 1857, he was still referring to it (in his personal inventory) as the "Sam. E. Mack House," although he and his family had been living there for two years, and Samuel F. Dickinson, his father, and not Samuel E. Mack, had originally built the mansion on Main Street. Since he still owed money on the property, perhaps he felt that he did not properly own it (he would not finally do so before 1863, when he made a payment of $4,000 in bonds to Harriet Mack, David's widow and Samuel's mother and legal representative).[14] Perhaps there are facts about his financial dealings that are not available to us: as a lawyer, Dickinson would have known ways in which money and property could be transferred and retransferred in order to disguise or to defer knowledge and the repayment of his borrowings.

The first version of "One need not be a Chamber – to be Haunted" was written (according to both Franklin and Johnson) in 1862. The uncertainty I have attributed to the poem may derive in part from uncertainties related to the ownership of the mansion. Although Dickinson almost always speaks with affection about home as a haven, during the time (1840–55) in which she lived on Pleasant Street (or North Street, as it was then known), the Homestead seems to have called up more ambiguous feelings:

> Prof Jewett has come and is living with his wife east of Gen Mack and *his* wife. Pretty perpendicular times, I guess, in the ancient mansion. I am glad we dont come home as we used, to this old castle. I could fancy that skeleton cats ever caught spectre rats in dim old nooks and corners, and . . . [the pilgrim fathers are] sitting stark and stiff in Deacon Mack's mouldering arm chairs.[15]

When she writes of pretty "perpendicular times," Dickinson does so from the experience of her own childhood, since her father's family had effectively lived as paying tenants in what had once been their own home from 1833 to 1840. The home, including the cellar and the garret, was divided in half, with the Mack family (the new owners) living on the west side and the Dickinsons on the east side. That division of the property line, as Jean McClure Mudge has pointed out, encouraged "two ways of looking at the Mansion" as well as at the world outside it.[16] On Dickinson's return to the same house some fifteen years later, though, the memories of that division, the sense that the house still half belonged to someone else (to the ghosts of David Mack or Samuel Fowler Dickinson, or to the living presence of Edward Dickinson, for whom the house was managed, or to Samuel E. Mack, who held a mortgage on the property) may have led not only to hauntings (or to potential visitations, which is how most of us experience the supernatural) but to a questioning of the foundation on which the Dickinson sense of identity was built. As Helen McNeil writes, the Homestead was "an over-determined place, carrying a heavy burden of other people's desires and projections, even before Dickinson wrote a word about it." As McNeil then goes on to observe, the Homestead was also an unsafe place for Dickinson, in that it (like the mind) offered no protection against "death, objects of fear, or the gaze and acts of others."[17] Her remarks are borne out by the following letter:

The nights turned hot, when Vinnie had gone, and I must keep no window raised for fear of prowling "booger," and I must shut my door for fear front door slide open on me at the "dead of night," and I must keep "gas" burning to light the danger up, so I could distinguish it – these gave me a snarl in the brain which don't unravel yet, and that old nail in my breast pricked me; these, dear, were my cause.[18]

The relations between the absence of a family member and the fear of potential visitation is typical of many of those Dickinson letters that describe ghostly happenings, but what interests me here is the mental disequilibrium caused by those fears. ("Booger," incidentally, refers to "any ghost, hobgoblin, or other frightening apparition," and "gas" is probably a self-consciously literary reference to candles, whale-oil or kerosene lamps: at the time the letter was written—1863—it is unlikely that the Dickinsons would have had gas lighting indoors.)[19] In the poem, and in many of Dickinson's writings about home, something similar happens: anxiety produces a questioning of home as sanctuary, and the word therefore becomes the site of multiple, contradictory, and mutually antagonistic perspectives (site of horror and haven of writing).

Dickinson herself once wrote (in a prose fragment that Johnson includes in his edition of her letters): "As there are apartments in our own minds that . . . we never enter without Apology – we should respect the seals of others."[20] But this Gothic poem deconstructs fine and genteel distinctions between private interiors and public exteriors: the entire poem dramatizes the breakdown of selfhood and the experience of subjectivity (to adopt the language of postmodern critical approaches). Coercive and destructive forces from *without* are so successfully assimilated that they take on the character and intensity of *inner* compulsions. Despite the clarity of the opening statement, though, an understanding of the poem depends in part on our recognition that the speaker (but not the writer) fails to see that at times there is no essential difference between the ghosts of the world and the ghosts of the mind—it may seem as if external ghosts have internal origins and that internal ghosts have external origins, but both emerge from the encounter of an individual sensibility and a complex network of social relations. Perhaps this explains the deliberate misreading of the first line, where the speaker (or writer) would appear to deny that the events of Gothic literature have any kind of inner correspondence or relevance. One is tempted to ask what it means to say that a mind, like a chamber, can be haunted, when one knows that the chamber is haunted by the mind in the first place (or can only be haunted in the presence of a human being, which is to say that a chamber cannot by definition be haunted on its own, which is to say that the speaker's point is therefore a strange one). It is precisely because the origin of such thoughts cannot be traced that they are so mysterious and terrifying, and why they cannot be legislated or protected against. Whether they constitute the internalization of coercive forms of moral or ideological authority or fears about the permeability of social facades, the poem demonstrates the confusion that results from the self's invasion by its own personalizations of sociohistorical forces.

"Ghosts," writes Arac, "arise from human actions and may be dispelled by them. They are not supernatural at all; their explanation is social." For Emily Dickinson, hauntings usually coincide with the absence of one or more members of the family: her ghosts derive from what Arac calls "displacements in social relations."[21] In 1851 it was Austin who was gone:

> The breakfast is so warm and pussy is here a singing and the teakettle sings too as if to see which was loudest and I am so afraid lest kitty should be beaten – yet a *shadow* falls upon my morning picture – where is the youth so bold, the bravest of our fold, a seat is empty here – spectres sit in your chair and now and then nudge father with their long, bony elbows. I wish you were here dear Austin – the dust falls on the bureau in your deserted room and gay, frivolous spiders spin away in the corners. I dont go there after dark whenever I can help it, for the twilight seems to pause there and I am half afraid, and if ever I have to go, I hurry with all my might and never look behind me for I know who I should see.[22]

As Wardrop notes in *Emily Dickinson's Gothic*, the "gay and frivolous spiders prepare us for a tone of jocular gothic, and yet the passage shifts midstream to acknowledge a real fear which the letter writer must hurry with all her might to escape."[23] Human beings who temporarily disappear leave behind them the premonition of their final loss, perhaps, or of a sequence of losses which (again) foretoken the ultimate and inevitable separation of death. What I intend to argue in the rest of this chapter, however, is that Austin's move away from the family home on Pleasant Street, motivated as it was by the economic necessity of finding a career and (later) gaining the kind of professional training that would make him marketable, shows that the invasion of the home by forces mediated by the market is one of the primary causes behind episodes such as this in Dickinson's life. I do not mean that what Dickinson fears to see in this instance is a representative of the market, but that the market sets in motion a sequence of changes related in Dickinson's mind to separation and death. In the letter above, the formal shift from comic beginnings to somber endings is the stylistic equivalent of the loss of control and integrity Dickinson feels when outside factors disrupt her life. Her letters at this time are not only individual sites of anxiety about social status, the breakup of the family, and the definition of home: they are also symptoms of the social phenomenon that caused this anxiety, namely the extraordinary geographical and economic mobility of the day.

Dickinson herself was caught up in the flux of that mobility. She wrote the following letter in 1851, when she and Lavinia were returning home to Amherst after visiting Austin in Cambridge:

> It was fortunate for the freight car, that Vinnie and I were there, our's being the only baggage passing along the line. The folks looked very funny, who travelled with us that day – they were dim and faded like folks passed away – the conductor seemed so grand with about *half a dozen* tickets, which he dispersed, and demanded in a very small space of time – I judged that the *minority* were travelling that day, and couldn't hardly help smiling at our ticket friend, however sorry I was at the small amount of people, passing along his way. He looked as if he wanted to make an apology for not having more travellers to keep him company.
>
> The route and the cars seemed strangely – there were no boys with fruit, there were no boys with pamphlets – one fearful little fellow ventured into the car with what appeared to be publications and tracts – he offered them to no one, and no one inquired for them, and he seemed greatly relieved that no one wanted to buy them.[24]

The train journey Dickinson describes could have taken place on any one of several routes: via the Boston and Worcester (which began operating in 1834) or the Western (which from 1839 would have enabled her to continue on from Worcester to either Palmer or Springfield). Instead (as Johnson suggests in his edition of the letters) she probably traveled from Boston via the Fitchburg, and then the Vermont and Massachusetts, Railroad to Grout's corner (Miller's Falls) and then by stage through Sunderland, which is north of Amherst.[25] (It seems unlikely that she would have traveled past Amherst to get to Sunderland from Palmer or from Springfield: going through Sunderland from Grout's Corner seems more plausible—though there is always the possibility that the trip to Sunderland and the one to Amherst from Boston took place on separate days.) The number of trains and routes available to Dickinson reflect the rapid improvements in locomotive and carriage technology (not until the 1840s was the superiority of steam power widely accepted), the rise of private enterprise as an alternative or supplementary source of funding new systems of transportation, and the necessity of finding a cheaper and faster means of distributing both raw materials and finished products across the country, especially in those areas not immediately accessible by river or canal.[26] As Alan Trachtenberg puts it, the "industrial system also requires a movement of resources. . . . Thus the railroad fulfilled inner necessities of capital, and it is this alone that accounts for its unhindered development in the nineteenth century."[27]

Dickinson is not known for her close attention to social details, so it is unusual that the letter is full of the minutiae of nineteenth-century railroad travel. Daniel E. Sutherland confirms that on most trains a boy "ranging in age from eight to eighteen, passed down the aisle about once an hour selling candy, fruit, newspapers, and magazines."[28] But the letter is a valuable historical document not only because of what she mentions but because of what she leaves out: she makes no mention of the landscape as the train progresses through the Connecticut Valley, which is interesting given the poet's usual interest in natural scenes. There are several (possible) reasons for this: one is that the journey (or the experience of journeying) through the countryside is now so routine that it does not attract her attention or merit comment—and indeed, the collective impression of reading her responses to trains and to train travel is one of familiarity and even (for the most part) enjoyment. (Of course, had she been talking to Lavinia for most of the trip, there may not have been much time left for observation: but she notices some details, and one wonders therefore why she chooses to ignore others.) The other reason is technological: because the train was capable of reaching and sustaining much greater speeds than stagecoaches, it became more uncomfortable for travelers to view whatever might pass by the window. In particular, objects in the foreground were almost impossible for the eye to register. Increased velocity made it more difficult to look at the landscape for any period of time without feeling tiredness and strain. Indeed, this is one reason why reading materials were sold on trains and at stations: passengers (especially those who used this mode of transport regularly) had to compensate for the difficulties of looking outside by looking at something inside. One might even speculate on whether this has anything to do with Dickinson's perception of her fellow passengers as "dim and faded like folks passed away": such fatigue may be a consequence of watching a moving spectacle, or it may (as Wolfgang Schivelbusch records) part of the "pathology of the railroad journey" brought about by the combined effect of vibrations, noise, and stressed vision.[29]

The letter describes an essentially modern and industrial experience—seated within the car, Dickinson is no longer the sole self in a mythic room of her own, but a member of the public subject to all of the privileges and demands of the market. In her letter, she may (typically) attempt to differentiate herself from the "majority" who usually traveled by train and from the "baggage," which was carried separately in the freight car, but for the railroad companies there was, strictly speaking, little difference between passengers and parcels. The increasing presence of market pressures in nineteenth-century life is evident from the description of a journey where not only necessities such as food and tickets are on sale, but also luxury items such as newspapers and (advertising?) pamphlets. In subsequent pages, I will look in greater detail at these pressures and at how they invaded Dickinson's own inherited and constructed zones of privacy—those of the home and of her poetry. But for now, I want to look at the implications that arise from the necessity of having to take a train and write a letter to her brother in the first place. For travel and correspondence both presuppose the absence of the person who is visited or written to, and in that sense her letters not only respond to but are symptoms of social phenomena, in this case the extraordinary mobility of the day.

The most striking discovery of recent social research is the astounding frequency with which Americans moved from one place to another. In his study of Boston, Massachusetts, Peter Knights discovered "incredible fluidity." Between 1850 and 1860, 61% of the heads of households in Knights's sample moved out of the city. During each ten-year period from 1830 to 1860, more than one-half of the household left Boston. . . . Even more people moved within the city (about 30% annually changed their addresses). In any given year, then, about 14% of the population moved out of town, 30% moved within the city, while eager newcomers entered to compensate for the 14% loss and produce net population growth.[30]

One might ask how these rates of mobility relate to Emily Dickinson and to the town of Amherst, whose population remained remarkably stable during the period covered by Knights's study, and the answer would appear to be that, although the *figures* stayed stable, the *individuals* counted by the census did not. This was the case even in the Dickinson family. Dickinson's mother, Emily Norcross, had moved from her father's house in Monson when she married Edward in 1828, and the letters to her sister Lavinia Norcross after the marriage refer openly to her homesickness: instead of being with her father, mother, brothers, and sisters, she was often left alone (or with the children), while Edward pursued his career. In addition, all of Emily's uncles and aunts on her father's side, as well as her paternal grandparents, left Amherst: William and Elizabeth settled in Worcester; Samuel Fowler Jr. and Timothy in Georgia; and Frederick in Ohio; Lucretia moved to Cambridge, while Catharine and Mary relocated to New York. On the maternal side, her uncle Joel Norcross moved to Boston and her aunt Lavinia (a favorite) settled in Cambridge, Massachusetts. In addition, a number of her girlhood friends left, including Eliza Coleman, Emily Fowler, Jane Humphrey, Abiah Root, and Abby Wood. Rev. Charles Wadsworth's move from Philadelphia seems to have distressed Dickinson, as did Samuel Bowles's journeys overseas. The list is by no means complete (and does not include those who were removed because of death), but it does serve to remind us that the national, regional, and local patterns of social migration affected this alleged recluse on a personal level. Although she underwent extended absences from home because of an eye complaint (in 1864 and 1865), Dickinson herself moved only twice, from the Homestead to North Pleasant Street (when she was five) and back again (when she was twenty-five). Nevertheless, the last move (of less than a mile) seems to have been traumatic for her (something which I will look at in greater detail shortly).

Of course, Dickinson's correspondence with Austin about the coming of the railroad to Amherst was necessitated by his absence: having entered Harvard Law School on 9 March 1853, he was then living just outside Boston. In fact, she had been writing letters to him since his departure on Saturday, 7 June 1851, when he began a year's engagement as a teacher in the boys' section of the Endicott School in the North End of Boston, then settled largely by Irish immigrants who had fled the potato famine in 1847.

These letters are interesting not only in terms of the biographical information they yield about the poet, but also as cultural documents expressive of larger class-related and ethnic preoccupations, which are not exclusive to the poet or to her immediate family. Here, for example, is her response to Austin's description of his first week's work at the school:

> Father remarks quite briefly that "he thinks they have found their master," mother bites her lips, and fears you "will be *rash* with them" and Vinnie and I say masses for poor Irish boys souls. So far as *I* am concerned I should like to have you kill some – they are so many now, there is no room for the Americans, and I cant think of a death that would be more after my mind than *scientific destruction, scholastic dissolution*, there's something lofty in it, it smacks of *going up!*[31]

Betsy Erkkila, in her groundbreaking essay on Dickinson and class, mentions the xenophobic and "seemingly genocidal attitude towards foreigners and the masses" displayed in a letter that also features sectarian parody (masses for the dead are a Catholic tradition), stereotypes (working-class and poor Catholics have more children than upper-middle-class Protestants), and a potential reference to social climbing in the last line: Austin's imagined "killing" of the Irish boys results in an improvement of his (and by extension, his family's) social standing.[32] It needs to be conceded, though, that this letter by a young Dickinson is addressed to a homesick brother, and remarks made privately and jokingly to a family member cannot necessarily be taken at face value (and Erkkila does not mention the allusion to the celebrated murder of Dr. George Parkman by Dr. John Webster, a Harvard medical professor, which explains the references to scientific and scholastic methods of killing). Nevertheless, these remarks reveal Dickinson's familiarity with a cultural sensibility that viewed resident aliens with suspicion and fear. Acculturating such children through brutalization was therefore consoling—and indeed, schools at this time were seen as important "agencies of socialization."[33]

But as Richard Brodhead points out, using severe corporal discipline as a means of controlling children already was questioned by some in the 1850s: even before this, a series of books (by Lydia Sigourney, Lyman Cobb, Mary Peabody Mann, and Horace Bushnell) offered nonviolent, personal strategies of presenting authority. There were two sides to the issue of "bodily correction"—and the letters of Emily to Austin Dickinson show that the latter was allied with the more conservative and authoritarian faction.[34] It is important to see, though, that Austin's adherence to traditional disciplinary practice is not simply (or even necessarily) a personal expression of his attitude to lower-class and immigrant children (he may, like Thoreau, have been required by his employers to use force), but part of a larger process of cultural or ideological assimilation. Amherst seems to have been more authoritarian generally in its attitudes to discipline: in 1872, the school board voted "that hereafter the only corporal punishment to be inflicted upon pupils of the school shall be by a rattan or ruler upon the hand, and that no other corporal punishment shall be allowed."[35] Education was an important means of eliminating as many potentially disruptive cultural, linguistic, and religious differences as possible and replacing them with obedience and conformity: punishment was the means of instilling a proper respect for an impersonal authority.[36] Nevertheless the tensions between those who favored a more lenient approach and more authoritarian elements are recorded in Amherst native Lucius Manlius Boltwood's complaint (entered into his diary for Tuesday, 9 April 1844) that he had heard "only a few weeks ago of a young man by the name of Robbins being turned out of the Academy at Meriden in this State [Boltwood was working as a teacher in Connecticut] simply for whipping a disobedient boy—We may well exclaim with the Roman orator 'O tempora O mores'!!"[37] The form of assimilation which Emily Dickinson at this still relatively young stage of her life and most of her family seem to have found comforting and even amusing identifies them potentially with the forces of reaction in American society and politics—though of course such forces are not always as clear as they might appear, especially in the Connecticut Valley at this time.[38]

The public debate about corporal punishment emerges from a historical conflict between residual, patriarchal ideologies of authority and the emergent "feminine" doctrines of domesticity and also as a response to dramatic increases in the number of immigrants coming to America at this time. Knowing, for example, that during the 1850s, the numbers of Irish immigrants rose to about 60,000, more than one-third of Boston's population of (around) 175,000, and that they spilled over from the North End to the West End (where the Norcrosses, Dickinson's aunt and uncle, lived), eventually forcing their upper-middle-class white Protestant neighbors to move to the South End, helps the reader to understand the Dickinson correspondence at this time, without condoning it.[39] In such circumstances, Emily Dickinson's murderous posturing is an exaggerated and comic expression of deeper socioeconomic anxieties about, and solutions to, this rapid demographic change. Thus, the emphasis on discipline is typical of an era and a class that responded to new patterns of immigration by creating institutions where disorder could be contained—prisons, schools, lunatic asylums, and poorhouses (on one of her trips to Worcester in 1844, Dickinson's father had urged her to visit the lunatic asylum there). These institutions helped "members of the upper-classes to control and manipulate persons in lower social strata and to imbue them with values congenial to upper-class interests in the new social order."[40] Whipping schoolboys, like whipping horses (or servants), was a way of ensuring the compliance needed to maintain social equilibrium. Indeed, part of the joy of "I like to see it lap the Miles" is precisely the sight and sound of this alien monster with its strange accents and potentially superior force being reduced to dumbness and docility in front of the squire's stable.

Robert Doherty has described how members of established elites responded to the threat to their power by newer ethnic and manufacturing groups by turning to voluntary activities, such as reform, personal exploration and challenge, literature and art in order to maintain a sense of social influence and stature and to promote continued meaning in their lives.[41] In Amherst, Edward Dickinson was a member of the economic elite, but that elite expanded during his lifetime with the rise of people like the Macks, the Hills, the Kelloggs, and the Fearings, together with the continued success of Luke Sweetser, his merchant neighbor. In response to a perceived threat from these recently wealthy families, Edward became a founding member of the East Hampshire Agricultural Society (but never its president, and not always a member of its executive board), trustee of the Northampton Lunatic Asylum, one of the forces behind the Amherst, Belchertown and Palmer Railroad Company (and president at a time when it was less than prestigious), treasurer of Amherst College from 1835 to 1873, member of the Massachusetts House of Representatives in 1838–1839 and 1873–74, and of the U.S. Congress in 1853–1855 (although he declined the invitation of the newly formed Republican Party to be their candidate for lieutenant governor of Massachusetts in 1861, because of his loyalties to the defunct Whigs). He served as a state senator in 1842 and 1843, and was a member of the Massachusetts Governor's Council in 1842 and 1843.[42] His political career was largely over by the mid-1850s and by the end of the 1860s, Edward was a man whose party had ceased to exist nearly a decade earlier.

His son, Austin, was equally busy, but his sphere of influence was more local. He succeeded his father as treasurer of Amherst College, was responsible for the building of the new First Congregational Church, planned the layout of Wildwood Cemetery, was one of twenty-two petitioners who were granted permission to form the Ornamental Tree Association under an 1853 General Court Act (and was largely responsible for the relandscaping of Amherst Common), and helped to found the Amherst Gas Company in 1877. In March 1868, Austin was appointed to a committee of three whose brief was to "report a code of bye-laws . . . for directing and managing [Amherst's] prudential affairs and preserving peace and good order and maintaining the internal police of such town." Polly Longsworth draws some pertinent conclusions: "Implicit in the very need for by-laws is recognition that mutually held values, certain ways of behaving heretofore generally accepted by residents of the village, were undergoing change, were no longer known to all."[43]

There is a certain continuity between the legal responsibilities of Austin Dickinson's civic maturity, and his clumsy attempts to beat boisterous Irish schoolboys into submission and obedience in 1851. He responded to change with violence in the first instance and later with the more abstract disciplines of law, voluntary associations, and public institutions.

Significantly, there is evidence to suggest that, although often homesick, especially at the beginning of his stay in Boston, Austin began considering a more permanent move west at this time. When instead he moved "East" (as Emily put it), it was to a new house (in the grand style of an Italian villa) adjacent to the Dickinson Homestead, paid for by his father as a wedding present. The stability and permanence of property, family, and a high-status occupation, which his grandfather and father had turned into a tradition, offset the excitement of a fresh start elsewhere. For Dickinson too, home offered the same possibility of stability (though with the significant difference that the main career option available to her at this time—marriage—would mean its loss). Her letters to her brother during his stay in Boston are, understandably enough, often structured around a similar opposition between home and the traditional relations of father, mother, and children and an alien environment that threatens the stability of those relations. In a letter written after a special dinner was prepared for a visit from Austin, which didn't occur, she described the table laden with food as a "melancholy emblem of the blasted hopes of the world."[44] And after visiting Austin, she again wrote:

> We have got home, dear Austin – it is very lonely here – I have tried
> to make up my mind which was better – home, and parents, and coun-

try; or city, and smoke, and dust, shared with the only being I can call my Brother – the scales dont poise very evenly, but so far as I can judge, the balance is in your favor.[45]

Mobility is perceived to undermine established order not only in New England but in Dickinson's mind as well. She is not considering a literal migration here, but the enforced disruption of an internal hierarchy of values—an identity—which is imagined as a landscape, a location, even a nationality (the reference to country covers both a rural and a national sense of place). In some ways, the personal experience of change results in a kind of betrayal of the self: Austin's absence compels her to think of him and Boston rather than her parents, sister, and Amherst. Such dislocation of normal loyalties and priorities resulted very clearly in a spirit of reaction, which was as political as it was personal:

Home is a holy thing – nothing of doubt or distrust can ever enter it's blessed portals. I feel it more and more as the great world goes on and one and another forsake, in whom you place your trust – here seems indeed to be a bit of Eden which not the sin of *any* can utterly destroy – smaller it is indeed, and it may be less fair, but fairer it is and *brighter* than all the world beside.[46]

The scales seem to have tipped the other way here: the breach of faith that she entertained before has now been dismissed, and Dickinson resorts to contemporary discourses about the sacredness of domesticity. This is as close as she ever comes to being a spokesperson for the culture of her times: the first sentence might have been scripted by Catharine Beecher or by other conservative social theorists of women's role. Although Dickinson never formally joined the church, this passage seems to express a secular and gendered version of the conversion experience, where she accepts that the female sphere is linked to the home. Dickinson's poetry can be defined, almost literally, as domestic fiction: it is produced at home, often takes home (or friends, or family, including those members of the family—like Susan—related to her by marriage) as its subject, and is frequently addressed to family and friends. Home offered Dickinson physical continuity—she would not have to move away—as well as a cohesive view of the self and of the self's relationships with others. But this very sentimentalization is, paradoxically, a token of the threat that both the family and the home were under at the time from urbanization, industrialization, immigration, and the expansion of the frontier. These forces produced domestic tensions and social tensions which the Cult of Domesticity was intended to relieve—not only for Dickinson, but for the nation as a whole. As one women's journal put it in the 1850s: "Without home, without the domestic relations, the love, the cares, the responsibilities which bind men's hearts to the one treasury of their precious things, the world would be a chaos, without order, or beauty; without patriotism, or social regulation, without public or private virtue."[47]

Dickinson's letters to Austin at this time show not only an emotional dependence on him, but also an ideological dependence on home as a refuge from dramatic and disruptive social changes. Threats to family bonds, similarly, produce an expression of her desire for the permanence of those bonds. There are inconsistencies here (or perhaps they are the beginnings of a negotiation with prevalent definitions, which would eventually produce a compromise): on the one hand, Dickinson's letters and poems show, at times, that she was clearly critical of the kinds of duties that domestic ideology expected of women; on the other, her recourse to an image of home as an enduring hermitage in times of flux and mobility are entirely typical of her day and age. As we shall see, however, home itself could offer no escape from the values, inconsistencies, and pressures it was symbolically constructed to oppose.

Economic instability was a feature of everyday life in nineteenth-century Amherst during Emily Dickinson's lifetime. Instances of failure and bankruptcy were most spectacularly illustrated during the financial panics of 1837, 1847, 1857, and 1873, but the cycle of fluctuation was endemic before, between, and after these years. The threat of fire was additionally constant, and there were serious conflagrations at "Factory Hollow" (to the north of the town), which resulted in the destruction of several textile establishments in 1842, 1847, 1851, and 1857. In the town itself, there were major fires in 1838 (11 February), 1851 (3 February and 26 July), 1879 (4 July), 1880 (23 April), 1881 (4 April), and 1882 (29 March). The 1879 fire was possibly the most devastating, since, according to W. S. Tyler, historian of Amherst College, "most of the business part of the town, hotel, Post Office, Savings Bank, book stores & principal shops . . . burned out during the night."[48] But the fires of 1880 (when both the Hills and Fearing factories beside the railroad depot burned down) and 1881 (when Phoenix Row—where Austin Dickinson had his law offices and records—was destroyed) were spectacular and close enough to be terrifying.

In 1837 (when she was seven), Dickinson was probably too young to have fully understood how nature, arson, and—especially—the market affected the local economy. In his excellent study *The Roots of Rural Capitalism*, Christopher Clark explains how Amherst suffered more than most towns from the reverses of 1837:

> The collapse of a Boston firm triggered a succession of failures, among them a large carriage-making company, a firm of gun manufacturers, the stove dealer Oliver M. Clapp, and the merchant and palmleaf-hat manufacturer Leonard M. Hills, who had been a large endorser of local paper. Clapp and Hills would recover; others did not.[49]

In fact, the problems were generated partly from within Amherst's own economy: the carriage makers Knowles and Thayer, who employed up to 150 workers and delivered their merchandise to Presidents Jackson and Van Buren had been financed by the stove-making firm of Clapp, Spencer and Company, which was forced to "withdraw its endorsements in an unsuccessful attempt to cover for the reckless speculations in mulberry trees of its senior partner, Oliver M. Clapp." Ebeneezer Dickinson, a prosperous farmer who built one of the first cotton mills in 1809, was "hounded by creditors" and forced to flee to Ohio in 1812. The cutlery shop of Morrill, Mosman and Blair went under in 1837, reorganized briefly as Mosman and Blair, and collapsed again in 1839. Truman Nutting's tool factory set up business in the 1830s and went bankrupt in 1852.[50]

There were notable successes too—the Cushman paper factory, the Kelloggs tool business, and the Hills and Fearing companies were among the most successful in the country—but economic activity in Amherst gave evidence of some instability. An increasing number of people were moving away from agriculture and into manufacturing and commercial occupations, among them Edward Dickinson, whose fortune was generated not so much from his professional income as a lawyer (which at four hundred dollars a year was quite modest) as from property, stocks, and shares.[51]

By the time of the next panic, in 1847, Emily was seventeen and she was well aware of the implications of market fluctuations for the family economy. Again, it is Austin she writes to:

> I had almost forgotten to tell you of a dream which I dreamed. . . . Father had failed & mother said that "our rye field which she & I

planted, was mortgaged to Seth Nims." I hope it is not true but do write soon & tell me for you know "I should expire with mortification" to have our rye field mortgaged, to say nothing of it's falling into the merciless hands of a loco!!![52]

The comic tone is both disguised ignorance and indifference: as a woman, Dickinson knows that business is none of her business, but that it potentially has very real implications for the kind of life and choices available to her. Again, despite the distancing effect of the quotation marks, the phrase "expire with mortification" accurately reflects the stigma of social embarrassment that financial obligations and the burden of debt carried with them (when Tyler says in *History of Amherst College* that Samuel Fowler Dickinson "became embarrassed" he means both that he experienced severe financial difficulties *and* that public shame accompanied these reversals).[53]

There is a fascinating similarity between Emily's letter to Austin, and one written by Edward—absent on political business at the General Court of Massachusetts (in Boston)—when a fire in 1838 prompted correspondence between him and his wife, Emily Norcross Dickinson. It was she who reported the fire (and her fears during it) to him; this was his response:

> It is singular – tho' true, that about 4. or 5. o'clock, on Sunday Morning, I awoke from a distressing dream, in which I thought there was a great fire devouring my friends in Amherst – and I awoke in the same manner on the morning before that. What connection there was between the fire & my mind, or how it was caused, I know not – but so it was. . . . The scene must have been awful & sublime beyond any thing that you witnessed before, and I do not wonder that the terror overcame you.[54]

What the two letters clearly demonstrate is how father and daughter shared and submerged feelings of anxiety caused by the threat to their security offered by such unknown factors as nature and the market.

At times Dickinson could see her father's absences as a threat in themselves to his business, herself, and the family as a whole. Edward was often away from home during the years in which he held elected state office, and therefore absent from his law firm in Amherst. Using language that echoes her comments in the letter about New London Day, Dickinson again writes to Austin: "Caesar is such 'an honourable man' that we may all go to the Poor House, for all the American Congress will lift a finger to help us."[55] Historian David Rothman has been summarized as arguing that fluidity "and grandiose ambition destroyed family cohesion and communal solidarity," and Dickinson's comments show her awareness that neglect of his legal business could have consequences for Edward's family as well as for himself.[56]

Samuel Fowler Dickinson's ambitions (which included the building of Amherst College) meant that he increasingly neglected the legal business that was the original foundation of his wealth and status in Amherst, and its subsequent failure led to the physical dispersal of his family. The house on Main Street, which was built by Dickinson's grandfather in 1813 (on the site of a frame wood-frame house), is a symbol in miniature of the cycles of financial debt and recovery experienced by the Dickinsons over the century.[57] Like many houses in the area, it had two storys, but its architectural details contained nuanced social codes, which the local population would have readily understood. The location became important only later, when some of the largest and finest buildings in the town were built in the vicinity of Main Street. The edifice itself was a "country version of the elegant Federal period style"[58] and the "granite blocks of [its] deep cellar [were] a first sign of the owner's wealth."[59] This statement tells only part of the story: it is true that the house is thought to be the first in town built of brick, and because brick was the raw material of city architecture, it suggested urbanity and sophistication and was an immediate and visible sign of the owner's emergent wealth and taste. But because nearby Amherst College was being built with bricks at about the same time, there was a surplus of available materials and workmen, so brick was a sensible choice as well. Eventually, in Edward's time, the house would have "five chimneys when the dictionary of townsman Noah Webster made a house a mansion with four."[60] The rectangular shape of the house allowed for a central passage and doorway, themselves explicit symbols of "status . . . and a statement of power," with two rooms opening on each side of the central hall, connoting symmetry and order.[61] According to Guy Leighton, "scars in the brickwork on the facade indicate the outlines of a fanlight over the doorway and of a Palladian window on the second floor, both popular features of the Federal period."[62]

But as Dickinson's poems and letters sometimes obliquely suggest, all of this was a facade—quite literally, because, as Tara L. Gleason has pointed out, the house that faced onto Main Street in 1813 consisted of two rooms at the front and two upper rooms only: the back rooms were added later, perhaps even over a decade.[63] The house records the financial instabilities of its first owner in the different materials used at the various stages of its construction, and in the history of its ownership, which is more complicated than hitherto supposed: biographers Polly Longsworth and Al Habegger have both suggested that Samuel Fowler Dickinson probably lost the house during the 1820s, almost ten years before received wisdom would have us believe. In the records for property dealings at the Registry of Deeds for Hampshire County, Northampton, Samuel Fowler Dickinson mortgaged the "tenement in Amherst aforesaid, whereon I dwell, containing two acres more or less with all the buildings on the same, . . . to Nathaniel Smith," along with "my houses and land, on Mount Pleasant so called" and other property and holdings for six thousand dollars to Oliver Smith of Hadley, on the 20 May 1825.[64] On 29 October 1828, Oliver Smith sold large parcels of land—mostly in Hadley—to John Leland and Nathan Dickinson for twenty thousand dollars. Among his properties in Amherst which are included in the transaction is "the dwelling house of Samuel Fowler Dickinson together with the lands and buildings attached to the same the land being about two and a half acres."[65]

In other words, there was no golden period of relative financial stability in the Dickinson household, which was ruined in the 1830s. The pattern seems to have been one of transferring debt from one person to another, until Samuel's financial distress moved into its final period. On 30 March 1830, Edward bought "the west part of the home lot on which Samuel F. Dickinson now dwells, & that part of the dwelling house in which he lives in . . . Amherst" from John Leland Esq. and Nathan Dickinson (a goldsmith and watchmaker who was also a distant relative).[66] His father, then, continued to live with his wife and remaining dependent children in the eastern half. Edward paid fifteen hundred dollars but on the same day mortgaged his side of the property *back* to Leland and Dickinson for eleven hundred dollars (before taking up occupancy in April).[67] Cynthia Wolff explains why:

> [The] resale had a significant provision: Edward retained an option to buy back his half of the house if within three years he paid roughly one-half of the amount he had received and if within five years he made up the rest. Although it may seem an example of New England eccentricity, this buying and instantly selling back, it actually made perfect sense to the Dickinson men. If Samuel Fowler Dickinson was

forced to declare public bankruptcy, at least half of the house would be safe from Father's creditors. If things took a turn for the better and Samuel Dickinson wanted to secure ownership, he would be able to pay off the mortgage on *his* half of the house, comfortable in the knowledge that the other half was at option to his son. Since Edward had a legally binding option to buy his half of the house, he may have had oral assurances that he would have first refusal of the other half. In the meantime, by moving his family into the Homestead, Edward relieved his father of a large portion of the interest payments.[68]

But within three years, an advertisement in the *Express* on 27 February 1833 stated that the entire brick house on Main Street was for public sale—probably less because of bankruptcy (which had already happened) than for reasons of expediency. On 13 May 1833, Edward sold his half to Leland and Dickinson for twenty-one hundred dollars, unwilling or unable to take up the option of buying the other half of the house:[69] Leland and Dickinson then sold the entire property to David Mack Jr., a merchant from Middlefield, Massachusetts. In yet another twist to the family drama, Edward moved, not out, but sideways to the eastern (and more roomy) half of the house, which formerly had been occupied by his father, where he continued to live as a tenant until 1840. Fifteen years later, on 27 April 1855, Samuel E. Mack sold the entire Homestead back to Edward for six thousand dollars.[70]

When Edward bought the house, he immediately set about enlarging it (even though the number of occupants had decreased since his father lived there) and making functional and decorative changes: a "front entrance and portico in the Greek Revival style" were added, together with a cupola (more typical of the Italianate style, which was then becoming popular) and a new two-story wing on the east side—the increase in size being another important statement of Edward's improved social status.[71] As J. Ritchie Garrison informs us, the "Greek Revival style was common enough in Massachusetts by the late 1830s, in houses owned by elites," and Edward's renovations were associated with both increased prosperity and a knowledge of new forms.[72] The addition of the new wing created a dining room, kitchen, washroom, and shed. Further modernization included the removal of the Palladian window on the second floor, and the addition of "a fashionable wood fence," which helped to demarcate physically the sense of family exclusiveness.[73] Though Jean McClure Mudge goes on to point out that the house was painted in order to cover up the scars of the changes made to its appearance, I would want to modify that statement by adding that paint served other practical and decorative functions as well. For instance, it acted as a defensive barrier from the weather, for local brick was soft and needed protection. It also unified the different details of the house: although paint was not in itself unusual, the soft or pale yellow color chosen was especially fashionable, and therefore a sign of taste.[74] It also helped to harmonize the Homestead with the Evergreens, which was painted in buff, a very similar color. Though architecturally different, the houses would present a fairly united family front to the onlooker.[75] Finally, it served as a sign that the house had a new owner.

When the changes to the mansion had been completed and the family moved back in, the *Hampshire and Franklin Express* congratulated Edward on his renewed success:

> The elegant place where the late venerable Dea. Mack resided for upwards of twenty years, has been recently sold by his son, Samuel E. Mack, of Cincinnati, to the Hon. Edward Dickinson, whose father, Samuel F. Dickinson, formerly owned the place. Thus has the worthy son of an honored sire the pleasure of repossessing the "Old Homestead."[76]

There is a delicious irony in the facts of the Homestead's sale and resale, for when Samuel Fowler Dickinson was forced to sell his half in 1833, he then moved as far away as was conveniently possible, to Cincinnati, Ohio; twenty years later, Edward managed to repurchase the house from the son of the man who had eventually purchased the house in its entirety because he (Samuel E. Mack, who had moved to Cincinnati in 1848) "had just lost everything he had, & a great deal more, through endorsing for his business partner, so he had to sell the dear old place immediately to turn the proceeds to meeting his partner's debts."[77] Samuel had been "connected with the general agency, in that city, of the Protection Insurance Company of Hartford Conn., and continued those relations until the suspension of business by that company, in 1854."[78] But Edward might have appreciated the symmetry in his father's loss and flight to Cincinnati being balanced by the recovery and return of his son's fortunes, occasioned by another instance of financial loss in the same city. And his neighbors clearly felt that there was an element of deft (albeit underhand) and preemptive skill in the circumstances of the repurchase:

April 27, 1855. Mrs Hannah Terry reports to her sister, Mary Shepard:
Sam. Mack has sold beautiful home of his Father to Edward Dickinson for $6000 *six* Thousand Mr. Terry felt as tho, he would have purchased it. Many purchasers were waiting for terms, but Sam made a secret sale. Dea Smith of Enfield Mass wanted it, and it would have brought much more, Sam has no judgment & is wasting all his Father left him.[79]

But the truth, as always, was slightly more complex that the triumphant return reported by the newspapers and local inhabitants, who estimated that in 1855 Edward had spent over "five thousands to repair" his former childhood home.[80] For on 2 May of the same year, Edward took out a mortgage on the house, which was secured by Samuel Mack. Edward may have needed the cash to pay for alterations and improvements made to his own house or to help offset the price of building another house next door (for Austin and Susan), but at any rate his ambition involved certain costs and not strictly financial ones. Although Emily Dickinson describes this final move (from Pleasant Street to Main Street) comically in a letter to Elizabeth Holland, about 20 January 1856, her imagery not only relates the change to more widespread forms of removal and relocation, but also shows how deeply the fear of enforced removal operated in her consciousness. One wonders exactly how much she knew of Edward's business transactions.

I cannot tell you how we moved. I had rather not remember. I believe my "effects" were brought in a bandbox, and the "deathless me," on foot, not many moments after. I took at the time a memorandum of my several senses, and also of my hat and coat, and my best shoes – but it was lost in the *mêlée*, and I am out with lanterns, looking for myself.

Such wits as I reserved, are so badly shattered that repair is useless – and still I can't help laughing at my own catastrophe. I supposed that we were going to make a "transit," as heavenly bodies did – but we came budget by budget, as our fellows do, till we fulfilled the pantomime contained in the word "moved." It is a kind of *gone-to-Kansas* feeling, and if I sat in a long wagon, with my family tied behind, I should suppose without doubt I was a party of emigrants!

They say that "home is where the heart is." I think that it is where the *house* is, and the adjacent buildings.[81]

Despite the humor, there are associations drawn between moving, death, loss of social accoutrements, identity, and status, and the wider patterns of population migration. And Dickinson's final definition of home as a *physical* location demonstrates the clear link between, and even dependence upon, property and a feeling of security. In fact, there *was* a statistical relationship between economic, ideological, and geographic stability in Massachusetts at that time.[82] This would have been impressed on Dickinson by her grandfather's failure: not only did he lose the family home, but all of his sons (with the exception of Edward, who may have been reluctant to stay but whose sense of familial honor and responsibility would not allow him to do otherwise) left Amherst, which Wolff's biography makes clear was related to the financial difficulties of their father.[83] As Mudge carefully and convincingly establishes, however, home for Emily Dickinson meant, more often than not, the Pleasant Street building which her father offered for sale in the *Express* of November 1858.[84] The public may have seen Edward's return to the Homestead as tangible evidence of his renewed prosperity and success as a lawyer and a statesman, but I suspect that for both Emily and her mother (who had some kind of nervous breakdown and suffered from what seems to a twentieth-century reader like depression for four years after leaving their dwelling place in Pleasant Street) the move represented the opposite: a cosmetic exercise and calculated risk, which placed the family in debt and exposed them again to the threat of ruin, disgrace, and (possible) removal.[85]

Biographers Richard Sewall and Cynthia Griffin Wolff, in addition to Vivian Pollak (in her notes for *A Poet's Parents*), argue convincingly that Edward Dickinson's relentless social aspirations were driven by the humiliating experience of his father's failure, disgrace, and death in exile. But his father was not the only one to fail in Amherst, and there were a number of ways in which people coped with the stresses of market life. Religious revivals were one: reform activities another. Edward's interest in the temperance movement, for example, which followed his reception into the First Congregational Church in 1851, seems a characteristic gesture to stabilize his own economic and moral destiny (and that of his family) by eliminating alcohol as the unknown factor in the economic equation. The abuse of liquor was said to lead to irregular expenditure, ill health, loss of the ability to work and to support oneself, domestic violence, debt, imprisonment, poverty, and the dissolution of the family. Although popular, the temperance movement began "as an elite attempt to maintain social control, calling on employers and parents to set examples of sobriety for their hired laborers, servants and children" and it was firmly "associated with well-established stores, substantial employers of labor and their business associates"—such as David Mack, who owned both a store and a hat factory.[86] As a lawyer and politician, Edward Dickinson was in the forefront of the temperance movement, and therefore a public target of proliquor advocates—who often resorted to burning property in an attempt to protect their livelihoods. The *Hampshire and Franklin Express*, 27 September 1850, reports a "Temperance Festival" held at Amherst where Edward Dickinson delivered an address to the Cold Water Army of North Amherst. "Pledging public hate to all that can intoxicate" helped make one a good candidate for credit.

What Dickinson's biographers overlook is the possibility that the same threat of embarrassment might have fueled both Emily's choice of writing unpublished (in the sense of printed) lyrics as a career and a significant proportion of her imagery.[87] In a sense, both she and her father are united in a search for stability and security, though they attempt to find it in different zones. The relationship between the physical architecture of the house and Dickinson's poetry is already widely documented, and is evident in the details of P#1234D (J#1182; I employ the copy sent to Higginson in 1871), "Remembrance has a Rear and Front," which includes a reference to "the deepest Cellar / That ever Mason laid." But the degree to which Dickinson's writing was influenced by the history of financial transactions surrounding the sale and purchase of the Homestead has gone largely uncharted. It may partly, but not fully, explain why Johnson or Franklin assign no poems to the years 1855 to 1857, and why Dickinson disappears from the family papers in 1857 as well (missing letters may always show up, of course). It is clearly possible that this absence can be explained again with reference to Emily Norcross Dickinson's nervous illness: both the daughters would have had an increased burden of domestic responsibility, and there would naturally have been less time (and energy) for the demands of writing. In addition, Susan and Austin married in 1856, and took possession of the Evergreens next door, and that event must have prompted a great deal of reflection on Emily's part about her relationships with Susan and Austin, both singly and together, and with her own parents and younger sister. It was largely Edward who had paid for the building of the Evergreens as a wedding present for the newly married couple and an incentive for Austin to stay in Amherst and continue the family line, while also securing the ownership of the family property, and this must have represented a considerable strain on his finances. In addition, 1857 was the year of more fires at Factory Hollow (which destroyed the woollen and cotton mills there) and of yet another financial panic. By then, Dickinson (who was twenty-seven) would have been fully sensitive to the potential horrors of "over-speculation in railway securities and real estate" that resulted in the collapse of nearly five thousand businesses in the United States as a whole ("by 1859 nearly 13,000 went under").[88]

The extent to which such events permanently invade and inform Dickinson's profoundly home-based literary production is obvious from the following definition (from a letter to Maria Whitney in early 1879), where she states, "Consciousness is the only home of which we *now* know. That sunny adverb had been enough were it not foreclosed."[89] Mudge, in her excellent study, *Emily Dickinson and the Image of Home*, quotes this same excerpt, and identifies foreclosure as an image for death.[90] I have no quarrel with the accuracy of her statement, but I would suggest that it needs to be amended slightly, for the word would have had a very precise social and historical force for the daughter of a lawyer and the granddaughter of a bankrupt whose own mortgage was foreclosed in 1833. Dickinson's own copy of Webster's *An American Dictionary of the English Language* offers the following definition: "*To foreclose a mortgage*, in law, is to cut him off from his equity of redemption, or the power of redeeming the mortgaged premises, by a judgment of court." The word receives much of its charge from its legal and economic significance: death resembles dispossession (and the traditional literary and scriptural image of the body as a temporary home enabled that notion) because it was the greatest imaginable equivalent to the devastation of one's personal and social identity (or because the family history might have led her to associate dispossession with death).[91] It is perhaps for this reason that "home" and "house" appear so often in Dickinson's work (86 and 74 times) as sites of property about which there are conflicting claims of ownership—economic and imaginative. In the fourth chapter, I intend to look more closely at the vocabulary of the market in certain poems that take flowers as their theme, but for now perhaps it is enough to point out how P#417A (J#424), "Removed from Accident of Loss / By Accident of Gain," typifies a literary consciousness that is aware of, and draws from, the element of chance and unpredictability that fluctuations in market forces brought to nineteenth-century life. I should add that I am not interested in establishing a causal relationship between economic instabilities and Dickinson's verbal indeterminacies. It is difficult to be absolutely certain of how direct or involuntary the connection between material conditions and stylistic features might be, but it should be obvious that Dickinson's inclusion of terms drawn from economic and legal discourses show that she was aware of their impact.

The following unfinished poem demonstrates the relation between the disturbances of the age and Dickinson's writing:

Paradise is that old mansion
Many owned before –
Occupied by each an instant
Then reversed the Door –
Bliss is frugal of her Leases
Adam taught her Thrift
Bankrupt once through his excesses –

Division 1 that| 3 each| 4 the| 5 of| 6 her| 7 through|
p#1144A (J#1119)

Believed to have been written about 1868, the poem shows that the language of the market was not always a threat to Dickinson: at times, it existed as an impetus and provided her with new metaphors for essentially psychological states. At the same time, the introduction of the Edenic myth structures the idiom of bankruptcy and gives the situation described (which is both subjective and social) a historical and theological depth. Apparently random economic processes and their effect on individuals (the poet's grandfather, for example) are given a certain coherence because of that: if history repeats itself in different forms, it at least demonstrates the possibility of a pattern, a series of resemblances, which betray a kind of order. The difficulty of blending these patterns in a convincing way, of course, is ultimately what brings the poem short: if bankruptcy is filtered through the lens of faith, then it signifies the immorality of the person who goes bankrupt, and perhaps the personal implications of that possibility were too painful to be carried through.

The pressures of the market are again reflected in a letter from Dickinson to James Clark in 1882: "No Verse in the Bible has frightened me so much from a Child as 'from him that hath not, shall be taken even that he hath.' Was it because it's dark menace deepened our own Door?"[92]

I do not offer this as an exclusive interpretation of the passage, but I think commodification of scriptural discourse, the merging of biblical speech with the language and standards of market exchange, can be detected here. What is doubly significant is that, in the same letter, Dickinson goes on to make her famous statement, "A Letter always seemed to me like Immortality, for is it not the Mind alone, without corporeal friend?" The desire for a disembodied letter is also a convenient metaphor for the woman of letters in search of an artistic zone free of the pressures and demands of capital. Thomas Johnson has described 1858 as the year when Emily "became seriously interested in writing poetry," though it would take some four years before (his argument goes) her most productive years.[93] If her literary productivity can be linked (though not exclusively) to years of extreme financial and political instability in her family, then it should be clear that Emily's flight from history is in itself a profoundly historical act. Her writing and circulation of manuscripts has its own architectural nuances, its own cultural codes.

Dickinson's withdrawal from the literary market may well have been influenced by (among other things) her experience of the property market. I am not trying to suggest that she was unable to distinguish between the two, but that she may have feared the kinds of instabilities, changes, and humiliations that the market visited upon published writers. One is reminded at this stage of Keats, and the second stanza from "Ode on a Grecian Urn:"

Heard melodies are sweet, but those unheard
  Are sweeter; therefore, ye pipes, play on;
Not to the sensual ear, but, more endeared,
  Pipe to the spirit ditties of no tone:

John Keats was a professional poet, subject to editorial comment and revision, and someone who did not expected his writing to remain unheard and unread, but available and even vulnerable to critical reaction. Part of the meaning of this stanza derives from this tension between the fixed sense of the poem as it appears in type and the free, fluid discourse of ideas as they appear to the mind before inscription. This can be extended into a defensive trope: the nuances of poetry as they are presented in print leave the poet open to negative reception, whereas the poem in its unpublished state remains private, unconsumed, and somehow innocent—because as yet untouched and untainted by the market. Dickinson may have never experienced unpleasant or disapproving reviews in the literal sense of having her poems evaluated critically in printed and public fora, but nonetheless she did suffer the humiliation of having several of her poems altered (without her permission or consultation) for publication in periodicals. For the speaker of the next poem, then, the thought of publication presents a remarkably similar dilemma to that of Keats:

Publication – is the Auction
Of the Mind of Man –
Poverty – be justifying
For so foul a thing

Possibly – but We – would rather
From Our Garret go
White – Unto the White Creator –
Than invest – Our Snow –

Thought belong to Him who gave it –
Then – to him Who bear
It's Corporeal illustration – sell
The Royal Air –

In the Parcel – Be the Merchant
Of the Heavenly Grace –
But reduce no Human Spirit
To Disgrace of Price –

Division 5 would I 9 who I
P#788A (J#709)

When Dickinson complained that her poem "A narrow fellow in the grass" (P#1096 [J#986]) was "robbed" by unasked for interference with her punctuation, the essential point she made is correct: the meaning of those lines (or more properly, the meanings of those lines) was compromised by the changes. Critics rightly go on to point out how acute her observation was and also how her concern alerts us to the significance of line positioning, grammar, and punctuation generally in her work. But they tend to overlook how Dickinson invokes the discourse of private property when she describes the changes made to her work.[94] In short, her choice of words fits in with the idea of writing poetry as a private activity, written poetry as a personal possession, and editorial change as an act of theft. The poem above uses a similar idiom when discussing the issue of publication. Especially, it addresses the crisis of ownership that arises when an artist releases her or his products to the world: to publish, it is stated, is to leave oneself open to the possibility of someone else (an editor, a reader, a critic perhaps) gaining control over one's work (this control may be understood literally, as the right to alter or to make textual changes, or figuratively, as the right to understand the poem differently from the way in which it was intended to be understood). This problem centers on the conflict between the prior claims of the artist and the interests of the consumer (in the broadest sense of that word), and underlying this is an extreme anxiety about the demands made upon the writer by the marketplace.

There are tensions in the poem that are not confined to Dickinson alone, but that may be related to her class; as I have said, her own family history was overshadowed by her paternal grandfather's loss of fortune and forced sale of the family property. Sewall records that the *Hampshire and Franklin Express* congratulated the family for restoring the house to its rightful owners, and that notice surely demonstrates how much anxieties about ownership were shared in Dickinson's social class, but it also reinforces how public and degrading the sale of one's possessions to pay off debtors could be.[95] Dickinson's language is redolent of this shame, for her speaker associates publication with a form of literary prostitution (echoing Pope's distinction in "The Dunciad" between the "Unstained, untouched, and yet . . . Maiden sheets" of a pure muse and the "smutty sisters [who] walk the streets"). Only extremes of poverty could justify publishing for money, it is suggested, and even this excuse is called into doubt by the intervening space between the first stanza and the archly suspicious "Possibly" of the second. For Dickinson, publication is equivalent to a bankruptcy auction, in the sense that it calls into question the social or literary status of the person doing the publishing or selling. Refusing to publish becomes a way of authorizing one's work, imparting to it a kind of stability and permanence at a period when the power and influence of established New England families were beginning to decline (sometimes abruptly, as a result of failed investments and speculation, especially in land) and when the reputation of a writer was in part dependent on a volatile literary economy.

The idea of literature as property is extended in the third stanza, which most critics read as saying that an idea (or set of ideas) belongs first to the thinker and then to the person who carries that thought (or those thoughts) as they are inscribed in written discourse. If they are shared to some extent by the writer with the reader, then this is a matter of choice, and the choice is generally a limited one, so that there is a single reader and not an audience, a public and plural network of consumers. But it is also possible to read this stanza as saying precisely the opposite—that the idea that the poem can belong to anyone other than the writer is as absurd as selling air (or air used by a king; or a national anthem; or the inspired breath of the poet as it is translated into words). This may not be what Dickinson intended, but this renegotiation by the reader is precisely what the speaker says she wants to avoid, and it is therefore quite interesting, especially since the manuscript version of the same poem makes this confusion no clearer. Because no matter how much the speaker might claim that publication is a disgrace, she runs the risk of losing control over the poem as soon as it is sent out to another person (perhaps even before this; there is the sense sometimes that Dickinson sees meaning multiplying and escaping her control even when only she is reading the poem). Of course, it may be that Dickinson has another form of publication in mind here (the kind defined extensively by Martha Nell Smith in *Rowing in Eden*): the private or personal variety where a manuscript is included in a letter and sent to a close circle of friends or to one friend in particular. But even then, the kind of misreading I have just demonstrated is always possible, which is either a misunderstanding or simply a different understanding from that sanctioned by the poet. As George Eliot puts it, signs "are small measurable things, but interpretations are illimitable."[96]

In other words, there is a kind of tension here between the fear of publication and the attraction of writing, between the desire to rein in and retain meaning and the fact that the poem is eventually sent out in a letter, a parcel even, and therefore turned over to the mercy of the recipient. Perhaps we can go even further to suggest that there is a contradiction at work in the poem, and that this contradiction emerges most clearly in the second stanza. Again, a variety of readings suggests themselves (even if there is only one reader, and that person the poet herself): the poem can be seen as describing the soul of the speaker (it therefore has a religious meaning) or as referring to the writer and her poems (it therefore has a literary significance)—and these are not necessarily mutually exclusive. As a religious poem it is quite conventional: the speaker would prefer to remain as pure and innocent as possible, and if this innocence is read as sexual, it can therefore be read as a profession of virginity. In addition, the speaker can be saying that as a poet she prefers to remain unseen and unknown (a blank) and that this anonymity has a religious purpose or explanation (it is in honor of the White Creator, presumably). But if that is the case, then why is the page not left blank? Surely there is an opposition between the act of writing on the page and the desire to leave the page empty, uninscribed?

These are contradictions of which Dickinson herself may well have been aware. For example, if we choose to read this stanza as religious, then it appears to communicate a Christian cliché: the best that we can do is to return to God what he has already given us, to use our talents in a way which glorifies him in some way. But another Dickinson poem (P#953A [J#848]), "Just as He spoke it from his Hands," actually contradicts this commonplace: it suggests that such a view of any creative enterprise is limited and limiting. In addition, the refusal to "invest – Our Snow" runs contrary to the parable of the talents (Matt. 25.14.; Luke 19.12.), where the servant who returns exactly the same amount originally given to him is defined as wicked. With this in mind, it is possible to put forward the idea that Dickinson might be ironizing what the speaker has to say: for a writer to expect control over her materials is absurd and nonsensical. The religious reading and the literary one coincide: the third and fourth stanzas express a sectarian scorn for Catholic practices (for example, the image of the service of the sacrament indicated by the parcel of royal air or heir: that is, Jesus Christ, son of God, which is opposed by the image of the snow, white and almost immaterial), which put intermediaries between the soul-speaker and the creator. Protestant worship, with its emphasis on an individual relationship with the deity, leads to a purer, more direct devotion.

With the notable exception of feminists, readers have for the most part remained remarkably uninterested in the relationship between Dickinson's writing and politics, but in the context of nineteenth-century American slavery, the reference to auctions, the buying and selling of human souls, the corporeal illustration (like a brand), and the repeated use of color as a designation of worth all accumulate to suggest that this issue may further contribute to the poem's critique of the merchandising of literature.[97] And Dickinson herself was, after all, from the North—her sentimental affection for (and presumably her allegiance to) that side is expressed in many extremely conventional poems and letters. It can be argued, then, that knowledge of the horrors of slavery reinforces the poem's claims that selling and buying human ideas is a barbarous activity, and explains in part why color can give a certain status, which is ultimately, if accidentally, preferable to becoming a cipher in a scheme of economic exploitation. In this reading, the potential abuse of the black print mirrors the actual abuses inflicted on colored victims of the slavery system, and this fits in with the poem's ostensible message, which strongly resists the idea that human worth can be calculated or measured in financial terms. Gillian Brown notes something similar in Harriet Beecher Stowe's objection to slavery, which is principally because "slavery disregards this opposition between the family at home and the exterior workplace. The distinction between work and the family is eradicated in the slave, for whom there is no separation between economic and private identity."[98] For both writers, slavery exists as a metaphor for the intrusion into private life of capitalism's public aspects.

Of course, the designation of color in the poem is a conscious choice, and while enlisting the reader's sympathy by echoing such crimes, Dickinson encourages us to see only the personal implications: she moves the frame of the debate from the public to the private sphere. In other words, the speaker draws on imagery that can be related to slavery, but instead makes it refer to the self: rather than comment directly on social malpractice, she transfers sympathy to her own plight. In a sense, the poem's uneasy vacillation between engagement with history and evasion of it fits in with the other readings: the rejection of engagement (in the sense of an arrangement that leads to marriage) and the refusal to engage with a wider audience by making one's work more widely available.[99] The irony is that the speaker's rejection of the world of capital expresses a belief that investment in the spiritual or symbolic world results in the accumulation of a different, and finer, capital (artistic fame in a literary afterlife or heavenly reward in a religious afterplace). A Marxist reading of this poem would detect a class reflex at work here, the intelligentsia responding to a perceived failure to influence reality and retreating instead to the safety of observation and fantasy. A withdrawn sensitivity to imaginative issues rather than an active involvement with social topics becomes the defining characteristic of artistic excellence and integrity. Speaking of Hobbes and Locke in a way that throws some interesting light on Dickinson's poem, Perry Anderson says that "the very meaning of freedom . . . was unintelligible outside their notion of property: freedom . . . *was* property of one's own person in a market society where he who sold his capacities (his labour) ceased by . . . definition to be free."[100] For the speaker of "Publication-is the Auction," freedom is defined in a similar way: the right to withdraw one's services or talents from the public sphere (although this is significantly gendered, so that virginity is preferable to biological production or prostitution, for instance). Creative production becomes a specialized location set apart from all other commercial or material enterprises, the site for an activity that is employed and enjoyed, not for reasons of economic survival or political initiative, but for its own sake as a ludic exercise liberated from the necessities of didactic, mimetic, or waged discourse. Art derives its values from internal criteria and remains independent of conditions outside its immediate field. As Pierre Bourdieu has argued, "The denial of economic interest . . . finds its favourite refuge in the domain of art and culture, the site of pure consumption. . . . The world of art [is] a sacred island systematically and ostentatiously opposed to the profane world of production, a sanctuary for gratuitous, disinterested activity in a universe given over to money and self-interest."[101] In this context, it is worth pointing out that Dickinson's brother, Austin, paid for a substitute to take his place during the Civil War; whatever his motives, the fact that he could afford to do this and could make the choice to not take an active part in the conflict provides an interesting gloss on a poem that both Johnson and Franklin date from 1863. Emily's father was opposed to slavery, but when he writes (in 1855) that "by the help of Almighty God, not another inch of our soil *heretofore consecrated* to freedom, shall *hereafter* be polluted by the advancing tread of slavery," his comments are conservative and (perhaps naturally, given that he was a lawyer) very cautious.[102] Dickinson herself was seldom actively involved with public issues of any kind, and only rarely remarked directly on events of shared historical significance: indeed, this is replayed at the critical level by a biographical preoccupation with the "war between the houses" (the alleged tension between the Dickinson home and that run by her sister-in-law, Susan, occasioned by Austin's affair with Mabel Loomis Todd) rather than the war between North and South.[103] And her poem appears to refuse any kind of intercourse—social, sexual, or textual. Or does it? Perhaps the distinction to be remembered is that, no matter how the speaker might profess her disdain for publication, as soon as she inscribes this thought in language it begins to echo with other voices, other texts, and other contexts—even (perhaps especially) to her.

What is also interesting about the poem is its location of the "garret" as the site of the speaker's production (or nonproduction) of her "Snow" (her unpublished poems). There are shades of Edward Taylor here (writing as a form of communication with God), shades of Anne Hutchinson, even, and of Samuel Johnson's *The Vanity of Human Wishes*, but shades too of an eminently sensible revision of Thomas Chatterton's more spectacular withdrawal from public life: here silence is chosen before suicide. The garret, of course, is the top story of the house, and it therefore connects

Dickinson with an artisanal and domestic theory of creative enterprise at a time when work was increasingly being moved out of the home (or hidden inside it) and into the factories. (This is also one of the areas of the house where live-in servants were housed: the choice of the garret is therefore resonant with anxieties about loss of class status.) Dickinson's own choice of publishing her poems through a network of friends rather than through the media of newspapers and printed books seems to link her with a preindustrial or anti-industrial economy of local exchange that is firmly embedded in the social fabric of rural life and that therefore opposes the impersonal and long-distance transactions of the market. The unstated assumption underlying the poem (and the choice of an alternative strategy of self-promotion and publication through the distribution of her poems in letters) is that she had sufficient class privilege to protect herself from market demands. She did not have to compromise her artistic integrity, bluntly, because she could afford not to (though she is prepared to accept—just—that lack of money brings with it a new set of economic needs and relations). Unlike servants, having a garret enables the speaker of the poem to *produce* without having to *sell:* private virtue is predicated upon private property.

This does not signify that I have a narrowly deterministic and mechanistic view of the relationship between Dickinson's class status and her poetry. After all, I have argued so far that the same status had an economically unstable base—and that as a consequence the ideological superstructure (to continue the metaphor that seems appropriate to a chapter on houses) was seriously shaken at times. It is, however, to state that *in her own mind* Dickinson shifted the foundation of her own sense of class difference from an economic base (which, however unreliable, still served as the primary anchor of that difference) to a cultural one. It is because of this that she describes consciousness as a "Pyramidal Nerve" and Emerson's *Representative Men* as "a little Granite book you can lean on": it is also because of this that she writes "While Shakespeare remains Literature is firm" (to Higginson in November 1871.)[104] The choice of stone for the Emerson reference is not accidental: literature was to Dickinson what private property was to her grandfather, and politics, the legal profession, religion, *and* property were to her father and brother—each connoted distinction (of different kinds), gentility, and depth.

Austin took a six-week trip through the South and West in 1887, and it is instructive to note the effects of the journey and his reaction to mingling with the emergent and lower classes, the self-made men and the poor: "If there is anything beyond this I shall need new senses to take it in. I am dizzy and bewildered – all the strange variety of this variegated country is too much for a single month – adjective are unavailing. I hope New England is not the dream and this the reality."[105]

Austin's response to an alien landscape and the values of its inhabitants is a kind of ideological disequilibrium—the questioning of his own values and identity. And he reacts, like his sister in her letter to him three decades earlier, with a politics of reaction, which is then expressed as a flight to culture (like Emily by the Irish, Austin is sickened by "niggers, poor whites, and other trash" and is grateful—like the speaker of P#256 [J#285]—that he was "born in New England"): "Money, land, cattle, corn, railroads, sudden futures, are all that is talked of in the west, or thought of. A man is a man for the cunning or chance by which he has siezed upon more than his part of the heritage of this world. It is unnutritious to me, and it is repulsive. I would^{nt} give a volume of Emerson for all the hogs west of the Mississippi."[106]

There is an interesting anecdote in Martha Dickinson Bianchi's *Emily Dickinson Face to Face* that reveals, I think, how the Dickinsons' keen sense of "being unlike most everyone"[107] found support in a pursuit of cultural excellence: "Austin's passion for pictures kept him without some other comforts, for he could not resist them; and once, after spirited bidding at a picture sale in New York, he was being carried beyond his depth, when a stranger whispered to him, 'Excuse me, Sir, but do you know you are bidding against A. T. Stewart's agent'?"[108]

"What makes a few of us so different from others?" wrote Emily in 1853.[109] As she grew older, that sense of difference would have been harder to maintain, as her father's political career began to ebb in the mid-1850s (significantly, perhaps, the time when he repurchased the family mansion), and as both he and Austin struggled to maintain the family finances. But Austin's comments and Bianchi's story show how taste was one way of preserving the family's uniqueness. In language that to some extent mirrors the criteria of "Publication is the Auction" (starving for art, for example), Bianchi shows how her father's love of painting drove him to compete with those with more money: in a sense, his failure is irrelevant, for culture gives him a symbolic capital that is superior to financial means. At the same time, the commodification of art—its circulation through a system whereby money became one of the chief criteria of its aesthetic value— leads to his exclusion. And yet, Bianchi clearly takes pride in this episode—her father's defeat is worn like a badge of honor. There are convoluted signals here: social marginalization in an era when power began to be centered in the city and in capital leads to an interest in aesthetic objects as a means of differentiating oneself from philistinism, and yet at the same time even high culture cannot entirely escape the language and the practice of the market. Given this curious mixture of arrogance and potential humiliation, Austin established his collection of art as an alternative to those housed by the great museums, institutions, galleries, and private collections:

> He was so familiarly known at the New York galleries of Shaus and Goupil, whose place in the art world was later filled by Knoedler, that they often telegraphed him to come down and see a new treasure before it was put on public sale. When he did buy a painting and get it home, he sometimes kept it upstairs in the guest-room with the door shut for weeks before showing it to his father, whose taste in art ran— or rather walked—to steel engravings, and who might well consider such doings of Austin extravagant, if not unduly fanciful. Of course, when he was ready, Sue and Emily were the first to peep at each one, propped up against a chair to catch the best light. A picture in itself, those three standing there, Austin and Sue flushed and excited, Emily revelling in a new emotion of color as she gazed.[110]

There are enclosures within enclosures here: framed paintings inside the locked chambers of a private home are transformed at the end into a painterly scene within the verbal frame of the narrative. Perhaps the point to make is the coincidence of domestic and aesthetic spaces: both provide a privileged zone free of the vicissitudes of public life. The Dickinsons housed their art at home, and found a home in art. Dickinson's rejection of the world in her "Home is a holy thing" letter is self-consciously *stylistic* or *rhetorical:* the rhythms and reversal of the final lines suggest that she was starting to think of *language* itself as a potential site for stability and as a refuge from the world's temptations and intrusions. It is interesting to compare how Edward entertained at social occasions that were often public and civic (supper for commencement week, for instance), while Susan and Austin presided over smaller evening gatherings (sometimes with Emily) that were more in keeping with "a literary and artistic salon."[111] In other words, in the space of a few generations, the base on which the Dickinsons founded their sense of preeminence became smaller and

shifted from the ownership of land and property to owning works of art—
or, in Emily's case, to retaining ownership over her own artistic works.

On a visit to Washington, Dickinson responded to the "jostle . . . scram-
ble and confusion" of her time there by visiting an art museum, writing
about the emptiness of the world at large, and feeling homesick. Her own
gallery of lyrics was privately produced and privately displayed; those who
read her handwritten manuscripts, enclosed within envelopes for solitary
viewing, were personally chosen. But even if she kept the work from the
world, she did not—perhaps could not—keep the world from the work,
as I have argued in previous chapters. And the privatization of art has its
own complicated social codes. The discipline of writing poetry and letters
(evidence that she composed many drafts of both letters and poems is contained in another early letter to Austin where she says "This is truly extem-
pore, Austin – I have no notes in my pocket"),[112] as well as the dignity that
the choice of the lyric genre symbolically conferred on her, did not so
much remove her from the potential trauma of social flux as provide her
with an alternative means of marking her own sense of distinction.
Whereas her father and brother responded to the erosion of their economic power by seeking to consolidate it through the choice and performance of their profession and through political mechanisms of influences
such as voluntary associations and public institutions and the collection of
art, Emily Dickinson tried to find her versions of stability, significance,
and status in the institution of culture.

CHAPTER THREE

HOUSING POSSIBILITIES

Dickinson and the
Institution of Culture

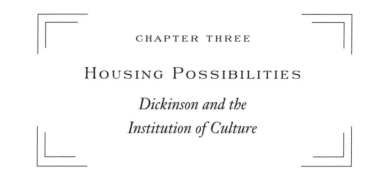

W H E N Emily Dickinson wrote her second letter to Thomas Wentworth Higginson on 25 April 1862, she responded (we infer) to his question about her reading, and gave him this list: "You inquire my Books – For Poets – I have Keats – and Mr and Mrs Browning. For Prose – Mr Ruskin – Sir Thomas Browne – and the Revelations." She did not mention drama, but in a later (1870) meeting with Higginson at her father's house in Amherst, she is reported to have said that she read Shakespeare and wondered aloud "Why is any other book needed?"[1] And yet, as Jack L. Capps and others have shown, Dickinson's reading was not confined to these writers. There were many others, including Lydia Maria Child, Harriet Beecher Stowe, Ik Marvell (Donald Grant Mitchell), Bret Harte, Helen Hunt Jackson, Elizabeth Stuart Phelps, Rebecca Harding Davis, Henry Longfellow, and a host of other (named and anonymous) poets who published in the newspapers and periodicals the Dickinson family received.[2]

Dickinson's statements (even if attributed, and therefore not verifiable) are interesting, not the least because, as her biographer Richard B. Sewall points out, they were misleading: "Ruskin and Browne seem to have been of minor importance to her" and both Thoreau and Emerson (in addition to the writers listed above, whom Sewall does not mention) were missing.[3]

In reality, Dickinson seems to have had very eclectic reading habits, and one wonders why she would want to give Higginson the idea that only these few writers were important to her.

A number of possible answers suggest themselves, but the one that most immediately comes to mind is that she did so in order to impress him. Sewall himself goes on to speculate that Browne and Ruskin were mentioned because Higginson had referred to them in his April 1862 *Atlantic Monthly* article, "Letter to a Young Contributor," and Dickinson may have omitted mention of Shakespeare in her first letter to him because he had praised Keats's "winged words of expression" at Shakespeare's expense.[4] In addition, the writers listed by Dickinson were all British, and they may have been deliberately chosen with the purpose of convincing Higginson that the four poems that she had enclosed with her first letter to him were worth taking seriously. As a literary commentator, Lawrence W. Levine argues, Higginson defined culture in "a resolutely classical and European-orientated manner and often . . . with the adjective 'high' appended."[5] Dickinson's value as a writer could be attested in part by the value of the company she kept as a reader.

The implications of this need not be confined to the immediate historical environment of Dickinson's epistolary relationship to Higginson. Even if she read almost indiscriminately, she had a keenly developed (and, judging by the list of names, a culturally conservative) sense of what did and did not constitute literary merit and importance. Like many of her day, she operated with a vertical model of writerly excellence, and, rather like a pyramid, it had a broad base and a narrow top.[6] Like pyramids, the best books immortalized the minds of their creators, and, as her sister, Vinnie, once said, Dickinson was very discriminating: she was "always watching for the rewarding person"—in literature as in life.[7] Her judgments about which monuments best preserved the memory of their architects did not always coincide with that of the literary cultural establishment, but generally speaking George Eliot, Charles Dickens, Robert and Elizabeth Barrett Browning, and the Brontë sisters represented a kind of literary aristocracy for her, whereas she had problems acknowledging the value of someone like Whitman—who was "disgraceful."

This is not to say that British writers influenced Dickinson more than American ones: the work of Sewall, Karl Keller, David S. Reynolds, and Joanne Dobson, among others, argues the very strong links between Dickinson and (some of) her contemporaries. But it is to say that (especially in her later years) she admired more British writers than she did American ones. Part of this, it may be conceded, was an accident of the market: in the nineteenth century, because of the absence of international copyright laws, books by established British authors were cheaper to publish and easier to distribute, advertise, and sell than those written by promising but unknown local writers (whose rights were protected by the federal copyright act of 1790). It is also an accident of history: many Americans in the nineteenth century believed that Britain had an established literary tradition which they lacked. But Dickinson's list of names is significant because, in the context of contemporaneous literary debate, it seems to align her with a Whiggish or conservative faction of American intellectuals who advocated an aristocratic and pro-British theory of literature in opposition to those who favored a democratic and national ideal—Poetry for the People, as it was sometimes known, or Literature for the Millions.[8] A number of Dickinson poems would appear to support this possibility, while her preoccupation with images of royalty and various forms of nobility would also appear to suggest that she may at times have agreed with establishment and elitist definitions of the artist and her or his function. But one needs to be careful about confusing the author with her rhetorical performances: her "posthumous" poems, by which I mean those that are spoken by a persona who is clearly dead, remind us that her work often involves a dramatization of psychic and social possibilities that should not be literally translated as representing her exact views. In addition, even a critic like W. A. Jones, spokesperson for a radical sociopolitical view of literature in the years before the Civil War, could write that "democratic as we are, we yet contend right loyally and reverently, for the sovereignty of mind, the aristocracy of genius, the high rank and precedence of talent."[9] Nevertheless, Jones believed that the highest forms of poetry would be essentially philanthropic, whereas Dickinson's poetry does not appear to take an interest in bettering or even describing social environments.

Indeed, Dickinson's use of the word "disgraceful" to dismiss Whitman is revealing, because it implies a moral and not an aesthetic judgment, and again would seem to suggest a view of literature more closely aligned with the conservative right than with the newly emergent theories of Young Americans like E. A. Duyckinck and W. A. Jones, who both wrote for the *Democratic Review*. It is true that there are instances when Dickinson's poetic practice would not contravene Jones's 1846 statement that "the imagination is the most religious of our faculties, and consequently the grandest."[10] Her poem P#533A (J#569) "I reckon – When I count at all – / First – Poets – Then the Sun – / Then Summer – Then the Heaven of God – / And then – the List is done – " seems to embody an even more radical version of this sentiment. But the Jones quotation is taken from an article printed by the conservative *Whig Review:* its appearance there suggests that such opinions were not unacceptable to both sides. The Young American view that literature should be democratic in spirit, so-cially progressive, and sympathetic to the oppressed seems, however, much more alien to the stance taken by Dickinson in some of her poems and letters. (One could argue, though, that it is the flip side of the same impulse: Jones wants to use culture *for* the masses; Dickinson wants to save culture *from* the masses.)

Dickinson's distance from the view of culture as a transforming, civiliz-ing medium can be teased out by comparing the following quotation (again from a letter to Austin) with Jones's espousal of "people's editions, cheap libraries without end,"[11] and his vision of a day when business and government would unite in making culture available to everyone:

> [Pat] asked me tonight if I had a newspaper – Why, said I, "Pat, can
> you read"? "Yes marm" he answered – I asked him what kind of a one
> he thought he should like – "Oh" said he with the utmost gravity "I
> want to read the *newses.*" I gave him two *Lawrence Couriers*, at which he
> seemed quite overcome – I presume it was a munificence very grand
> to him – [12]

Dickinson's patronizing interrogation of her father's servant makes embar-rassing reading for a twentieth-century reader (unless one somehow be-lieves that "with the utmost gravity" is neutral description rather than comic belittlement, that "he thought he should like" is the exact equivalent of "he should like," and that the donation of two minor provincial newspa-pers constitutes an act of true generosity). But it is a reminder, perhaps, that culture is not a neutral field and that it contains within it the same kinds of conflicts that are played out in social and political life generally. The subtleties and nuances of Dickinson's narrative act as a watermark of her own superiority.

Such a sense of superiority often carries over not only into her writ-ing but also occasionally into her reading. And yet, it is at odds with the American emphasis on equality, on shared standards and practicalities. In the following poem, Dickinson's speaker uses death as an image for such equalizing tendencies (or cultural and political equality as an image for death, perhaps):

Do People moulder equally,
They bury, in the Grave?
I do believe a species
As positively live

As I, who testify it
Deny that I – am dead –
And fill my Lungs, for Witness –
From Tanks – above my Head –

I say to you, said Jesus,
That there be standing here –
A sort, that shall not taste of Death –
If Jesus was sincere –

I need no further Argue –
The statement of the Lord
Is not a controvertible –
He told me, Death was dead –

Division 11 taste| 12 sincere – || 13 further| 14 the| 15 controvertible] controvert-| ible 16 Death|
P#390A (J#432)

The poem's opening question reveals an anxious puzzlement which is never quite resolved, and those who argue for the primacy of manuscript over printed text would find evidence to support their views here, for despite the apparent acceptance of the conclusion as it is printed in the neat stanzas of both the Johnson and the Franklin editions, the manuscript seems to show the poem stuttering to a halt, falling apart under the weight of its uncertainty, its careful architecture of quatrains undone in particular (physically and semantically) by the word division in what Franklin represents as the fifteenth line. The poem follows a pattern that, initially at least, seems formulaic: doubt is displaced by an assertion of faith, which the speaker then attempts to illustrate with the aid of a simile, and it is at this stage in the manuscript that the language of the poem appears to deconstruct itself. Not only is the end word in Dickinson's autograph eighteenth line (Franklin's fifteenth) split apart, but there is a blank space after "Death" in Dickinson's nineteenth line that suggests a missing referent, an absent verb or phrase that calls certainty into question.

The manuscript evidence is not always as clear cut as this would make it appear. For instance, both Franklin and Johnson insert a gap between the twelfth and thirteenth lines in their text, whereas in the manuscript (as it is reproduced in *The Manuscript Books of Emily Dickinson*, where the poem takes up two pages, as it did in the original) there is no such interval of space. Now, it could be argued that having the two lines so close together actually *reduces* the element of ambiguity that is introduced by the gap in the printed text. Because the lines are continuous in the manuscript (the argument might continue), they form part of one tonal or emotional unit and support each other's meaning: they are essentially orthodox. In the Franklin and Johnson editions, there is a space, a delay that separates the two and makes them oppose each other much more. And in the second page of the manuscript (which contains the final part of the poem running from "I need" until the close), there is clearly less physical room, so the poet is reduced to about three words per line where before she could fit four to six fairly easily.

I digress momentarily from the argument of this chapter because it seems to me that those who support the view that manuscripts contribute visually to a poem's meaning believe in a much closer relationship between language and meaning than the speaker in the poem does. If Dickinson deliberately divided the word "controvertible" in order to communicate a collapse of faith, then surely this means that language as it is inscribed on the page is still fully adequate to the meanings assigned it. In other words, the poem would demonstrate a formal commitment to linguistic sufficiency while at the same time disputing that sufficiency thematically. Such ocular onomatopoeia is a cheap trick that contradicts the poem's own uneasiness about discourse. For the logic of the poem (as I understand it) would appear to be that language is in fact an insufficient basis for belief. The comparison that the speaker offers is essentially a false one: posthumous survival is likened to the physical act of breathing, life after death matched with life before it. The simile has a symbolic charge, of course, for the tanks that supply the speaker's lungs are positioned above her or his head, and may therefore signify an influx of grace rather than air, spiritual as opposed to physical oxygen. In such a reading, it is the experience of conversion supplied by God that certifies that the promise of immortality is a real one. Nonetheless, the terms of the equation do not fit: present life is no guarantee for postmortem existence, and the use of such a simile underlines the fact that evidence for continued and continuing consciousness after death can only be offered verbally, not materially. As the poem develops, so too does its preoccupation with the media of belief: testifying and denying (lines 5 and 6), saying (twice in line 9), stating (line 14), and telling (line 16). Since all discourse is subject to abuse or inaccuracy, then faith must always be haunted by the knowledge of its own provisionality, its own subjunctive state. And if belief is a contract that depends on the believer's accepting the sincerity of the redeemer's discourse, then questions of intention and authority come into play. The speaker becomes confused about whether Christ was employing rhetorical-literary or functional-transparent language, and as if to embody and to exacerbate this confusion, Dickinson ends the poem by echoing the last line of John Donne's "Death, be not proud, though some have called thee," the tenth of his Holy Sonnets, which includes the formulation "Death, thou shalt die."[13]

Of course, implicit in P#788 (J#709) "Publication – is the Auction" (discussed in the previous chapter) is the outraged fear that commercial success calls into question aesthetic merit: Dickinson's own failure to follow up her many opportunities to publish is haunted by the fear that compromise in this life would mean failure in the next. The echoes of Christ's resurrection has clear implications for Dickinson's own choices as a writer because he (like her) "is sacrificed in this world and consecrated in the next." It has to be said, though, that this literary economy of short-term loss in return for long-term gain is based on a literal economic fact, and one Pierre Bourdieu nicely sums up: "it was still (inherited) money that assured freedom from money."[14] This is one of a number of complex reasons why Dickinson's works lack a sustained sense of explicit social commentary or concern (at a time when such engagement provided women authors with a primary motive and justification for writing in the first place); why she wrote lyrics and not novels; and why she could write almost two thousand poems but not publish them. Unlike many of the women writers of her day, she did not write because she needed the money (though she may have feared that possibility, and one wonders sometimes if she stored her fascicles for just such an eventuality). The convergence of spiritual election and literary immortality in the poem is therefore underpinned by social and economic segmentation: indeed, without the existence of class differences, an artistic afterlife would be unthinkable, for poetry can only survive the death of its author if there is a reading public who has been educated to believe in the significance and value of poetry itself as a mark of distinction and taste. No poem can be spoken by itself: the "I" that proposes her- or himself as proof of an afterlife depends in turn on a reader to enunciate and perform that possibility. Indeed, the tanks of oxygen that lie above the poem belong properly to precisely these readers, who are placed physically above the page as they read or speak it (echoing the famous letter to Higginson where Dickinson asked if her verses breathed).

In this interpretation, the first line contrasts the process of physical deterioration with the gradual decline in a writer's posthumous reputation, where composition becomes decomposition. The anxiety about depending on the goodwill and understanding of a future readership is not a new idea, and indeed can almost be said to be as old as writing itself: Shakespeare's sonnets promise the same permanence beyond the moment of composition, and many of Dickinson's own poems appear to express similar sentiments. Nevertheless, such assertions are occasionally undermined by ambivalence (as they are here): for example, the last four lines of P#772B (J#675), "Essential Oils – are wrung" (I reproduce the later and better-known version, rather than the one sent to Susan) claim that

The General Rose – decay –
But this – in Lady's Drawer
Make Summer – When the Lady lie
In Ceaseless Rosemary –

Echoing Shakespeare's sonnets in both the apparent message and in the reference to "Summer," the quatrain suggests that there is an essence in poetry that survives its maker, but (if read literally, as critics often do) the penultimate line is in fact untrue, for it is not the lady's bodily self that reclines eternally in rosemary, but her substituted representation ("this" can be the poem or perfume which she has distilled). That the line suggests the lady is "Ceaseless" is the kind of "lie" that fiction can help to fabricate—not a falsehood exactly, but an invention made possible by literary discourse. The bodily decomposition of the poet is disguised by the intervening body of composition, which is the poem: this may be a corruption, but it consoles the actual knowledge of corruption in the flesh with the felt truth of desire for permanence.

Many of the same ideas, it seems to me, are being discussed in P#390A (J#432): the relationship between scriptural and textual immortalities, and the fear of transience are particular areas of concern. What interests me here is not the psychological aspect of these writings, but their relevance to the present discussion of publication and nonpublication. For in both poems the preoccupation with religious versions of immortality finds its analogue in involvement with literary forms of timelessness. In other words, there is an interest in the fate of the poem after the poet's death, and Dickinson's refusal to publish can be read as a rejection of the kinds of contamination connected with the poem's appearance in the historically contemporary world, where reputations are dependent on the majority taste of other writers, publishers, readers, reviewers, teachers, and critics. What Dickinson attempted to evade, then, is the ephemeral nature of the popular, the brief life and death of the best-seller. This effort to distinguish her writing from current literary productions partly explains the concern with class, which is evinced in the poems above (and indeed in many others): in P#772B (J#675), the speaker differentiates the "Lady" (a word that implies gentility or noble birth) from the ordinary round of women, the "Essential Oils" from the "General Rose" (itself at a remove from the more common mass of plants); whereas in P#390A (J#432) the crisis in language and belief is triggered by the commonplace of death the leveler, which the speaker clearly finds disturbing. Particularly in the latter poem, the imagery betrays a profound unease about the democratic tendencies of the day, for the speaker's worry about the thought of extinction is expressed in hierarchical terms; there are some who are superior to others, and the poem hopes that this will carry over into, and beyond, her (or his) demise.

This anxious awareness of Death the Democrat is also shared by the speaker of P#1189A (J#1112), a poem that seems, superficially at least, to be one of the most vicious in the Dickinson canon.

> That this should feel the need of Death
> The same as those that lived
> Is such a Feat of Irony
> As never was achieved –
>
> Not satisfied to ape the Great in his simplicity
> The small must die, the same as he –
> Oh the audacity –

Once again, there is a preoccupation with event or experience as a symbolic property, although in this instance there appears to be no subtlety in the speaker's attitude; only seven lines of powerless invective, a sequence of comments recording the persona's dissatisfaction with the common-place of death as leveler, the great equalizer.[15] Christ's crucifixion is seen as conferring a special status on death, as the rite of passage through which the community of saints travels to their eternal reward. Such a privilege, the poem argues by implication, should not be extended to others; instead, it should be reserved for the few, although the speaker recognizes that, however unmerited, there is nothing that can be done to reserve mortality in such a way that it is experienced only by the elect. As if to underline the hierarchical implications of any religious institution that insists on divid-ing the regenerate and the unregenerate and assigning them to positions of superiority and inferiority (the upper and lower levels of heaven and hell), the poem uses a verb ("ape") which seems to repeat wider cultural caricatures of the working classes, in particular the assignment of simian features to Irish laborers and African Americans. And the last word of the entire poem, "audacity," depends for its effectiveness on an acceptance of the discourse of genteel courtesy with which the upper classes differentiate themselves from other lives. As with other poems, irony becomes the weapon of the disaffected and disfranchised bourgeois; the speaker's dis-missive sarcasm is the identifying mark of her own superiority.

Whether Dickinson writes or speaks this poem is perhaps the crucial question: the second word of the first line, "this," remains teasingly ambig-uous and uncertain: it is not at all clear, for example, that a corpse is the referent, and it is just as possible that the "this" can refer to the poem itself. Dickinson uses sacramental imagery elsewhere in her letters and poems to describe the power of language to survive the moment of its utterance (especially in script), and other references to the smallness of her poems make it feasible that this poem concerns itself with a competition between the immortality offered by poetic text (which is dead when fin-ished, but reborn each time it is read anew) and that offered by Christian-ity (represented by the speaker, who is antagonistic to the poem he or she is reading). In this complex interpretation, the work is uttered not by the writer but by the reader of another poem that (presumably) expresses the desire that the work will outlive the poet. There is a double irony here; the sarcastic speaker who notes this is ironized in her or his turn by the writer.

Still another possibility presents itself if we recover the Elizabethan pun on death as orgasm; with this in mind, we can imagine a reading where the speaker of the poem is a male complaining about female desire. Those that live are presumably men who conduct much of their lives in public, while the imagery of smallness recovers other images assigned by Dickinson to her female speakers. Such an interpretation is not entirely convincing, perhaps, for the death of Christ does not seem to have a direct relevance (in the poem) to the issues of gender and sexuality; nonetheless, it is not impossible, for the indeterminacy of "this" in combination with "Irony" (suggesting the possibility of a reverse reading) leaves spaces in the poem for voices other than that of the speaker. Indeed, this is one of the features of Dickinson's poetry; written by anyone else, the above poems would seem conventional and even cruel, but since they are drafted by her, they remain open, multivocal, and unresolved. It is easy to overlook the fact that some poems, P#390A (J#432), for example, are internalized dialogues: the first question is followed immediately by an answer, and this reply is then scrutinized in its turn. We can further observe that, although the poems reveal so little about the private life or experience that generates them, they do furnish a series of oblique impressions that function to instigate a kind of dialogue between the reader and the speaker.

Trying to tease a political position from Dickinson's poetry can be a risky business, then, because it draws one into making firm interpretive judgments about a writer who was and is notoriously difficult to classify. As an example of her slipperiness, one could cite another exchange of opinions conducted between Dickinson and Higginson, after the latter had published an *Atlantic Monthly* article (in January 1867) entitled "A Plea for Culture," in which he called for a truly American art while simultaneously complaining that the conditions for such an art did not yet exist: "American literature is not yet copious, American scholarship not profound, American society not highly intellectual, and the American style of execution, in all high arts, yet hasty and superficial."

Dickinson answered his article (privately, in another letter) by writing:

Bringing still my "plea for Culture,"
Would it teach me now?[16]

Dickinson readers will recognize the familiar and deferential pose of the ignorant scholar addressing the elder teacher, but for me the question seems to sum up the full uncertainty of her social and literary situation, for on the one hand she identifies herself almost playfully as the American artist or intellectual in need of refinement (and therefore in a potentially oppositional relation to Higginson's definition of culture) while on the other, she appears to seek instruction and guidance on Higginson's terms.

It may even be that, in an indirect way, she is inserting herself as a possible answer to the malaise he (and others like him—Henry James, Charles Eliot Norton, James Fenimore Cooper, Nathaniel Hawthorne) wrote about. There is ambition in her lines, but also anxiety: she does not yet possess culture (as Higginson defines it), but she aspires toward it. Although Dickinson is playing with Higginson here, she does not openly disagree with his judgments, and indeed there is a profundity and weight of intent to be detected here beneath the playfulness: for her, Culture is a very high and serious business, almost a vocation, and it is one she very consciously wants to pursue.

Dickinson's flight to culture is, I would argue, both a result of her class status and a consequence of its increasing marginalism and threatened erosion. Her nonpublication is a radical sign of a split between mass and elite culture, an indication "of the relative decline of a shared public culture, which in the second half of the nineteenth century fractured into a series of discrete cultures that had less and less to do with each other."[17] The rapid progress of industrialization and urbanization, the accelerated intake of millions of immigrants with their alien cultural practices, all brought with them a threat to the established order, and Dickinson's escape is typical of wider efforts to cope with this threat. (Those who believe that living in Amherst protected Dickinson from these phenomena should look again: although the population remained fairly stable during her lifetime, and although there is a highly visible continuity and cohesion in terms of those who "ran the town, held the political offices, supported the churches, and owned the stores and factories," this stable group was also joined by highly transient subgroups made up of African Americans, Irish, and French Canadians.)[18] It is exactly parallel with Austin's beating of Irish schoolchildren and establishment of by-laws, and with her father's purchase of a home with which he could symbolize the return of the family fortunes and a political career wherein he could attempt (and fail) to gain influence of some kind. Levine sums up these parallels nicely:

> [These] worlds of strangers did not remain contained; they spilled over into the public spaces that characterized nineteenth-century American life and that included theaters, music halls, opera houses, museums, parks, fairs, and the rich public cultural life that took place daily on the streets of American cities. This is precisely where the threat lay, and the response of the elites was a tripartite one: to retreat into their own private spaces whenever possible; to transform public

spaces by rules, systems of taste, and canons of behavior of their own choosing; and, finally, to convert the strangers so that their modes of behavior and cultural predilections emulated those of the elites.[19]

The celebrated difficulty and indeterminacy of Dickinson's writing, as I have said before, is the stylistic equivalent of this escape: it guarantees that only readers with sufficient leisure, capital, and a certain standard of higher education can approach the work. (Henry James once wrote in a letter that "the difficulty itself is the refuge from vulgarity," and one suspects that Dickinson would—at times—have agreed, though she was much more capable than James of identifying her own position in terms of society's outcasts.)[20] Like the home in which she lived and the family who lived there, poetry was an oasis of excellence in a wasteland of the common, even though many of the poems continued to chart the struggle against modern life's pressures in terms of imagery, vocabulary, and patterns of concern. Those poems that express the purity and power of their speakers also situate that power and purity only in the textual space of the poems themselves, which serve as an antidote to feelings of alienation and impotence in daily life.

Clearly, though, indeterminacy is a standard of literary excellence in modern fiction, and one wonders at this point how much Dickinson's alleged ambiguity can be explained in terms of her work's circulation in differing historical environments. If we return to "Publication – is the Auction" for answers to that question, and look at the phrase "Disgrace of Price" in the final line, it seems at least possible that ambiguity inheres within the poem itself, rather than occurring in the encounter between reader and poem. "Disgrace of Price," after all, could mean either that the person whose property (or self) is *being* sold, or that the person *doing* the selling, is humiliated and degraded by the act of sale. Instances of such ambiguity are common in Dickinson's poetry, as scholars have pointed out before me. Cristanne Miller convincingly shows how "multiplicity [and] indeterminacy" result from very specific grammatical practices.[21] David Porter observes "the indefiniteness of the poet's purpose" in specific poems, and his careful formal analysis reveals a poet more attuned to "the dance of tropes" than mimetic intentions.[22] The point to make, then, is that ambiguity in Dickinson's writing seems to be a fully conscious and deliberate strategy and not simply an accident of the fact of her nonpublication (which could conceivably explain why, in Sharon Cameron's memorable phrase, Dickinson "chooses not choosing": not having to prepare a text for final publication in conference with editors meant that she was not obliged to clear up slippages and obscurities of meaning).

Finally, the indeterminacy and ambiguity that a number of scholars have attributed to Dickinson's work may to some extent be a side-effect of the time in which she lived, when the relative stability of local exchange and barter between people known to each other personally was steadily eroded and then replaced by the exigencies of less visible, and sometimes long-distance, conditions of supply and demand: a crisis of confidence in one's readership results then in a conscious obfuscation of poetic discourse (I am aware that this would suggest that Dickinson's audience was *not* the present one she included poems in letters to, but a *projected* one of the future). Dickinson's concern with whiteness in "Publication – is the Auction" has fairly clear associations with debates about ethnicity, women's status, and literature, but it may also be seen as invoking a point of view that either rejects printed paper (that is, cash, or credit, or even deeds of property such as mortgage agreements) as a token of exchange or argues in terms that can lead one (perhaps at some stage of the argument's progression outside the poem, for example) to imagine the speaker and the poet capable of entertaining such a rejection. Allied to this is an unambiguous refusal to consider payment or profit as a motivating factor for her work (partly because it then leaves one open to the charge that the writing was done out of necessity, which undermines respectability and integrity). Poetry is its own reward, its own justification, its own (to borrow an image Dickinson too borrowed) capital—though again with the proviso that such a set of ideas depends on the condition of one (or one's family) having sufficient capital in the first place.

I am not about to say that ambiguity is a kind of superrealism caused by uncertainties in Dickinson's economic life (though that is a possibility I cannot rule out, and one that Marx and Engels accepted as a valid benchmark for great literature), or that there is a causal or deterministic relationship between one and the other. What I do say is that this characteristic of her work goes some way toward explaining Dickinson's apparent isolation from history and her dislike for the actual. For example, consider once again the speaker of "I like to see it lap the Miles" who is positioned *off* the train, watching it—perhaps even fearing it—but not intervening to alter its progress in any way or indeed to adopt any kind of direct response to it at all. Consider, also, the speaker of "Publication – is the Auction" who observes enslavement only to make it refer to the potential commodification of the literary self, and whose recommended course of action against such slavery is to refuse it (a strategy that demonstrates sympathy but no understanding of the exact circumstances under which historical individuals suffered under slavery). Consider, finally, the speaker of P#260A (J#288), "I'm Nobody! Who are you?" who criticizes public performance but recommends a privatized strategy of opposition into withdrawal and whispering. The latter poem in particular associates refinement with quietness and political oratory with crudeness and vulgarity—as does "I like to see it lap the Miles," which draws a similar distinction between a "horrid – hooting stanza" and the speaker's own suggestive removal. In all three poems, it is the speaker's *disengaged* consciousness that is sufficient guarantee of her superiority, and this is clearly significant.

Disengagement *from* history can function as a form of consolation for the impossibility of engaging *with* history in the first place. Dickinson's class position is clearly relevant here, for it was an ambiguous one: as a *woman* she is both a part of and apart from the rural elite her family aspired to. In Bourdieu's formula, she belongs to the dominated half of a dominant provincial class.[23] When Betsy Erkkila accuses feminist critics of writing ahistorically (so that Dickinson is often represented as a woman operating in opposition to a generalized patriarchy, rather than within a specific set of social relations during a particular period of nineteenth-century American capitalism), one applauds the originality and accuracy of her insights, but is then confronted with Erkkila's own unambivalent assertion of Dickinson's loyalties to masculine ideologies, which surely would have been complicated by her gender.[24] It is of course true to say that gender is socially constituted, but the accident of her biological identity would have prevented her from fully accepting the imperatives and institutions of nineteenth-century politics—or would at least have placed her in a more distant relation to its activities—if only because nineteenth-century institutions and imperatives excluded her on the grounds of that identity. In addition, as I have tried to argue, the Dickinson class status was not as fixed as it appears to us in the twentieth century, when it has the semblance of a finished narrative. Since class is always defined in relation to other sections of the population, it is always (though not always radically so) fragile, changing, and under constant threat. There is an Irish joke that tells of how two farmers who disputed the ownership of a cow tried to settle the argument in a contest of strength: one pulled the cow by the tail, the other by the horns, while a lawyer sat in between them and milked for all he was worth. Edward Dickinson could milk too, but he would have been uncomfortably aware that he too owned a cow, and that sometime, someone else could do the same to him. The family never experienced the kinds of housing conditions suffered by Irish workers in nearby Holyoke, but it did suffer the shame of having to live in a duplex arrangement with others (in the Widow Montague's house, in Samuel Fowler Dickinson's house, in David Mack Jr.'s house), and eventually of being forced to sell the family mansion. And Emily Dickinson was denied power because she was not consulted on such basic matters as where she wanted to live, for example, or about the duration of her education. There are no records of her ever having conducted financial transactions, or having full control over her travels outside Amherst (she was sometimes sent away at times of emotional distress). Nor can we be sure that her visits to Boston for treatment to her eyes were entirely voluntary. In later years, after the death of her father, the evidence points to her exercising greater choice over her relations to medical practitioners: even at the time of the illness which brought about her death at a comparatively young age, she refused to let Dr. Bigelow in the same room with her. Poetry provided her with an alternative arena of empowerment and valorization. Writing without publishing embodied an aspiration to be free of social determination or authority, class allegiance as well as economic dependence on the market: handwritten lyric poems derive their legitimacy from other sources (the genius of the writer, the beauty of the language, the truth of the insights expressed). At the same time, such a removal is partly enforced, in the sense that poetry (although acknowledged as the highest form of the written arts by most critics) was gradually being displaced and segregated by the more popular and socially influential form of the women's novel.[25]

In his preface to *Portrait of a Lady* Henry James wrote that "the house of fiction has not one window, but a million—a number of possible windows not to be reckoned, rather."[26] In the following poem the house symbolizes the aesthetic consciousness grounded in real ownership (in the sense of either property or economic sufficiency) and that therefore affords the possibility of detached and multiple-sided perspective, but that is also superior to ownership in the sense that it is not subject to the fluctuations and demands of the market. Texts, like houses, are differentiated according to architectural integrity, stylistic details and the viewpoints they enable.

I dwell in Possibility –
A fairer House than Prose –
More numerous of Windows –
Superior – for Doors –

Of Chambers as the Cedars –
Impregnable of eye –
And for an everlasting Roof
The Gambrels of the Sky –

Of Visitors – the fairest –
For Occupation – This –
The spreading wide my narrow Hands
To gather Paradise –

8 Gambrels] Gables –

Division 7 everlasting | 11 my |
P#466A (J#657)

The history of American writing and publishing in the nineteenth century shows a sudden and rapid enlargement of the market in the period leading up to the Civil War. Technological advancements and mechanization made it possible for more (and bigger) books to be printed for comparatively less money. Railroads made it easier for the final product to be circulated more cost effectively to different regions, and growth in both the size and the literacy of the population meant an increased audience and enlarged profits. Whereas a successful writer could expect to sell perhaps five or six thousand copies in the 1820s, by the 1850s such a limited print run was a sign of relative failure: *The Scarlet Letter* reached this figure whereas other writers (and women writers in particular) "regularly sold sixty, eighty, or even a hundred thousand copies in a year."[27] In the 1820s, just over a hundred novels were published, but one thousand were printed in the 1840s, so that literature had become a market, with the result that there was more (and more aggressive) competition between authors, genres, and publishing houses. The market (in the shape of publishers, critics, and a middle-class audience, which demanded, and got, a certain product) exercised a greater amount of control over literary productions, as well.

The opening statement of P#466A (J#657) depends for our understanding on an awareness of conflicts and uncertainties that accompany the transformation of literature into a commercial economy. The increased competition between writers and genres is clearly a factor here, and it produces a reactionary statement of poetic priorities: unlike the prose books (Catharine Maria Sedgwick's *Home*, Susan Warner's *The Wide, Wide World*, Louisa May Alcott's *Little Women*) and magazines (such as *Home Journal*, *Home Monthly*, *Home Missionary*, and *Arthur's Home Magazine*), which take domesticity as their subject but which also compete for sales in an extradomestic environment, this poem is intent on gathering in "Paradise" rather than readers or royalties. She takes nature, and not human nature, as her subject, and this self-enclosed world of self and subject replicates the ostensible direction of the domestic environment (which is inward and spiritual) but not necessarily its ideological purpose (which is to provide a haven for the male worker and for the family, but also a place where women act as hosts for other visitors and thus provide a sense of community and social cohesion).

But a literary reading of the poem is certainly not the only one made available by its architectural imagery. Typically, the poem situates itself as the location for an activity that exists in opposition to those that occur in real houses, though that activity simultaneously draws on a matrix of the middle-class values of this time, such as the emphasis on leisure and privacy encoded in the Cult of Domesticity. Whereas houses (especially for women) are sites of ideological, economic, and physical confinement—prisons almost—with limited numbers of windows, doors, and chambers, Nature provides an unlimited access to visionary experience and thus the potential for participation and personal (interior) enlargement. (It is assumed that the speaker is female here mainly because the reference to the "narrow Hands" recovers similar imagery of feminine smallness in Dickinson's writing.) The mutability of domestic exteriors is contrasted with "Cedars," a singularly appropriate tree, in that it connotes the Bible, local and universal nature, as well as longevity and stability.[28] In a study deriving from 1892, there are a number of interesting features attributed to the red cedar:

It is a striking feature in the landscape of eastern Massachusetts, especially near the seashore, but it is rather seldom seen here. Within our limits it occurs only in comparatively isolated specimens. It may be seen in the Village Cemetery, near, and almost in front of, either entrance. The wood of the Red Cedar is very valuable. Being extremely aromatic, it is much used for moth-proof chests. The extreme durability of the deep red heart-wood makes it highly prized for fence-posts; and it is the wood of a southern variety of this species which is used in the manufacture of lead pencils.[29]

It is tempting to think that Dickinson had some of the same aspects in mind when she wrote her poem: the relative rarity of the species makes it an apt symbol for the speaker's originality and value, while the connections with the afterlife (the cemetery) and artistic activity (pencils) are also convenient, as is the reference to fence-posts, for the "building" in which the speaker dwells, like a two-way mirror, affords her protection from prying eyes while enabling her to see outward at the same time. (The mansion on Main Street was also protected by a picket fence, it might be added, and by three gates that—according to house rules—were always to be kept closed. But it could not be protected from other intrusions.)[30] This information is clearly useful, but not necessary: on its own, the cedar tree stands as a symbol for solidity and permanence (it is an evergreen and an exceptionally durable tree).

Privacy, the denial of the actual, and the preoccupation with perception are typical Dickinsonian motifs, indicating a familiar distrust of the merely accidental or contingent features of domestic spaces. If "This" can be seen as referring self-consciously to the poem itself (or to the occupation of writing or reading: the spreading of the hands to hold a book, for example), then the poem can also be seen as attempting to find in nature *and* in culture a site of dignity and stability that is an alternative to those enclosures prescribed by society.

Rather than being "a totally self-contained experience," then, I would argue that the poem depends on economic and historical definitions for much of its charge.[31] It begins with a self, an I, who defines herself and her nonproductivity in opposition to contemporary definitions of the female sphere and role (occupying a "House" but having no economic occupation within it), but who still inhabits a private space that is separate from commercial enterprise (it is interesting that the Amherst census of 1870 describes Emily Dickinson as being "without occupation," which carries with it a recognition of Edward's economic status as well as betraying society's ambiguous relationship to unmarried women who remained at home). Viewed through the lens of nineteenth-century domestic ideology, the poem seems to flit in and out of focus, at one hand appearing to contradict it, on the other hand reworking its priorities to the speaker's own advantage (and at the same time coming dangerously close to affirming that *this* woman's marginalized position is acceptable). The poem establishes its own world-within-a-world, a scene of domesticated nature rather than natural domesticity. And yet the poem is as sentimentalized as the cult of the Angel in the House: this angel defines her own importance in similarly spiritual terms (gathering flowers, gathering words, embracing "Paradise").

Similar points could be made about the poem P#407 (J#670) which I discussed toward the beginning of the previous chapter, "One need not be a Chamber – to be Haunted." When Dickinson makes a distinction in that poem between a "Haunted . . . House" and the chambers of the mind, she is drawing on, but distancing herself from, public modes of expression. Increase and Cotton Mather believed that Indians, demons, and witches were able to adopt noncorporeal selves, but in the nineteenth century a series of scientific investigators argued that ghosts did not exist independently of their perceiver.[32] Those shapes that did occur outside the self were products either of the (literary or hallucinatory) imagination or of the illusory effects of technology, such as the magic lanterns (and their equivalents), which were capable of projecting specters (or scenes of urban and foreign life) onto external screens for a paying, public audience.[33] Included within the poem's opening statement is an implicit opposition between those apparitions produced for consumption in the literary marketplace and the inner disputes of the lyric poet alone in her chamber. The poem (it might be argued) dramatizes an essentially economic or class-based conflict between the published literature of sensationalism and the sensitivity of an artistic mind that is faithful to the struggles enacted within consciousness itself. The "Superior[ity]" of the "Spectre" in the penultimate line (like the "Superior[ity]" of line 4 in "I dwell in Possibility") is not just in relation to the person who has barred the door but to those cheap and garish projections of texts and technologies directed by the commodified imagination.

In "One need not be a Chamber – to be Haunted" is therefore (in part) a poem about the differences between private poetry and public, published prose (the more explicit theme of P#590A (J#669), "No Romance sold unto / Could so enthrall a Man / As the perusal of / His individual One –"), between specters in stories and what Dickinson elsewhere termed the "spectral power in thought."[34] It is also a poem that dramatizes a wider shift in historical thinking: as Terry Castle puts it, from "an initial connection with something external and public (an artificially produced "spectral" illusion), the word [spectral] has now come to refer to something wholly internal or subjective: the phantasmic imagery of the mind."[35]

Thoughts, then, are more terrifying than real ghosts because they cannot be protected against: consciousness may guard itself against the posthumous appearances of the dead (or against supernatural appearances), but it can only defend itself from thought through its own cessation. Again, one of the effects of the distinction that the poem insists on is the creation of a hierarchical architecture of intellects: the more troubled one is by doubts, fears, and anxieties, the more sensitive one is (and vice versa—the equation is reversible). One of the poem's points, however, would be that thoughts are as substantial as houses: here, clearly, this is a negative attribute, because there is no protection against thinking (at least no *material* means of defending oneself; there may be a suggestion that other strategies are possible). But in other contexts the very materiality of thought clearly has potential as a location for significant and permanent creative enterprise—it may not afford rest and comfort in the shape of real chambers, but the "pretty rooms" of verse do offer an alternative site for a domicile of the mind. (It is easy to overlook the significance of a statement such as "The brain has Corridors surpassing / Material Place": it effectively displaces property as the single token of social value or excellence.) In other words, the poem provides us with the negative contours of Dickinson's faith in the imagination: at its worst, it may terrify, but the very power that makes it so terrible is also what gives it its power and attraction.

Both poems contain within themselves a declaration of high moral seriousness, and "I dwell in Possibility" in particular exemplifies the process by which art became sacralized in the latter half of the nineteenth century. As is often the case, a poem that resists the idea of art as a commercial or didactic activity depends for its position on the benefits of economic advantage. People with houses find it easier to protest their indifference to houses than people without them, it might be said. But almost immediately, one thinks of a qualification to this statement, for perhaps the dismissal of prose properties in the poem proceeds instead from a different kind of necessity: given her biographical circumstances, Dickinson may have felt that she had to define her significance in ways that were different from those of inheritance, entitlement, and ownership, precisely because those values no longer represented stable currency. At any rate, poems such as these are rationalizations of leisure, which define their own purpose and importance in opposition to materialist practices. Thus Dickinson's speaker remains enclosed in the invisible space of anonymity, whereas others open the curtains and give a voyeuristic public unlimited access to their own homes and minds. In a sense, Dickinson's nonpublication (or her choice of circulating the poems among a small and fairly elite circle of sympathetic friends) is the guarantee of the poem's integrity: even if we do not suppose that she is the speaker (though there are reasons for feeling that the writer may at least have identified partially with her persona), the fact that the piece did not appear in print functions as a kind of warrant for its sincerity.

The weight of historical evidence does not necessarily enable us to fit Dickinson into a political or social scheme: she (or her speakers) may voice conservative, even reactionary, opinions, but she also demonstrates opposite tendencies. She may align herself with a literary elite, but she read (and enjoyed) popular forms—newspapers, serialized novels, biographies, short stories, and sentimental fiction. She chose to write lyric poems, a decision that has clear political as well as aesthetic implications, for lyric poetry is primarily the genre of privilege and prestige, the expression of the bourgeois self who can afford the time and leisure to write about herself rather than others. But she also read sociological and realist fictions— Rebecca Harding Davis's "Life in the Iron Mills," for instance, as well as Harriet Beecher Stowe's *Uncle Tom's Cabin* and its Native American equivalent, Helen Hunt Jackson's *Ramona* (both of which were literary extensions of women's reformist activities during the nineteenth century). My own view is that Dickinson's position as a disfranchised woman who lacked the power to speak publicly, to publish publicly, and to influence public events in the same way as her father and brother results in a literary point of view that privileges noninvolvement, strategic withdrawals, and the weaponry of a difficult and indirect discourse. Her poems often describe or enact deferral, seeing rather than doing, knowing rather than participating.[36] For Karl Mannheim, the condition of "homelessness in society" is one of the identifying characteristics of the unattached intellectual. Though speaking of a later era, Mannheim does acknowledge that the intelligentsia in the Age of Romanticism subscribe to a "broad, dynamic mediation of conflicting points of view"—albeit from a conservative perspective.[37]

We often think of Emily Dickinson as particularly home-bound, but she was also capable of a kind of skepticism about domesticity: Higginson reports her as asking "Could you tell me what home is" in 1870, and in 1883, the year after her mother's death, she described a state of being "Homeless at home" (P#1603A [J#1573]), which replicates her July 1875 statement (again to Higginson) that "Home is so far from Home, since my Father died."[38] This condition of homelessness is not simply a result of the loss of her parents, but also a recognition that uncertainty and doubt were (in part) definitions of being alive in a market economy. Indeed, in many poems "ownership" is itself equated with death: "I am alive – because / I do not own a House" says the speaker of P#605 (J#470)—"I am alive – I guess," while the first stanza of P#1050 (J#1090) reads "I am afraid to own a Body – I am afraid to own a Soul – Profound – precarious Property – / Possession, not optional – ." Clearly the house of the first quotation is the "long home" of the grave, and the second quotation expresses the dreadful certainty of death and the fears that attend the individual's responsibility for her or his own moral purity and transcendence. Nonetheless, *economic* realities inform these same fears: at the very least, the presence of these terms reveals how intimate a part of Dickinson's vocabulary and consciousness the property market was. The poems about "home" show it to be the very opposite of everything the nineteenth century defined it as: sanctuary, haven/heaven, refuge. It is, in short, a place haunted by conflicting forces and pressures that have their origin outside the self.

This much is evident in a famous quotation (attributed to Lavinia), which shows the members of the Dickinson household finding their own ways of marking their difference from other, competing classes. Though they lived together during all their childhood and for much of their adult lives (even Austin coming almost every day after his marriage to eat breakfast with his sisters) each of them had intensely separate spheres:

> Father was the only one to say "damn." Someone in every family
> ought to say damn of course. As for Emily, she was not withdrawn or
> exclusive really. She was always watching for the rewarding person to
> come, but she was a very busy person herself. She had to think – she
> was the only one of us who had that to do. Father believed; and
> mother loved; and Austin had Amherst; and I had the family to keep
> track of.[39]

This description of the family's different interests fascinates not least because it mirrors the increasing segregation of nineteenth-century American life generally. The institutions of faith, local politics, the religion of love, culture, and domesticity are all significant but separate avenues for self-realization. They are also, I argue, zones where the members of an established elite responded to economic and social competition and change by finding a compensatory sense of personal worth and influence: women in particular found dignity and a sense of empowerment in conducting the daily business of the affections, "so much so that the cultivation of close relations might be said to *be its* productive activity."[40] Such cultivation also included writing letters and poems and sending flowers.

In reading Dickinson's lyric enclosures, we seem privileged to oversee and to overhear (as Northrop Frye puts it) the thoughts of someone "who turns [her] back on [her] audience," but this should not detract us from recognizing that many of the alleged contradictions and inconsistencies of Dickinson's writing emerge from adjacent historical polarities.[41] It is therefore possible to read her recourse to home in the first place as (again, in part) an ideologically conditioned reaction to the fluctuations and intrusions of the market and the increased competition and mobility of her age. Her home-based and nonutilitarian production of literature can also be seen as an extreme version of a general characteristic whereby members of the middle and upper middle classes sought to define a sense of social difference and superiority through aesthetic detachment, stylistic difficulty, intellectual intensity, psychological depth, and moral refinement. This is certainly not the only way of understanding such a strategy, but it is interesting and instructive given the relative lack of attention paid to the relations between social formations of culture and Dickinson's apparent privatization of writing and textual circulation. Her poems have more to do with issues of class, immigration, ethnicity, industrialization, the mass-market, and democratic politics than first appears. The proliferation of alien perspectives and languages necessitates finding new grounds for social preeminence, but to achieve this eminence one must constantly sift through those languages as they appear in order to define the precise but shifting coordinates of one's own difference and identity. At the same time, however, I hope to have demonstrated that even if the poems can be constructed as existing in political reaction to her own times, opposing voices and viewpoints are stubbornly, and I think deliberately, present in the work, disturbing and invigorating, challenging and energizing. To separate those voices from Dickinson's is, I believe, to lose much of the reason for her writing those poems in the first place.

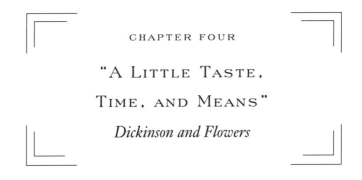

CHAPTER FOUR

"A Little Taste, Time, and Means"

Dickinson and Flowers

"If you have no further use for this," the reader is instructed in L. W. Goodell's *Catalogue of Choice Selected Flower Seeds and Bulbs for 1878*, "please hand it to some friend who is interested in the culture of Flowers."[1] Goodell's Flower Farm ("Pansy Park") was situated in Dwight, Massachusetts, but the address Goodell gave for himself was in Amherst, and he may well have been one of the suppliers of bulbs and seeds for the Dickinsons, all of whom seemed to enjoy gardening (or gardens) in one form or another. "I have long been a lunatic on bulbs," wrote Emily in May 1883, to acknowledge a gift of bulbs from her neighbor Cornelia Peck, wife of John Howard Sweetser, Luke and Abby Tyler Munsell Sweetser's only child.[2] Taken together, her statement and that by Goodell allow us to make a number of generalized observations that are germane to the concerns of this chapter. First, both assume the existence of a shared culture of exchange in which flowers and texts about flowers can be circulated as gifts, primarily among women. Often, this system of exchange is thought of as existing in opposition to economic practice, but both the commercial and the cultural promotion of flowers coincide in their appeal to class distinctions: the specimens offered by Goodell are "choice," "carefully selected," and "of the first quality."[3] Of course, one would hardly expect a merchant to say anything else about the products he is trying to sell, but in fact the application of scientific principles to the selection and breeding of indoor plants at the end of the eighteenth and beginning of the nineteenth century meant that flowers were less neutrally fixed in the domain of "the natural" than they had been before: they were now divided up (and priced) according to their rarity and beauty, which made it easier for them to reflect class differences and values.

Goodell's catalog claimed that his stock sold for as low a price as "seeds of the first quality can," but looking through its pages for references to the kinds of flowers that Dickinson is known to have liked, one finds that they were still not cheap: lilies sold for between twenty-five and fifty cents (each), packets of alyssum, for five to ten cents, the primrose for between ten and fifty cents, the heliotrope for fifteen, the carnation for twenty-five, the mignonette for between five and ten, the gilliflower for ten, the pansy for between fifteen and twenty, and the crocus for between ten and fifteen. Not all of the flowers thought to have been grown by Dickinson are contained in Goodell's catalog, however, which suggests that those that weren't had to have been either picked from the wild (by a woman whose education taught her where to find them, which ones to value and why, and how to cultivate them) or shipped from nurseries farther afield (in Connecticut, Minnesota, New York, and Vermont), which meant that they would have been rarer, more expensive, and therefore more valuable in ways that were simultaneously economic and aesthetic.[4] John T. C. Clark, in *The Amateur's Guide and Flower-Garden Dictionary* (1856), points out the relationship between economic status and taste: "Where flowers are planted, a home becomes a tasteful residence, while its intrinsic value is greatly enhanced. Cultivated taste gives beauty and value to property, and the small cost of a flower-garden, so far from being a useless expense, as some assert, adds to the money-value of a property."[5]

The "culture of Flowers," then, is one way in which a specific class can promote and preserve its constituent beliefs and reaffirm its collective identity. Indeed, the words "culture" and "cultivation," according to Webster's *American Dictionary of the English Language*, could apply simultaneously to the management of plants and to the practice of self-improvement.[6] Horticulture, like culture itself, was a measure of refinement—though it was not available to everyone (or, more accurately, it was available at prices that differed in ways that reinforced its segregation according to the boundaries of social class). The indulgence in flowers, which could cost between twenty-five and fifty cents each, was in many ways a parallel activity to the purchase and perusal of genteel magazines, which sold for an average of thirty-five cents.[7] The cultivation of flowers was part of the display of taste, as was the reading of premier magazines: both were expensive pastimes with very specific social implications:

> Amherst's periodical and newspaper lists demonstrate that it was primarily women of the middle and upper classes who were reading these publications. If a household received any periodical, it was most likely receiving more than one. This suggests that those people who read these magazines and newspapers not only had the time to sit down and read every month or every week or every day but that they also had the money to pay for multiple subscriptions.[8]

According to the *Periodical and Newspaper Lists* for Amherst's post office between the years of 1860 and 1865 (as they are indexed alphabetically by name of recipient), the Hon. Edward Dickinson subscribed to fourteen publications, which is about three times as many as would be expected for a family with a real estate value of over $10,000, and twice as many as most clergymen subscribed to.[9] Among them, of course, was the *Atlantic Monthly*, the "most prestigious venue for quality fiction" in the United States (it sold for twenty-five cents a copy).[10] Dickinson's decision to write to Thomas Wentworth Higginson after his "Letter to a Young Contributor" appeared there in April 1862 shows in part how she conceived of her own art and what kind of audience she (might have) projected for it.[11] Writing about flowers in poems and letters and enclosing cut flowers as gifts to friends are part of a broader cultural and social continuum that includes the periodicals one chooses to read and the people one decides to circulate one's letters and manuscripts to. This chapter looks more closely at the correspondences between Dickinson's flowers and her poems—those "flowers of the muses"—as well as at their significance for a politico-literary aesthetics.[12] In order to do so, I will stress some of the rather obvious, but often overlooked, processes and conditions that made Dickinson's authorship and gardening possible: her literacy, for example, which allowed her to be so knowledgeable about botany and natural history, but which distinguished her very clearly from other sections of the population; her comparative leisure (because she was economically disfranchised but supported and comfortable);[13] and, finally, the effects of technological innovation that broadened the domestic spaces available to the family, eased the lives of its members, increased the privacy available to them, and made the home and its commodities a suitable subject for a particular kind of middle- and upper-middle-class literature written by nineteenth-century American women. This is not to advance an unproblematic relationship of causality between the material circumstances of Dickinson's life and her creativity, for that would be to deny her the right of human agency. Rather, it is an attempt at recording the full and complex experience of her engagement with history as she lived it—sometimes compliantly, sometimes combatively—through the myriad locations of her poetry.

It is easy to overlook how Emily Dickinson's sentimentalization of the homes she lived in during the 1840s and 1850s coincides with, and depends in part on, technological advances in the instruments that made domestic interiors more comfortable. Candles, for example, had been largely replaced or supplemented by oil lamps, which burned brighter and more evenly—an important consideration for a writer who often worked at night.[14] When the family moved back to the Homestead in 1855, Edward Dickinson improved the old house (it is believed) by installing cast-iron fireplaces, or Franklin stoves, in several rooms, including the poet's bedroom, which made the business of writing poems a year-round activity: without that stove, the astonishing production of 1862 and 1863 (as conjectured first by Thomas Johnson and subsequently by Ralph Franklin from changes in the poet's handwriting) may not have been possible.[15] Had she been productive thirty years earlier, the ink she used (when she used ink) would have frozen overnight during the severest stretches of the New England winter, and even writing with a pencil would have been a laborious enterprise. The family would have been capable of operating with ease—and writing letters—only in those limited areas where large fires afforded communal warmth.[16] Indeed, when Dickinson writes to Austin in 1853 that she misses "the long talks most, upon the *kitchen stone hearth*, when the just are fast asleep," she expresses a very typical nostalgia for a select community of her own but also the difficulty of finding a private space in a house where the warmth was largely confined to shared family spaces.[17]

Franklin stoves were not cheap, but they were economical in the long run, because they "burned far less wood than open hearths . . . at least one-third."[18] They also enabled the family to live separately from each other—and thus afforded the poet the privacy necessary to her writing. Finally, they facilitated an extension not only of the poet's poetic but of her horticultural zones as well, for Dickinson also grew plants in her bedroom: indeed, as Jane Nylander has argued, stoves made the growing of plants easier, but plants in turn provided the now dryer room in which they had been installed with necessary humidity and oxygen.[19] (In *The American Women's Home* of 1869, Catharine Beecher recommended growing house plants for precisely this purpose).[20] Evidence of Dickinson's early interest in botanical pursuits is provided by correspondence dating from her time at Pleasant Street: on 2 November 1847, when she was at Mount Holyoke, she mentions her plants in a letter to Austin, and at the same time reflects on the combined difficulties that the Massachusetts climate and architecture posed for amateur gardeners: "How do the plants look now & are they as flourishing as before I went away? I wish much to see them. Some of the girls here, have plants, but it is a cold place & I am very glad that I did not bring any, as I thought of doing."[21] She is probably referring to indoor plants, and the fact that she could expect her own to be still alive in November is testimony to her conformity to conventional tastes (women who could afford to were encouraged to occupy their time by caring for plants), as well as to her or her mother's exceptional skill and dedication as a gardener. Finally, it indicates the presence of sufficient heat to keep bulbs and plants from freezing overnight. Before the move to the Homestead and the purchase of open stoves, however, it seems unlikely that many plants would have been placed in Dickinson's bedroom: they were probably kept in the kitchen or in one of the family rooms, which adjoined the great central chimney.

> Brick chimney stacks retained some heat throughout the night,
> keeping at least a portion of the rooms through which they passed
> somewhat warmer than the outside walls. If such heat could keep the
> temperature above freezing, indoor plants and flower bulbs could be
> forced into bloom. There is little evidence of this in eighteenth-
> century households, but after about 1820, many people developed
> an interest in indoor gardening.[22]

Anything left outside in small gardens would not have lasted long, as Dickinson acknowledges in a September letter to Abiah Root written two years before her letter from Mount Holyoke: "I have had a beautiful flower-garden this summer; but they are nearly gone now. It is very cold to-night, and I mean to pick the prettiest ones before I go to bed, and cheat Jack Frost of so many of *the treasures* he calculates to rob to-night."[23]

Stoves (and the money it took to provide them) created an atmosphere where both plants and poetry could flourish, as her niece, Martha Dickinson Bianchi, confirms:

> She would perhaps be by the dining-room fire, or better still up in her own room, forever associated for me with the odor of hyacinths, for the way of a bulb in the sunshine had an uncanny fascination for her, their little pots crowding all four window-sills to bring a reluctant spring upon the air. From the first prick of the green above the earth she detected every minute sign of growth.
>
> There I would find her reading or writing, while the slow glow of the open Franklin stove added another deceptive hint of spring warmth.[24]

Bianchi's description clearly dates from the later years at the Homestead, and (like the letter to Root) shows that domestic interiors—like poetic ones—provided the poet with an artificial zone for the exercise of a degree of control over external forces and processes, a zone that was dependent in turn on its financing and furnishing with the instruments that facilitated leisure. That same environment also enabled her at times to withdraw her poetic constructs from the world outside. Writing at the age of nineteen, for instance, in a Valentine poem published anonymously in *The Indicator* (an Amherst College magazine), Dickinson very typically shifts attention from social necessities and programs to a world of linguistic display (where society, in an image that echoes the first chapter of *The Scarlet Letter*, is a kind of weed, which can be torn up by the roots and thrown away):

> But the world is sleeping in ignorance and error, sir, and we must be crowing cocks, and singing larks, and a rising sun to awake her; or else we'll pull society up to the roots, and plant it in a different place. We'll build Alms-houses, and transcendental State prisons, and scaffolds – we will blow out the sun, and the moon, and encourage invention.[25]

As Joanne Dobson also notes (in a superbly balanced essay on social issues in Dickinson), "the paragraph restricts itself to the universe of its own potential"—as language.[26] It is not motivated by a desire to action, but instead draws attention to its own ludic propensities. Of course, the genre of the Valentine letter does not encourage mature reflection on economic inequities. But the careless importation, for the purposes of comic effect, of those institutions built by society for the alleviation of poverty and the punishment of wrongdoing (by incarceration and death) suggests a consciousness that is aware of their existence but unaware of the depths of degradation and suffering that their existence entailed. The writer clearly knows that charity and reform are part of an important moral agenda for people of her class, but she prefers to satirize that impulse; instead, society is imagined as a flower-weed that requires transplantation to another location outside the immediate confines of the local.

Such marginalization of social issues is typical of many comments made by a very youthful Dickinson where she co-opts the public for private concerns: in that sense, poems about flowers function as manifestos of poetry, a genre of the sociopoetic. They also dramatize her perception of the necessary distance between aesthetic representations and external realities. At this stage of her life, she is fully prepared to write the social out of her literary formula, and it therefore seems appropriate that she uses a flower to express the idea: flowers enhance the message of the poem by removing any anticipation of explicit social content. Alan Liu writes that genre "tells the story of a poet's relation to history," and in this case the selection of both lyric genre *and* botanical subject achieves the same effect, though Dickinson also breaks out from the circle of social expectations others have for her by writing in a genre that precludes any such demands (although other women could, and did, use poetry as a discourse with which to address and redress social ills).[27]

The poet's cultivation of flowers (both in the bedroom and in the conservatory that her father had added when the family returned to the Homestead in 1855) provided her not only with images for her writing but also (and this is the point) served as a useful metaphorical equivalent to the writing of lyric manuscripts: both were conducted privately, and both ended up with products that were "small, but *so* full of meaning."[28] (On 17 October 1851, she writes to Austin "here is a *brighter* garden, where not a frost has been, in its unfading flowers I hear the bright bee hum, prithee, my Brother, into *my* garden come!" in a way that playfully links epistolary, erogenous, floral and poetic zones).[29] Her niece wrote, "more and more she turned to the warmth of her world within, and the little conservatory where her ferns and yellow jasmine and purple heliotrope made an atmosphere more tropical for the dwelling of her imagination."[30] Bianchi's collusion with those who promoted her aunt's withdrawal as the action of a woman too acutely sensitive for the real world seems, almost, to suggest that Dickinson was a flower herself: exotic, beautiful, self-sufficient, and living by preference in an environment constructed solely for the purpose of sustaining her imaginative talent.

Dickinson's conservatory may not have been intended for public display or consumption: nonetheless, its products were often sent to selected individuals and, whatever the messages they carried, were a means of demonstrating not only good taste and individual talent but also a household with sufficient knowledge and means to select and purchase the flowers and enough leisure and energy to invest in their growth and care. Though Dickinson's flowers are not necessarily tokens of social ambition (as gardens often were for the middle classes), they *do* function as signs of social status. For, as Jack Goody has argued, there was a "class aspect [to] the conspicuous expenditure on flowers," and the cultivation of plants for reasons other than necessity is evidence of a culture of luxury that is itself a product of hierarchical divisions within society.[31] Having money, then, made it possible for the creation of a domestic environment in which both poetry and plants could survive. Dickinson's interest in flowers (like her playing of the piano or her sitting as a child for a portrait with Lavinia and Austin) is similar to her dedication to poetry, in that it has inescapably social (and political) signs.[32]

Dickinson's interests in, and gifts of, flowers were neither peculiar nor particular to her: instead, they functioned as part of a network in which women belonging primarily to the middle and upper-middle strata of society shared their advantages and affinities. "There is no employment which harmonizes more pleasantly with taste and amusement than the cultivation of Flowers," wrote Mary Adéle Allen. "It unites grace with purity, health with virtue and affords an agreeable occupation for all gentle, refined and cultivated minds."[33] Flower viewing is a mental occupation, not a manual one: it is an affair of the educated imagination, and not of the hand. "Our man has mown today," Dickinson wrote to Joseph A. Sweetser in the early summer of 1858, "and as he plied his scythe, I thought of *other* mowings, and garners far from here."[34] Dickinson's social perspective at this stage of her life is usefully illustrated by the passage, which moves automatically from agricultural labor to religious allegory: what is emphasized is not the actual work of the person who does the mowing, but *an image of mowing*, which draws attention to the person doing the imagining.[35] We are given a remarkable insight into how nineteenth-century agricultural society functioned in this image: the professional classes pay laborers to tend their property and harvest their products, while their educated daughters transform these raw materials into scenes of sentimental morality for intellectual consumption. The erasure—or transcendence— of physical labor for the sake of a mental effect is, of course, typical of pastoral poetry, "Annihilating all that's made / To a green Thought in a green shade" as Marvell put it in "The Garden"—although Dickinson is also thinking of the scriptural phrase that "all flesh is grass." What I find intriguing about such levels of imaginative contiguity is that Dickinson was not a town dweller writing from a geographical and intellectual distance about agricultural events and characters: for her immediate society, and for her family, harvesting was a very important and highly visible annual activity. But her writing leaps immediately to the abstract or metaphorical equivalents of such activity in ways that erase their social or economic specificity. Her imaginative alignment is not with the land and its laborers, not with *the actual*, but with a universal tradition of writing, and I find this suggestive of her poetry in general. As far as biographical evidence can allow, Dickinson left the heavier *physical* work in the garden to the hired man and to her sister, Lavinia, while she focused her energies on the "luxury of apprehension"—choosing, growing, picking, arranging, and sending flowers for display and as emblems of taste, or transforming them into "flowers" of speech. Nor could one necessarily expect otherwise. But the point to be made, once again, is that this is not an unmediated, innocent response to the natural environment in which Dickinson lived: it is situated within, and collaborates with, ideological perspectives on the same environment as these were disseminated in part by the Bible and by pastoral poetry (both of which transfer raw social issues into the realm of abstract ideas and therefore tend to neutralize them if not to deny their significance altogether).[36]

Knowledge of flowers (and especially of their figurative potential) was one means by which the middle and upper-middle classes distinguished themselves from proletarian and agricultural views of nature—and from nature itself: flowers might have been freely available to everyone in their wild state, but cultivating them for domestic and ideological interiors gave them "a superior charm."[37] "There were a number of small private conservatories" in Amherst, writes Allen, but they were clearly limited to that section of the population (in 1860, almost 50 percent of taxable wealth was in the hands of 10 percent of the population) who could afford them.[38] Guy Leighton has pointed out that, facing south and east (and protected from the worst winds), the brick at the back of Dickinson's conservatory would have retained the heat generated by the sun during the daytime and released it at night.[39] Its proximity to the dining room, where there was a fireplace, also afforded an extra source of warmth. Having material means, as much as education, talent, and imagination, provided the conditions by which the creation of an arena separate "from the mass of minds" was made possible.[40] The vulnerability of flowers can describe, for example, a perception of the importance of beauty and the need to preserve it—not only literally in the form of herbariums, but also figuratively in the shape of a culture that increasingly promoted the appreciation of the beautiful as a way of distinguishing itself from the rest of the population.

Reading Dickinson's writings about domesticated nature can tell us a great deal about the value system that produces such decorative aesthetics in the first place. Bianchi's descriptions of the Dickinson garden, and Emily's floral preferences in particular are pertinent here, because they are saturated with the language and suppositions of class division, as when Bianchi states (of Lavinia's garden) that "self-sown flowers of humbler origin elbowed and crowded their more aristocratic neighbours."

> Emily's own conservatory was like fairyland at all seasons, especially in comparison with the dreary white winter cold outside. It opened from the dining-room, a tiny glass room, with white shelves running around it on which were grouped the loveliest ferns, rich purple heliotrope, the yellow jasmine, and one great Daphne odora with its orange-bloom scent astray from the Riviera, and two majestic cape jasmines, exotics kin to her alien soul. She tolerated none of the usual variety of mongrel houseplants. A rare scarlet lily, a resurrection calla, per-haps—and here it was always summer with oxalis dripping from the hanging baskets like humble incense upon the heads of the household and its frequenters.[41]

We need to distinguish here between Dickinson's practices and her niece's interpretation of those practices for her own later purposes (and between the different historical frames they inhabit), but the quotation is still useful: it illustrates the poet's preference for the decorative and uncommon rather than for the utilitarian; its description nicely merge the sacred and the floral; and it assumes an investment of money and leisured energy that produces a separate and rarified atmosphere of mysticism, taste, and exclusivity which is sometimes replicated in the poems themselves (and, just as significantly, in subsequent readings of those poems).

The flower mentioned most often in her poetry—the rose—appears forty-four times.[42] It is at once one of the most exclusive and one of the most traditionally popular (her choice of the daisy, an apparently more humble flower, still has many of the same hierarchical implications, as I shall explain later):

> On the ornamental side, bulbs and roses have always been popular American flowers starting with the earliest settlements and extending to the present gardens. Daffodils, crocuses, scillas, and may other bulbs . . . were very early introduced into Europe and brought here by the colonists. Roses, such as Sweetbriers, Province, and Moss, were favourites in ancient gardens mainly for their fragrance.[43]

Dickinson's fondness for roses was partly inherited in the sense that the society in which she lived valued and marketed them, and in the additional sense that her own mother purchased and grew them: when Emily Norcross Dickinson was absent on a trip to Monson in June of 1829, Edward wrote her, "Your plants are all safe & flourishing – the roses in the door-yard are in blossom. . . ."[44] But a number of historically contemporary books on flowers also defined the rose as both "pretty" *and* "genteel,"[45] and the poetry often reflects that sense of distinction: P#897B (J#991) "She sped as Petals of a Rose" defines it as a "frail Aristocrat of Time," and the following poem proceeds from the same sense of fragile exclusiveness:

> Essential Oils – are wrung –
> The Attar from the Rose
> Be not expressed by Suns – alone –
> It is the gift of Screws –
>
> The General Rose – decay –
> But this – in Lady's Drawer
> Make Summer – When the Lady lie
> In Ceaseless Rosemary –

Division 3 Suns – | 7 the |
P#772B (J#675)[46]

"Literature," wrote Higginson, "is attar of Roses, one distilled drop from a million blossoms." The statement comes at the end of a passage (in "Letter to a Young Contributor") about the differences between the ordinary mass of men and those "few men in any age [who] are born with a marked gift for literary expression, . . . have access to high culture, . . . [and] have the personal nobleness to use their powers well."[47] The distinction between "one" and "a million" is interesting, of course, given the then current debate between a Whig sociopolitical theory of literature that championed the genius of Wordsworth and Shakespeare and the Young American (or Democrat) avowal of "Literature for the Millions." In the poem, there is a similar consecution of levels that reflects wider social hierarchies: the rose is (presumably) selected because of its superiority to other flowers, and the "Essential Oils" are distinguished from both the "General Rose" they derive from *and* the "Lady" (not the woman—the word has exact social nuances) who owns and uses them.

"The scent of her cape jasmines and daphne odora is forever immortalized to those who breathed it," wrote Bianchi of her aunt's conservatory, "transporting them back to the loveliness of her immortal atmosphere."[48] Bianchi's description and the poem coincide to this extent: both become specialized zones that protect their inhabitants from the contamination of the immediate. Both are concerned with distilled essences that clarify and intensify experience, and that also transcend the immediate physical presence of their creators: as Wolfgang Schivelbusch reminds us, the use of perfumes first emerged in the eighteenth century when "people gradually became aware of the bad odors resulting from deficient personal hygiene and began to consider them an unpleasant odor." And, he continues, "the first boom in the perfume industry [was] less an expression of some new positive olfactory sensibility than an effort to escape the odors of the body."[49] For the speaker of the poem, what is feared is decay—the putrefaction of the corpus of her work, perhaps, as much as the disintegration of her corporeal self. The antidote, again for both, is to be found in the ability to remove from an object something that is a part of it and yet apart from it—either scent or symbolic meaning. But the difference between the two is that the speaker of the poem knows that extracting (or "express[-ing]") essences is not a leisured or even sedentary activity: it involves intense and sustained work (having to be "wrung")—even work that is imagined as technological or mechanical in nature (the "gift of Screws").[50] Leisure is what happens after death: what precedes it is a kind of labor. Indeed, the value of the poem is clearly dependent not only on the insights the writer brings to her text (the illumination suggested by the reference to the "Sun"), but also on the craftsmanship invested in it (or in her talent). Literature that is essential, like character, and like social position, is not achieved in a day: it evolves over time even as it seeks to vanquish it (the emphasis on hard work, self-denial, and the gradual accumulation of cultural capital has obvious political or ideological overtones in an age when vast fortunes were made and lost overnight, and when best-sellers could catapult a writer to fame—sometimes within a matter of days). It is the process of struggle and application that guarantees quality and produces the finest results.

Clearly, then, Dickinson conceived of her writing as a form of discipline—and strict discipline at that. Just as clearly, she subscribed to a hierarchical view of cultural productions: the self-conscious assertion that "this" (the poetic text, or body of texts represented by the fascicles, a term that was also used by botanists to signify a "bundle") will survive where the "general rose" (the mass of ephemeral texts produced casually for the market) will decay is breathtakingly arrogant (though in terms of this century's canon of literary texts, it is also accurate).[51] What enabled this kind of confidence in the superiority of her own literary output and the certainty of its survival? A number of possible answers suggest themselves, though one needs to add that this is still a work of fiction, an imaginary construct rather than a personal confession, and that the speaker balances the certainty of posthumous success with the knowledge of its cost (the language of the poem is dominated by images of torture and suffering). Fiction, after all, is a kind of "lie"—for it is not the lady herself who endures, but the essence she had created for herself. Nonetheless, the answer to Dickinson's speaker's confidence in the poem resides at least in part in this reference to "Rosemary," traditionally associated with Christmas (on the basis of faulty etymology, since rosemary derives from "the Latin *ros* and *marinus*, meaning 'dew of the sea'"), and thus with the birth of Christ and the promise of immortality. Rosemary is additionally and appropriately linked with memory: in *Hamlet*, as Robert Fleissner points out, Ophelia says "There's Rosemary, that's for Remembraunce; / Pray love remember" (act 4, scene 5, lines 174–75).[52] Almira H. Lincoln's *Familiar Lectures on Botany* (1815), identified by Richard Sewall as Dickinson's botany textbook at the Amherst Academy, includes a section, "The Symbolical Language of Flowers," which defines "Rosemary" as "Keep this for my sake. I'll remember thee."[53] In other words, it is the speaker's confidence in the permanence of a set of social values that is simultaneously traditional (herbs and flowers have a history of symbolic meanings attached to them) and contemporaneous (there exists a consensus about the values associated with this knowledge which is maintained and transmitted—primarily by ladies—in the form of other genres of cultural information, including poetry) that means she does not need or seek to justify her own claims to immortality. The poem assumes the acceptance of the system of belief that underwrites it as being legitimate, natural, and (to some extent) eternal. It takes cultural continuity for granted, as well as the constituent beliefs of that continuity: the love and appreciation of flowers, the knowledge of their importance and meaning, and the recognition of the skill and taste of the speaker who enfolds them within her poetic texts—either literally, in the shape of fresh or pressed flowers, or metaphorically, in the guise of images and allusions.

What enables the speaker to be confident about the survival of her product is precisely this assumption of the inevitability of a shared matrix of cultural references and priorities, and the centrality of flowers to this feminized, middle- and upper-middle-class, nineteenth-century culture is evident in Dickinson's extensive use of them in letters, and in poems such as the following, which Johnson finds was enclosed as a note together with a bouquet of flowers presented to Perez Dickinson Cowan, her cousin.[54]

Partake as doth the bee
Abstemiously
The Rose is an Estate
In Sicily

p#806b (j#994)

Nineteenth-century tracts on deportment such as *The Young Lady's Friend* gave very detailed instructions on the rituals and etiquette of dining, and the quatrain extends these rituals (playfully) into the realm of visual consumption: the food-rose is rare, the manner of eating-viewing delicate (and as far removed from an act of physical necessity as possible), and the pleasure to be derived from the consumption is intellectual—even the language is pared down to a kind of culinary-floral minimalism. The lines function in much the same way as an arrangement of flowers, in that it is the skill of the writer that best brings out the particular attractions of the flower, heightening its distinctiveness by explaining that in Sicily (which in the nineteenth century experienced such levels of poverty and economic instability that a rose would very literally have been equivalent to the estate of many peasants) it has a value that its conspicuous availability in America tends to diminish.[55] Typically, Dickinson's poems fight against the attenuation and even vulgarization of an object's value by its accessibility: she invokes poverty only in a highly figurative sense as a mechanism by which exclusivity can be reattached to the everyday. Essentially, the poem is didactic: it reaffirms and seeks to perpetuate certain hereditary values and priorities—refinement of sensibility, high thinking, and an appreciation of quality even in the midst of democratic quantity.

This poem is typical of what might be termed, to modify a phrase of Bianchi's, "poems of occasion," which were written for a particular event or purpose, or—at times—were written with the purpose of fitting another purpose at some later date. The sending of flowers in these instances functioned almost generically, in that such a gift impressed upon the recipient as well as the sender their mutual adherence to codes of generosity and gentility. They are to the sender what the "oil" is to the "rose"—a substitute for the self. And like the letters in which they are enclosed, they re-present the absent writer, as in this one to Emily Fowler Ford: "My flowers come in *my* stead, today, dear Emily. I hope you will love to see them, and whatever word of love, or welcome kindly, you would extend to *me*, 'do even so to *them*.' They are small, but *so* full of meaning, if they only mean the *half* of what I bid them."[56]

As indoor gardening became more important in the first half of the nineteenth century, tracts about the subject emerged to satisfy a middle-class public who had been made familiar with the significance (meaning and importance) of flowers through their education and through the increasing diversity of plant types made available by the market. Dickinson's message to Perez is conventional enough, because by the time it was written there existed a sentimental culture of flowers that relied on the Western scholastic and folkloric traditions but that also modified it for nineteenth-century purposes. Throughout the middle decades of the century, there appeared a series of floral glossaries or dictionaries, which included poems by way of illustration and thus served doubly as anthologies. Sarah Josepha Hale's *Flora's Interpreter; or the American Book of Flowers and Sentiments* (1832); Charlotte Elizabeth's *Floral Biographies; or Chapters on Flowers* (1842); Mrs. J. Thayer's *Floral Gems, or the Songs of the Flowers* (1846); Mary Chauncey's *The Floral Gift, from Nature and the Heart* (1847); and Lucy Hopper's *The Lady's Book of Flowers and Poetry* (1848) all have sections that discuss the "language of flowers" (also the title of a book edited by Miss

Ildree in 1865).[57] Some of the meanings are predictable enough: the laurel (as Dickinson also notes in a poem sent to Higginson [P#1428C (J# 1393)], "Lay this Laurel on the One") "has ever been the symbol of glory or fame." But others are slightly more complex (at least to the uninitiated), such as "our hopes," the daffodil "is brightly colored; like them too it quickly fades." Lilacs mean "forsaken." Fuchsias represent "Trusting love" or "Humble love." Given that Lavinia Dickinson placed two of them in the coffin of her dead sister to take to Judge Lord, it is interesting that heliotropes are taken (by one of these writers) as meaning "devotion."[58]

The relationship between such popular flower publications and Dickinson's own nonpublished writing about flowers is more complex than George Whicher allows when he admits to disappointment that Dickinson "did not entirely escape the contagion of the popular sentimental approach to nature which verged on the mawkish."[59] If the existence of such publications indicates a common, conventional, and traditional vocabulary of ascribed meanings which she could draw from and rely on, it is also the case that Dickinson contended and engaged critically with that tradition at times. Flower glossaries limit their appeal to a range of emotions linked to either love or virtue, but Dickinson's poems involve the exploration of a much broader set of relations between horticultural, linguistic, psychological, emotional, moral, and ideological concerns. Despite the proliferation of books, the market offered relatively uncomplicated translations of floral symbols, whereas Dickinson's messages are typically dense and discreet—the one to Emily Fowler Ford suggests that only half of the contents she had silently inscribed in the flowers will be divulged by them. Clearly, this mirrors Dickinson's own relationship to nature, which she found enigmatic for most of her life. By extension, it reflects her circumspection or need for indirection. Finally, it indicates a need to differentiate her flowers in some way from others: hers carry secret messages, which at some level will always elude the person who receives and views them. In the same way, Dickinson's letters and poems about flowers (and with flowers) can be seen as versions in miniature of her rejection of the printing industry (which publishes anthologies—from the Greek, meaning a garland of flowers—of poetry as well as collections of verse, the flowers of speech, written on particular types of flora): hers—like the one to Perez—are home produced, hand-made, and all the rarer and more valuable for that. Certainly, her withdrawal from the market can be seen, paradoxically, as a sensible promotional strategy: it contributes to the rarity of her productions and thus increases their potential (market and literary) value.

The sense of an intersection of personal and social concerns emerges very clearly from the following poem:

> Bloom – is Result – to meet a Flower
> And casually glance
> Would cause one scarcely to suspect
> The minor Circumstance
>
> Assisting in the Bright Affair
> So intricately done
> Then offered as a Butterfly
> To the Meridian –
>
> To pack the Bud – oppose the Worm –
> Obtain it's right of Dew –
> Adjust the Heat – elude the Wind –
> Escape the prowling Bee –
>
> Great Nature not to disappoint
> Awaiting Her that Day –
> To be a Flower, is profound
> Responsibility – [60]

3 cause one scarcely] scarcely cause [one]

Division 1 Result – | 3 one | 5 the | 7 a | 9 Bud – | 10 of | 11 Heat | 12 bee – ‖ 13 not | 15 is |
P#1038A (J#1058)

As I have noted previously, one of the intriguing things about Dickinson as a poet of nature is that she omits the daily *human* labor associated with the agricultural environment in which she lived except, in a figurative sense. "Almost everything which anyone *does* in the countryside" is missing, writes James Turner of the pastoral tradition in English poetry, in terms that have an obvious bearing on Dickinson's work.[61] In Turner's formulation, it is nature, and not human nature, that labors in this kind of poetry. What flowers work at is goodness—though they do this best by doing nothing, or by being themselves, or "by unconscious influence."[62]

Flowers provide spiritual and moral lessons: though humans are forced to lower their gaze to see them (thus learning the value of modesty and humility), "their own faces [are] raised to heaven, [and] set us the example of looking thitherward."[63] Dickinson's poem (like many others) stresses the plant's physically inferior stature at the same time as its propensity for moral example. But what was formerly known as morality is also known today as ideology—the existence of a set of values that reflect, engage with, and respond to relations of power. An ideological reading of the poem might emphasize the differences it explores between what may be called "organic" theories of human character, which are rooted in the idea of biological and environmental (and hence involuntary) factors as crucial determinants in a person's make-up and the insistence that character is an affair of will and individual development a deliberate, conscious effect. There is a very obvious sense of the flower as something (or someone) that (or who) is exemplary in some fashion—from the very beginning of the poem its life is intensely visible and subject to scrutiny. Again, one has to acknowledge that a religious reading is also feasible, though the two approaches do not necessarily cancel each other out: "saints" in Amherst were "visible" (their account of grace being made publicly in church), whereas the gentry saw its own role as one of providing models for the emulation of social excellence and stability. In Christianity, as in democratic society, accidents of birth and position count for less than an individual's responsibility for the success of her or his own soul and self. Dickinson's poem reflects this. Potentially egalitarian, this belief also had its corollary in the conviction that material circumstances were in some way a reflection of moral condition, however, and the poem quite clearly subscribes to the belief in a natural aristocracy made up of members who have an obligation to themselves and to their maker. Again, if the belief in the self-made individual in the era of aggressive individualism and the single-minded pursuit of commercial success is echoed here, this is surely accidental: the poem very deliberately begins by distinguishing between the flower's outward appearances and its inner strengths—it competes for "Great Nature" and not for personal gain. Note too the highlighting of the bloom's discipline and courage—which are moral qualities, not material ones. The quest motif that structures the poem also underlines these qualities, as well as those of perseverance, duty, and faith. It enacts the triumph of vocation over the conditions, actions, and individuals that threaten to disrupt or disable it. At least in this poem, the writer finds an emblem for personal fulfillment within a context that would have been approved by the social order she derived her status from: although Wendy Martin reads the poem as demonstrating "Dickinson's evolution from conflict-ridden adolescent to independent woman," the flower's concerns with prowlers, false seducers, and responsibility is surely a sign that the poet's identity is very much caught up with social definitions of her role.[64]

There are times, in 1859 for instance, when Dickinson's speakers appear to relate toward flowers as if they were the standard bearers of high morality and culture: they even possess "a system of aesthetics – / Far superior to mine" (P#95B, J#137). And again, in 1862 (I employ the first of two variants, received by Eudocia Converse Flynt on 21 July 1862):[65]

All the letters I could write,
Were not fair as this –
Syllables of Velvet –
Sentences of Plush –
Depths of Ruby, undrained –
Hid, Lip, for Thee,
Play it were a Humming Bird
And sipped just Me –

Division 1 could | 6 Thee,‖ 7 a | 8 just |
P#380A [J#334]

This is double-speak: insight masquerading as inadequacy. For the poem that performs its own failure to emulate the language of nature indicates a decorous reverence before a higher form of expression and related set of meanings. That certain truths must remain unspoken is a roundabout way of saying that one knows what these truths are (or that they exist), and that one observes the propriety of their being represented only by Divine or esoteric tokens. Thus, when Dickinson writes (in P#849A [J#797]) that "By my Window have I for Scenery / Just a Sea – with a Stem – / If the Bird and the Farmer – deem it a "Pine" – / The Opinion will do – for them – ," the refusal to articulate an explicit alternative meaning suggests the speaker possesses a superior knowledge beyond utilitarian language. The negative account of other, pedestrian speech forms, like the admission of naturally superior discourse in "All the letters I could write," is not only a way of recognizing (and sharing one's recognition) of a reality that lies beyond ordinary words, but also of communicating a sense of appropriate restraint in one's own writing.

The cultivation and appreciation of nature is part of a larger system of cultural capital that distinguishes its initiates from the rest of humanity. It is significant, I think, that in the poem above, Dickinson employs the discourse of luxury and wealth to define the flowers that her speaker claims not to be able to contend with: indeed, there may even be a distinction made between letters that are reference oriented (those of the alphabet) or message oriented (correspondence) and the letters of the flower-poem, which are geared only toward display, and whose display *is* the message— their beauty and symmetry suggest the symmetry and beauty of the mind who created them (or the mind who mediates this creation to others).

In this context, it is interesting that nowhere in her writing does Dickinson allude to an interest in *artificial* flowers, for one of the chief occupations for young ladies of leisure in the nineteenth century was the making as well as the growing of flowers. *The Ladies Manual of Art, or Profit and Pastime*, though published after the poet's death (it appeared in 1887), is typical of previous decades in that it includes separate chapters on the art of paper-, wax-, and feather-flower making, as well as embroidered flowers and the preservation of natural ones.[66] In his *Plain and Pleasant Talk about Fruit, Flowers and Farming* (1859), Horace Ward Beecher identifies such artificial pursuits as one of the auxiliary reasons for the fact that too many women in his day "are afflicted with nervous disorders." As part of the cure, Beecher recommends the growing of flowers and house plants:

A woman's perception of the beauty of form, of colors, of arrangement, is naturally quicker and truer than man's. Why should they admire these only in painting, in dress, and in furniture? Can human art equal what God has made, in variety, hue, grace, symmetry, order and delicacy? . . . We are persuaded that, if parents, instead of regarding a disposition to train flowers as a useless trouble, a waste of time, a pernicious romancing, would inspire the love of it, nurture and direct it, it would save their daughters from *false taste*, and all love of meretricious ornament. The most enthusiastic lovers of nature catch something of the simplicity and truthfulness of nature.[67]

The issue of *false tastes* is crucial here (Beecher numbers reading novels, playing on the piano, and writing certain kinds of poems among them): time spent close to nature takes women farther away from the artificial occupations society has constructed for them and closer to a kind of instinctive perception of beauty and form, which is the foundation for a true aesthetic and religious sense. Never mind that this concept of nature is in itself an ideological construct and that Ward's view of nature is little more than a mirror of his own viewing position: the embrace of simple forms confers a sense of righteousness on the person doing the embracing. One is reminded here of P#519A (J#441), "This is my Letter to the World," where the speaker defines her significance exclusively in terms of the message given to her by Nature. As many readers before me have pointed out, the "tender Majesty" of the fourth line in that poem can refer back to Nature (the source of the message), or forward to the speaker (the conveyor of the message): in a sense, though, the phrase does both. There is a kind of closed or circular logic to Dickinson's proposition in the poem: the courier is important because the contents of the message she carries come from Nature, and Nature is important because of the contents of the messages it sends (and the couriers who carry them).

Nature confers a kind of distinction upon those who confer distinction upon it. Writing poems about flowers is therefore a prestigious activity: mentioning roses in a poem about poetry, indicates to the reader that the poet, too, is a "lady." Mention anemone (3), buttercup (10), clematis (1), clover (21), crocus (3), daffodils (13), daisies (27), dandelions (7), fern (1), fuchsias (1), gentians (6), geraniums (2), lilacs (5), lilies (8), primroses (1), rhododendron (1), rhodora (1), and violets (9), however, and the poet does something more than just display botanical knowledge: she sends out quite sophisticated signals that say that only those initiated by the combined circumstances of educational background and moneyed leisure can expect to understand and appreciate her texts. She also provides such initiates with an indication of her values and priorities in life—not just flowers, but the entire cultural apparatus that privileges lyric and aesthetic sensibility generally above (say) other human lives:[68]

> Good-night! I can't stay any longer in a world of death. Austin is ill of fever. I buried my garden last week – our man, Dick, lost a little girl through the scarlet fever. I thought perhaps that *you* were dead, and not knowing the sexton's address, interrogate the daisies. Ah! dainty – dainty Death! Ah! democratic Death! Grasping the proudest zinnia from my purple garden, – then deep to his bosom calling the serf's child.
>
> Say, is he everywhere? Where shall I hide my things?[69]

The passage makes painful reading, and is quoted by Betsy Erkkila, who finds the equal ranking of a workman's child and a flower less shocking than the fact that Dickinson "placed her own loss an aristocratic and 'purple' notch above the loss of the 'serf's child.'" She continues by alleging that Dickinson's "psychic and metaphysical fear of 'democratic Death' begins to merge with a material and historical fear of losing the Dickinson property, goods, and name. . . ."[70] ("I had some things that I called mine (P#101 [J#116])" debates many of these issues slightly more playfully.) Erkkila is undoubtedly correct in her assertion that Dickinson takes it for granted that social distinctions are natural, though one feels like adding the caveat that this is not so much Emily Dickinson as the affected young woman who signed herself "Emilie" at the end of this letter and whose most mature and complex epistolary and poetic productions had not yet emerged with any degree of consistency. One would like to think, even as one concedes the accuracy of Erkkila's statements, that the later Dickinson would not have been capable of this kind of callousness in the service of a sentimental literary effect, though one notes that exactly the same dehumanization is present in the reduction of the gardener's very real physical labor to the clichéd image of death as the grim reaper: both convert the subject into imaginative property. The death of a flower and the death of a young girl were conventional pieties at the time Dickinson was writing this letter, but (to take the obvious example of the "Lucy" poems) the person described is just as, if not more than, important as the vehicle of the description: in this instance, there is no such (social or metaphorical) parity. Indeed, part of the infuriating blindness of the passage is that the death of a worker's child is imagined as part of the natural order of things, whereas in fact (as many of the newspapers of the day acknowledged) it was more often a result of poor standards of health and housing: Austin would survive because he and his family could afford proper medical intervention in a relatively sanitary environment, whereas Dick Matthews could not offer the same for his children. But Dickinson's is not a consciousness that is sensitive to such issues: unlike those of Helen Hunt Jackson, Dickinson's deaths (at least at this early stage: later, especially after Gilbert died, is a different story) are manipulated for the effect of pathos, not reform.

Flowers are part of a repertoire of social and cultural identification. In such poems where they appear, and especially where they are enclosed together with (or instead of) a note, the aesthetic text and the agricultural context in which Dickinson lived collide, for flowers are beautiful but (to a large extent) useless—except as markers of taste and gentility. Indeed, establishing a flower garden was also a means by which a reputation and even a sphere of influence could be secured, as Mary Allen attests to in her following remarks: "Miss Emily's garden had a touch no one else's had. I think that others planted gardens with lemon verbenas, jockey club, sweet clover, and star of Bethlehem because Miss Emily had them in her garden."[71]

The "Miss" which is prefixed to Dickinson's name is honorific, a title that automatically indicates status. The flowers are badges of excellence: they are a means of showing taste, the cultural mechanism that reflected and promoted the social differential that was her claim to respectability. Flowers are the equivalent of the horses Dickinson's father and brother rode, exhibited and judged at the annual agricultural fairs: they are explicit symbols of money employed in the pursuit of nonutilitarian occupations. Dickinson's flowers are not grown to be eaten or sold, but for the pleasure of being displayed (privately or in local fairs) or sent to friends and relations. As such, they are perfect emblems for a literary art that strives toward self-sufficiency and is dismissive of social concerns: like lyric poems, flowers are attractive and autonomous, but they *do* nothing (except, famously, to provide the reader-viewer with a very powerful but localized experience which is simultaneously cerebral and corporeal—but emphatically asocial). In one poem, Dickinson puns on the commonness of clover ("the Purple Democrat") to indicate her preference for a decorativeness that is not geared toward public display:

Her Public – be the Noon –
Her Providence – the Sun –
Her Progress – by the Bee – proclaimed –
In sovereign – Swerveless Tune –

P#642A (J#380)

Ornamental without being ostentatious, the clover is disguised by its ordinariness: being so visible renders it practically invisible (the clover is an abundant flower found in pastures, but the assignation of the color purple, which Dickinson associated with royalty, clearly makes it a kind of aristocrat in disguise). In many other Dickinson poems, there is a much more obvious separation of the boundary between public life and private experience, but here the clover deliciously suggests that one assists the other. The implications for a Dickinson poetic (if there are any) might be this: the sense of title or rank that accompanies the single, and single-minded, production of music; the choice of nature as the scene of singing/writing/ display, and the dismissal of the need for an audience, except an audience of peers, or equals, who exist in single relation to the flower (*the* Noon, *the* Sun, *the* Bee, rather than noons, suns, or bees). If there is any hint of social consciousness here, it is only in the sense of a person who defines herself in opposition to activities that are in any way orientated toward a social program but who is otherwise socially exemplary.

Flowers in Dickinson's poems do not, then, exist in a kind of vacuum any more than their mistress alone with them in her bedroom. In seeking to describe them, Dickinson often resorts to recognizable social situations and language:

> The Flower must not blame the Bee –
> That seeketh his felicity
> Too often at her door –
>
> But teach the Footman from Vevay –
> Mistress is "not at home" – to say –
> To people – any more!

Division 1 the⏐
P#235A (J#206)[72]

Though this is a slight poem—perhaps little more than an extended witticism—Rebecca Patterson points out that it "so perplexed her first editors that they refused to publish it."[73] In a plausible paraphrase of the poem, Patterson claims that understanding it depends on our accepting that it is spoken by the bee, who then installs himself as the lady's footman and rejects all future lovers. The joke, however, is that the message of the rose (as this is conventionally constructed) is "love" or "beauty," which means that it is against its nature not to attract lovers/bees. In a sense, instructing the rose to refuse visitors is asking it to do the impossible, and this absurd suggestion is mirrored formally by imposing a discourse of social etiquette on the natural scene: the discrepancy between them is the occasion for the humor.

But the reverse of the poem's message is that there are good reasons *in the human realm* for having formal codes of behavior with which to regulate relations with other people. There are no mechanisms by which blossoms can protect themselves from bees because there is no need to, but the rituals that serve to segregate people of different social strata from each other *are* necessary if the system underlying those rituals and divisions is to be maintained and preserved. The moment when the "Mistress" of the house asks hired staff to lie on her behalf is a key part of her role in protecting the domestic environment from social undesirables. The bee in the poem embodies all kinds of threats to elite integrity and although the humor minimizes the fearfulness of social conflict or antagonism, there is a serious message: If you do not insist on distinguishing yourself from the poor, or the immigrant, or the working class, you can hardly expect sympathy when they abuse your familiarity. The poem's glee, then, might be satiric: homogeneity breeds homogeneity, and vice versa (quite literally: the bee carries with it the familiar sexual potency of the foreign or ethnic other). But to anyone reading the poem who happens to make a living from knocking on doors and persuading people to buy a product or pay for a service, the message is pretty clear: This poem is not for you.

Like P#176A (J#179), "If I could bribe them by a Rose," the following poem plays with the idea of flowers as a kind of capital asset.

What would I give to see his face?
I'd give – I'd give my life – of course –
But *that* is not enough!
Stop just a minute – let me think!
I'd give my biggest Bobolink!
That makes *two* – *Him* – and *Life*!
You know who "*June*" is –
I'd give *her* –
Roses a day from Zinzebar –
And Lily tubes – like wells –
Bees – by the furlong –
Straits of Blue –
Navies of Butterflies – sailed thro' –
And dappled Cowslip Dells –

Then I have "shares" in Primrose "Banks" –
Daffodil Dowries – spicy "stocks" –
Dominions – broad as Dew –
Bags of Doubloons – adventurous Bees
Brought me – from firmamental seas –
And Purple – from Peru –

Now – have I bought it –
"Shylock"? Say!
Sign me the Bond!
"I vow to pay
To Her – who pledges *this* –
One hour – of her Sovreign's face"!
Extatic Contract!
Niggard Grace!
My *Kingdom's worth* of Bliss!

14 Dells] *the* D *over another letter* 25 Her] *the* e *made from another letter*

Division 1 to | 2 life – | 4 me | 15 in | 18 adventurous‖ 19 firmamental | 26 Sovreign's |
p#266A (j#247)[74]

The poem begins with a moment of crisis: as a woman, the speaker has no independent means by which she can pay for things. In a sense, she has no credit rating, and the rest of the poem playfully elaborates on establishing an alternative form of exchange. Describing flowers as her fortune might have its lighter side, of course (though it also indicates the truth that tokens of barter begin as organic materials, which are inserted into economic systems and thereby acquire a symbolic value separate from any intrinsic usefulness), but it does (we surmise) reflect the seriousness attached to botanical pursuits in the feminized sphere. Growing, knowing, and writing about plants are acceptable ways of establishing validation at a time when many public avenues of proficiency were normally not open to women.

I have been arguing so far that poems about flowers might tempt us into considering them to be zones of aesthetic detachment from the world in which they were written. But the poems above show Dickinson *including* references to social antagonism, law breaking and the market—precisely those forces that one expects them to ignore or to exclude. Clearly, a more flexible approach to their function in the poems is therefore necessary. What I would suggest is that the discourse of the market and the law are introduced within the poems only on the terms of their aestheticization and that their enclosure serves as a way of exercising a degree of imaginary control over them. Dickinson transplants the language and motifs of commerce into the poems and gives them a new orientation: in doing so, she attempts to alter, but simultaneously acknowledges, the strength and direction of their authority over her. This works in two ways: on the one hand, it seems to belittle the solemnity of (in this instance) the discourse of buying and selling, but on the other it indicates (I suspect) the continuous presence of social concerns and pressures in Dickinson's consciousness: even as she trivializes them, she recognizes their centrality and power.

Even the ephemerality of flowers—a common enough trope in the literature of plants—is often reported in terms that transfer fears about the insecurity of property to the natural realm (as in the earlier letter of 1845 to Abiah Root where she refers to Jack Frost robbing her treasures):

> The Frost was never seen –
> If met, too rapid passed,
> Or in too unsubstantial Team –
> The Flowers notice first
>
> A Stranger hovering round
> A Symptom of alarm
> In Villages remotely set
> But search effaces him
>
> Till some retrieveless night
> Our Vigilance at waste
> The Garden gets the only shot
> That never could be traced.
>
> Unproved is much we know –
> Unknown the worst we fear –
> Of Strangers is the Earth the Inn
> Of Secrets is the Air –
>
> To Analyze perhaps
> A Philip would prefer
> But Labor vaster than myself
> I find it to infer.

16 Secrets is the] Travellers the

Division 1 was| 2 too| 3 unsubstantial] un-| substantial 4 Flowers| 5 hovering| 6 of| 7 Villages| 8 search| 8 him‖ 9 some| 10 at| 11 gets| 12 could| 13 much| 14 the‖ 15 is| 15 Earth the| 16 is| 16 Air – ‖ 18 would| 19 Labor| 19 than| 20 to|
P#1190A (J#1202)

In a brilliant reading of the poem contained in an article, "Law, Property, and Provincialism in Dickinson's Poems and Letters to Judge Otis Phillips Lord," James Guthrie argues that the poem's imposition of a legal discourse on a set of natural circumstances "ultimately serves to interrogate, or even parody, the aims of man-made law."[75] If Guthrie is correct, then one finds oneself being pulled into a familiar structure of opposition that privileges the eternal truth of nature over the empty fabrications of society. There is no doubt that such an opposition might potentially exist in the poem, but what I would want to adjust in Guthrie's reading is the conclusion that he draws on behalf of the speaker. Because the poem is informed by very real fears held by the middle and upper-middle classes of Dickinson's day in Amherst: the newspapers are full of references to the presence of tramps, unemployed laborers, and aliens who are often jailed on the night of their arrival (or detection) and then expelled from town. Believing that killers are "natural-born" is not necessarily a critique of any attempts to legislate moral and social behavior; it is rather erecting a barrier beyond which the speaker refuses to travel. Instead of probing too deeply into the motives and consequences of lawlessness, the speaker withdraws (in the fourth stanza) to a politics of ignorance and laissez-faire; overscrutinization, the poem seems to imply, might lead to a more far-reaching disclosure of the factors that lead to criminal behavior.

I am not quarreling with Guthrie's assignation of preference in the poem: Dickinson's speaker clearly sides with nature. Nor do I fully disagree with his conclusions: nature exposes human laws as inadequate. But I would suggest that she is more fully implicated in the terms of this debate than might be immediately apparent. Of course, frost functions most often in Dickinson's poetry as the agent of death, and in that sense there is a very obvious reason why the speaker might be implicated more directly in the processes she describes. But there are additional sides to this: I have already suggested one approach, but another might be that using natural imagery to describe criminal or political (mis)behavior—random murder, the assassination of presidents, political intrigue, revolution even—is a roundabout way of saying that the historical is an extension of the natural, and therefore legitimating the female speaker's intrusions into a sphere (the public or historical) that would normally be interpreted only by male historians (or by the makers of history). But the logical (political) corollary of a belief that history is a natural phenomenon and that both nature and history are ultimately unknowable is a kind of fatalistic withdrawal, a superior resignation: to analyze, intervene, or act is foolish because nature, politics, or history cannot finally be understood. The commitment to uncertainty produces a theory of nonintervention, privileging the perception of a principle of incomprehensibility over attempts to investigate, change, or draw any conclusions about the mysterious. The speaker's powers of observation derive, paradoxically, from a real powerlessness: she can watch the processes of natural (and human) behavior (and misbehavior), but she cannot do anything about them. Nor would she appear to desire to do something: her ability to acknowledge the inevitability of natural and historical processes is sufficient, which is another way of saying that such knowledge, and not understanding, is what she considers to be truly valuable. It is for this reason that Dickinson's poems describe or enact a moment before or after action, which is why many of them, like flowers, do not *do* anything: the explosions they describe are more often than not deferred, potential, internal, or past. As I suggested in the previous chapter, a combination of gender and socioeconomic reasons can help us understand why this is the case: many women in the nineteenth century did not have direct access to economic and political power, and may therefore have privileged perception over action.

Still, flowers can be acted on, and there are some poems that describe the aftermath of action, even as they avoid acting themselves. In this poem, the desire for social and botanical exclusion coincide, and combine with the knowledge of the problems that accompany such a desire.

Did the Harebell loose her girdle
To the lover Bee
Would the Bee the Harebell *hallow*
Much as formerly?

Did the "Paradise" – *persuaded* –
Yield her moat of pearl –
Would the Eden *be* an Eden,
Or the Earl – an *Earl*?

2 lover] *the* l *over another letter*

Division 1 loose| 3 Harebell|
P#134 (J#213)

In a reading that anticipates some of the comments made by Guthrie, Nancy Walker argues that the poet "acknowledges the conventional transformation of 'good woman' into 'bad woman,' and her extension of this convention to the 'innocent' world of bees and flowers testifies to its absurdity."[76] Like Guthrie, Walker presupposes (on Dickinson's behalf) that natural relations expose social constructions of human nature as fraudulent. While tentatively agreeing with the possibility of this reading, I wish to amend it slightly, for it is clearly possible that the explosion of human conventions may be more troubling for the speaker than Walker supposes. Rather than see the poem as a dramatization of questions related to sexuality, it might be that this is also a poem that investigates the socially leveling implications of a democratic system: if the upper classes relaxed the conventions of restraint by which they distinguished themselves from the lower orders (including the conventions by which people of distinct social or ethnic background do not marry each other), the poem might be construed as asking, Would there be a concomitant loss of the respect and deference that were normally accorded to them? This may be an overliteral translation of the poem's concerns, but it seems legitimate given that the poem itself (unusually for poems with this kind of thematic concern in her work) posits an explicit relationship between the loss of sexual and social status for women. In fact, given that this is one of the few works to employ a specifically social discourse to describe an apparently natural encounter, it is worth considering that it is primarily the *social* rather than the sexual aspect that most concerns her. As long as bees invade the private territory of flowers, the act is inconsequential, even celebrated, but on the occasion of its description in terms of social stratification and systems of deference, such a breach of etiquette becomes more disturbing and has wider implications.

When Dickinson celebrates consummation or gratification in nature, it is usually because it is appropriate in that environment. But generally speaking, her poetry tends, if not always to celebrate, at least to broadcast the pleasure and the power that derives from the deferral or denial of gratification—like the bee that "hums and lingers [over the fragrant flowers], and hums *more* for the lingering."[77] Such a literary manifesto is again a product of economic, historical, religious, and personal circumstances, I would argue. "Renunciation – is a piercing Virtue – " (P#782A [J#745]) is a typical expression of this view (I quote the second half of the poem only (lines 10–16), so not all of Franklin's notes are immediately relevant to my discussion):

Renunciation – is the Choosing
Against itself –
Itself to justify
Unto itself –
When larger function –
Make that appear –
Smaller – that Covered Vision – Here –

9 Outvie] Outshow • Outglow – 16 Covered] flooded – • sated –

Division 1 piercing |
P#782A (J#745)[78]

Whatever the other aspects of the principle of abnegation, it is based on an economic fact: renunciation of society depends on having an economic base from which to do the renouncing (one that combines privilege with limited influence, status without extensive power). To argue that "The Banquet of Abstemiousness / Defaces [variants: debases *or* surpasses] that of Wine – " (P#1447A, J#1430) is one way to console oneself for not having the opportunity to participate more fully, and although previous critics have chosen to comment on the religious or gender-specific aspects of the poem (in ways I do not contest, and that in fact should intersect with class-based readings), it is also possible to read imagery and poems such as the following in different ways:

I would not paint – a picture –
I'd rather be the One
It's bright impossibility
To dwell – delicious – on –
And wonder how the fingers feel
Whose rare – celestial – stir –
Evokes so sweet a torment –
Such sumptuous – Despair –

I would not talk, like Cornets –
I'd rather be the One
Raised softly to the Ceilings –
And out, and easy on –
Through Villages of Ether –
Myself endued Balloon

By but a lip of Metal –
The pier to my Pontoon –

Nor would I be a Poet –
It's finer – Own the Ear –
Enamored – impotent – content –
The License to revere,
A privilege so awful
What would the Dower be,
Had I the Art to stun myself
With Bolts – of Melody!

3 bright] fair 7 Evokes] provokes 11 the Ceilings] Horizons 12 out,] by – 14 endued]
upborne • upheld • sustained 21 privilege] luxury

Division 19 content – ‖ 23 stun ∣
P#348A (J#505)[79]

Dickinson's class provides us with a powerful explanatory framework for
contextualizing poems such as these that describe an inverse ratio where
the failure to be allowed to participate or act is translated into a consola-
tory denial of the need to act or participate in the first place. For this
speaker, *doing*, in whatever form, is crude, as my friend and colleague Jeremy Hawthorn puts it in his *Cunning Passages:* "It is delayed or denied
gratification which is the mark of refinement . . . renunciation was a necessity which was turned into a virtue, a mark of caste."[80]
     There is no denying the force of desire that prompted the poem to be
written in the first place, but the initial impetus is canceled by the poem's
circumlocutions: the physical "fingers" that become "celestial" in the
next line, the paradoxical pairings of "sweet . . . torment," "sumptuous –
Despair," and "privilege . . . awful." Painting and certain forms of speech
are replaced by the (piano and flute?) music in the first and second stanzas,
which transforms desire into an abstract but elevating medium; these in
turn are replaced by the more passive form of listening. It might be suggested that there is an onanistic aspect to the poem, what Paula Bennett
would call an "autoerotic" quality: it contemplates and postpones consummation rather than attempting it.[81] This is more fantasy than gratification,
and the implications for a literary art (after all, the poem very consciously
addresses the benefits and shortcomings of all the major forms of creative
expression) can be read in ways that correspond to Dickinson's social posi-

tion as the privileged but disfranchised daughter of rural gentry in an age when significance was often measured in terms of actions and achievements: for the speaker of the poem, impotence and "content[ment]" are equated in ways that only make sense within a culture that defined potency and the pursuit of power as vulgar. Marjorie Levinson, writing of Keats, draws a link between masturbation and a kind of middle-class aesthetic of nonparticipation:

> Masturbation . . . is a holding action: a way of holding on to a holding off. The formula could be recast in temporal terms. Masturbation, that unnaturally hasty act, dreams of a "slow time": a duration which neither wastes nor realizes, at once history's negation and fulfilment. "Deathwards progressing / to no death was that visage." (Or for a categorical association, "purposiveness without purpose," Kant's definition of aesthetic experience.) Many of our fondest moments in Keats's poetry describes this condition: "Their lips touched not, but had not bade adieu." (The very time signature of "To Autumn" is a code for this kind of *durée*; it is also the subject and object of this *undying* poem.)[82]

In a letter to Higginson, which Bennett also quotes, Dickinson writes that "Emblem is immeasurable – that is why it is better than Fulfilment, which can be drained."[83] Poetry, or any literary art that privileged indirect, abstract, or "symbolic representation" (as Bennett puts it), is superior to other forms of discourse that are exhausted of meaning because the (political, social, personal) contexts they grapple with have a limited applicability to other times and places. For instance, in her second (known) letter to Higginson about "Hills," "the Sundown," and her dog "Carlo," Dickinson remarked, "They are better than Beings – because they know – but do not tell," suggesting the privileging of indirect over direct speech, suggestiveness rather than statement.[84] Her poem, and in particular the emphasis on paradox and indeterminacy, demonstrates the same predilection for telling "all the truth but tell[ing] it slant" as the persona in P#1263 (J#1129), as if plain speaking was a sign of shallowness and superficiality. The social meanings of this literary aesthetic can be teased out from another letter written to Higginson in the same year:

> Of "shunning Men and Women" – they talk of Hallowed things, aloud – and embarrass my Dog – He and I dont object to them, if they'll exist their side. I think Carl[o] would please you – He is dumb,

and brave – I think you would like the Chestnut Tree, I met in my walk. It hit my notice suddenly – and I thought the Skies were in Blossom –

   Then there's a noiseless noise in the Orchard – that I let persons hear – [85]

Being embarrassed by indecorous speech is a sign of heightened sensitivity and therefore social prestige, and in this passage there are a series of displacements that link the forms and subjects of linguistic usage with social status: far from being a token of incapacity, Carlo's inability to speak in human terms is the metaphorical equivalent of Dickinson's own decorous refusal to do so on any terms other than those sanctioned by the protocols of polite discourse (it is also a devastating piece of social satire that privileges an animal over human beings). The switch from the human to the natural toward the end of the passage is also a way of showing (without telling) that Dickinson possesses aesthetic competence or literacy: it too is an index of distinction. What is important here is that Dickinson's explanation of her seclusion is simultaneously social and linguistic, and it shows her awareness of competing definitions of literary practice as being embedded within wider social struggles. At the very end of the passage (as I quote it) she memorably defines "a noiseless noise in the Orchard" as a superior form of speech: again, she uses a sophisticated literary device (oxymoron) to illustrate nature's capacity to contain and communicate truths that lie beyond literal articulation. In an interesting reversal, a highly educated and cultured form of discourse asserts that the best way to approximate the extralinguistic realm of nature is either by silence or by a form of figurative language that effectively silences itself by dealing in contradictions. Noise (with its connotations of empty discordance) is what mobs make: a "noiseless noise" (or musical tone) lies beyond the sounds humans make to each other but not beyond the social boundaries they create and the linguistic practices that reflect those barriers. Finally, note that Dickinson situates herself as a translator of nature's messages, an occupation that confers a kind of symbolic importance through association on her, and that she conveys these messages to "persons," and not to an undistinguished and anonymous mass of people.

Emily Dickinson's writing on flowers serves as a valuable lens with which to look at political aspects of her poetry as a whole, but also at cultural ideology in the nineteenth century. The culture of flowers became widespread at the same time as there was an increase in the numbers of women in early nineteenth-century America who had a comparative surplus of leisure time and means at their disposal, and needed recreational activities to occupy themselves. Dickinson's choice of poetry as a career, like her interest in flowers, could be sanctioned by her family and by her society because it was seen as a respectable domestic activity. Social values found their expression in the performance of these twin rituals of indoor gardening and lyric poetry, and Dickinson's choice bespeaks a partial acceptance of those values—and not, as many critics have suggested, a rejection. Growing flowers at home, and writing poetry there, was never in practice a challenge to contemporary ideologies of the feminine, but was more an accommodation acceptable to both fathers and daughters. Although more conservative male commentators—including the poet's father—worried about the effect that literary careers could have on the character of a woman, and women writers themselves worried about the effects of publicity on an identity and integrity increasingly defined in association with the private and domestic, the majority did not take issue with women who pursued anonymous and homebound careers. Indeed, writing poetry and growing flowers in her bedroom was an indirect reflection of Edward Dickinson's status, because it meant that he could afford to keep his daughter at home, a situation that Thorstein Veblen discusses.[86]

But it would be false to say that Dickinson's writings about flowers represent a form of escapism, for that cheapens and distorts the very real concerns which they often embody and trivializes their potential to represent adequately the complexities of experience. In addition, as David Schuyler writes, "by the mid-1840s, horticulture had become big business: the value of the national produce of gardens, orchards, and nurseries for 1847 was $459,577,533. During the antebellum years horticulture emerged in the Northeast as an important response to the mechanization of agriculture and the transport revolution."[87] Flowers could never represent an unproblematic refuge from external forces and pressure because as instruments of leisure they were dependent on finances that were in turn dependent on the forces of the market. Dickinson's poems about flowers may reflect not so much a preference for the beautiful as a need for it, but they also contribute toward a sense of life's precariousness—a sense that was derived as much from the agricultural environment in which Dickinson lived, where the fluctuations of the seasons were obvious metaphors for the transience and vulnerability of flowers and human beings (and even sometimes for the lives and deaths of those who found their employment and sustenance there). Flowers, and poems about them, may embody fairly explicit social agendas (for example, the strengthening of character through the trials of adversity, pietistic clichés, and the desire for an afterlife that is confirmed by the regeneration of spring), but they also express very opposite conditions: intense sexual longing, anger, and the vulnerability of the individual to external forces and pressures. Invisible threats surround her conservatory and gardens, suggesting their fragility and transience:

Dear Hollands,

Belong to me! We have no fires yet, and the evenings grow cold. To-morrow, stoves are set. How many barefoot shiver I trust their Father knows who saw not fit to give them shoes. . . .

This is September, and you were coming in September. Come! Our parting is too long. There has been frost enough. We must have summer now, and "whole legions" of daisies.

The gentian is a greedy flower, and overtakes us all. Indeed, this world is short, and I wish, until I tremble, to touch the ones I love before the hills are red – are gray – are white – are "born again"! If we knew how deep the crocus lay, we never should let her go. Still, crocuses stud many mounds whose gardeners till in anguish some tiny, vanished bulb.[88]

The passage usefully summarizes some of the concerns and conclusions of this chapter. To begin with, there is the insulation from social realities which "a little taste, time and means" provide the writer with. Dickinson's decision to oppose the seasonal progress of the year coincides in part with the prospective arrival of the Hollands, but also (and just as important) with the domestic environment that protected her from the elements with the technology used to keep it warm and comfortable. When the stoves are lit (in the bedroom and in the dining room beside the conservatory), a kind of artificial or imaginary summer is possible. From her soon-to-be-heated room, she feels a measure of sympathy for those who cannot afford such luxury, but immediately abnegates responsibility of any kind for their condition: it is the "Father" who has decreed that they be "barefoot," not she (or her society). Indeed, it is doubtful if the reference to "shiver[ing]" creatures is primarily human: Dickinson more often reserves this kind of attention, and uses these kinds of phrases, to describe birds.

The use of flowers as analogues for human states and emotions—both positive and negative—is also a typical strategy in Dickinson's letters and in her poems. Daisies—one of the commonest flowers in her epistolary and literary vocabulary—are associated in fairly uncomplicated ways with summer. The onset of winter, and, by extension, the passage of time, is announced by the appearance of the gentian, which "flowers in August and September" and which "forms a striking and rather lonely contrast with the exhausted herbage around it."[89] The crocus stands for "cheerfulness," according to at least two contemporary authors, but also represents spring because it is one of the earliest flowers to bloom (one other writer interprets it as "youthful gladness," which strengthens the sense of regeneration).[90]

Flowers provide Dickinson with a vehicle for discussing and distancing herself from some of her central concerns, for example, the transience of life and the importance and fragility of beauty. By "distancing" I mean she does two things: she employs a vocabulary with connections to a world of feminine culture so that she doesn't appear to be pretentious, or threatening, or indecorous; she discusses matters of weight at a remove so that their implications are less immediate and makes the discussion less intimate or self-referential. (Whatever else Dickinson meant when she wrote that her poems were spoken by a supposed persona, her statement suggests that she was uneasy about having them read as her own thoughts.) It also needs to be repeated, however, that Dickinson *enjoyed* growing and caring for flowers and that she also derived pride, self-esteem, and personal satisfaction from sharing the results of that knowledge and skill with others. Like the writing of poems, the nurturing of plants was essentially a way of nurturing her sense of an inner self: it gave her a way of validating herself in an environment that provided her (and other women) with few other outlets for expressing and sustaining excellence and authority. Flowers are vehicles of self-realization, and their cultivation an approved pastime that she also happened to be good at. In that sense, her choice of flowers as a suitable subject for poetry is historically conditioned but simultaneously subjective: it bespeaks both limitation and empowerment.

It is probably safe to say that Dickinson's writing about flowers (and home, for that matter) emerged from a sense that domestic pursuits provided fairly new and appropriate subjects for a middle-class and home-based literary art: as Harriet Beecher Stowe wrote in *Hearth and Home*, the rituals of domesticity are "a subject matter which woman, and only woman, could possibly be able to present."[91] In that sense, her choice does not differ significantly from the interests of people around her: the world of flowers may seem to be a world apart, but it does have fairly precise social coordinates. Previous critics have rightly emphasized the flower's embedding in a feminine culture of gift-exchange, which is opposed to the masculine pursuit of material comfort and advancement—though it should be recognized that the domestic itself was an ideology that was not shaped by women alone, but was fully sanctioned and partly designed by men. (In addition, some of the poems use imagery from masculine professional spheres, for example, working at a forge or monumental architecture, in ways that are intensely competitive and self-assertive.) By and large, however, Dickinson's poems about flowers are figured as sites that exist beyond the economic life of nineteenth-century New England, where women forged meaningful and supportive links based on their shared cultural tastes and expertise. Exchanging gifts of flowers is clearly a way of expressing personal affection, but these exchanges also provided a supportive and nurturing network for aesthetic interests and practices. As critics have now begun to acknowledge, especially after the work of Martha Nell Smith, Dickinson did not work alone: her poems gain much of their dignity and authority from an epistolary community of friends who appreciate (and often reciprocate) the learning, skill, and taste that are invested in them. It may seem like stating the obvious, but Dickinson could only write about the environment in which she lived because she knew from her own experience and upbringing that others would find her subjects worthy enough to be written about. The domestic environment was judged to be a suitable subject for serious literature as long as it was a superior one: fitted with objects of value and taste, it replaced the church as a site of sacred significance (which is perhaps why Dickinson could stop going to church and write instead, in 1870, that "Home is the definition of God": it is also why her niece, Martha, described her conservatory as a kind of floral cathedral to good taste).[92] She might have chosen to write about flowers because she wanted to, but that choice was made from within a specific field of historically preconditioned possibilities.

The Clover's simple Fame
Remembered of the Cow –
Is better than enameled Realms
Of notability.

Renown perceives itself
And that degrades the Flower –
The Daisy that has looked behind
Has Compromised it's power –

6 degrades] profanes

Division 7 looked | 8 it's |
P#1256A (J#1232)

The scene described here is one of localized and privatized consumption, an exchange between the passive clover and the cow who eats or sees her— indeed, the purpose of the clover can be paraphrased as being nothing more impure or externally orientated than its own consumption. The poem works (to my mind) on two levels. On the one hand, it is riddled with class anxieties and prohibitions: the instruction to remain content with one's situation, the fear of ambition, which is translated into a judgment against vulgarity, and the assertion that power is power withheld, nonindulged, immobilized, all of which have fairly clear origins in class tensions. On the other hand, the poem can be read as expressing a kind of gentleman's view of art, which asserts that writing is an activity engaged in for its own purposes and rewards, and for a limited audience: as William Empson writes on Shakespeare in *Some Versions of Pastoral*, it—the flower—"may do good to others though not by effort or may simply be a good end in itself (or combining these, may only be able to do good by concentrating on itself as an end)."[93] The person who becomes aware that literature might yield fame has immediately "compromised" (like "degrades"—and its manuscript variants, "profanes," "pollutes," and "defiles"—a verb with specific associations with status and its loss) their creative and social integrity.[94] The poem also reworks traditional (and sexist) images of female vanity: once the clover sees itself, or turns to see if it is seen, it dramatizes its own vice (or inquisitiveness: there are echoes of Lot's wife here). And yet, the poem is not unselfconscious, even if it claims to promote self-denial: it propounds its own self-sufficiency, its own justification for being, in opposition to literary hype and celebrity.

"The Clover's simple Fame" was written (it is conjectured separately by both Johnson and Franklin) in 1872, by which time there were many competing definitions of the literary, dismissed by "high" cultural practitioners in ways that equate fame with notoriety, a word that suggests exposure or public knowledge in a negative sense. Dickinson's own home-based perusal of flowers is situated in between fully functional and autonomous definitions of literature as these operated in the first and second halves of the nineteenth century. Dickinson may not have written to improve the condition of those of her fellow human beings who were less fortunate than herself (like Stowe, like Hunt Jackson, and like Sedgwick), but she did seem to believe that her withdrawal met with some measure of Divine approval (rather like the speaker of Milton's "How Soon Hath Time," she found that "measurement"—the writing of metrical language—*was* God's purpose for her). That is why she co-opts elements of Scripture for her scriptural career, writing poems like P#1751 (J#1651), "A word made Flesh is seldom" (with its memorable fusion of sacramental and poetic visions) and P#1223A (J#1205), "Immortal is an ample word" (almost a palindrome in the sense that the word itself is as ample and immortal as "immortal" is an ample word). It provides us with a historically mediated and mediate definition of literature, as her Valentine letter *and* the one to the Hollands show: writing is not judged by its social usefulness alone but also by its more intrinsic qualities and merits. Like many of Dickinson's poems, the following one is an act of communication and a communication about art.

This is a Blossom of the Brain –
A small – italic Seed
Lodged by Design or Happening
The Spirit fructified –

Shy as the Wind of his Chambers
Swift as a Freshet's Tongue
So of the Flower of the Soul
It's process is unknown –

When it is found, a few rejoice
The Wise convey it Home
Carefully cherishing the spot
If other Flower become –

When it is lost, that Day shall be
The Funeral of God,

Opon his Breast, a closing Soul
The Flower of Our Lord –

5 Chambers] Lodgings

Division 1 of| 3 or| 5 of| 6 Freshet's| 7 Flower of| 9 a| 10 it| 12 become – ‖ 13 Day| 15 a|
P#1112A (J#945)

We see again here the indivisibility of spiritual and aesthetic discourses:
although it seems fairly clear (to a twentieth-century reader at least) that
the first line refers to the poem itself, and by extension to the creative
talent that made it possible, it is not at all clear how this text-talent can
be distinguished, say, from the process whereby the experience of grace
changes human life and charges it with meaning (poetry seems to have
replaced the religious life as a vehicle for expressing faith, though). One
can see, however, why someone who could write such a poem could also
decide to absent herself from the world: poetry is equivalent to a "calling,"
a spiritual vocation, which requires the kind of nurturing and dedication
that are traditionally defined as female values. The poem is very much a
portrait of the miniature artist as a young woman: she conveys the "blossom" home (to a feminine sphere, which is then made all the more sacred),
employs the flower as a principal image because it corresponds to her own
experience and to her value system and demonstrates the kind of patience,
care, and devotion, which are also characteristics of the nineteenth-
century lady. So the poem justifies the attentions lavished on it in ways that
comply with the cult of domesticity but also differ from it: the discipline of
writing does not justify the ways of God to man (or woman), or effect
social change on behalf of a moral agenda, but it is an end in itself: indulg-
ing one's talent is a way of extending the life of divine creativity on earth
(if not replacing it entirely). And taking care of flowers, one might add, is
a kind of training for a literary career conducted, as Adrienne Rich puts
it, on Dickinson's "own premises."[95]

Emily Dickinson's ambitions were not limited ones: she too aspired to
excellence, to "immortality," to being a major poet rather than a poet of
the majority. Her exclusion of explicit reference to historical circumstances and social contexts is a sign of her long-term ambition, her desire
to weed out the merely accidental from the essential. Adapting Empson
to our own purposes, one might say that the flower in Dickinson's work
represents "beauty, vulnerability, [a] tendency to excite thoughts about the
shortness of life, self-centredness, and [the] power . . . to give pleasure."[96]

It is more than just the vehicle for an especially dense form of class propaganda. Dickinson's choice to use flowers as metaphors (or as subjects) in her poetry is just that—a personal choice, perhaps even an *urge*, for the sheer number of her writings proves that there is such a thing as a *need* to write that cannot be explained solely in terms of social conditioning. But that choice also needs to be situated within the field of historically constituted cultural perspectives on nature from within which it was made. At the very least, for instance, there had to be a market for domestic flowers and for writing about (domestic and wild) flowers: the cultivation of flowers for small and indoor gardens was still a relatively recent economic and cultural phenomenon—as Ann Leighton points out, the first publication on gardening in the United States (Bernard M'Mahon's *The American Gardener*) did not appear until 1806—and one that was not available to all sections of the population.[97] When Emily Dickinson wrote about flowers, she did so for a number of reasons: because gardening was taken as a serious cultural pursuit in the nineteenth century, and seen as an index of refinement; because her education had taught her that flowers carried significant and profound messages, and that caring for them was part of a genteel woman's most important accomplishments; because she genuinely liked them; and because she knew how to pick and grow them, where to find them, and how to preserve and arrange them, and what names to assign them (in Latin and English). Flowers are therefore crucial elements of a vocabulary that empowered Dickinson as much as it may appear to delimit her historically today. All of this establishes the boundaries of Dickinson's writing not in order to denigrate it or her, but more fully to define her humanity. Being a member of the leisure class who had the time and means to look after flowers does not fully explain Dickinson's poetry, because (and the formulation is not mine) not everyone who looked after flowers and was a member of the leisure class wrote poetry—especially poetry like hers.[98] But trying to see beyond the perfected image, the *completeness*, which death sometimes gives to people from the past, is (I feel) to approach closer to the partiality, the complexity, and the contradictions of that Dickinson we know from the poems and the letters—not some angel of the house, some pure unmediated consciousness existing in splendid isolation from social and political constraints (direct or indirect), but a *complete* personality with prejudices, dislikes, fears, and desires. To approach the general boundaries of her art is, I hope, to see more clearly the extent and depth of the landscape behind them.

CHAPTER FIVE

LETTERS FROM HOME

Dickinson and Publication

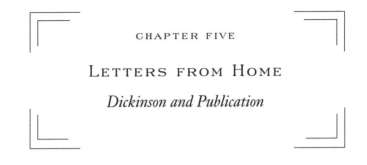 OVER the past decade, critics increasingly have come to view Dickinson's nonpublication as a choice she made in the interest of preserving the textual integrity of her work. In particular, Martha Nell Smith has looked at a cluster of statements made separately by Dickinson and Susan that suggest a common poetic manifesto.[1] "I had told you I did not print," Emily wrote to Thomas Wentworth Higginson in early 1866, complaining that the published version of "A narrow Fellow in the Grass" had been altered in the 17 February edition of the *Springfield Daily Republican.*[2] In another letter to Higginson, which Smith also quotes, Susan wrote that the poems "will ever be to me marvellous in manuscript or type." Finally, Smith alludes to this passage from Susan's letter of 18 February 1891 to William Hayes Ward, editor of *The Independent:*

> Dear Sir.
> Thank you for spending so much time over my letter. I recognize fully all Miss Emily's lack of rhyme and rhythm, but have learned to accept it for the bold thought, and everything else so unusual about her.
> I think if you do not feel that your own literary taste is compromised by it, I would rather the three verses of the "Martyrs" should be published if any. I shall not be annoyed if you decide not to publish at all. I should have said *printed.*[3]

The cumulative effect of these quotations as Smith understands them is an expression of skepticism about the medium of print itself, or about its technological limitations—its rigid typefaces, inflexible lines and margins. Kamilla Denman supports this view when she says that Dickinson's "reluctance to publish was based, at least in part, on an aversion to the conditions of print."[4] I examine these claims to an antagonism to print more closely in my next chapter by looking at the kinds of evidence available to us from the manuscripts of Dickinson's correspondence with Higginson. There I argue that examining the historical (manuscript) context of individual poems and letters can affect our method of reading the poems. In this chapter, I want to look at publication in larger terms and to consider Dickinson's decision not to print in light of my previous focus on her social and economic situation. Although I do not deny the possibility that Dickinson may have wanted to preserve the chirographic, generic, and grammatical liberty of her texts, it seems equally allowable that she might not have wanted to publish for reasons that have as much to do with class as with a concern for artistic control. I would therefore alter the path of Denman's and Smith's emphases somewhat and say that the statements made by Susan and by Dickinson are also about the *ideology of print*. It is legitimate to say that, like the snow of "It sifts from Leaden Sieves" (P#291A [J#311]), print buries the unique characteristics of handwriting under a blank uniformity. But character can refer both to individual personality and to handwriting, so that print compromises character in a social as well as a textual sense. We can be fairly certain that Emily and Susan were not comfortable with the *idea of publication;* Dickinson's letters and poems, and her nonpublication (however much that changed from year to year), testify to that. And Susan goes on to say in her letter to Ward that she had thought of "a vol. to be printed at my own expense" and circulated privately. But a strong motive behind this was to avoid moving Dickinson too much into the public sphere, as well as to prohibit the advertising of "personal detail" and "peculiarities." Susan also wrote, "I sometimes shudder when I think of the world reading her thoughts minted in deep heartbroken convictions," showing an aversion to the consequences of publication that is remarkably similar to Higginson's nervousness about the publication of "Wild Nights" (though he is criticized for being patronizing when Susan is understood as being protective).[5] The emphasis here is on issues of *privacy* and *propriety*, not on the significance of scriptural detail—and Smith has also rightly pointed out that Susan would have had these misgivings. Where I differ from Smith, and from others, is in the degree of my emphasis: my own opinion is that Emily and Susan reacted not just as nineteenth-century women, but as nineteenth-century women of a certain class and ethnic background. It was their economic and social alignment as much as their gender that determined their responses to publication. For there are unmistakable traces of class prejudice here: Susan's shuddering is the reaction of a refined sensibility to the intrusive gaze of the unrefined.[6] Indeed, the whole letter is deeply preoccupied with the rights of property, literary and otherwise: Susan is dazed by the announcement that "stranger hands were preparing [Dickinson's poetry] for publication."[7] Issues of propriety are also reflected in other letters from Susan to Ward: "I wish I could persuade my daughter [Martha] to send you an Easter poem she has just written—but she is immovable, *having a most feminine horror of print*" [italics mine].[8] In fact, there never has been a biological reason for women not to print, and Martha's horror is a properly dignified advance rejection of the impulse to publish commercially, which might have brought with it potentially shameful speculation about the financial status of the woman author's family. Emily's and Susan's objections to print may therefore be seen as part of an internalized middle-class ideology of the feminine that insists on domestic privacy for women as an important aspect of a family's identity and respectability. As Susan wrote, "(after all the intoxicating fascination of creation) she [Emily] as deeply realized that for her, as for all of us women not fame but 'Love and home and certainty are best.' "[9] Publication brings publicity, which threatens personal and familial integrity: exactly how much print threatens the aesthetic integrity of the poems is still an open question. (My viewpoint on publication should not be taken as signifying that the publishing history of those texts has not included serious and consistent misrepresentation of different kinds: it is intended to mean that at the present cycle of her reception, we are still not clear what the extent and significance of Dickinson's textual misrepresentation might be—or indeed if we might not be perpetuating it in another way.)

I want to probe further the ideological implications of Dickinson's failure to publish by asking if her rejection is not a politically conservative and culturally hierarchical gesture; an attempt, in other words, to exclude wider social discourses and realities in favor of an individualized idiom of emotions, abstractions, and essences. If this is indeed the case, if the poetry can be seen as a consistent attempt to deny literature's existence as a social phenomenon, one might also ask what such a private and privatized art tells us about the interpretive communities that privilege its strategic withdrawals.[10] "Subjects hinder talk," Dickinson once wrote in a letter to Susan, and the phrase has a typical resonance and indeterminacy.[11] It can be read as a kind of dismissive, imperious pronouncement: actual topics or issues ("the subject matter of a discourse" as Webster put it) impede important, significant expression. The statement is inscribed with the kind of class consciousness that asserts that writing about contemporary matters results in an inferior product. Another possibility is that it is the self that hinders full expression; in other words, a lingering sense of anxiety or even embarrassment at the prospect of self-exposure leads to a stylistic and distributive circumspection. Given this alleged nervousness it is therefore interesting that, in the following poem, there is what many critics see as a typically Dickinsonian refusal to publish the private self. The poem can be read as an antilyric (a comment either on the genre and other practitioners of that genre, for example, or on expectations we have about the genre) and as a denial that any fully revealed presence can ever be made available in the words of a lyric. Either way, reading the poem can allow us to explore some of the reasons for Dickinson's reticence, as well as the complexity of her relations to readers and to historical contexts:

I'm Nobody! Who are you?
Are you – Nobody – too?
Then there's a pair of us!
Dont tell! they'd banish us – you know!

How dreary – to be – Somebody!
How public – like a Frog –
To tell your name – the livelong June –
To an admiring Bog!

4 banish us] advertise   7 your] one's

Division 4 banish| 7 livelong|
P#260A (J#288)

We often think of poets as unburdening their souls in writing: the term "confessional poetry," though specific to a number of mid-twentieth-century American poets, is emblematic generally of the kinds of expectations we have of lyric poets in particular. In this poem, that first expectation is immediately defeated, for instead of being a poem about the writer, it becomes about us, the readers. A statement about the poetic self is replaced with a string of questions addressed to ourselves: who we are and what relationship exists between us and the speaker are two immediate areas of concern. Another example of this kind of effect is given by William Empson in *Some Versions of Pastoral*, where he quotes Alexander Pope's couplet engraved on the collar of a dog presented to Prince Frederick:

I am his Highness' dog at *Kew;*
Pray tell me Sir, whose Dog are you?[12]

As Empson points out, "Frederick himself would [have been] the first to read it," and the playful suggestion is that as son of the monarch, the prince is in his own way under someone else's charge. And Pope himself, as the poet, speaks through the dog to say something about his, or any other writer's, dependent status in the system of patronage. That this is meant as a joke, rather than a serious critique, is argued by the note of comic confidence communicated by the couplet. What is useful for the purposes of the present discussion, however, is the switch in interest from the writer-speaker to the reader. The questions in Dickinson's poem function in a number of similar ways, at once suggesting sympathy (like the dog speaking to other dogs, this is a nobody speaking to another nobody), superiority (the dog does after all belong to royalty, and the nobody refuses to reduce her- or himself to the level of frogs); and a kind of troubled and troubling riddle ("whose Dog are you?" becomes "Who are you?"). At one level, the questions seek to establish a conspirational affinity between the person who speaks and the person who reads, an alternative and exclusive community, which is threatened with "banish[ment]," and this may be why Dickinson preferred this verb ahead of "advertise." At another level, they undermine whatever thoughts the reader might have entertained about poems and about what they reveal about their authors or authorial selves. This also sets up a possible alliance between writer and reader, this time on the basis of now shared interests in unconventional types of poetic practice: the "you," it will be noticed, is not seen as part of the "admiring Bog," and the addressee is therefore not part of the public audience. By asking what kind of readers we are, and simultaneously denying access to the self, the writer specifies the terms for contact between sender and recipient.

What the first stanza effectively offers is a contrast between competing definitions of writing and reading poetry: while others are quite happy to "advertise" (as Dickinson suggests in her variant for line four), to turn their selves into poetic merchandise, repeating or revealing personal information, which then becomes public property, this speaker feels it necessary to initialize contact but to avoid any further communication. This is all very playful, and to some extent the poem is a tease: by telling us nothing, we are invited to find out much more. But it is worth remembering that such anonymity is also a defensive gesture: separated from, and uncertain about, her audience, the first-person speaker wants to protect her or his identity from prying eyes. It is possible that the persona is feminine, and that assertion is made on the grounds that the need to protect the self from possible criticism was potentially greater for woman writers in the nineteenth century than it was for men. Here it is useful to note the difference between Dickinson's poem (with the persona's sense of existential absence) and the quoted couplet, which oozes complacency (both Pope's and the dog's). Although it is true that a male writer like Hawthorne disguises the source of *The Scarlet Letter* in "The Custom-House" for reasons that include anxieties about the reading public at large, it is not the case that his gender was a point of possible contention, as it was for Dickinson. Issues of authority loom large in her writing: many of her poems adopt conventional nineteenth-century "feminine" attributes (timidity, modesty, invisibility) in order to anticipate and deflect potential cultural antagonism.

In the second stanza, "Nobody" is contrasted with "Somebody," the speaker's order not to "tell" with the Frog "tell[ing]" its name, and anonymity with "public[ation]." One possibility is that the poem ironizes writers (Whitman's poetic self comes to mind here, but there were presumably other contenders, including those described by Keats as "careless hectorers in proud, bad verse"), who endlessly and effortlessly proclaim their self-importance (perhaps by the simple fact of publishing, which carries with it the assumption that one deserves to be published). Margaret Dickie, speaking more generally about the poet herself, sheds some insight on the persona of this poem: "She would never be convinced either of the perfect sympathy between poet and listener that the English Romantic poets celebrated or of the conviction of her compatriots Emerson and Thoreau that the poet was the namer and sayer for all men."[13]

Dickie indicates that ordinarily writers try to persuade, to open up a debate, to elicit a response, or to influence the audience in some way. In other words, they take it for granted that they do have an audience, a reader whom they can address, cajole, scold, and converse with. What the poem above suggests is that the identity of its potential (as opposed to desired) readership is uncertain and even problematic: the speaker makes introductions inappropriate by denying her own identity (and thus the necessity of having a self in the poem at all) and transferring attention to the listener, and although she works very hard in order to create the conditions for an environment where appellations (or titles) are first deferred and then made unnecessary, she also allows the reader to create the speaker almost in her or his own image. The poem can be understood as a critique of the cult of personality: instead of names, or the sounds that confer and confirm identity, an anonymous speaker asks us to think about ourselves as readers and to reconsider not only the kinds of poetry and poets we are accustomed to hearing but even the nature of literary authorship, authority, and audience.

The poem can also be read as taking self-importance so much for granted that it ceases to be an issue; being "nobody" suggests a choice which "somebodies" do not have the intelligence to aspire to. Or, to put it another way, the poem satirizes those who would make a name for themselves and suggests that such puffery is a sign of shallowness and therefore banal and degrading. In other words, the poem reverses the normal equations so that "nobodies" form an exclusive and secret nobility (a meritocracy paralleling Dickinson's social position), while "somebodies" expand their chests only to announce their self-important desires to an unanswering bog (or to other, unreflecting frogs) and therefore to (and in) a kind of vacuum. What is more, since the speaker distinguishes her communication (which is free of information about the self) from that of the frog, which communicates with the function of alerting other members of the species to its nearness, the implication is that the human is distinguished from the animal by precisely this difference in their use of sounds; one is liberated from the tyrannies of presence and purpose, the other trapped within them.

It may be that the speaker is not thinking of animals either; Amherst Common, which was set aside for "public or particular" use—including political meetings—in the 1750s, was adjacent to a large frog pond. If we see the first and second stanzas as indicative of more than a struggle between forms or genres of poetic expression, and as communicating a perceived contest between political rhetoric (or public speaking) and lyric (or private speech), then the poem can be seen in a different setting, that of the larger tradition of debate about the relationship between the artistic and political spheres. "I'm Nobody" can be read as a variation on Shelley's statement in *The Defence of Poetry* that poets "are the unacknowledged legislators of the age," with the emphasis on "unacknowledged": for Dickinson's speaker, to be known, to be a "name," is somehow crude and debasing. The consolation for not being a celebrity is that, if popular taste is coarse, then being popular is a sure sign of one's vulgarity (in 1851 Herman Melville wrote privately to Evert A. Duyckinck that the true "test of distinction is getting to be reversed; and, therefore, to see one's 'mug' in a magazine, is presumptive evidence that he's a nobody").[14] Read in this way, the poem can be seen as profoundly reactionary and antiegalitarian, for it establishes a hierarchy whereby politicians and fashionable authors-speakers are ridiculed at the expense of the restricted, privileged company of the retiring writer and her private reader.

In such a reading, Dickinson's lyric poetry becomes the last refuge of a rejected bourgeois mind. "I'm Nobody" in particular (and another on frogs, P#1355, J#1379, which begins "His Mansion in the Pool / The Frog forsakes – / He rises on a Log / And statements makes – ") can be said to recover the disdain of particular images deployed by William Cullen Bryant in "The Embargo; or, Sketches of the Times" (1809), his poetical garroting of Thomas Jefferson, then the outgoing president of the United States:

Go, search with curious eye, for horned frogs,
Mid the wild wastes of Louisian bogs;

Geography and form have social aspects: Bryant's elegant and educated couplets proclaim the northern Federalists to be sophisticated and urbane, while the emphatic rhyme of frogs and bogs communicates an imperious judgment of Jefferson and his voters as an undistinguished mass living in a southern wasteland. This is not to say that Dickinson had Jefferson in mind when she wrote her poem, but it does situate her in an American tradition of thought and writing that expresses a distrust of, and even a disgust with, the populist excesses perceived as latent in the democratic system. Confirmation of the political overtones of "I'm Nobody! Who are you?" was provided to me unexpectedly while attending a recital in Massachusetts where the speaker read the poem aloud and (after speaking the last line, with its reference to "an admiring Bog") suggested that this was probably a poem that Irish people would have enjoyed: in Massachusetts, the Irish were historically known as bog-trotters. I have to admit that I am not entirely convinced that this alleged reference to the Irish in the poem was not in fact intentional: Dickinson had an earthy sense of humor, and the targets of that humor may occasionally and almost inevitably have included other ethnicities.[15]

George Washington Peck, conservative critic and writer for the *Whig Review*, complained of the Young Americans, Jefferson's political descendants, who sought to extend radical democratic ideology into the world of literature, that there "are demagogues in letters as in politics" and thought that it was "the interest of a radical, no less in philosophy and letters than in politics, to be noisy." The Whig Party, which Edward Dickinson belonged to and which elected him in 1852 to the Congress of the United States, effectively constituted a reformation or regrouping of the Federalists, and they advocated essentially conservative policies: belief in strong central government; support for the established business concerns of the Northeast (such as industry and transport, the latter a particular interest of Edward Dickinson); and resistance to the growing economical power and populism they associated with the opening of the frontier. The Dickinson poems we have just looked at may not commit themselves to such party political programs; at best, they can be said to reflect a larger cultural debate about the meaning and efficacy of a democratic system, and the repercussions such a system would have on the literary enterprise; at worst, they reveal elitist dismissal masquerading as poetic humility.

It seems to me that there is both arrogance and modesty in the poem, and that these are held in a creative tension that fully reflect the perceived polarities of Dickinson's socioeconomic position. Political conservative or literary radical: whichever we choose, we can be accused of imposing external criteria on essentially "private" matters like Dickinson's style and subject matter (in reality, though, style is not separate from other signs of social status). The point is that such categories are relatively crude and misrepresent the simultaneity of historical options and an individual's experience of them. As a middle-class rural woman in nineteenth-century America, Emily Dickinson could occupy positions of oppression and privilege at the same time, and therefore exist in a critical relationship to some aspects of society and a conformist one to others. Social aspects of linguistic style raise interesting questions and are important to my project of following through all the implications of Dickinson's decision not to publish—not just the ones that seem most appropriate to the critical moment.[16] Insistence on the poet as an innovative, experimental writer must always be discomfited by the knowledge of the historical person's elite position in Amherst society as the daughter and sister of two of its most important and respected citizens. It is going much too far to suggest that, as for living, Dickinson's servants did that for her, but she did have servants and choices available to her that were not available to (for example) a working woman of the time. In fact, Dickinson *did* use her Irish servants to give messages and gifts to people who visited but who she refused to see. "Unlike Eliot and the Brontës," Wendy Martin observes, "Dickinson did not have to work at unrewarding or humiliating jobs to support herself, nor did she have to marry for pragmatic reasons."[17] Can she be blamed for this; can the accident of her birth as a white, upper-middle-class woman be held against her? Clearly, there is little point in expecting Dickinson to observe late-twentieth-century models of political and social behavior, but there is also no reason to overlook or to ignore those sides to her writing that may have larger implications for her publication (or lack of it) and its subsequent reception. For, as readers, how are we supposed to respond to the nuances of disdain and condescension toward a certain type of audience which are revealed in "I'm Nobody! Who are you?" And with "Publication – is the Auction," how are we as readers to react to a poem that claims that the very enterprise that makes it available to us in the first place is socially debasing? Can we divorce the initial act of material consumption (buying the book) from our subsequent acts of interpretive consumption (reading the book)?

By the close of "I'm Nobody!" we may feel that the early disavowal of status and title are mere shams, since the speaker subscribes to an ideological position where not having to (or wanting to) struggle with the goal of attaining social prestige or attention is the true sign of superiority. Rather than criticizing privilege, the speaker reverses the methods of assigning distinction, so that self-exclusion becomes the means by which excellence is identified and conferred. Irony and paradox become the signs of that excellence: modesty enables arrogance; anonymity confers selectiveness. If the poem can be interpreted as a poetic equivalent to Dickinson's own seclusion, her refusal fully to take part in the public side of the age she lived and wrote in, then the suggestion is that such a circumstance was not necessitated by the perceived rejection of the poet by her society, but arose from an artistic commitment to a disinterested aesthetic based on a ludic language that conferred status on the genius who produces it. Economically dependent, and yet a member of a professional upper-middle-class family in nineteenth-century New England, Dickinson held a position that was full of contradictions, which also emerged in her relations with the literary world of her day—and in her art. Her recourse to writing without publication can be seen as an act of secession, which established her difference from the concept of art as a site of labor or production—as a commodity the value of which could be determined in a market defined by the contemporary tastes of printers, reviewers, and readers. Her privileged social position meant that she was at a comfortable remove from material needs, in a place where she was safe enough to reject what demands the age might otherwise have made of her, in order to write for subsequent, or posthumous appreciation:

> Some – Work for Immortality –
> The Chiefer part, for Time –
> He – Compensates – immediately –
> The former – Checks – on Fame
>
> Slow Gold – but Everlasting –
> The Bullion of Today –
> Contrasted with the Currency
> Of Immortality –
>
> A Beggar – Here and There –
> Is gifted to discern
> Beyond the Broker's insight –
> One's – Money – One's – the Mine –

P#536A (J#406)

Although the playful, ironic inversion of economies appears to be relatively straightforward in this instance, where spiritual worth is made into a metaphorical commodity, many of her poems reveal a profound ambivalence about aspects of literary eternity, such as in the following:

> The Robin for the Crumb
> Returns no syllable,
> But long records the Lady's name
> In Silver Chronicle.

Division 1 for | 3 records | 4 Chronicle] Chron- | icle
P#810A (J#864)

The normal economy of consumption and production is evaded here: the speaker first denies that it is demand in the form of food that induces the bird to supply the song. Here too the material "Crumb" is transformed into the abstract value of birdsong, which is pure sound, containing no language (though, crucially, rendered linguistically in the poem). The music escapes the material circumstances of its production, just as the poem itself avoids expressing either its own origins or the urgency of the need, which the image of the bird suggested. Music can be defined as the melodious arrangement of sounds into meaningful patterns, and the poem aspires to that definition: the repetition of "r," "cr," "l," and "s" sounds (Robin, Returns, records; Crumb, Chronicle; long, Lady's; syllable, Silver) are foregrounded for reasons of sound more than sense. At the same time, the rhymes are not particularly harmonious, and this tension between sound and the necessities of sense may be rendered intellectually as indicating a strain between the desire to create an abstract essence free of the moment and the felt need to have one's real self maintained in that essence (or, alternatively, a tension between thought and forms of linguistic usage). In addition, despite the fact that the bird's song does not contain words, it is said to preserve the lady's name, which seems a logical impossibility, except in the sense that the stimulus to give the bird food in the first place is immediately translated back into the sheer impulse of its music. So there is a cost to fame, which many of Dickinson's poems express, for although one's name may be converted into symbolic capital (the "Silver Chronicle"), this is only achieved after one's material present/presence has disappeared. Perhaps there is a pattern to be discerned here: Dickinson's withdrawal from the sounds of her poetry (both in her refusal to publish and her erasure of the self in many of the poems) reveals an anxiety about the value of literary performances and the nature of celebrity in a market where status is transitory and contingent on (changing) public tastes. The poems constitute and often communicate an alternative economy whereby investment in writing is rewarded afterward with cultural or spiritual accreditation (recuperation and valorization by later readers, or subsequent acknowledgment by God).[18] This act of poetic segregation is a sign with a variety of potential, and often contradictory, meanings.

Many of Emily Dickinson's poems *did* have an audience, because Dickinson included them in letters to people she knew—over 250 to Susan Dickinson (according to Franklin), 71 to Louise and Frances Norcross, 31 to Elizabeth Luna (Chapin) Holland, 16 to Sarah Eliza Sigourney (Cushing)

Tuckerman, 13 (in four years) to Mabel Loomis Todd, and 11 to both Helen Hunt (Fiske) Jackson and Maria Whitney. And that audience was not confined to private women: she also sent about 40 poems to Samuel Bowles, editor of the *Springfield Daily Republican*, 6 to Dr. Josiah Holland (including one to him and his wife), founder and editor of *Scribner's Monthly*, 8 to Thomas Niles, editor of Roberts Brothers, the publishers, 3 to Otis Phillips Lord, judge of the Supreme Court, and 1 to Daniel Chester French, the sculptor. Although that audience was (numerically, and in terms of ethnic background and class) a limited one, and although it is always difficult to say with certainty if the person who received the poem was the intended (or implied) reader, nevertheless it is clear that Dickinson's poetry was circulated privately and that might therefore suggest that she was interested in having her poems read and responded to. (Even if she had published, of course, it is not at all certain that the class and ethnic background of her readers would have been very different—though Dickinson herself could not have been sure of that.) Indeed, enclosing poems in letters can be seen as a strategy for controlling and limiting the social environment in which one published and of guaranteeing *posthumous* literary survival within the cultural terms and conditions privileged by the same social circle. The wider and more influential the net of her recipients became, the greater the chance that her poetry might be circulated in other circles, recognized, and eventually published. (This strategy is not as cynical as it might appear: Dickinson wasn't exploiting her *correspondents* so much as her *correspondence*, because letters have a way of surviving the original matrix of their inscription and reception.) There are more letters to women than to men: women, Dickinson knew, would have been especially careful to preserve personal documents and to pass them on to the safekeeping of daughters.

All of this suggests that Dickinson preferred an audience of people she knew and trusted to one she did not know at all. But the evidence also suggests that Dickinson thought of different kinds of audiences, rather than of one in particular. For along with the loose poems discovered posthumously by Lavinia in her sister's cherry drawer, there were forty other packets of manuscripts, which had been threaded together (probably in the early sixties), as well as a further fifteen groups that had been left unsewn. Many of the poems in the fascicles do not appear in her correspondence, and these "unpublished" collections may show us Dickinson consciously preparing for future textual or print distribution, perhaps during her own lifetime. This project was probably abandoned with her subsequent realization (or decision) that this would not happen.

But this evidence of a will to publish is conflicting. There are references in her correspondence to such a desire: in a letter of 1861 to Susan, Dickinson writes: "Could I make you and Austin – proud – sometime – a great way off – 'twould give me taller feet – " which suggests perhaps that she wanted them to be proud of her as a recognized writer while they at least were still alive.[19] And she also responded to Higginson after his 1862 *Atlantic Monthly* article "Letter to a Young Contributor" seemed to invite submissions from unknown—and female—authors. Five of her poems appeared anonymously in 1864, in a variety of newspapers and journals, some of them (as was then the practice) being subsequently reprinted elsewhere.[20] But there is the elitist dismissal of the contamination of print culture and the market expressed by speakers in poems such as "I'm Nobody" and "Publication – is the Auction" as well as Dickinson's own outraged comment to Higginson that "A narrow Fellow in the Grass" (published in the *Springfield Daily Republican*) had been robbed from her and "defeated" by an alteration to the punctuation in the third line.

What are we to make of these alleged contradictions? Perhaps one approach would be to say that they represent an intersection of *person, gender,* and *social history:* very few who wrote in the nineteenth century shared Dickinson's situation as (eventually) the unpublished author of 1,789 poems (the most recent estimate), but many women (as Richard Brodhead brilliantly demonstrates) found themselves caught up in changes in the literary and social fields, as entertainment became more visible, commercial, and public at the same time that the Cult of Domesticity urged females to remain economically inactive and invisible except at home.[21] In other words, it is possible to see Dickinson herself (or her nonpublication) as the site of competing ideological discourses. Let me try to illustrate what I mean by quoting part of a letter she wrote in 1880 to Higginson, asking his advice after someone had requested that she release some of her work for publication:

Dear friend,
Thank you for the advice – I shall implicitly follow it –
The one who asked me for the Lines, I had never seen –
He spoke of "a Charity" – I refused but did not inquire – He again earnestly urged, on the ground that in that way I might "aid unfortunate

Children" – The name of "Child" was a snare to me and I hesitated –
Choosing my most rudimentary, and without criterion, I inquired
of you – You can scarcely estimate the opinion to one utterly guide-
less –

Again thank you –

Your Scholar –[22]

Dickinson had succumbed to such a request once before, in March 1864, when three of her poems were included in *Drum Beats*, a Civil War anthology for the benefit of soldiers. And it is believed that, although Higginson advised her to give only one (if any), she did allow another three of her poems to aid "unfortunate Children"—although the particular publication has never been found or identified. Nevertheless, what interests me in this instance is the curious appeal to poetry as an extension of middle-class women's traditional activities of social aid and reform, and at the same time the fear that such charity is a kind of snare, a Trojan horse that bespeaks some kind of threat to the other sphere of female activity—the home and its (architectural and mental) interiors. Note too that although Dickinson is tempted to release some of the slightest of her texts (not the least of the letter's fascination is the idea that she herself had some idea of what constituted her best and worst productions), she does not want to take responsibility for the decision to publish *alone:* she relinquishes that right in a manner that resembles that subgenre of prefaces where women explain that they are publishing reluctantly at the behest of a third person (usually male) or on the grounds of social or financial necessity. Clearly the pressures that would prevent Dickinson from giving three relatively unimportant poems to a deserving cause are (I think) cultural and pertain to definitions of men's and women's separate roles during the emergence of nineteenth-century capitalism.

The parallels between Dickinson's letters of 1864 and 1880 provide us with the potential framework of a narrative about her attitude to publication: under certain circumstances, and on the condition of anonymity, she allowed herself to publish for reasons of compassion and social expediency. Indeed, in one of her poems (P#982A [J#919]) her speaker claims that "If I can stop one Heart from breaking / I shall not live in vain." But in a letter written to her cousin Louise in 1872, the scaffolding of that narrative gives way:

Of Miss P—I know but this, dear. She wrote me in October, requesting me to aid the world by my chirrup more . . . I replied declining. She did not write to me again – she might have been offended, or perhaps is extricating humanity from some hopeless ditch . . .[23]

This is typical of the kind of causal cruelty that Dickinson critics call her wit but that is in fact a means of demonstrating her social superiority. By dismissing women's efforts to alter or to aid the predicament of the underprivileged, turning social tragedy into comic advantage, Dickinson displays her disengagement from the world. So how are we to reconcile this statement with the utterly sentimental speaker of "If I can stop one Heart from breaking"? The answer may be that these contradictory voices dramatize the century's own ambivalence toward women's roles and women's writing, and that Dickinson never fully controlled those voices: instead, they sometimes controlled her. The two letters enact a range of positions with regard to publication and to women's culture. Dickinson satirizes Miss P. because to distance herself from the sentimentalized (but socially concerned) current of women's writing helps establish her own claims to high cultural dignity and artistic seriousness. She appears, however, to align herself noncritically (albeit in the highly fictionalized world of her correspondence with Higginson) with the tradition of female intervention in the world of children's deprivation. One must believe either that Dickinson was schizophrenic, or that she responded differently to prevailing social currents: in any case, the lack of consistency is not a sign of character weakness but of the power of forces of social determination.

In the introduction to this book, I referred to the image of Emily Dickinson, on a "Largely Literary" T-shirt, as a woman hiding or imprisoned in a small room, which I took to be representative of the popular conception of her as a recluse. The multiple ironies of an unpublished poet being transferred onto a location which is rarely free of (often commercial) messages and signs, the aloof loner occupying this most public of all garments, are intriguing, for among the many possible motives for Dickinson's decision not to have her works printed was the desire to avoid precisely this kind of commodification, thereby ensuring that her poems would be subject neither to the demands of the market (in the shape of unknown readers, critics, and editors) nor to its fluctuating tastes (compromise for or by one audience meaning rejection by a future one). But the image of the poet within her room has further anomalies: Dickinson may have written at home, but she circulated individual letters and poems among a wide and select group, constructed "manuscript miscellanies" (or fascicles), and showed a preoccupation in some of the works with issues of posthumous fame and strategies for its successful realization.[24] It seems to me that Dickinson's habits of textual collection and transmission suggest different needs and audiences: the first (writing itself) corresponds to a personal imperative; the second (writing to friends) indicates that her poetry could function beyond the domestic and within a limited social environment; and the third (collating poems for fascicles and sets) bespeaks her awareness of a larger nexus of relations between herself as a writer and an unknown audience of the future (the existence of "scraps" and "fragments" of poetry and prose also suggests that she stored language for specific occasions and correspondences).

In other words, Dickinson's appearance on the front of a mass-produced garment may not be as discordant as it first appears: her poems may not have been printed widely in her lifetime, but her work often had a social character, which Arthur Marotti usefully summarizes:

Lyric poems served as instruments of social intercourse: they could be passed personally to friends and family members, performed in social gatherings, sent as verse epistles or as accompaniments to prose letters . . . used to celebrate births, commemorate deaths, pursue a courtship . . . express gratitude for favours received, present (or serve as) gifts . . . [and] cement the bonds of friendship.[25]

Marotti catalogs the social significance of English lyrics written largely by men in the seventeenth century, but in ways that seem uncannily apt for a nineteenth-century American writer who sent poems in, and in lieu of, letters, read and declaimed others in the kitchen, sent more as notes to accompany the births and deaths of family, close friends, and acquaintances, composed (and published) Valentines, and enclosed lines, stanzas, and full verses with, and instead of, customary gifts of flowers and food. Such usage can be occasional and ephemeral, but the construction by hand of manuscript editions of the poems as well as the highly wrought quality of the language itself argues for something else: a desire for permanence, which seems to take for its model the endurance and reach of *printed* texts. These poems divulge themselves of their social contexts and instead construct alternative relations with both one another and an unseen readership of the future: as I wrote before, they are not letters alone, but letters to the world. To borrow Marotti's language for our own purposes, these poems are not only "instruments" but also "durable artefacts" that extend the sphere of their applicability and usefulness to other ages and audiences, as the following poem might seem to suggest:

The Lamp burns sure – within –
Tho' Serfs – supply the Oil –
It matters not the busy Wick –
At her phosphoric toil!

The Slave – forgets – to fill –
The Lamp – burns golden – on –
Unconscious that the oil is out –
As that the Slave – is gone.

2 Tho'] *written* ⟨'⟩Tho'

Division 3 busy | 7 oil |
Emendation 4 phosphoric] phosporic
P#247A [J#233]²⁶

Ralph Franklin identifies this poem as having been written in 1861, when Irish immigrant Margaret O'Brien was still employed by the Dickinson family: her work, as Aífe Murray was the first to point out, included cleaning and refilling lamps (with whale oil) daily, and trimming and replacing wicks.²⁷ As Murray further documents in "Kitchen Table Poetics: Maid Margaret Maher and Her Poet Emily Dickinson," where she alludes to this poem, such activity is largely invisible and yet necessary to the production of poetry. If O'Brien and Maher had not maintained the oil lamps and performed other domestic tasks, Dickinson could not have produced the volume of poems that she did.²⁸ Murray's point might lead one to believe that normal class boundaries have been blurred by the poet's apprehension of herself as a kind of domestic laborer with the responsibility of ensuring that the devices that enabled others to see themselves and their immediate material and cultural environments more clearly would burn brightly and evenly. What we see here instead, I would argue, is a fusion of essentially Romantic ideas of poetic inspiration and illumination (the inner light of genius, which is represented in contemporary cartoons as the lamp bulb above the thinker's head) with the nineteenth-century middle-class desire to hide labor and protect the privacy of the family as well as privacy within the family. In architecture, domestic space was organized so that the kitchen and washrooms were at the rear and the bedrooms out of sight upstairs. There is a continuity here: Dickinson may appear to identify with the serf, but in reality she is approving the division of social spheres that separates owner and servant, private life and poetic product. In order to be successful in society, one must give the illusion that one does not have to labor. In order to be successful in art, one must hide all evidence of manufacture and origin. Labor becomes visible only at the point where its product ceases to function properly. (Indeed, one wonders what the implications of this poem might be for current work on Dickinson's manuscripts.) Dickinson is identifying sympathetically with servants and workers less than she is offering an approving vision of a stratified domestic universe, where the physical labor of domestic servants mirrors the symbolic labor of domestic poetry but is not equal to it.[29] These are layered projects, hierarchically arranged: one downstairs and strenuous, the other upstairs and mental. Dickinson's remoteness *in the poem* from contemporary Irish servants and African American slaves is demonstrated in the terms she uses and in the focus suggested by their deployment. The "Serf" introduces a historical distance that makes the "Slave" Roman not southern, universal not particular. And the focus of the poem is on the lamp, but not on the servant who supplies it with oil.[30]

Lamps created small worlds of visibility. Reading and writing in these circles of light, Dickinson would have been struck by the potential parallel with her own small instruments of illumination. The poem shows Dickinson's thorough appropriation of domestic particularities for her own purposes: "the development of the Argand lamp in 1798 and its successor, the 'astral lamp'" led to a "dramatic improvement in illumination" and her poem clearly aligns itself with the benefits of such devices, while also demonstrating her independence from them.[31] Somewhat appropriately, perhaps, Ami Argand, the Swiss scientist who invented the lamp that bore his name, died in poverty in Geneva in 1803. But it is less the lamp itself than the necessity of the social arrangement by which it has to be maintained that interests Dickinson, I suspect.[32] "The Lamp burns sure – within" deals with the paradox of a manufactured object of value whose smooth functioning effaces both the method of its construction and the means by which it operates successfully, but it approves of this paradox. At least in this poem Dickinson is complying with the idea that the effacement of the slave-scribe is inevitable to the proper running of household implements-poems.

The ideological components of a literary work can never be assumed to relate smoothly and one-dimensionally to a discernible social class, however. Figurative or allegorical descriptions of social situations do not have to correspond exactly to the writer's own views. By extension, an individual can occupy a complicated and even contradictory position within a specific group, which can be said to be the case with Dickinson who was a member of the local gentry in Amherst, but also a woman who had been taught from a very early age that unpaid domestic labor was a part of her familial responsibilities. It may even be that anyone who subscribes to a view of poetry that erases its own origins in order to survive must be troubled by the thought that the personal self also disappears in the same process of erasure. Nonetheless, the poem displaces perspiration in favor of perspicuity, and this relates fairly directly to a nineteenth-century bourgeois desire to conceal domestic labor (waged and unwaged) and to present elegant facades of leisure to the public. As stated before, in order to become timeless the poem must give the impression of being perfectly self-contained, even though such an impression can only be achieved by the application of intense labor.

Or perhaps it is simply a reflection on the paradox of a product of consciousness that is not conscious itself: the poem cannot exist alone, but it can stimulate a further response in the consciousness of others long after the consciousness which originated it is gone, as the following poem also suggests:

The Poets light but Lamps –
Themselves – go out –
The Wicks they stimulate
If vital Light

Inhere as do the Suns –
Each Age a Lens
Disseminating their
Circumference –

Division 1 but | 3 they | 5 the |
P#930A (J#883)

This may be a revision of the earlier poem, a metaphoric improvisation on a similar theme. Again, it addresses the paradox of a material thing that survives its human origins, though this time the social aspects of this idea are less obvious. There is instead a biological or dynastic element: the poem perpetuates itself in the same way that male human beings (sons) perpetuate themselves by fathering more sons (the process of dissemination, which is to "scatter for growth and propagation, like seed").[33] Taken together, however, both poems imply to some degree that the terms of a text's success can be measured by its capacity to generate the greatest number of readings over the longest period of time. Conventionally, to happen, utterance depends on the immediate presence of a speaker and a listener: literary discourse transcends this dependency (as well as its origins) by being able to communicate across great distances of time and space. This definition is not unproblematic, at least to someone for whom the social conditions that might have helped bring the work of art about in the first place are an important means of understanding its significance, though it seems to me that Dickinson's image of the lens allows for the possibility that the poem must be open enough to suit various critical interests and historical environments, without losing its integrity. But it is uncertain where Dickinson places the burden of responsibility for this longevity. Is it a strategic indeterminacy within a poem (and therefore formal), or some inherent truth that remains immutable and capable of infinite recovery and attenuation (and therefore a matter of content)?[34] Perhaps it is both. Traditionally, the study of literature has meant the study of authors, and Dickinson's correspondence reveals her interest in the biographies and autobiographies of the writers she liked best. But her poetry shows that the text should be independent or autonomous of biographical determination, even if the skill of the work and its truth content lead the reader back to the invisible presence of the artist who fashioned it. In both the poems under discussion, however, the implication would seem to be that the conditions under which it was produced (by which I include the various stages of its development in manuscript form, as well as the social and economic factors, which may have helped to determine it) are irrelevant to its future study. One hesitates to construct a rule from two poems, but these pieces are valuable reminders that Dickinson may have never intended us to look at all her manuscripts or to take the unfinished ones seriously as aesthetic objects worthy of close textual scrutiny. Who knows, she might have concurred with Baudelaire as Roger Shattuck quotes him: "Does one show to a now giddy, now indifferent public the working of

one's devices? Does one explain all those revisions and improvised varia-
tions, right down to the way one's sincerest impulses are mixed in with
tricks and with the charlatanism indispensable to the work's amalgam-
ation?"[35]

Both poems subscribe quite clearly to the idea of aesthetic autonomy
and can be related to the image of the unpublished poet in the garret of
"Publication – is the Auction": interestingly, the garret is also the place
where live-in servants stayed, and the ideas of both the servants who remain invisibly active and the poet whose genius informs her work of art
are part of an ideological continuum. Dickinson's virtual nonappearance in
print can be understood as a deliberate disavowal of literature as a market
commodity: instead of subjecting herself to judgment (and social compromise) in the shape of contemporary arbiters of literary taste or the book-
buying public, Dickinson commits herself to a longer-term investment in
a future community of interpreters, drawn largely from her own kind of
ethnic, socioeconomic, and cultural background, whose members would
privilege poetry above prose and her privatized art above those published
and morally partisan writings of which her age approved. The writer's sacrifice of herself for her art is a token of its sincerity (and hers): the integrity
of both is guaranteed by their removal from a wider public sphere.

Dickinson may not have been famous in her day, but her preoccupation
with fame, both in letters and poems, is partly explicable as an engagement
with the moral and therefore social consequences of the increasing celebrity attached to the literary profession. This engagement in turn can be
understood as part of a historical complex that included increases in population and literacy, rapid improvements in printing technology (where
iron-frame presses could produce the same number of impressions in half
the time of a wooden press) and systems of transportation, all of which
resulted in the replacement of genteel traditions of authorship with a competitive marketplace economy where a larger section of the community
than had ever done so before began to produce, respond, and exercise
influence over the type of literature it wanted. In this enlarged and competitive arena, definitions of literary success were no longer measured
solely by familiarity with traditional forms and genres, or by the skill with
which one worked within these, but additionally by one's sales figures and
popularity. Dickinson seems at times to have identified with alternative
constructions of literary excellence based on the heroic refusal or failure
to succeed in these terms (see, P#112A [J#67], "Success is counted sweetest / By those who ne'er succeed"). Newspapers and magazines increas-

ingly became arenas of literary performance, and as literature became more professionalized, it took on greater public dimensions and responsibilities. Editors enforced the moral and stylistic codes their audience demanded: Dickinson's (whimsical but serious) response was to insist that she was interested only in "Bulletins . . . / From Immortality" (P#820A [J#827]). Typically, however, she borrowed from the language of the press only to adjust its primary focus of attention: even her sensational first lines seem sometimes like the very stuff of advertisement features (P#401C [J#365], "Dare you see a Soul at the 'White Heat'?").

The forms of Dickinson's private production and transmission can be related, in other words, not just to the writer's own preferences and personal experience, but also to external conditions and processes, which may not appear directly in the writing itself. At the same time, relating the poems to their material contexts does not always reduce their ambiguity, I am persuaded. The existence of letters and poems by Dickinson that appear simultaneously to celebrate and critique the ideology of the domestic reminds us that there were contradictions in the social performances of that ideology, which also manifested themselves in her work. Similarly, the real meanings of Dickinson's privatization of literary practices may be much more complicated than we imagine. The existence of the fascicles, for example, is a sign we are not properly equipped to understand: Dickinson left no convenient messages explaining their purpose, no banners proclaiming that her letters to the world were meant to be read by people of only one ethnic and economic identity. The historical contexts, which include the fact of her epistolary mode of distribution and her dissatisfaction with print, allow for such a possibility, as do pronouncements within specific poems. But this is only guess work. It is equally possible that by leaving the fascicles behind when she died (when ladies' manuals explicitly stated that it was the individual's responsibility to destroy anything that was personal), Dickinson wanted them to cut across barriers of time and social class in ways that she herself could not do when alive. It seems to me that these possibilities are not mutually exclusive. That Emily Dickinson may not have written to us directly had we been alive when she was does not exclude her writing indirectly to us in our lifetime. A historical reading of Dickinson (or of any other writer for that matter) must attempt to negotiate with a sense of her foreignness, her strangeness: it must attempt to recognize the otherness, the pastness of the past. Lyric poems tend to enfold us in an illusory relationship of intimacy; they speak directly to us as one confiding self to another. They speak to us, I believe, because there are certain subjects and emotions that remain constant in human life, even if those constants are experienced and responded to in distinct ways by individuals living within specific historical environments and further differentiated by circumstances of gender, class, and age. And yet it is important to keep in mind that the person who wrote Dickinson's poems is no longer alive, even as she lives again every time we impersonate her voice during the act of reading. The perspective I am trying to describe involves negotiating between the position implied by the title of a detective novel, *Emily Dickinson Is Dead*, and that enacted by a piece of graffiti recorded at the 1996 Amherst Book and Plough Festival, where someone had written "Emily D. lives." The truth, for any reader, is situated dynamically somewhere between these two poles.

CHAPTER SIX

GATHERING BUDS

Dickinson's Autograph Anthologies

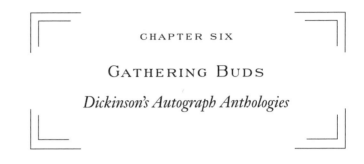 THIS chapter deals with a more specifically textual aspect of Dickinson's publication, namely the manuscript *collections* of the poems known as the fascicles or miscellanies. After the poet's death, some eight hundred poems were discovered, many of which had been gathered together in hand-sewn booklets containing approximately nineteen to twenty poems each. A series of articles and books have made these booklets or fascicles their object of study—in the not unreasonable assumption that such collections represent the best possible (or only available) approximation of the writer's own desires when it comes to the arrangement and sequence of the main body of her poems. A number of scholars have argued that the fascicles are integral editions, with poems composed or arranged as part of an overall structure of meaning that can operate either at the level of the single edition or at that of all of the editions as a whole. Clearly, such an argument potentially invalidates the standard collected editions of Dickinson's poetry (those of Thomas Johnson and, most recently, Ralph Franklin). For Johnson and Franklin present the poems chronologically, rearranging the order and sequence that Dickinson gave them in the fascicles, imposing a very different structure—and thus a context of interpretation—on Dickinson's poetry *as a whole*. In the next chapter, I look at the extent to which levels of meaning are (or are not) lost for *each* poem when it is transposed from the author's handwritten original to a printed translation. Clearly, these two issues are related inasmuch as they both deal with

the transition from manuscript to print, but are otherwise relatively independent of each other (which is why I have given each a chapter): whatever one decides about the first issue has no necessary bearing upon the second issue, and vice versa.[1]

The sheer size of Dickinson's work has allegedly made it difficult to discern any development and consistency of perspective or attitude. Often (so it seems) four poems will form a tentative rule, which the fifth one will break completely.[2] At a point near the end of *Dickinson, the Modern Idiom*, David Porter reflects on this fact and compares Dickinson's poems with those of Robert Lowell, noting the "absence of a project, the impossibility of wholeness, the inevitable turning with the power of language to separate moments" which he detected in both.[3] Ever since this observation was made in 1981, critics have tried to come to terms with Porter's evaluation in different ways—and with varying degrees of intensity and success— by accepting, modifying, or attacking it. And yet, it seems to me that his description is incontrovertible as it applies to the experience of reading the printed versions of her texts edited first by Thomas Johnson in the 1950s and subsequently by Ralph Franklin at the end of the 1990s.[4] Porter himself goes on to claim that print "gives the impression of orderliness and continuity," which distorts the experience of reading Dickinson's manuscripts, and it would be possible to develop that statement by saying that print imposes a different order or that it removes any original semblance of order entirely (even if one understands original order to mean the discontinuous state of many of Dickinson's manuscripts and fragments). In other words, the chronological arrangement of the poems based on the logic of changes to the writer's handwriting (though a truly stunning scholarly achievement) can also be seen as a rearranging or even as a disarranging of the bound and unbound packets of poems Dickinson left behind at her death. Reading the 1,775 poems in the sequence Johnson created for them, or the 1,789 poems that Franklin arranges in a different order, has a disorientating effect—it takes an exceptional or a partisan mind to read through them and to find there a consistent aesthetic program (presuming in the first place that finding a coherent program is a necessary function of literary criticism).[5]

The size of Dickinson's opus, its presentation (especially in the one-volume edition) as a single mass of undifferentiated print, rather than as a series of smaller volumes, does present a problem (though some of the responsibility might be said to lie with Dickinson herself, who left no explicit instructions on how to assemble her texts for publication).[6] The work of the British poet Philip Larkin presents a useful point of comparison, for after the posthumous issue of his *Collected Poems*, one objection raised by reviewers was that their chronological arrangement distorted the sequence and meaning of those poems that had appeared before under separate covers: to group them in this way, it was alleged, was seriously to abuse the integrity of Larkin's earlier work. If one extends this argument to Dickinson, a similar problem can be observed: gathered together in a reconstructed sequence of their composition in time, they lack an identifiable principle of organization, the kind of shared thematic or imagistic concern or approach that is possible to detect in a shorter edition. It follows that part of the difficulty we may experience reading her work— especially reading it straight through, in succession, is textual (in the literal sense of the word): we can't be sure what relations—if any—individual poems have with others, and we can't be sure if the words we are reading are the words she would have wanted us to read (or indeed, that she would have wanted us to read any of her poems in the first place).[7] What some readers, experience, then, is the kind of disorientation reported by Joyce Carol Oates: "By way of voluminous biographical material, not to mention the extraordinary intimacy of her poetry, it would seem that we know everything about her; yet the common experience of reading the work, particularly if the poems are read sequentially, is that we come away seeming to know nothing."[8]

This feeling of incompleteness exists partly as a problem of editorial procedure, then, but partly also as a problem of meaning within individual poems. For often, too, there are several different versions of each poem, and after a while, even single copies of poems will have what appear to be alternative words written above, below, or beside certain words in the text: later still, these are marked with a cross (+) to indicate the presence of variant words or phrases at the bottom of the lyric. Whitman and Yeats were two other poets who revised and changed poems (though for different reasons, one suspects: Yeats because he wanted to improve, to perfect; Whitman because the poem was always in process, unfinished), but in this case there is the feeling—as Sharon Cameron puts it in the memorable title of her second book on the poet, Dickinson was "choosing not choosing"—that alternative words were included in the margins because the writer herself increasingly came to discard the belief that the poem was something bound, framed, or self-sufficient.[9] Her procedures run contrary to the idea of the lyric as an organic whole, a unit complete unto itself. But if one takes this argument seriously (and most Dickinson critics do), then it would appear to multiply the difficulty of ever finding coherence within Dickinson's texts. For example, if I substitute one word "in the poem" for another supplied "on the page" (and one of Cameron's arguments, as Martha Nell Smith puts it, is that there is no such thing as an "inside" and an "outside" on Dickinson's pages), it would be possible to say that a new poem has been created—and this is especially true if one accepts Smith and others' argument that the "variant" words are not always simple synonyms or antonyms, but discursive units that exist at oblique angles to their originals.[10] In these instances, a field of tension is established between the constituent elements of the text and their replacements, for they promise and threaten to alter the orbit(s) of the poem's significance. It as if each poem has within it at least three levels on which meanings proliferate before the reader even approaches the text: those of the poet, those of the poem, and those of the poem's variants (or those of Dickinson the writer, Dickinson the reader, and Dickinson the rereader). When one considers that variants sometimes reach double figures, a vertiginous scenario opens whereby Dickinson's *Complete Poems* would verge on the tens of thousands.

All of this might be seen as intensifying the need for what Porter in *The Modern Idiom* described as not being there, and indeed since his book appeared in 1981 (and even before then), a number of scholars have followed his advice and turned their attention once more to the collections of manuscript poems known as the fascicles, arguing that they enact the kinds of principles that Porter fails to discover in Johnson's edition of *The Poems of Emily Dickinson*. In her privately printed *This Edifice*, Martha Lindblom O'Keefe argued that "the basic unit of [Dickinson's] work, for at least the first half of her work, is not the single poem but the fascicle."[11] What O'Keefe found there was sequence, thematic unity, and structures built from metaphor and parallelism: poems existed in consecutive pairs of opposites. In her exhaustive *Emily Dickinson's Fascicles: Method and Meaning*, Dorothy Huff Oberhaus claims that the fascicles represent a complex but coherent narrative of conversion (both she and O'Keefe draw very similar conclusions about the importance of the Christian tradition to Dickinson's writing, and both tend to see her as an epic poet working with lyric forms). According to Oberhaus, the fortieth fascicle (which is the main subject of her book) is a tripartite meditation on the protagonist's relationship to Christ, and her pilgrim's progress "from renunciation to illumination to union, and then, after many conflicts, to her contentment with this union."[12] A less solemn but no less serious interpretation of the logic enacted by the fascicles is William Shurr's *The Marriage of Emily Dickinson:* he feels that they tell the story of a secret love affair or "marriage" between the poet and Charles Wadsworth, and even suggests that this union may have resulted in an illegitimate child (or the fear of an unwanted pregnancy).[13]

By concentrating on the fascicles, Shurr is implicitly saying that Joyce Carol Oates's disequilibrium is an accidental side-effect of reading the wrong text (rather than reading the text wrongly). According to him (and Oberhaus, O'Keefe, and others) it is the fascicles that impart a sense of order: sewn together with string, they are also linked internally by physically invisible but discernible patterns. "Each bound unit replaced multiplicity and confusions," wrote Franklin, and critics have interpreted his comments slightly differently from the way they were intended: instead of the material or physical tidying of scraps and work sheets Franklin referred to, scholars have extended his ideas to mean that the fascicles erase the alleged multiplicity and confusion of the poetry as a textual unit organized along the principle of chronology.[14]

But the assumption that all these critics make is that there is an unproblematic relationship between Dickinson the person and Dickinson the writer, and that the fascicles represent a species of lyric autobiography, the growth of the poet's mind. If we were to operate with this assumption when approaching P#409A (J#303), "The Soul selects her own Society," to take a familiar example, then an understanding of the poem would best be effected by reading it in relation to the other poems within Fascicle 20 where Dickinson placed it, and then in relation to the other fascicles within which it would form part of a larger narrative structure. In order for this to work successfully, one would have to accept that the poem is an apologia for Dickinson's withdrawal from the world.

But of course there is some ambivalence in the poem, though we can still in theory continue to understand this ambivalence as being personal, related to the historical individual known as Emily Dickinson. In the first stanza a choice made between society and self involves the necessary loss of one or the other. The sense of exclusiveness is balanced by the knowledge of exclusion. So there is a struggle between opposing impulses in the poem. There is a conflict between shutting and opening, between closing off and allowing access, between doors and entrances, between rejecting and admitting. Selection leads to a measure of both gain and loss. Increase or benefit in one area leads to decrease or reduction in another. The final stanza describes again the process of preferring the single way to all others.

The soul focuses only on one. The valves can refer to the heart or to the mind. And stone can suggest solidity, strength, and self-reliance. But it can also connote immobility, hardness, or coldness (exactly the same ambivalence toward single-minded purpose or devotion to a cause is expressed by Yeats in "Easter 1916" when he writes that "Too long a sacrifice / Can make a stone of the heart"). Again, the suggestion is that fixing the attention on one person or being or idea leads to being fixed in some way. I am not claiming that Dickinson prefers one way over another (my colleague at Trondheim Jeremy Hawthorn points out that the last line could contain a potential reference to the stone that blocked the entrance to the cave where Christ was laid after his crucifixion, a possibility that again opens up the final image for other readings). It seems to me that Dickinson very playfully exploits formal devices and linguistic associations in order to get across this struggle between openness and closure. She seems to undercut the speaker's insistence on the self as a sufficient majority with other voices that are not reconciled to this view. It is as if the practice of the poem stands in opposition to the option taken by the soul. Or, to put it another way, the speaker offers one perspective while the text (or the writer) appears (or can be construed as appearing) to offer another.

This last possibility opens up another way of approaching (at least some of) Dickinson's poems, seeing them perhaps not as lyrics (the private thoughts and emotions of a person who is not obviously distinct from the writer) but as *dramatic* lyrics (where the speaker is a character, or at least a persona who exists at one remove from the writer herself, or who is different from her in some way). Sandra Gilbert and Susan Gubar, for instance, have put forward the idea that Dickinson's poems might be seen as "an elaborate set of dramatic monologues," and the statement is helpful when considering a poet who many critics have described as speaking in character, employing disguise, masks, and assumed identities.[15] Fernando Ferrara is useful here:

Much of the so-called "lyric" is nothing but poetry through character which must be attributed to the author who proposes his own poetic persona . . . as the protagonist. One must imagine it as being recited not by the author but by that character whom the author proposes as interpreter. . . . In the case of the lyric "I" would tend to have the so-called "inspiration" coincide with the assumption of all those recognizable elements (poses) which constitute the characterization of the "I" which is the protagonist and voice of the lyric.[16]

Of course, Dickinson's poems do not *look* like dramatic monologues, and even if the poet speaks in character, it is not character in itself that appears to be the main focus of interest: there is often too little time to develop a sense of personality, much less a sense of psychological makeup, motivation, or formation. In addition, not all of Dickinson's lyric monologues can be said to be dramatic, and even those which are (I am thinking here of P#591A [J#465], "I heard a Fly buzz – when I died," or perhaps even the pathetic figure of the so-called Master letter) may be said to intersect at some point with the poet's own presence. Instead, they seem poised uncertainly somewhere between, so that the person who speaks is not obviously different from, nor similar to, the person who writes. This is not to say that none of Dickinson's poems is related in any way to her as a human being. Instead, I am suggesting that the ability to write imaginatively includes the possibility of inhabiting other selves, other perspectives. Or to put it another way, the poems are not always her own utterances: they are also potential impersonations of a self that she might have wanted to be, or thought others might have wanted her to be, or constructions of a self that she thought that she was but then discovered that she wasn't, in the process of describing that self in a given poem.

It seems to me that these comments should be borne in mind when we come to read the fascicles. As I have said, "The Soul selects her own Society" appears in number 20 (as it is listed in R. W. Franklin's edition of *The Manuscript Books of Emily Dickinson*), together with seventeen others, many of which take survival (after death, after emotional or psychological upheaval) as their subject.[17] Like "The Soul selects her own Society," again, most of the poems have two quatrains with alternate lines of tetrameter (or pentameter) and trimeter together with a loose *abcb* rhyme scheme (some of the poems also employ a very playful form of intellectual rhyme, so that in P#396A [J#1725], "I took one Draught of Life"—to take the first one in the sequence—"Life" rhymes with "existence"). At least two of them (P#411A [J#528], "Mine – by the Right of the White Election!" and P#401C [J#365], "Dare you see a Soul at the 'White Heat'?") are thematically quite similar and appear to describe a semi-ecstatic condition of possession-empowerment by some outside force (perhaps grace or the muse). Both are also boastful and provocative, and even come close to performing a kind of subjective violence on the reader. Many of us read poems (at least to begin with) as if they were (or could have been) spoken by ourselves: but how many of us can say that "Mine – by the Right of the White Election!" affords us that opportunity? Again, it needs to be said that not all Dickinson's lyrics behave like lyrics: in the case of these two poems at least, they exist (potentially) at right angles to ourselves, as discrete, alternate worlds. As such, they have what Roland Greene calls "completeness in thought and feeling":

> In fact [the poem's] completeness is realized only in the continuous process of the work where it appears, because it is a completeness of response, a temporary exhaustion of one pose or stance toward the extant issue. A fresh orientation toward topic and auditor, nothing less, will bring about another utterance, and so goes the work. On this supposal, all utterances are the constituents of a dialogue, even when . . . the other voice is fully received into the single speaker's dramatic awareness, and has no independent, perspicuous life. The literary utterance is the product of a submerged dialogue in the mind of the author, of hidden reconnaissances of his or her purposes and positions, the terms of which can be mastered only from attention to the entire work.[18]

Greene writes about sequences of lyric poems occupying a kind of intermediate territory between poetry and prose (a space he designates as lyric fiction), and what emerges from reading all eighteen of Dickinson's poems consecutively is the impression that, although they constitute a series of improvisations on a related theme, and although many are formally quite similar, they also contain very diverse and divergent—even contradictory—views. Again, if we look at the first poem in this group, "I took one Draught of Life," and compare it with the last, P#413A (J#370), "Heaven is so far of the Mind," then it can be seen that these poems appear to engage in a kind of dialogue with each other. The first poem is a potentially sectarian comment on religion as a kind of economy whereby Heaven is priced as being exactly equivalent to one's life, while the last would seem to suggest that the idea of an afterlife is precisely that—an idea, or state of mind, rather than an empirically proven or provable location.[19] The first poem has "Heaven" as its last word, while the last has it as its first. Whereas the first situates "Heaven" as something that is given to the person in exchange for her or his existence, the last identifies it very much as a projection of the imagination (perhaps even literally, for the "Here," which the speaker locates as the site of "Heaven," is potentially the poem itself). The speaker of the first poem seems slightly naive and credulous (which does not necessarily invalidate what he or she has to say: Dickinson often employs the voice of naiveté for satire), while the speaker of the last seems more sophisticated and self-reliant in the sense that he or she trusts not in the external trappings of faith but in the capacity of the imagination to construct adequate structures of aspiration for itself. The last poem indicates that Heaven is almost an intellectual property, while the first dramatizes (and, through the agency of dramatic distance, satirizes) the point of view of someone who believes (or has been taught to believe) that Heaven is a commodity that can be weighed, measured, and priced. Finally, given that one of the main concerns of this book is with the degree to which Dickinson's writing engages or does not engage in dialogue with her time, it is interesting that the first poem fuses the discourses of religion (and possibly transcendentalism), the temperance movement, and the market economy, while the last does not (or does not appear to) engage in any dialogue at all.

Indeed, if we work from the hypothesis that the poems are deliberately arranged as a sequence to exist in a protodialogic relationship to each other, then the second poem in the group (P#397A [J#1761]), "A train went through a burial gate," can be seen as a parodic revision of the first.

A train went through a burial gate,
A bird broke forth and sang,
And trilled, and quivered, and shook his throat
Till all the churchyard rang;

And then adjusted his little notes,
And bowed and sang again.
Doubtless, he thought it meet of him
To say good bye to men.

Emendation 8 good bye] good-by

Whereas the first poem can be interpreted either as a typically Dickinsonian attempt at grafting a simple language onto the experience of death (the distance between the words used and the experience defined resulting in an increased sense of death's mysteriousness) or as the simplistic rendering of death by a consciousness duped by the discourse of nineteenth-century entrepreneurial capitalism (or Catholicism, or both) into thinking that everything has its price, the second poem begins by describing a funeral procession and then suddenly switches focus to the sound of a bird's singing, which coincides with the coffin's progress through the entrance to the graveyard. Of course, the movement through the "burial gate" stands as a potential type of the movement of the soul from one world to the next, and indeed the bird itself (a traditional Romantic symbol of transcendence or aspiration, and in New England, once a popular inscription on gravestones) intensifies the possibility of the soul's flight. But Dickinson's use of the connecting "and" (it appears seven times, or almost once every line) imparts a sense of immediacy—the here and now rather than the hereafter—to the poem. The bird's dramatic presence does not necessarily reinforce but may in fact oppose the possibility of the soul's continuing presence elsewhere. Indeed, it is interesting that the dead person all but disappears in the poem: the reference to a train (which seems disembodied or dehumanized; there is no direct indication of mourners or even of a coffin containing the remains of a human being) seems to hint at a universe that continues almost mechanically and indifferently on its course, with no consideration for human affairs or rituals.

The imagery of the poem is rather cute: the flapping of the bird's wings is likened to a conductor adjusting the sheets of a musical score, and there are other signs of a (literal) musical performance. On its own, this personalization would seem to be closer to Walt Disney than to Emily Dickinson, but the cuteness is misleading: situated after "I took one Draught of Life," the poem provides us with another perspective on death, this time one where nature continues its activities with complete disregard for human events and concerns (this disregard should not be seen as willed callousness, however). Although the last lines suggest that the bird is an elegist, the truth is that the song's beginning coincides only accidentally with the body's entrance into the graveyard, and that any pattern or message of immortality it might offer the listener-reader is therefore produced rather than observed. Dickinson's insertion of the adverb "Doubtless" at the opening of the third line in the second stanza is therefore crucially important, for although it ostensibly means "probably," it can also suggest a religious or theological certainty, which the bird's performance otherwise calls into question. The shift in this poem from the human to the nonhuman perspective suggests the possibility of a skeptical point of view at odds with the certainties communicated in the first poem (and associated symbolically with the bird). It is difficult to say if the last statement in this poem is intended as a sentimental personification (the bird paying its tribute to the deceased) or is meant to be ironic, a deliberately trite version of the bird's song, which hints at a gulf between its activities (singing, flying) and the constructions popularly put on them.

The idea of a gulf between nature and humanity is developed in the next poem in the sequence, P#398A (J#364: there are differences between the two editions—Johnson has "Woe" instead of "Wo" in the first line, and "And" instead of "The" in line seven).

The Morning after Wo –
'Tis frequently the Way –
Surpasses all that rose before –
For utter Jubilee –

As Nature did not Care –
And piled her Blossoms on –
The further to parade a Joy
Her Victim stared opon –

The Birds declaim their Tunes –
Pronouncing every word
Like Hammers – Did they know they fell
Like Litanies of Lead –

On here and there – a creature –
They'd modify the Glee
To fit some Crucifixal Clef –
Some key of Cavalry –

3 rose] *marked for an alternative, none given*

Division 11 Did they|

Like the first two poems, this one addresses the theme of survival, though unlike them what is survived is not death (at least, not the death of the speaker) but some kind of emotional or psychological trauma (perhaps grief following the death of the speaker in the first poem, or that of another, unnamed person). Like the second poem again, there is a gap between human affliction and the continued activities and energies of the natural world, though unlike it, its tone is not cute but solemn and even bitter. Finally, both the second and third poem feature musical imagery, and given that the purpose of this present section is to look at the degree to which Dickinson's poems endlessly revise each other (at least in the fascicles), it is worth looking more closely at differences that emerge in the deployment of this imagery. The third stanza of this poem, for instance, continues the comparison between the singing of the bird(s) and a musical performance, but instead of the rather precious imagery of "A train went through a burial gate" there are a series of terms that belong to the vocabulary of music but whose meanings are twisted to such an extent that they come to refer to very different experiences. The "Hammers" in line 11, to take the first example, indicate that the tunes played by the birds are not as pleasurable as notes produced when the strings of a piano are struck with piano hammers, but instead that they inflict pain in a way that can be likened to physical blows: this encounter between the voices of the birds and that of the speaker is likened to torture, or "a structure of *in*equalities inimical to dialogue as Bakhtin idealizes it."[20]

Throughout the poem, there is the submerged presence of Christian discourses: the (possible) reference to the resurrection in line 3, for example, and even the likened assault with the hammers which may (or may not) function as a subliminal reference to Christ's fixture to the cross. However, the conventional or even chronological significance of this narrative of death and resurrection is altered: the poem *begins* with a number of references to rising or resurrection but *ends* with an equal number of references to death by crucifixion (or an intensity of suffering, which is likened to it). In addition, it seems to suggest that nature's message of continuation (morning after night, joy after pain) is inappropriate and unacceptable: but it is difficult to say whether the speaker objects to the purely physical (and therefore meaningless) activity of waking displacing's the metaphysical act of resurrection (the rising of the sun rather than the Son rising) or to its existence as a trite type of the resurrection (and therefore something that demeans the speaker's despair by suggesting that it is without value, even redundant). Instead, the speaker calls for nature to act with a kind of decorum and restraint, respecting human torment and altering its activities accordingly. There is a kind of inversion at the end of the poem, for the imagery of crucifixion is used not to argue for the possibility of resurrection (or the lessening of anguish over a period of time, a succession of mornings) but for the integrity of pain: the music called for is meant to reflect suffering rather than survival. The Christian imagery does not therefore serve as a form of consolation (the poetic equivalent of harmony), but is appropriated to symbolize an experience of extreme, intense, and individual distress.

The sequence of puns in the poem reinforce the possibility of this interpretation: instead of "Litanies" or prayers that "Lead" (by which I mean "to guide") upward to Heaven, the noise of the birds occasions a falling momentum: the heaviness of "Lead" (by which I mean a base metal) rather than the lightness of Heaven. (I do not rule out the possibility that the mention of flowers, hymnlike tunes, and prayers describes or disguises a church service rather than the singing of birds.) Similarly, the speaker's call for music in the key of her or his suffering seems to deny the potential comfort to be drawn from events subsequent to Calvary: a key (like its French equivalent, "clef") can refer to an instrument that affords the opportunity for gaining access to somewhere else (an afterlife, for example, or an alternative explanation of events, the key to all mythologies), but in this poem it seems as if any such solution to human misery is precluded. Instead, Dickinson's use of "Crucifixal" comes close to indicating the status of that event as fiction rather than fact—and therefore material that can be appropriated and applied to different situations.

It seems to me that there is clear evidence of the dialogic in this poem, in the sense that there is a conflict between the relentless solemnity of the speaker and the noisy, carnivalesque enthusiasm of the birds: one detects the consolations of evangelicalism or perhaps transcendentalism here at odds with either a skeptical intelligence or a late Puritan worldview that questions the reliability of Nature's messages. Bakhtin would argue that the poet's position is privileged above the others, but such a interpretation depends on our accepting that this is a lyric spoken by the writer, whereas I have been arguing that it occupies a more uncertain generic position. As a dramatic lyric (or as lyric fiction), the poem's tensions are unresolved, and therefore truly dialogic: this tendency is increased when one considers the multidirectional play of meaning occasioned by the poem's relationship to other poems in the sequence.

Almost unnoticed, the word "tensions" slipped into the final sentence of my analysis and discussion in the preceding paragraph. "Tension" is one of the keywords of the New Critical approach to literature, and I am aware that "heteroglossia" can come to be equated with and employed as a formalist and even Derridean play of meanings. (Paul deMan argued that the concept of "dialogue" itself was a trope.)[21] The danger of approaching Dickinson's poems as a series of dramatic monologues, which endlessly rehearse and revise a number of positions toward ideas, experiences, events, and ideologies, is that such an approach can easily lead to an emphasis on (for example) imagery at the expense of their specificity as historical documents or their capacity to refer to anything outside the poetic world itself. In this respect, it is perhaps useful to look at the practice of her poems in relation to existing aesthetic codes and conventions, for Dickinson's "spasmodic" meter, her flexible and playful use of rhyme, and her almost total deviation from norms of punctuation are all important departures from the available and predominant forms of poetic expression. Bakhtin claimed the opposite: for him, rhythm "serves to strengthen and concentrate even further the unity and hermetic quality of the surface of poetic style, and of the unitary language that this style posits."[22] Nevertheless, the shape and rhyme scheme of Dickinson's poems (as many critics have previously noted) echo those of the hymn, and her distance from the kind of messages normally encoded in those songs (and her distortion of their images) establishes her verse (again) as a location for ideological conflicts—conflicts not always resolved, but more often than not simply performed within the poem. As Yuri Lotman puts it in "The Text within the Text":

The play with meaning that arises in the text, the slippage between the various kinds of structural regularities, endows the text with greater semantic potential than have texts codified by means of a single, separate language. . . . Culture is not a chaotic collocation of texts but a complex, hierarchical functioning system. Every text inevitably appears in at least two perspectives, two types of contexts, opposed on the axis homogeneity-heterogeneity.[23]

Even the transformation of Christ's suffering into a mirror of personal suffering, which can be seen either as an audacious imaginative appropriation or as a greedy exploitation (and perhaps both), is also a response to shifts in nineteenth-century theological thinking, which saw Christ transformed from abstract deity to a kind of everyman figure. Given, for instance, the Unitarian insistence that Christ was a human prophet and not a divine one, Dickinson's privatization of his execution does not look as completely innovative as it might appear. By extension, her image of Nature, with its carnivalesque imitation and mockery of the acutely sensitive self of the poem resonates with the class distinctions of the day. The third stanza argues that if the birds only knew better they would not do what they do, but the point is that they do not know better because they know nothing: consciousness is something reserved for the speaker of the poem, her mental anguish being opposed by their manual labors. Levels of literary interpenetration (to borrow I. A. Richards's phrase) also occur within and across the poem: there are echoes of Keats's "Ode on Melancholy," for example, though there is also an interesting variation on the movement there from joy to sadness: Dickinson's speaker progresses *from* sadness *to* sadness, and joy is situated as an emotion outside her. Both speakers, though, appear to communicate a sense that melancholy is a higher sensation: for Keats, it increases sensitivity to other experiences, while for Dickinson it implies a consciousness that is already acutely sensitive to the full range of those experiences.

Whatever we might say about the meaning(s) of this and the other two (or eighteen) poems on a one-to-one basis, it is possible to argue that, taken together, this fascicle constitutes a species of lyric cubism. A subject or loosely linked topic is seen (separately but not always sequentially) from the perspective of differing ideas, emotions, or personae, all of which have their own integrity and all of which interact to a greater or lesser degree with each other. The overall effect is cumulative, which is not to say that the poems enact a narrative, develop toward a conclusion, or represent a totality of positions with regards to the subject that either generated their composition or provided Dickinson (as editor) with a principle of grouping them together after they were written. Rather, they seem to exist in a relationship to each other that can be compared to that of characters in a work of prose fiction, some of whom may be conjectured as being closer to the author's own position than others, but none of whom can be treated as being coterminous with her (or with truth). As a friend of mine puts it, the speakers in some of these poems can be likened to a child's imaginary friend, who is in some sense clearly a part of the child's self but also, just as clearly, someone or something with whom to interact and converse with (in reporting this, I am not suggesting that Dickinson's thinking is childlike in any simplistic sense). Indeed, "The Soul selects her own Society" is in itself a useful example of Dickinson's apparently dialogic habit, not only in the ways in which it engages with poems such as "Mine – by the Right of the White Election" and "Dare you see a Soul at the 'White Heat'?" but also because it appears to inform us about a character who, like the poet, practices a gradual withdrawal from society, while at the same time undermining that choice and showing its costs. If this is *lyric* self-projection, then it is raised to the level of *dramatic* or *fictional* exchange, because the process of turning the subject into an object (if this is indeed what has taken place in that poem) enables Dickinson to engage in dialogue with herself: the description of the soul(sole)-self displayed can then be weighed from an outside position. Other poems begin (teasingly) by offering the promise of almost unmediated access to the speaking consciousness ("I think") before dissolving into a description of an external object: P#400A (J#525), which opens this way, then continues (in the Franklin reproduction of the manuscript) "the Hemlock likes to stand."

In the end, the fascicles supply us with one context of meaning, but only one. Although books by Oberhaus and O'Keefe have repositioned Dickinson in a tradition of Christian meditative and prophetic writing, one has to acknowledge that this interpretation is intimately related to their granting the fascicles a primary status among Dickinson's different modes of textual assembly and presentation.[24] They assume as a given something that we have no evidence for: that the manuscript miscellanies were organized with a fixed purpose both at the level of the individual collection and as part of a larger structure of significance. The result is a very different picture from the disparate and dissident selves presented in, say, Porter's *The Modern Idiom*, though Porter's view of Dickinson is equally informed by his use of the Johnson editions, where the chronological sequence isolates each poem from the next and gives the impression of a proleptically modernist, eminently nonconformist, and playful creative intelligence. Oberhaus and O'Keefe, together with William Shurr, offer us a comforting narrative sequence, a plot for the poems, which many other critics tend to ignore or disparage as embarrassing. The fascicles provide Oberhaus, O'Keefe, and Shurr with the possibility of definable patterns, which would be impossible to find in the larger body of poems: taken whole, Dickinson's poetry as it appears in the Johnson edition does not constitute a whole. But as John Gerlach reminds us, since there is a "human tendency to find pattern even in ink blots, the fascicles may simply be the Rorschachs into which all may read as they please."[25] Or, as George Eliot puts it:

Your pier-glass or extensive surface of polished steel made to be rubbed by a housemaid, will be minutely and multitudinously scratched in all directions; but place now against it a lighted candle as a centre of illumination, and lo! The scratches will seem to arrange themselves in a fine series of concentric circles round that little sun. It is demonstrable that the scratches are going everywhere impartially, and it is only your candle which produces the flattering illusion of a concentric arrangement, its light falling with an exclusive optical selection.[26]

The clusters of images that O'Keefe finds in Fascicle 20, for instance, are repeated in other fascicles also, so that the association of music with hammers and pain in "The Morning after Wo" has very definite echoes in P#477B (J#315), "He fumbles at your Soul" from Fascicle 22. This does not invalidate O'Keefe's thesis (which would make a very useful reader's guide, if it were ever to be made more widely available), but it does suggest that the kinds of oppositions and parallels that she detects *within* the fascicle also work just as well *without* it.

One of the features of Dickinson's correspondence with Thomas Wentworth Higginson is her tendency to include clusters of poems with apparently related themes or images, and which Thomas Johnson thought to have been written around the same time. In November 1871, for example, Dickinson sent Higginson four poems that Johnson numbered as 1181, 1182, 1183, and 1184.[27] This kind of evidence would have strengthened the arguments of those claiming that Dickinson composed according to a theme—or at least according to some kind of linkage of metaphor or subject. But the new Franklin edition of Dickinson's poetry suggests that Johnson's consecutive arrangement of these poems does not necessarily mean that they were consecutively composed: Franklin assigns them numbers 594C, 1234D, 1227D, and 1229B (though of course he may be wrong). The point to be made, however (and this has implications not just for those who favor using the fascicles but for others who group and then interpret poems according to their recipients), is that packaging poems in almost any way imposes on them a logic of relation they may never have had. The four poems sent to Higginson belong in addition to different autograph anthologies: in this instance, P#594C (J#1181), "When I hoped I feared," is an 1871 variant of a poem (594A) first placed in Fascicle 26 and dating from 1863. Another version (594B) was sent to Sue in 1865. Surely the logic of this is that neither the fascicles nor the human recipients are the true or single determinants of the poem's origin or reception. The same applies for P#1234D (J#1182), "Remembrance has a Rear and Front," which exists in four variants: A (now lost) exists in Susan's transcript, B (also lost) was transcribed by Frances Norcross, and C was recorded in Set 10 [a set is an unbound fascicle]. P#1229B (J#1184), "The Days that we can spare" was sent to Higginson, while A was collected in

Set 10, and C was written on a bifolium of notepaper, with no address or signature. Finally, P#1227D (J#1183), "Step lightly on this narrow Spot" exists in four versions also: A was sent to Susan in 1871, B was written in pencil on the flap of an envelope, and C was collected in Set 9 (which has only one other poem). What emerges from these revolving contexts is, I think, a mobility of potential referentiality, which is perhaps the defining characteristic of Dickinson's particular genius—the sense that, distinctive though they are, all her poems have different addresses and different addressees. Reading them as part of a sequence (of poems in a fascicle, of poems in a correspondence) is therefore to close down or to sentimentalize the very flexibility of relations with the world that Dickinson's own practices seem to insist on.

Another letter to Higginson, written toward the end of 1872, has the following poems (or excerpts from poems) as Johnson numbers them: 1206 (now P#1270C, "The Show is not the Show"); 1207 (P#1266B, "He preached upon 'Breadth' till it argued him narrow"); 1208 (P#1267B, "Our own Possessions though our own"); 1209 (P#1239C, "To disappear enhances"); and 1210 (P#1275C, "The Sea said 'Come' to the Brook").[28] Of these, "The Show is not the Show," "He preached upon 'Breadth,' " and P#1208, "Our own Possessions," do not appear in any fascicle or set at all, while a version of "To disappear enhances" is included in Set 10 and a version of "The Sea said 'Come' to the Brook" appears in Set 11. In 1873 and 1874, Dickinson wrote two letters in which she included poems that Johnson numbered as 1255 (now P#1298A, "Longing is like the Seed"); 1256 (P#1214B, "Not any higher stands the Grave"); 1257 (P#1299A, "Dominion lasts until obtained"); 1259 (P#1216D, "A Wind that woke a lone Delight"); and 1260 (P#1314B, "Because that you are going").[29] Of these five, three ("Longing is like the Seed," "Dominion lasts until obtained," and "Because that you are going") are not contained in any fascicle or set, while earlier 1871 versions of P#1214A, "Not any higher stands the Grave," and P#1216B, "A Wind that rose though not a Leaf" are both gathered in Set 8a.

There are a number of points here. First, the fact that versions of the same poem exist in different textual and personal contexts suggests that Dickinson did not necessarily *write* with some kind of improvised or unifying principle in mind (which is essentially what O'Keefe and Oberhaus have argued): poems could have been grouped together in, or left out of, fascicles and sets *after* their composition, according to editorial, formal, or interpretive criteria (the list is loose because it is not certain what the organizing principle really was, or indeed if there was or is one). Again, though, such a conclusion depends in part on our accepting that Johnson's and Franklin's assignation of numbers are more accurate than accidental—and although we can in principle, and do in practice, agree to separate the poems from one year from those of another year, it is more problematic to separate their order *within* a year. One might then go further and say that Johnson's and Franklin's numberings of the poems, though certainly valuable for ascertaining how many poems might have been written in a given year, are potentially misleading in the sense that the numbers can and do sometimes suggest an *intentional* relationship, which may never have existed in practice. Dickinson, however, often included poems in groups to Higginson, and Johnson's assignation of numbers to these was based on the not unreasonable hypothesis that they were written about the same time. L#413 includes one whole poem and one part: listed respectively, these are 1294 (P#1327A), "Of Life to own" and a variant of a new stanza from 1298 (P#1350E), "The mushroom is the Elf of Plants."[30] Another letter, written in 1876, finished with 1352 (now P#1387A, "To his simplicity") and enclosed a further five: 1353 (P#1380F, "The last of Summer is Delight"); 1354 (P#1381C, "The Heart is the Capital of the Mind"); 1355 (P#1384E, "The Mind lives on the heart"); 1356 (P#1369C, "The Rat is the concisest Tenant"); and 1357 (P#1386D, " 'Faithful to the end' amended").[31] Of these six poems, versions of three others—"The last of Summer is Delight," "The Heart is the Capital of the Mind," and "The Mind lives on the heart"—are included together elsewhere by Dickinson—in Set 14. Again, this first suggests that we should maintain a certain skepticism about their sequential relation to each other as Johnson and then Franklin numbers them, but second, that doubts about claims that the fascicles or sets were grouped according to an organizing element at the point of their conception cannot be universally applied: the titles, "The Heart is the Capital of the Mind" and "The Mind lives on the heart" surely suggest a relationship to each other, which is more than simply chronological.

The underlying logic of the fascicles is not, to my mind, a consistent one: poems within different miscellanies may have been related organically to each other, but it is just as possible in many instances that Dickinson grouped them afterward according to criteria that we can only guess at—their quality (which means, once again, that she had some idea of what was good and what was not) or some (vaguely or precisely) similar themes or images. Perhaps the point to make, however, is that the different groupings of the poems in letters sent to Higginson—or to Sue for that mat-ter—and in the fascicles suggest that the fascicles do not embody the final word on the relation of one poem to another: Dickinson's practice of send-ing quatrains from poems rather than full poems in letters suggests a much looser attitude to their potential applicability, a fluidity of potential range which I and others see as the quintessential genius of the poetry.

It also does not necessarily follow that the writer's own choices and ar-rangements within the fascicles were fully independent ones. Dickinson may have been thinking of which poems would be suitable for publication (the main body of fascicles having been gathered at a time when her liter-ary output was at its highest, and when she still could have entertained the possibility of having them appear in print), and as such, she may have had one eye on the age and the other on the manuscripts in front of her. This is clear, for example, in the letters, where the poet deliberately chose and even changed texts in order to suit the interests and tastes of the person being addressed. For example, after her first approaches to Higginson, she was careful to send him poems that were increasingly conventional by her standards: even if they were quite different from anything being written at that time, they often expressed (or can be construed as expressing) sen-timents that in many ways were widely held. The letters are important because they show us Dickinson making editorial decisions and com-promises, though ones that are not always consistent over time. In fact, Franklin and more extensively Martha Nell Smith have argued separately that the correspondence represented "the only external form of publica-tion [Dickinson] allowed herself during her lifetime."[32] If this is the case, then one wonders (with an eye to my next chapter on the status of individ-ual manuscripts) what the implications are of her decision to send what appear to be finished poems to her correspondents, and not versions of the poems with variants added?

Looking at the fascicles has its own kind of editorial and interpretative logic, of course. It cuts the amount of poems down to a more manageable size—slightly over eight hundred if you concentrate on the bound packets (still a considerable number, but only about one-half of the total collection in Franklin's new edition) or between twenty to thirty if you concentrate on one fascicle in particular (as both Cameron and Oberhaus do). Never-theless, what unites these revisionist efforts—and those of the editors of the Dickinson Electronic Archives presently engaged in bringing together, in separate but coordinated editions, collections of letters and poems sent to individual correspondents like Susan Gilbert Dickinson and Thomas

Wentworth Higginson—is rethinking the history of Dickinson's conventional publication in an effort to re-create the poet's own practices, both on the level of the individual poem as it appeared in manuscript form and on the level of what Martha Nell Smith (with Jerome McGann possibly the leading contemporary theorist of Dickinson's textual status) described as the poet's own system of publication—circulating manuscripts privately to an intimate circle of friends and hand-chosen acquaintances.[33] All of this confirms the sense that with Dickinson what we see in a poem depends very much on the kind of text and context that we are presented with or which we choose to read: the edition informs the view more than ever. And it is to a different set of issues related to manuscripts at the level of their individual presentation that I now move.

CHAPTER SEVEN

REVISING THE SCRIPT

Dickinson's Manuscripts

EMILY DICKINSON's poetry presents particular challenges, difficulties, and opportunities for a number of reasons, but chief among them in the current critical climate arises from the fact that her poems remained largely unpublished (in the sense of being typographically fixed in a printed text) in her own lifetime. This chapter deals with individual versions of poems in manuscript and examines the extent to which levels of meaning are or are not lost for particular poems when they are transposed from the authors's handwritten originals to printed translations. The manuscripts of the majority of *published* writers, may be understood as notes toward a final, printed version, but with Dickinson's manuscripts, which are in a very different, and potentially more sophisticated, medium, print has been seen as seriously misrepresenting the work. It has been suggested that the printed page, with its blank background and uniformity of script, regularizes her poetry in the same way that her first editors regularized her "idiosyncrasies" of grammar, punctuation, meter, and rhyme—in this case by erasing its graphic aspects. For Martha Nell Smith, the most visible and outstanding of a new generation of Dickinson textual scholars, physical or chirographical features of Dickinson's work are part of the poet's project of "destabilization."[1] This chapter tests the accuracy of that observation—and looks also at what the manuscripts' material attributes might tell us about Dickinson's relationship to commercial culture and ideology. Clearly, any study that claims that Dickinson's poems generate meaning from the manner of their inscription has serious implications. At least potentially, such studies call into question the validity of all printed editions of Dickinson's poems and letters.

That Dickinson intended the printed versions of her words to reproduce all the details of her manuscripts is not at all clear. She left no explicit instructions on how her texts were to be assembled and presented, and the evidence contained in the manuscripts themselves is not consistent. Nevertheless, there is, broadly speaking, a consensus of international scholarly opinion that holds that a return to the manuscripts is necessary to establish a reliable corpus of her poems, and I should declare that, by and large, I am caught up in this critical momentum. But I should also declare that I have misgivings about the kinds of positivistic assumptions that underpin such a project, or, more accurately, misgivings about the lack of published attempts to measure the accuracy of claims being made on behalf of Dickinson's manuscript practices. It is not that I think such claims are necessarily wrong but more that certain problems of approach (and some of the conclusions already drawn) have not yet been thought through or sufficiently debated. I am therefore testing out the assertion that Dickinson's manuscripts are the most reliable guide to her meaning(s)—and that they demonstrate a proleptic textual radicalism—by looking closely at how Dickinson presented her work to others. I close this chapter by examining some of the available evidence on how the woman championed by Smith, Ellen Hart, and others as Dickinson's closest friend and literary ally, her sister-in-law, Susan Huntington Gilbert Dickinson, appears to have interpreted formal aspects of Dickinson's poetry. Details of punctuation, capitalization, indentation, and lineation, as well as the relationship between lines and between words at the end of a line and the right-hand edge of the page, will also be attended to in an attempt to provide readers with enough detail to draw independent abstract or theoretical conclusions.

Voices opposed to the contemporary emphasis on the manuscripts as agents of a new poetic and scriptural enterprise are too often dismissed as anachronistic. Ironically, one of those voices belongs to the man who, perhaps more than anyone else, was responsible for generating much of the new interest in the manuscripts with *The Editing of Emily Dickinson: A Reconsideration* (1967) and *The Manuscript Books of Emily Dickinson* (1981).[2] Ralph Franklin does not believe that Dickinson's work sheets, drafts, and fair copies possess the detailed aesthetic significance attributed to them by later scholars, though his comments have often been interpreted as if they support such a view.[3] In *The Birth-Mark*, Susan Howe paraphrases correspondence with Franklin on this question, in which he expresses antipathy to the project of making manuscripts the primary object of Dickinson scholarship:

> [Franklin] told me the notebooks were not artistic structures and were not intended for other readers; Dickinson had a long history of sending poems to people—individual poems—that were complete, he said. My suggestion about line breaks depended on an "assumption" that one reads in lines; he asked, "what happens if the form lurking in the mind is the *stanza*?"[4]

Another conscientious objector is David Porter. In a review of William Shurr's *New Poems of Emily Dickinson*, Porter contests Jerome McGann's claim that Dickinson's "surviving manuscript texts urge us to take them at face value, to treat all scriptural forms as potentially significant *at the aesthetic or expressive level*":

> In the aesthetics of her scriptural forms, then, what is the function of Dickinson's disabling eye trouble and the probability that, as she wrote in pen then pencil, her impaired peripheral vision could not measure out spaces or reliably ascertain a sheet's edges where her hand-written lines began or finished or were interrupted?[5]

Porter and Franklin, as I understand them, appear to unite in resisting Howe's observation that after "the first nine fascicles, lines break off, interrupting meter" and the implication that this represents a deliberate strategy on Dickinson's part.[6] But if the manuscripts *do* include certain features that are then normalized or even excluded (accidentally or on purpose) from the published editions of Dickinson's work, then the printed versions of some poems (perhaps even the majority) misrepresent essential parts of their meaning(s). Such at least is the argument put forward by McGann in *Black Riders: The Visible Language of Modernism*, in which he illustrates his conclusions by taking as examples two versions of the opening stanza of P#760 (J#650); the first is the version that appears in Johnson's one-volume edition, the second, McGann's transcription of Dickinson's manuscript copy:

1.

Pain – has an Element of Blank –
It cannot recollect
When it begun – or if there were
A time when it was not –

2.

Pain has an Element
of Blank –
It cannot recollect
When it began – or if
there were
A time when it was not[7]

McGann says that it "does no good to argue, as some might, that these odd lineations are unintentional—the result of Dickinson finding herself at the right edge of the page, and so folding her lines over. Her manuscripts show that she could preserve the integrity of the metrical unit if she wanted."[8] Whether McGann's certainty derives from empirical research (a statistical study of the number of times Dickinson divides a given metrical unit into two lines for reasons that can be construed to be conscious, as opposed to the number of divisions made necessary by the length of a word, its proximity to the right edge of the page, or both) is not stated. It is hard to know if such a scientific approach could be objectively sustained, but one would want, nevertheless, to question some of McGann's conclusions. Does it follow, for example, that the "integrity of the metrical unit" is compromised by having it occupy two lines of a manuscript rather than one? And while there is no reason to doubt his claim that the blank space that follows the word "Blank" is a kind of pun, is it not possible that the same pun exists in the "regularized" version? Moreover, if this pun is truly intentional, why did Dickinson not accentuate it by omitting the dash, which interposes itself between the noun and the space that follows and which may be read as leading us to the next line rather than to that space? Finally, if McGann is so concerned with the misrepresentation of Dickinson's technique entailed by any failure to present her texts exactly as she wrote them, why does he ignore the plus sign (+) after "A" in line 6 of the manuscript version, which signals the presence of a variant ("Day") for the word that comes after it ("time")? Indeed, why not point out for that matter that "began" in line 4 looks very much like the "begun" that Johnson transcribed it as? Are we to assume that this ambiguity is accidental where all the rest are not? And why omit the dash that appears to follow "not" in the manuscript version? Where are we to stop when it comes to judging which inscriptions make a deliberate contribution to the meaning of the poem and which do not?

Peter Campbell makes many of these same points in his review of *Black Riders*, and he goes on to suggest that her line breaks could indicate that Dickinson was not at all interested in the physical properties of the poem, a possibility that may be difficult for twentieth-century editors and readers to accept, but that cannot be dismissed.[9] In this context, Dickinson's correspondence with Thomas Wentworth Higginson, the manuscripts of which are presently lodged at the Boston Public Library, can be instructive, for a number of reasons. The correspondence was carried on from 1862, an early peak year in Dickinson's creative enterprise, to 1886, the year of her death, and is therefore quite comprehensive. At the same time, it comprises a limited number of texts and a manageable yet reliable body of evidence for close textual investigation. Finally, it combines both poems and letters, which one can compare for common characteristics, for as Ralph Franklin has claimed, "any special theory of Dickinson's mechanics will have to fit both poems and letters."[10] And there *are* common features. For example, in the manuscript of L#441, written in July 1875, Dickinson twice splits words (ironically enough, because Johnson has been criticized for not reproducing these features, both occur in his transcript of the letter): on the second page, she writes "She asks / for my / Father, con- / stantly," and on the third page, "I am pleased / that what / grieves our- / self so much."[11] On the first and second pages of her January 1876 letter to Higginson she tells him, "I had read [page break] 'Childhood,' / with compunc- / tion that / thought so / fair – fall / on foreign / Eyes – " (L# 449; GC: Ms. Am, 1093 [58]). In February or March of the same year, she asks "Could you / pardon the / Elderly gentle- / man, who / entrusted / the circumstan- / ces to you" (L#452; GC: Ms. Am. 1093 [66]). Again, in L#458 (GC: Ms. Am. 1093 [69]; spring 1876), she writes:

Dear Friend,
    Your
thought is
so serious
and cap-
tivating,

In L#486 (GC: Ms. Am. 1093 [78]; about 1877) she writes on the second page, "In a dissem- / bling hue" and "Please re- / member me." These two word breaks are especially interesting because the first forms part of a poem, while the second is in the letter itself. Of the two, the second might seem to have the more semantic potential, though it is likely that it was accidental. Dickinson is asking to be remembered to Mrs. Higginson, and there would seem to be little point in punning on the letter as a kind of *disjecta membra*, which is then reconstituted in the living speech of the recipient to his wife. On the fourth page of the same letter, she talks of how "I thought / your appro- / bation Fame – / and it's with- / drawal Infamy." In L#488 (GC: Ms. Am. 1093 [79]; early 1877) she refers on the third page to looking in vain for Higginson "in the Mag- / azines, where" once he wrote. The examples continue (and I have not included all of them): "per- / haps" on the third page of L#622 (GC: Ms. Am. 1093 [99]; December 1879); "con- / venient" on the second page of L#674 (GC: Ms. Am. 1093 [101]; November 1880); "can- / not" on the third page of L#735 (GC: Ms. Am. 1093 [106]; about 1881); "im- / measurable" on the second page of L#819 (GC: Ms. Am. 1093 [107]; late April 1883); "Biogra- / phied" on the second page of L#972 (GC: Ms. Am. 1093 [111]; February 1885); "Super- / scription" on the second page of L#1007 (GC: Ms. Am. 1093 [112]; August 1885); "en- / tered" on the first page, and "no- / tices" on the third page, of L#1042 (GC: Ms. Am. 1093 [113]; spring 1886); and (finally) "acclama- / tion" in L#1043 (GC: Ms. Am. 1093 [114]), written in late April 1886. The patterns are clear enough: in the years I have looked at in which word separation occurs in Dickinson's correspondence, the ratio of letters with instances of division to letters without is about one to two. However, if we include those years between 1876 and 1886 when there is no division at all (1878, 1882, 1884), the ratio is closer to two to five (twenty with, forty-eight without). The occurrences seem largely accidental, however; they do not appear to have been deliberately manipulated for semantic purposes.[12]

Now letters are not poems, even though a great deal of thought (and often revision) went into Dickinson's correspondence. There were frequently drafts of letters (and even of short notes), and Dickinson seems to have kept little scraps with images and phrases that she subsequently incorporated into her communications when they were appropriate for the occasion. In 1863 she included this version of the concluding stanza of P#243B (J#286) "That after Horror – that 'twas *us*" in a note to Higginson:

The possibility to pass
Without a Moment's Bell –
Into Conjecture's pres-
ence –
Is like a face of
steel
That suddenly looks into
our's
With a Metallic Grin – [page break]
The Cordiality of Death
Who Drills his
welcome – in –[13]

McGann claims that Dickinson's manuscripts urge us "to treat all scriptural forms as potentially significant," and one can, in fact, construct (or
reconstruct) a possible strategy behind the splitting of "pres-ence."[14] It
delays the encounter between the speaker and Death—heightening the
sense of dreadful anticipation—and perhaps also performs the desire to
postpone that final meeting. It would be nice to believe that Dickinson
intended such an effect, but it is impossible to say with any certainty that
she did, for the evidence of the photostat suggests that she broke the word
at this point because she did not have room enough to complete it.[15] What
is relevant for my discussion is that almost any feature of Dickinson's manuscripts can be interpreted to suggest a proleptic concern with the semantic
potential of the poem's visual properties, its line and word breaks as well
as its punctuation. But such interpretations—however interesting—must
remain conjectural, for there is as yet no solid evidence—in the shape of
a book-length study of these features—of a consistent attempt on Dickinson's part to exploit these aspects of linguistic inscription.

In other words, words divided between lines is not uncommon in Dickinson's writing (especially in the later years), and their occurrences in her
manuscript poems may not therefore be consistently deliberate. At least
in the letters to Higginson, there does not appear to be a pattern of words
being consciously split for an artistic effect. If one extends the insights
gained from her habits in the letters to the poems, then it might be argued
that instances of word splitting in the latter may have been equally accidental. If there is a tendency here, it is this: generally speaking, the material inscription of the letters that formed words and the words that formed

lines in Dickinson's correspondence with Higginson were not an important concern for this poet.

Among the many objections that might be raised against such a provisional conclusion, the most obvious is that Higginson (judging by his negative comments on formal aspects of Dickinson's style, as reflected in her replies to his letters) was profoundly conservative—even ignorant—when it came to literary innovation. But there is a sense in which this conservatism strengthens the conclusion I am proposing, for if Higginson was as conservative as he is made out to be, there would be no point in Dickinson's experimenting with lineation and word division in her correspondence with him. And if one objects to this line of argument by saying that such instances are not deliberate in the Higginson correspondence (as seems to be the case), why are they accidental only there and not everywhere else? For example, when Dickinson writes to Samuel Bowles (in November 1862) and splits "ar- / gument" between lines 12 and 13 of the second page; "super- / sede" between the last line of page 3 and the first of page 4; and "content- / tion" between lines 5 and 6 of the fourth page, does this mean that the split word ("econom- / ical") in the version of "Victory comes late" she sent to him in 1862 is similarly accidental?[16] If the letters were crafted with care (as they were) and yet feature nonsignificant word splitting, what does this mean for the significance of words split in the poems?

It might be objected that Higginson and Bowles were men of the world, public figures with whom Dickinson was not intimate enough to relax and reveal her truly innovative side. And there is some truth in this. The letters to Bowles, for instance, are more reserved than those to her sister-in-law and close friend, Susan Dickinson, which are casually inscribed on an array of different papers—envelopes and scraps as well as more formal stationery. It has been argued by Smith in particular that the scraps bespeak a "comfort-level" with Susan that Dickinson could never feel with Higginson or Bowles. The very materiality of these different texts, then, has a meaning. But precisely how this meaning can be formulated is difficult to say. Some critics see Dickinson's confidentiality enabling her to be experimental. But perhaps the opposite is true. Familiarity may mean that normal epistolary and literary regulations can be suspended. Perhaps Dickinson relaxed with Susan because the appearance of the writing on the page had no significance for either of them—except occasionally as Dickinson played with some accidental detail of the paper or fragment on which she was writing. In other words, in this instance the relevance of Dickinson's scripts can arguably be limited to the historical relationship she had with her sister-in-law. It might be a function of their friendship and have no importance for her poetry as a whole. With Bowles and Higginson, who offered the possibility of publication, access to the literary scene, and some measure of institutional literary respectability and esteem, her circumspection or self-control could be taken as a sign that, had she published, she would have normalized some of her lines and even accepted the conventions of print. She might even have given the poems titles. The "published" version of a poem like "Victory comes late" shows a willingness to compromise or negotiate her linguistic and scriptural forms.[17] Also, the fact that Dickinson complained to Higginson in 1866 that a line in "A narrow Fellow in the grass" had been "defeated" by the unsanctioned insertion of a comma in the third line of its printed version does not necessarily mean that she paid the same kind of minute attention to details of punctuation in all other poems. Variant copies of the same poem demonstrate inconsistency on this point (from another perspective, they are restlessly inventive).[18]

Another claim made about poems included in correspondence—and about the letters themselves—is that they break down the boundaries between poetry and prose. There are several ways in which this assertion might be understood, but for the purposes of this chapter I concentrate on the poems included in the correspondence without any apparent attention being drawn to their existence *as poems*. The argument is that these poems are thus not lifted out of their context or separated from the matrix of personal connections that constitute the relationship between the letter reader and the writer, as they were by Dickinson's editors. Again, Thomas Johnson's edition of the letters is usually blamed for imposing standards derived from the conventions of print on Dickinson's handwritten letters, thus obscuring the extent of her experimentation. To indicate the presence of a poem or a stanza within a letter, Johnson indents and therefore separates the poem physically and generically from its prose context.[19] Ellen Hart, who is among the critics who suggest that Dickinson was experimenting with generic boundaries when she included a poem in a letter without indicating formally that it was different, makes two central points:

First, Dickinson did not visually separate prose and poetry in her letters. Her prose lines and the lines of a poem are similar in length, she did not consistently divide poetry from prose through spacing, and she did not vary margins. A standard prose format for the letters results in visual inaccuracies, such as Johnson's paragraphing: Dickinson did not use indentation to indicate paragraphs. Second, the relationship between poetry and prose is so complex in Dickinson's writing that lineating poetry but not prose sets up artificial genre distinctions. There are no easily drawn periods in Dickinson's writing, no distinct point where it is possible to say, "Before this the genre of the letters is exclusively prose, and there is no need to lineate." Furthermore, when prose is not lineated, poetic devices that Dickinson uses in her prose may be deemphasized, muted, or obscured.[20]

Hart's arguments are cogent and bespeak a long familiarity with the manuscripts, though it is not absolutely clear to me (in the current era of the prose poem, the long line, and the letter-poem) that lineation is needed to detect the presence of the poetic in Dickinson's correspondence. But Hart's comments are not completely accurate when applied to a draft letter to Sarah Tuckerman about 1880:

Dear friend,
    I thought
of you, although
I never saw
your friend.
Brother of
Ophir
Bright Adieu – [page break]
Honor, the
shortest route
To you –
    Emily –[21]

The right-hand margins in this short note are relatively consistent for the *prose* part of the letter, but not for the *poem* (P#1462C [J#944]). The first five lines feature empty spaces from the end word to the right-hand edge of the page that measure approximately 1.3, 0.9, 2.3, 2.3, and 2.8 centimeters, so that there is no visual indication that the prose has ended and the poem has begun. Instead, prose and poetry run into each other, which may be an attempt on Dickinson's part to disguise the extraepistolary origins of the poem by suggesting an organic continuity between the two, that this is "a poem that has grown up in a field of prose, like tares among the wheat."[22] But the sixth line ends about 8.4 centimeters from the right-hand side of the page, and there are spaces of 4.6 and 4.3 centimeters after the first and third lines on the second page. Contrary to Hart's view, at this point there does seem to be *some* visual indication of a generic shift—though this is only one small example and Hart would rightly argue that her generalization applies to the majority of the poems in manuscript form (and even allows for such discrepancies). Nonetheless, the conclusion to be drawn from the Tuckerman note may be that Dickinson's prose linea-tion is caused by a combination of arbitrary factors: the size of the page, for example, and the length of Dickinson's words as they are written on the page. Within the poem, however, *some* aspects of the lineation are de-liberate, and we need to set up guidelines for knowing which.

If we look again at the correspondence between Dickinson and Higgin-son, this time in search of what conclusions can be drawn about the visual marking of generic shifts, the results are interesting. There are instances when Dickinson enclosed poems on separate sheets of paper within the same envelope as a letter. Most famously, when she wrote to Higginson for the first time on 15 April 1862, asking if her verse was alive, she in-cluded four poems on separate pages that did not form a continuation of the letter proper. In February 1863, however, she tried something slightly different. She enclosed "The Soul unto itself" (P#579A [J#683]) on two pages detached from the main body of the letter but also included "Best Gains – must have the Losses' test" (P#499A [J#684]) and "Not 'Revela-tion' – 'tis – that waits" (P#500A [J#685]) within the text of the letter it-self.[23] Both J#684 and J#685 are two-line poems according to Johnson, who indented them, and then assigned them numbers in his editions of the *Letters* and the *Poems:* Franklin also assigns them numbers, and indents them, in his new variorum edition. But Dickinson gives no indication in her letter that she intended the first of these to be read as poetry or inde-pendent of the prose that surrounded it (just as Hart leads us to expect). The second, which is written over four lines in the manuscript, is slightly different in that the space between the last word ("disclosed – ") in the line immediately before it and the right edge of the paper is appreciably greater than those after other end words on the same (fourth) page, and in that this space is then repeated in the second line of the poem as it is transcribed on the page, and again in the fourth line of the poem as it is transcribed on the fifth page of the letter (where it is the second line from the top). Listed consecutively, the distances measure approximately 6, 6, and 8.7 centimeters. Most of the other lines in the rest of the letter end within a centimeter or less of the right edge of the paper; thus the sequence of open spaces not apparently dictated by reasons of necessity tends to make the poem stand out more on the page. These spaces function almost as a typographic convention that signals the presence of a generic shift. Whether this is deliberate is another question. For now, it is perhaps enough to record that a reader would have been aware of some kind of shift in register, even if the poet did not indent or attach quotation marks or otherwise announce the fact that she was changing genre.

In 1863 Dickinson reverted to earlier habits by writing a short (one-and-a-half-page) note to Higginson, signing it, and then writing the second stanza of "That after Horror – that 'twas us" (P#243B [J#286]).[24] But in L#459, sent to Higginson (it is conjectured) in spring 1876, Dickinson included "The things we thought that we should do" (P#1279D [J#1293]) within the text of the letter itself; this is a useful example of those instances when she did not signal the inclusion in any obvious way (by assigning a title, or a new page, or by introducing it in the preceding paragraphs), but where the reader can nevertheless see that it is different. On the first page of the manuscript of this letter, the lines (characteristically) reach either very close to the right-hand edge of the paper or stop about one centimeter short. On the second, third, and fourth pages, line length is more erratic; this excerpt begins at the top of the second page, and is preceded by the words "I hope that you had a happy trip, and became"

refreshed.
Labor might
fatigue, though
it is Action's
rest.
The things
we thought
that we
should do
We other
things have
done
But those
peculiar
industries

Have never [page break]
been begun.

The Lands
we thought
that we
should seek
When large
enough to
run
By Speculation
ceded
To Speculation's
Son –

The Heaven,
in which we [page break]
hoped to pause
When Discipline
was done
Untenable to
Logic
But possibly
the one –
I am glad
you remember
the "Meadow
Grass."
That forestalls
Fiction.[25]

After the word "rest" in the fifth line, there is a space of approximately 6.9 centimeters. Normally, such a space is dictated by necessity, for example, by a long word that would not fit into the space left after the first word in the line, or by the need to indicate formally that a new paragraph follows. Hart is perfectly right in saying that Dickinson does not usually indent at the *beginning* of a paragraph, incidentally, but this is only half the truth; new paragraphs are usually indicated at the end of the previous one by blank space in the last line.[26] There is no long word following "rest," so it is likely that Dickinson is using the space to announce the beginning of a new sequence of ideas, which in this instance turns out to be a poem. The handwriting seems to me to become larger in the poem, especially on the third page, but what immediately interests me is the multiplication of instances where lines fall short of the right-hand edge (as they do not in the first page). Lines 8, 12, and 13 are fairly clear examples of this on the second page, while lines 8 (in particular), 10, and 12 are equally clear examples on the third. The distance between "run" (on line 8 of the third page), and "Son" (on line 12 of the same page), and the right-hand side of the paper are both roughly 8.5 centimeters, which is fairly substantial given that they do not precede new paragraphs. In addition, Dickinson skips a line between the stanzas of the poem. Normally, the gap between the bottom of one line and the top of the next is about 5 millimeters, but between the bottom of the last line of a stanza and the top of the next it is about a centimeter. In short, Higginson (or any other reader) would have been conscious of a change in the layout that corresponded to a shift from prose to poetry. The new paragraph beginning with "Labor" and ending with "rest" provides a kind of bridge between the conventional courtesies of the first page and the poetic density of the second, in the sense that it marks a change in register or tone (it is much more condensed) and breaks up the scriptural regularity of the page.

Dickinson regularly used capitals to indicate the beginning of a poetic line, so that, for example, although "By Speculation / ceded / To Speculation's / Son – " is arranged as four lines on the third page, these represent only *two* lines of poetry (which is how Johnson and now Franklin have correctly transcribed them). Much has been made of the potential significance of Dickinson's line arrangements, but in this case the combination of upper-case letters and iambic meter makes it seem reasonable that Johnson and Franklin were correct in assuming that here were three quatrains whose manuscript arrangement as thirty-two lines was not intellectually, semantically, metrically, or generically significant. Another example, this time a pencil draft that was complete but never sent (though Dickinson had written "Prof. [Edward] Tuckerman," on it), derives from 1883 or 1884, and is numbered P#1599C by Franklin (J#1622; I number the lines for the sake of convenience):

(1) A sloop of
(2) amber slips

(3) away
(4) upon an ether
(5) sea,
(6) and wrecks in
(7) peace a purple
(8) tar
(9) the son of
(10) ecstasy[27]

I have deliberately not indicated where Dickinson's capitals are because it is possible to reconstruct the poet's wishes with respect to the arrangement of lines from the alignment of words, margins, and spaces on the page. Although most of the lines come near the right-hand edge of the paper, lines 3, 5, 8, and 10 do not; they feature spaces of (approximately) 7.8, 8.7, 8.7, and 6 centimeters between the last vowel or consonant in a line and the edge of the page. Clearly, in all of these cases, the words are either written singly for the sake of emphasis or they are extensions of the lines that precede them. If for the sake of argument we consider these words less as units of meaning on their own than as elements of a larger unit (the poetic line), it is fairly easy to construct a plausible case for saying that Johnson and Franklin did not act unreasonably or against Dickinson's wishes when they arranged the lines in exactly the same way in their respective variorum editions (though their choice of punctuation may be another matter):

A Sloop of Amber slips away
Upon an Ether Sea,
And wrecks in Peace a Purple Tar,
The Son of Ecstasy –

j#1622[28]

A Sloop of Amber slips away
Upon an Ether Sea,
And wrecks in Peace a Purple Tar,
The Son of Ecstasy –

p#1599c

Does this mean that the broken line arrangements of the manuscripts can be ignored when transcribing poems to the page of a book or the screen of a computer? This is a difficult question, and the answer may depend on the intended audience and the kind of edition being prepared. But respecting Dickinson's wishes (a deeply problematic issue even if she had explicitly formulated them with regard to textual presentation, which she didn't) involves more than the exact reproduction of line arrangements in the manuscripts—even presupposing in the case of multiple variants of single poems that we know which best represents those wishes. The spaces between end words and the right-hand edge of the paper are also clearly significant, as are the capitals, the rhyme, and the meter (not all of which are as predictable as the examples I have chosen). Clearly, though, future editorial decisions will have to be argued on the basis of individual merit by general readers and academic specialists—which is perhaps one reason why the Emily Dickinson Editing Collective, established to produce more reliable and open editions of the texts, believes it may be able to improve on the efforts of its predecessors, since it will have the benefit of contributions and perspectives from several persons rather than one or two. It seems to me that the scholars behind this initiative—Martha Nell Smith, Ellen Louis Hart, and Marta Werner—are doing the international Dickinson community an immense service by attempting to make electronic copies of the manuscripts more widely available so that more and more readers can attempt, independently or in collaboration with others, to check the Johnson and Franklin editions of the poetry against Dickinson's autograph originals. But even here, there are problems. For when I write "check . . . against . . . originals" the implication is that Dickinson's autograph poems must be absolutely correct in their entirety and anything else a potential or actual corruption of those originals. On the contrary, the logic of the Higginson correspondence and some of the notes I have transcribed so far suggest that in fact we can and sometimes must present the poems in printed versions that do not literally reproduce line arrangements and word division as if they were fully intentional. In my view it is also our responsibility to make an attempt to produce working print editions of Dickinson's work for the larger, nonspecialist audience: not everyone has access to the Web, and not everyone has sufficient time or money to spend with the manuscripts (in original or reproduced form) to be able to tell which details are significant and which are not, or even to be able to understand Dickinson's handwriting. Furthermore, even the benefit of familiarity or multiple editors does not always guarantee accuracy or openness to other viewpoints. To take a tangential but related point: on the second part of a transcription of the first page of a handwritten draft of "Essay on Architecture" by Susan Gilbert Dickinson,[29] the editors appear to misread the verb at the end of the fourth line as "mean? [or] denote?" when it is in fact more likely to be "reveal." And although one concedes the practicality of providing simultaneously placed transcriptions of handwriting which, for convenience of reference, follow the line arrangement of the original, one wonders if it be possible and even desirable to produce a third stage in the reading of such materials whereby they were represented in a typed form. For, invaluable and eminently commendable as they are, the point of such pages must be to assist readers to form conclusions about the variety of ways in which Dickinson's texts including printed ones, can be presented and read. If this is not done, we are giving primacy to the autograph poems as the approved or final medium of study, which is to replace one form of alleged textual tyranny (print) with another (manuscript). Exactly how more democratic or egalitarian this is remains to be seen: it would be interesting if these Web pages included a site for public discussion at particular and theoretical levels, to see, for example, how editors respond to suggestions for change, and on what grounds.

One final example, "The Sea said 'Come' to the Brook" (P#1275B [J#1210]), is worth examining because, again, there are several versions of the poem, which Johnson dates to 1872. The "he" in the second stanza of the C version-poem (sent to Higginson in later 1872) is interesting because there is no reason for it to be on a separate line. Dickinson could easily have fitted at least one, if not both, words from the next line onto the same line if she had wanted to. Instead, the word's isolation indicates a pause that corresponds to the end of a poetic or metrical line.

The Sea said
"Come" to the Brook –
The Brook said
"Let me grow" –
The Sea said
"Then you will
be a Sea" –
"I want a Brook –
Come now" –
The Sea said
"Go" to the Sea –
The Sea said

"I am he
You cherished" –
"Learned Waters –
Wisdom is stale
to Me"

P#1275B[30]

The Sea said
"Come" to the
Brook –
The Brook
said "Let me
grow" –
The Sea
said "then
you will be
a Sea –
I want a
Brook –
Come now"! [page break]

The Sea
said "Go" to
the Sea –
The Sea
said "I am
he
You cherished" –
"Learned Waters –
Wisdom is
stale – to Me" –

P#1275C[31]

Another claim about Dickinson—made most persuasively by Susan Howe and Martha Nell Smith—is that she used letters of the alphabet visually. As Howe memorably formulates it, "Letters are sounds we see."[32] One of the examples used by both Howe and Smith is "The Sea said 'Come' to the Brook," where, according to Smith, the *S*'s are shaped like waves and the *T*'s formed to resemble choppy seas. Taken in isolation from the rest of the letters and poems, the argument seems convincing, and it is often repeated in other contexts as though it were established fact. Of course, Smith's point here is a part of a larger one, as she describes a writer challenging the rigidities of conventional printing; in Howe's view we miss this challenge by reading her poems in ordinary type form.[33]

But in fact the letter *S* is shaped in exactly the same way in many other manuscript poems and letters, and one may legitimately wonder whether the effect described by Howe and Smith is only that—an effect, not an intention. In a letter to Higginson in November 1871, for instance, there are several examples of *S* (and even *s*) shapes which are exactly the same as those in P#1275: "Shakespeare" on the third page of the manuscript is a very clear instance of this.[34] And in a poem enclosed within the letter, "Step lightly on this narrow spot" (P#1227D), written about 1871, the *S*'s in the words "Step," "Spot," "Seams," and "Step" are almost horizontal, while the *T*'s and *t*'s are slanted and crossed in such a way that they resemble *X*'s (or *x*'s). Interestingly, when Dickinson sent a copy of P#1275C to Higginson in late 1872, there were no real differences between the *S* and *y* shapes in the poem and those of the letter (the *y* in the word "you" resembles an *s* shape in both, which is why I mention it): again, the presence of a feature in a letter can and should be used as a means of verifying our impressions about manuscript characteristics in a poem or poems.[35]

Much has been made recently of Susan Dickinson's claim that she would have produced a very different edition, "rather more full, and varied, than [that of Higginson and Todd]" with excerpts from the letters and "quaint bits to my children."[36] It seems to me that Susan's mode of presentation would have been influenced principally by its limited readership, mainly friends and family who would have found the poems and excerpts from letters personally as well as aesthetically significant—like snapshots, interesting mainly to those who knew or were related to her. Susan's description implies a desire to reflect the range of her sister-in-law's talents but not necessarily her textual production: from this statement at least, there is no reason to suppose that she found the handwriting or layout of the poems and letters semantically significant—except in particular instances. But given the claims that are made on Susan's behalf, by Smith in particular, it would be useful at this point to look over Susan's shoulder, as it were, to see what implications her habits of reading and transcribing Dickinson's handwritten poems might have. For Susan was the recipient of almost three hundred poems, not just during the period of the writer's greatest creativity, but throughout her life. To put things into perspective: Johnson thinks that of the poems in Fascicle 20 (to take an example that I looked at more closely in the previous chapter), Susan received all of "Like some Old fashioned Miracle" (P#408B [J#302]) in 1862 (though Franklin thinks 1863); the first stanza of "The Soul selects her own Society" (P#409B [J#303]) in 1864 (though Franklin does not confirm this); and one copy of "One need not be a Chamber – to be Haunted" (P#407B [J#670]). Thomas Wentworth Higginson was sent a copy of "Dare you see a Soul at the 'White Heat'?" (P#401 [J#365]: text uncertain) in 1862. The ratio of poem(s) to recipient fairly reflects the biographical and creative importance of the two individuals to Dickinson herself: as Smith and a number of other critics have argued, Susan was probably more important to Dickinson as a reader, friend, literary collaborator, and editor than Higginson (who received about one hundred poems). If Smith is correct, then it should be possible to get some idea of what was significant in Dickinson's manuscripts from the ways Susan recorded them in her own hand as she prepared then for a volume of poetry she planned to edit. For if Emily and Susan were so close that writing was almost a mutual project, then surely there is a possibility that Susan would have known what her sister-in-law's preferences were in relation to her manuscript practices?

Some idea of Susan Dickinson's editorial methods can be recovered from the fragments stored with the Dickinson family papers at the Houghton Library, Harvard. Among these is Susan's manuscript for Emily's obituary, which was published in the *Springfield Daily Republican* on Thursday, 18 May 1886.[37] This is potentially useful because at its end Susan quotes the first stanza from one of Dickinson's earliest poems (P#18B [J#27] thought by Franklin to have been written in 1858):

Morns like these, we parted
Noons like these, she rose,
Fluttering first, then firmer,
To her fair repose.[38]

This is Dickinson's version, as I have transcribed it from its holograph form:

Morns like these – we parted –
Noons like these – she rose –
Fluttering first – then firmer –
To her fair repose.[39]

This is Mabel Loomis Todd's version, as it appeared in *Poems by Emily Dickinson*

Morns like these we parted;
Noons like these she rose,
Fluttering first, then firmer,
To her fair repose.[40]

Dickinson dash is first replaced with more conventional punctuation in Susan Dickinson's transcription of the opening stanza, and it says much about the strength of cultural norms about poetry and its appearance that Susan and Todd independently arrived at very similar presentations (or it indicates that Todd had access to Susan's versions, and copied them, which is not unlikely). Susan's version partly vindicates Todd's, in the sense that both appear to proceed from the assumption that Dickinson's manuscripts existed in a raw state and required editorial finishing before appearing in print. Given that Susan must have known of her sister-in-law's unhappiness about alterations to the punctuation of another poem, Susan's own changes show indifference, a sense that punctuation was not important in such an early poem, or an awareness that Dickinson's objections to changes in her punctuation were less generalized, less a manifesto than has been supposed. Another possibility is that Susan was more conventional in her tastes than Emily and not fully conscious of the extent of her friend's innovations. Still other factors may come into play here. Susan may be quoting from memory, or it may be that aesthetic considerations were secondary at this time of terrible loss—that what was important was that the sentiments expressed by the stanza be personally and generically appropriate. Having said that, it must be added that the obituary itself is a wonderfully controlled and careful piece of writing. As others before me have pointed out, Susan very consciously addresses and corrects many of the myths that had already sprung up about Dickinson (which reminds us again how public Dickinson's privacy actually was). In addition, Susan had several hundred manuscript poems to choose from, and she selected one that simultaneously promotes her sister-in-law as a literary authority, someone to be quoted, and downplays her lack of religious orthodoxy (and all this in bird imagery that had private associations as well as links to the wider vocabulary of feminine culture). Given this attention to detail, it seems surprising that Susan failed to reproduce Emily's punctuation—unless, as I have just said, it had little or no significance, either for her or Dickinson (at least in the specific instance of this poem).

In light of current assertions that Dickinson did not distinguish between poetry and prose in her letters, it is interesting that Susan did not separate the stanza graphically from the prose that precedes it, although the typesetter for the *Republican* did. This practice prefigures the later treatment of Dickinson's letters by her editors. But Susan made no attempt to undo the typesetter's change in layout when she received a printed copy of the death notice for proofing, although she made several other alterations. The implication is that some nineteenth-century writers left the responsibility for the typographical arrangement of their work to the printer and objected to changes only when the aesthetic or semantic integrity of the text had been seriously compromised. In this instance, Susan clearly did not feel that her intentions had been significantly interfered with, and one wonders what significance this might have for Dickinson's epistolary and poetic practices. Was Dickinson playing with genre, as some commentators claim, or is the alleged erosion of generic differences in her correspondence a function of their informality, their casual status a personal documents?[41]

What is clear from the papers owned by Harvard University is that at some point after Dickinson's death Susan began to prepare a volume of her poems for publication (again, this information is not new: it is my application of this information that carries some measure of novelty). Many of the texts listed in the third volume of Thomas Johnson's *Poems of Emily Dickinson* exist largely as transcripts made by Susan. The problem facing any reader attempting to reconstruct Susan's editorial policies from the copies that she made of Emily's originals is that in most cases only the copies remain. But there are exceptions. Here is "Remembrance has a rear and front" in two versions, the first approximating Dickinson's own, and the second as Susan transcribed another lost variant:[42]

Remembrance has
a Rear and Front.
'Tis something

like a House –
It has a Garret
also
For Refuse and
the Mouse –

Besides the
deepest Cellar
That ever Mason
laid –
+ Leave me not
ever there alone
Oh thou Almighty
God!

_____

+ Look to it by
Fathoms
its Contents
Ourselves be not
pursued![43]

_____

      front
Remembrance has a rear and
'Tis something like a house
It has a garret also
For refuse and the mouse
Besides the deepest cellar
That ever mason laid
Look to it by the contents
Ourselves be not pursued
      E[44]

It needs to be admitted immediately that the version of Dickinson's poem that I print is from Set 10 and may not be the same one Susan received. Nonetheless, several points can be ventured from a comparison. Familiarity with other manuscripts allows us to be fairly sure that Susan dispensed with Dickinson's own lineation, even though we cannot be certain exactly what changes she made. The broken lines characteristic of the handwritten poems from the eighth fascicle on have been replaced, and one neat eight-line stanza appears in their stead. The punctuation has also been omitted, as have the capitals, though Susan elongates the last letters of certain words in a way that might be mistaken as indicating dashes. However one reads the handwriting, it seems possible that these transcriptions were not final but were part of a process by which the poems were prepared for eventual publication. From the evidence at Harvard, it seems that Susan did not work completely on her own. Both her adult children, Ned and Martha, seem to have had specific tasks. Although we cannot know that this is so, it would appear that Susan compiled and then copied Emily's poems sent to her, tidied the lineation and some of the punctuation, and then gave them to Ned or Martha to type. When typing was complete, Susan proofread the typed copy against her copy, added punctuation if and when she saw fit, and sometimes supplied a title. In the following poem, for instance, most of the punctuation has been added to the typescript by hand, as has the title, and in the twelfth line "merry" has been written above a crossed-out "many":

> Afterward
> Besides the autumn, poets sing,
> A few prosaic days,
> A little this side of the snow,
> And that side of the Haze.
>
> A few incisive mornings,
> A few ascetic eves,
> Gone Mr. Bryant's Golden Rod,
> And Mr. Thomson's sheaves.
>
> Still is the bustle in the brook,
> Sealed are the spicy valves,
> Mesmeric fingers softly touch
> The eyes of merry elves.
>
> Perhaps a squirrel may remain
> My sentiments to share –

Grant me Oh Lord a sunny mind
Thy windy will to bear.

Emily Dickinson

Susan Dickinson was a poet herself, and given her intimate and continuous familiarity with Dickinson's writing, one wonders if a still clearer
view of the significance of details in Dickinson's manuscripts can be
gained through Susan's own poetic practices. For instance, there are two extant versions of a poem by Susan that begins "What offering have I, dear
Lord": one is handwritten, the other typed. (Since the time of writing, this
poem and others by Susan have been made available by Smith and others
on the Internet: the reader is welcome to look at these for comparison
with my own efforts at transcription.)[45] Here are the first two stanzas of
the autograph copy (I have underlined words that appear to be cancelled
with strikeout marks in the original):

> have I <u>oh</u> dear Lord
> What offering <u>can I bring</u>
> thee Lord
> To show I am thy child
> What service shorn of
> selfishness
> And not with sin defiled!

> ———

> The day is past for turtle doves
> For incense burnt in clouds
> Or even spikenard costly
> rare
> That bro't thy loving words.

> ———

Here is the typewritten version of the same poem, which I quote in full.

> What offering have I, dear Lord,
> To show I am thy child!
> What service shorn of selfishness
> And not with sin defiled?

The day is past for turtle doves,
For incense burnt in clouds –
Or even spikenard costly rare
That bro't thy loving words.

Thou art not poor as we of earth, –
All space and time are thine
Save one unyielded wealth I hold, –
The will that should be thine!

The twelve lines of the first two stanzas in the autograph version have been tidied up in the typewritten version, where they are neatly compressed to eight. Contemporary editorial procedure would suggest that had this been a Dickinson poem we would have retained the twelve lines. One hesitates to push the point too far, but I wish to consider that Dickinson would not have intended us to take similar phenomena in her own manuscripts as seriously as we do now. Like Susan's split lines, hers may simply be a function of their unpublished state (rather than features that prevented publication because she would not relinquish the right to use them in print). In the two versions of a poem by Susan entitled "Irony" (both are clearly works-in-progress), the handwritten copy often contains split lines that are made single in the printed copy. One might be tempted to say that if Susan ignored her own line arrangements when her poems were typed, perhaps Emily would have done the same. But Susan is a very different writer, and reading Dickinson through her habits is questionable procedure.

Nevertheless, what I hope to have established by now is that Susan's editorial methods (to the extent that they are recoverable from the Harvard collections, which are not extensive) provide us with insights that can be used in different ways. If one champions Susan as Dickinson's literary confidant, then it has to be admitted that one or both might have been more conventional than present-day scholarship would have us believe. It may be that Susan misjudged the extent of Dickinson's textual innovations, or perhaps she understood her well enough to feel that various graphic properties of the manuscripts had no significance. Still a third possibility is that she (like Higginson and Todd) felt that compromise was necessary to get Dickinson published.

McGann has made what is in many ways the definitive statement of contemporary critical consensus about the Dickinson texts, namely that they need to be read in their original form to be truly appreciated and understood: "Emily Dickinson's poetry was not written *for* a print medium, even though it was written *in* an age of print. When we come to edit her work for bookish presentation, therefore, we must accommodate our typographical conventions to her work, not the other way around."[46] In fact, McGann's assertion that the poetry was not written for print is significantly different from saying it was not printed. One presupposes an intention, the other reports a historical fact. McGann assumes as a given something that not all critics are agreed on: indeed, the existence of the fascicles by themselves might suggest that the poems were prepared for some form of publication (though of course publication need not always be synonymous with print). There is a need to modify McGann's claim, for although the majority of Dickinson's poems did not appear in print during her lifetime, it does not follow that they were not meant to be printed. The fascicles were not sent to any of Dickinson's closest friends in the way that individual poems were, a fact that suggests that their intended audience may not have been an intimate, or local, or even contemporaneous one. There is no evidence, for instance, that Susan knew about them. McGann's desire to avoid imposing twentieth-century typographical conventions onto Dickinson's texts is admirable, but it does not obviate the possibility that his own perspective derives from modernist experiments with the medium of print, which he then inscribes on a premodernist body of writing.

In "The Poet as Cartoonist," Smith compares aspects of Dickinson's "hand-made mode of production" and what she terms her cartoons—visual marks or appendages on the same page as a poem. She supports McGann when she writes that "our study moves her comic text into the public sphere and demands shifts in thinking about what can count as a cartoon"—and, by implication, what counts as a poem.[47] Nevertheless, we cannot be certain that Dickinson herself would have approved of either the move of her private documents into a public sphere or the idea that this constitutes a deliberate challenge to definitions of what constitutes a cartoon. In other words, it is possible that what we identify as significant when we look closely at the physical or material details of her manuscripts are the consequences of our own editorial choices and interpretative conventions. It may well be that the informality and playfulness manifested by some of her texts are functions of their status as private, unpublished texts. Giving them a wider set of implications may be imposing a potential significance that they were never meant to have. Emily Dickinson may not have been fully conscious of the potential her unpublished manuscripts possessed or would later come to acquire as published documents. Later scholars may invent or reconstruct that potential on her behalf. This is not the same as saying that critics misrepresent Dickinson. It is not even to say that Dickinson was ignorant of this potential for misrepresentation. But it does mean that when we give her privately produced papers a public significance, we are doing something that Dickinson herself did not do.

At stake, too, is Dickinson's place in the literary canon. If Dickinson is demonstrably not in control of, or not directing, the implications of her own textual practices, then she takes one step backward into the nineteenth century; if she is visibly (and visually) in control, she takes a step forward into (and perhaps beyond) the mixed and postmodernist media of the twentieth century. (One might wonder, though, if what is ultimately at stake is the belief that all artists are fully and always in control of their own meanings.) The contemporary preoccupation with Dickinson's manuscripts may be seen as an attempt to lift her texts out of history, to say that here was a poet who made eminently modern collages, using visual forms and using form visually. Claims that are made on Dickinson's behalf certainly put more distance between her and the century she lived in. In a sense, they establish her claim to what Northrop Frye called the "doodle" aspect of poetic discourse, which Jonathan Culler (quoting Frye) defines as the "'elaboration of verbal design,' as in shapes, stanzas, and conventional forms that create patterns for the eye" (and, I add, for the mind).[48]

Are we further misrepresenting Dickinson's poems by presenting them in manuscript form as if the manuscripts were constructed with the aim of public consumption and aesthetic experimentation? There are a number of ways in which the theorization of Dickinson's scriptural practices can be understood and formulated: as nineteenth-century graphic initiatives whose significance has been fully recovered by textual scholars only in the twentieth century; as the accidental by-products of a nineteenth-century home-based literary production not oriented toward publication and impossible to transpose into print at that time (because of technological and editorial limitations) but with implications for twentieth-century poetics and aesthetics; and as formal deviations that are interpreted as significant by twentieth-century readers and then inserted into the nineteenth century as fully deliberate graphic experiments. Are we reconstructing Dickinson's intentions, drawing our own conclusions for our own purposes, or behaving as if our conclusions were hers? The first possibility, it seems to me, has not yet been proved statistically, while the second and third are impossible either to prove or disprove. They are simply suspicions and doubts we must carry with us whenever we approach a Dickinson text, whether our primary interest is in its status as text or its significance as poetry. In the end, perhaps such questions can never finally be answered. We can only proceed in the hope that our reconstructions of Dickinson's texts approximate the range of choices Dickinson offered herself, and that we do not mar their integrity too much. The truth is that the visual characteristics of Dickinson's handwriting are not determinate, and it is impossible to recover their meaning with any degree of certainty. One feels that it will be always so with Emily Dickinson, who left no explicit statements about which methods of poetic presentation, assemblage, and transmission she desired. To borrow the image of the bee who avoids the chasing schoolboy in P#304B (J#319) sent to Higginson in April 1862, she continues to mystify and elude us. Long may she run.

CHAPTER EIGHT

Cordoning off Dissent

Dickinson's Monologic Voices

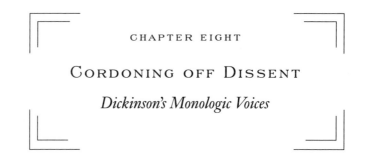 IN 1863, an elderly woman who wanted to look at a house in the vicinity of Main Street, Amherst, called at the Homestead, and was pointed by Emily toward the local, west, cemetery, in order (she explained later to her cousins Louise and Frances Norcross) to save her the expense of having to move ever again.[1] The story is told by the poet herself, and does reflect her own sense of humor, but it is a problematic image for any critic who wants to counter the idea of Dickinson as an antisocial writer. Here she opens one door only to close another: she removes a physical barrier to her presence only to erect a linguistic one in its place. The moment seems typical of a writer who likes to alter or play with the gravitational pull of social custom on the meaning(s) of words, preferring to emancipate language from conventional usage and (often) to replace its habitual orbits with new paths of her own. Here, then, is the point of departure for this chapter, for Dickinson's reply seems to indicate the rejection of normal social intercourse, but in fact depends for the success of its wit on straight questions, the presumption (in all the senses of that word) of an ordinary discourse comprising shared codes and intentions.

The movement of a woman who is said to have closed doors more often than she opened them, who withdrew from the world by withdrawing into words, is often represented as a flight from the public to the private sphere, an act of historical quarantine. But language, it should be remembered, is a shared inheritance, a medium that precedes and succeeds us and one that we can never exclusively call our own. We may not converse or practice discourse as a social activity, but its meanings are still defined and debated by people other than ourselves. It therefore follows that Dickinson's texts engage (sometimes consciously, sometimes unconsciously) in a kind of dialogue with nineteenth-century systems of meaning as these are communicated in, and by, language. Dickinson's preoccupation with home, to take the previously discussed example of a word that occurs eighty-six times in her poetry, appears on the one hand to confirm the writer's profile as a solitary exile from nineteenth-century American life, but on the other to reflect the larger social coordinates of women's roles and their foundations in politicoeconomic theories of domesticity. Publications addressed to middle- and upper-middle-class white females and written by women like Lydia H. Sigourney, Catharine Beecher, and Lydia Maria Child often centered on the subject of home. Even Martha Dickinson Bianchi's story of how her aunt would finger an imaginary key and say "It's just a turn – and freedom, Matty!"—such a classic statement of the space she found in confinement—is echoed (among others) by Helen Campbell's definition (in her *Household Economics* of 1898) of "a separate room [as] the right of every human being; a place where one can lock the door, be safe from intrusion, and in silence and freedom gather strength for the next thing to be done."[2] In other words, Dickinson's lifelong concern with home (in her poems, in her correspondence, and in her gradual seclusion) is not simply a private choice but one conditioned in part by economic, political, and (to some extent) regional factors.

It should now be apparent, both from preceding chapters and these opening remarks, that (like some Dickinson critics before me),[3] I take issue with Mikhail Bakhtin's proposition (expressed in "Discourse in the Novel") that the novel is necessarily the site of heteroglossia, and that poetry characteristically works to exclude alien vocabularies and historically specific languages: "In genres that are poetic in the narrow sense, the natural dialogization of the word is not put to artistic use, the word is sufficient unto itself and does not presume alien utterances beyond its own boundaries. Poetic style is by convention suspended from any mutual interaction with alien discourse, any allusion to alien discourse."[4]

In my view, Dickinson's work is pervaded with other voices and vocabularies, which suggests that it comes closer to Bakhtin's definition of the dialogic imagination as this is manifested in *prose* genres.[5] A poem like

"Publication – is the Auction / Of the Mind of Man" (P#788A [J#709]), for instance, grafts together imagery influenced by historically contemporary anxieties about property, the movement for the abolition of slavery, and reformist discourses on the evils of prostitution (all three of which had implications for women's rights). Many of her other poems begin with lines that appear to reply to some query or (spoken or unspoken) charge, even though they are not accredited or defined formally as answers: indeed, one has a sense, at times, that a poem is part of a conversation that has already begun outside its formal boundaries and that is not yet over by its end.

At moments like this, it seems that Dickinson is less speaking her poems than that the conflicts of her times are being spoken through them. Even in instances where she imports only isolated words, these then become centers of tension(s) and struggle. Perhaps the clearest example of this use of indirect speech is her practice of assigning quotation marks to a word, for instance, "Heaven," as a visual indication of the relationship between consciousness and context, individuality and social specificity, in the production of meaning. This is interesting in itself, of course, because as Gary Morson and Caryl Emerson point out, Bakhtin characterized novelistic style as speech "with quotation marks."[6] Words that are highlighted in such a way do not have their conventional meanings erased, but carry a number of historically predetermined significances, which the writer engages with. Quotation itself can even be thought of as a form of violent appropriation. But no matter how much Dickinson interrogates and disparages conventional meanings, her inclusion of them in her poetic texts indicates that she cannot ignore them. There is an argument for saying that she relies on other dialects to create often unstated alternatives, as a comic duo relies on one serious member to highlight the comedian. The typographic isolation of a word like "Heaven" suggests the problem Dickinson faced of understanding and communicating her own ideas in the context of an inherited discourse of the divine, a preexistent vocabulary of the spiritual. Her poems do not therefore appear to be monologic, though they may aspire toward that condition.

Here I think is the crux, for it may be argued that in placing those words in quotation marks, Dickinson's purpose is less to engage in dialogue than to segregate those words and to ironize them, thus rejecting their predetermined significances, in order to clear a space for a new and private meaning or meanings, which the poet often refuses to (or is unable to, or does not feel that she needs to) share with us. It is here that I differ from those critics who have found an unproblematic convergence between Bakhtin's theory of the dialogic and Dickinson's poetic practice. The speaker of P#700A (J#636), "The Way I read a Letter's – this," for example, sighs "for lack of Heaven – but not / The Heaven God bestow," while the speaker of another (P#544A [J#575]) claims that "Heaven' has different Signs – to me." The strictly theological or even conventional sense is replaced with an often unstated, and perhaps unstatable, alternative. The word ceases to have any clear-cut meaning and instead acquires a range of possible connotations, which are emancipated from the ordinary. To adopt the vocabulary of Bakhtin again, what we see here is an attempt to suspend the word from outside discourse—or perhaps to assimilate it to the poet's own purposes. But surely we are also seeing the inevitability of interaction with, and allusions to, alien discourse—precisely those things Bakhtin claims the lyric poem does not do? Indeed, it is even possible to argue that Dickinson reverses the assignment of heteroglossia to social discourses: it is society that closes down meaning, and the poet who attempts to open it up again.

In Dickinson's poetry as a whole, this apparent rebuttal of conventional language results from time to time in an attempt at a "social differentiation, a social stratification."[7] Sometimes it is a derisive silence rather than speech that characterizes this superiority: the speaker of P#179A (J#168), for example, asks "If the foolish, call them *'flowers'* – / Need the wiser, *tell*?," as if wisdom or poetic knowledge (the flowers may refer to the flowers of speech) were a kind of secret possession and power shared, or rather withheld, only by the wise or poetically skillful. But even here, it is possible to detect Dickinson's strategy of including other traces or accents, other verbalized preferences, in her poems, even as she (or her speaker) works to deny their significance. In such instances, her poems become in effect sites of ideological conflict. Bakhtin, again, is relevant here:

> All words have the "taste" of a profession, a genre, a tendency, a party, a particular work, a particular person, a generation, an age group, the day and hour. Each word tastes of the context and contexts in which it has lived its socially charged life; all words and forms are populated by intentions. . . . As a living, socio-ideological concrete thing, as heteroglot opinion, language, for the individual consciousness, lies on the borderline between oneself and the other. The word in language is half someone else's.[8]

Language itself, of course, is a common property, and literary language is no different: as Denise Levertov puts it, "poetry makes its structures, its indivisibilities of music and meaning, out of the same language used for utilitarian purposes."[9] Even lyric poetry (the most private of poetic genres, and therefore the one best adapted to a poetics of privatization) is made up of borrowed elements. The practice of combining sound structures and rhythmic patterns into ritual forms of creative expression did not originate with Emily Dickinson, no matter how original we think her particular utterances might be. (I will return to this issue at a later point.) The idea that language is a shared property, something that half belongs to someone else, is acknowledged by Dickinson when she puts words in quotation marks. But as I have argued, her procedure involves attempting to wrest control of those meanings out of the hands of those others: language, in short, is an ideological property over which there are competing claims of ownership. The early Dickinson of P#35A (J#13), "Sleep is supposed to be," rehearses a number of accepted explanations for the meaning of sleep and waking before dismissing them with the imperious declaration that "Morning has not occurred!" Although she cannot help stating directly here the difference between the banality of conventional definitions and the brilliance of her own, most poems record a more subtle progression away from common understanding to a more abstract and (presumably) higher level of usage. P#191A (J#300), " 'Morning' – means 'Milking' – To the Farmer," for instance, lists a number of possible perspectives, which culminate in the (failing) vision of a person who is either dying or going blind, and it is typical of Dickinson that she installs blindness or death as the last step in a process by which the self disengages with the world and approaches a condition of pure consciousness, beyond the specific language of the poem and the borders of language generally.

The tone in some of these poems is disdainful, even arrogant, and, taken together with their tendency to etherealize, to move away from the mundanity or materialism of ordinary existence to universal or abstract experiences, would seem to contradict my position that Dickinson's work can be described as dialogic. Indeed, even the alleged difficulty of her style can be seen as a product of her alienation from society, as a technique that forestalls the easy consumption of her texts, and thus appears to discourage dialogue (this time between poet and reader, though it is also possible to argue that it provides the formal conditions by which a certain kind of readership is specified). Perhaps, however, such a contradiction rests on the assumption of dialogue's mutuality, its egalitarianism, whereas Dickinson seems to suggest that it has its own hierarchies. In order to test out some of these ideas, I have chosen to look at one of her best known poems (P#411A [J#528]), and one that seems to deal thematically with issues related to the self in opposition to society.

Mine – by the Right of the White Election!
Mine – by the Royal Seal!
Mine – by the sign in the Scarlet prison –
Bars – cannot conceal!

Mine – here – in Vision – and in Veto!
Mine – by the Grave's Repeal –
Titled – Confirmed –
Delirious Charter!
Mine – long as Ages steal!

(1) in pencil, retraced in ink; alternative symbols in the text in pencil, not retraced in ink 8]
Good affidavit – 9 long as] while *(2) in ink; alternative symbols in the text in ink* 1]
marked for an alternative, none given 4 Bars] Bolts

Division 1 of| 3 in| 5 and|

An initial understanding of this poem proceeds (or can perhaps proceed) on the assumption that the speaker is not referring to the democratic process by which individuals (the poet's own father, for one) are chosen to represent certain constituencies in an institution such as Congress, but instead records the exhilaration felt by a speaker who is convinced that God has chosen her (or him) as one of the elect, thereby sanctioning her (or his) entrance into Heaven. However, the poem does not provide the kind of situating context that might have helped the reader to repossess the experience that generated it: there is a proclamation, which we are invited to witness but not necessarily to share. Indeed, this is the logical consequence of the speaker's expressed singularity, for the statement that one is of the elect carries with it the presumption that only the elect can understand one. The capitalization of words and phrases in the poem therefore serves the same purpose as the assignment of quotation marks: the conventional meaning(s) are potentially suspended and the phrases are reinscribed with new (but unstated) significances. This is why, for example, some critics feel that the poem describes the gift of grace less than the gift of the muse.

There is a thematic and stylistic convergence here, for the assertive concentration on the self is mirrored by the practice of redeploying institutional discourses so that they come to apply to only the individual who employs them. A statement of election, for example, normally precedes admission into the larger membership of the church, but the poem reflects no desire to join such a body. One might argue that the terms in the poem are almost in opposition to their religious and secular equivalents and that the speaker attempts to seal her consciousness off from the outside world in order to demonstrate her exclusiveness.

Nevertheless, other vocabularies are stubbornly (and perhaps consciously) present, for the poem is saturated with terms drawn from the legal profession: the use of the words "Seal," "Repeal," "Titled," and "Charter" and "Steal" contributes toward a preoccupation with ownership, which can be linked further to issues of autonomy and status. The possessive pronoun is used six times, and (combined with the insistent use of exclamation marks) the repetition has the effect of energizing this status, giving it an urgency and force that overcome any possibility of doubt or illegitimacy. There is a kind of paradox here, for the speaker employs terms of secular guarantee for an experience that gestures toward unworldliness. Uncertainty (or undermining) may be present here despite the authoritative posturing: the last line, for example, seems to suggest that the claims made by the speaker are in some way conditional on time, which is curious (perhaps even inconsistent) given that the poem as a whole appears to express the certainty of a status that operates outside it.[10] It may be that the sense of urgency or desperation with which the poem rehearses its hidden triumphs may be less an inner conviction than a response to other social voices (the language of evangelical religion, scientific skepticism, democratic politics, or the legal system, to name a few) from which the poem partly obtains its vocabularies.

It is interesting that the condition of spiritual or lyric autonomy, which the poem may appear to communicate, employs images that are borrowed, and simultaneously distanced, from both the legal profession and the world of politics. Perhaps the clearest example of the latter is in the very first line, with its insistence on election at a time when women did not possess the vote. Of course, Dickinson may be using the noun in its strictly theological sense, but it depends nevertheless for some of its impact on precisely its difference from the political significance of the word (something of the same impact through distance can be felt in the use of the term "Majority" in "The Soul selects her own Society," where the multiple—but private—opportunities available to the speaker are contrasted with the absence of any institutional opportunities for experiments in women's self-realization during "the age of majority"). The experience described distinguishes the speaker from the common democratic mass and instead confers on her a sense of nobility. While private experience is spiritually or imaginatively enabling and liberating, public experience denies women opportunities for electoral participation and political influence. The same line, however, may be suggesting indifference toward the question of women's suffrage—the poem relocates the authority and prestige of the speaker in a spiritual rather than a formal or institutional environment (such as the ones occupied by Dickinson's father and brother). Indeed the poem might be seen as a kind of snub or reply to the public success enjoyed by the men (and some of the women?) in her family, both of whom were lawyers and by 1862—the conjectured year of the poem's composition—professed members of the First Congregational Church in Amherst. Women were not full citizens at the time this poem was written, whereas free men (of all classes) were. Women's property laws were still in emergence. Yet the poem seems arrogantly indifferent to these issues and sure of the speaker's own importance. By locating women's power in a different, private sphere, Dickinson's speaker simultaneously asserts her version of women's equality (perhaps even their superiority) and appears to reject the need for women's rights in a public or formal context.

Nevertheless, this private rejection of society (the poem is not known to have been included in any letters to her favorite correspondents) is dialogic in Bakhtin's sense of the word, for it relies on a number of received discourses for much of its impact, even as it appears to reject their specificity. After all, the antagonistic relationship of the world and the spirit that the poem expresses is a fairly traditional and conservative one that privileges soul over body, or eternity over time. Although new alignments are also introduced—most notably the opposition between private and public spheres—these are (paradoxically, given the poem's preoccupation with timelessness) very time bound and historically particular. The nineteenth century defined the woman's sphere as that of the home, an oasis of moral values and stability in an otherwise acquisitive and precarious world, as well as a compensatory (or oppositional) site of women's power. Although gender partly explains the self-confident proclamation of spiritual status in the poem, there are also unmistakable signs of class conflict here: the speaker of the poem is like a member of some formerly privileged aristocracy imprisoned and condemned by an emergent proletariat—and even the language of the poem records a similar struggle between the literature of prose sensationalism and that of lyric supremacy. In a poem like this, one senses great social and historical forces, which compel Dickinson to speak: as Morson and Emerson put it, "perhaps the ideal speech situation involves not benevolent, voluntary exchange, but punishment, the *extraction* of answers; every time we speak, perhaps, the torture chamber haunts our discourse."[11] In the case of Dickinson's speaker, it is not the torture chamber but either the guillotine or a lingering death in confined spaces (the body, the room, the house) that produces this last will and testament, and it is interesting to speculate on what might have attracted the poet to such a politics of titular status and inherited wealth (however metaphorical). Of course, it has been pointed out that at the time Dickinson was writing, Victoria was queen of England, and the irony may be that social structures in Britain afforded women writers like her better paradigms of female achievement than the "democratic" system in America. Similarly, Calvinism, with its emphasis on individuals' responsibility for their souls, provided women with an ideological space where they could employ a discourse of empowerment.

Whatever the contents of the poem might be taken as signifying, Dickinson is communicating an intensely personal experience in a language that has an emphatically social and political nexus. Her poems may demonstrate a tendency to privatize or etherealize, but it is nevertheless important to recognize that Dickinson's writing offers a level of social consciousness, although that consciousness appears occasionally to exist in an antagonistic, oppositional relationship to popular culture and its institutions. Her apparently personal poems use an idiom that includes terms taken from the public world, and nowhere is this usage more apparent than in the vocabulary of suffering, which she acquires (in part) from the Civil War. It is a fact, as Daniel Aaron argues, that "the years between 1861 and 1865 proved to be [Dickinson's] most creative ones."[12] Even though, as Aaron and many others point out, Dickinson co-opts the facts of war for her private purposes, the coincidence of literary productivity coming during the most concentrated years of human carnage and slaughter suggests a writer who was at once receptive and wary of the world in which she lived (at a physical remove) and wrote.

In the following poem, discussed previously in the introduction to this book, withdrawal from the social sphere is once again an explicit thematic concern, but the poem carefully weighs both the benefits and the cost incurred by such an action:

The Soul selects her own Society –
Then – shuts the Door –
To her divine Majority –
Present no more –

Unmoved – she notes the Chariots – pausing –
At her low Gate –
Unmoved – an Emperor be kneeling
Opon her Mat –

I've known her – from an ample nation –
Choose One –
Then – close the Valves of her attention –
Like Stone –

3 To] On 4 Present] obtrude 8 On [her] Rush mat 11 Valves] lids –

Division 9 ample| 11 of|
P#409A [J#303]

Michael André Bernstein describes this poem as a fundamental "rejection of any universal dialogism" and (in a more extended and indirect reference) Morson and Emerson characterize the generic lyric poet as someone who "can speak alone, and does not require interaction with other consciousnesses and with other languages in order to say what he wants to say. He selects his own society—he *is* his own society—and then he 'shuts the door,' except perhaps to other poets and other poems."[13] Bernstein then goes on to argue that for a woman in the nineteenth century, withdrawal and reticence may have been dialogic responses to social situations. (I will develop this idea further at the end of the chapter when I come to look at issues raised by Dickinson's nonpublication.) Morson, Emerson, and even Bakhtin overlook this point, which shows the difference that considering gender can make to our reading of this text. The other point to make is that within the poem itself there is a double (Bakhtin would call it hybrid) perspective—represented formally by the simultaneous (but not necessarily analogous) presence of both a third- and a first-person pronoun. It is possible to argue that this polyvocality is reinforced in the manuscript and in both variorum versions, which include word variants at the end: in the one-volume and selected editions (where the variants are not included), there might appear to be less distance between the speaker, the writer, and the subject because the poem looks finished, organic, whole, seamless. In the handwritten and variorum versions of the poem, the presence of another point of view as it hesitates over which words to choose is clearly visible. Given the motivation, it is always fairly straight-forward to construct an almost formal or symbiotic relationship between the poem's appearance and its contents, and although this is certainly stim-ulating, it is not always necessary. For as Michael Bernard-Donals reminds us, "even if the author gives the [speaker] traits that mirror nearly exactly traits that exist in the author, the [speaker] is 'consummated' in the lan-guage of the text, and once the author finishes writing the life of the [speaker], the author's life continues: the 'I' of the aesthetic construct and the 'I' of the author are markedly different."[14]

It is for this reason that the poem describes exclusion as both an effect and a choice: internal exile (shutting the door) is followed by a sense of self-sufficiency (the soul has a divine majority, but is separate from it). Despite the sense of indifference and arrogance the poem (or more accu-rately the soul) imparts, there is security but also constraint here. The rep-etition of the adjective "Unmoved" implies that the woman (if woman she is) is unaffected as well as firm and resolute. But "Unmoved" might also mean incapable of being moved, and therefore a fixity which is at once strength and weakness, enabling and disabling power. One is reminded here of the final line from *Washington Square*: "Catherine, meanwhile, in the parlor, picking up her morsel of fancy-work, had seated herself with it again—for life, as it were." This last sentence about Catherine Sloper's life is in fact a self-imposed life sentence (or death sentence, indeed): the decision to absent herself is final, irrevocable, for ever. But the line is also ambiguous: it could suggest that Catherine makes her decision for the purposes of living, although this would suggest a very Jamesian definition of living—less to do with participation, and more with perception, obser-vation, a kind of refined detachment (separate, like the speaker in Dickin-son's poem, from the age of majority). Perry Anderson, in his essay, "Com-ponents of the National Culture," quotes Gellner on an intelligentsia "who differentiate themselves from the heartier rest of the upper class by a kind of heightened sensibility and preciousness, *and*, at the same time ... by a lack of interest in ideas, argument, fundamentals or reform," and although this seems pertinent, gender again has a large part to play in the decisions made by these fictional personae.[15] Given a choice, Catherine takes up her "fancy-work," her embroidery, her art, and gives up the social obligations which are conventionally understood as comprising a woman's life. Dickinson's poem appears to express a similar ambiguity. Many critics have pointed out how the image of the gate and the mat can stand for, respectively, the tombstone and the grave, so that the speaker is in a sense already dead, or at least no longer interested in the daily rounds of the living woman (with social duties, visits, or commitments of a wider kind). The "gate," "mat," and "valves," however, can similarly be understood as referring to parts of the female body, which the speaker refuses access to on the grounds that such withholding will allow her independence, even strength. The scenario suggests that marriage is unattractive to any woman who has a sense of her own dignity and worth and who in addition has her gaze fixed on a world other than the present one (or the one of presents, enticements, marriage gifts, and dowries). Presumably, the poem describes a rejection of the conventional roles of wife and childbearer and an embrace of spiritual or artistic realities, but in a way that communicates the cost of that decision for the speaker.

This reading reinforces the sense of the poem as a personal, even auto-biographical, document, with class as a primary determinating constituent both in its production and in our understanding of it. But if one links the language of closure to historically contemporary debates about immigration and nativism, the text has wider, more overtly political, connotations. It seems, for example, to parallel aspects of the foreign policy of the Know-Nothing Party with which Austin Dickinson has sometimes been associated. But one needs to be careful of such echoes, or at least to rank them in order of likely priorities to a woman who professed her indifference to institutional politics on many occasions. It seems more relevant, at least to me, that Dickinson's poems are saturated with the imagery of nineteenth-century gender ideologies: Horace Mann offered women dominion over "the empire of Home—the most important of empires, the pivot of all empires and emperors." And Thomas Nichols claimed that it was "the part of woman to accept or repulse: to grant or refuse. It is her right to reign a passional queen."[16] Dickinson's poem takes these formulations, designed to compensate women for the loss of external influence and action, and strips them of their social function, which is to encourage women to withdraw from the world in order to support their husbands and children. Typically, she engages with social choices only to modify them, as well as to examine their personal cost.

I began this chapter by arguing that Dickinson's texts engage in a kind of dialogue with nineteenth-century ideologies as these are communicated in, and by, language, and I attempted to set out who I thought that dialogue was *with* or *between*. The question that, in my mind at least, remains to be addressed is the one of (actual or imagined) audience: who, in other words, was this dialogue *for*? Are the poems meant like diary entries or notes to oneself, or are they aimed at an ideal imagined reader, or at actual people, or at a sense of self beyond the "selves" the poems explore? With the exception of some ten or eleven poems, Emily Dickinson did not publish during her lifetime, and it is not certain that all or any of these poems appeared with her agency or consent.[17] One wonders what the purpose of "moving through the network of discourses that constitute the sociosymbolic domain of language, interrogating and manipulating culturally determined voices" can be if the end product of such investigation is withheld from the public domain—the sphere in which such discourses circulate and have their force.[18] This is important precisely because the dialogic potential of these poems may be said to depend in part on their having an audience to engage in dialogue with, and it is the act of deliberate publication that normally establishes the conditions by which such a dialogue can take place. If the poems are withheld from publication, the implication is that the dialogue is then privatized, somehow removed from historical and political contexts: indeed, there is a biographical, generic, and politicoliterary convergence here in the sense that Dickinson's social withdrawal, choice of the lyric genre, and refusal to publish all appear to be consistent and coherent attempts *not to* engage in anything approximating dialogue during her lifetime. Again, at worst this seems to contradict my stated position that the poems are methodologically dialogic: at best, it presents us with something of a paradox. All the arguments I have enlisted in favor of her dialogic technique are minimized if not invalidated entirely if these poems were intended for Dickinson herself, rather than for others (though if the "self" which is being explored exists as a series of rhetorical performances, as characters in a form of "lyric fiction," then one might ask what "for herself" means).

For Joanne Dobson, that Dickinson addresses her own needs rather than those of an audience suggests a radical departure from "conventional nineteenth-century literary expectations" for women. She continues:

The arena of public concerns seems an unlikely one in which to investigate Emily Dickinson's life and work. A discussion of Dickinson and public issues is to some degree a discourse in negative terms, a chronicling of what isn't there. Dickinson is a quintessentially private poet. Although she was living and writing in a time of great social tumult, when major issues of freedom and responsibility—abolition of slavery, women's rights, urban poverty, exploitation of the working poor— were in frequent contest at the polls, in the press and the pulpit, and on the battlefield; her direct commentary on these matters is virtually nonexistent.[19]

Dobson goes on to say that Dickinson imports images and issues of social concern for the purposes of investigating and performing aspects of "her own psychological and existential situation."[20] Not writing about political and social issues can, of course, be seen as a social and political stance in itself, and Dobson interprets this positively, or liberally, as language- and self-orientated. But what does this mean in terms of a dialogue with the world—the kind of dialogue engaged in by professional female writers who were Dickinson's contemporaries?

Let me return to a remark I made previously about "Mine – by the Right of the White Election!" where I indicated that there is a proclamation we are invited to witness but not necessarily to share. I pointed out that the poem invites us to a performance, but leaves us in no doubt that we are spectators and not actors. We are doomed always, in my view, to read this poem from the outside, looking *at* more than *in*. The assumption then would be that Dickinson is writing this poem to, and for, herself, though one might wonder why she feels she has to (and the answer may be that she is only now, at the narrated time of the poem, conscious of the experience she describes and the authority invested in her by it; or that her dignity somehow depends on it). But much of the force of this poem lies in the assumption that it is providing information to *someone else* about her life, though it does seem more like telling than engaging in dialogue. Of course, one of the problems with a poet like Dickinson is the feeling that her poems will always partly elude us precisely because the experience that generated them seems so difficult to recover.[21] But the *language* of the poem does allow us to guess at its context: it seems as if the speaker is answering a statement or ideological position which (directly or indirectly) impinges on her in some integral way by calling into question her status or authority as a disfranchised woman, or as a nonprofessed Christian, or (perhaps) as a resident in a country that was becoming increasingly diversified along ethnic, racial, and class lines. And the act of writing the poem may function as a form of dialogue for Dickinson herself—she sees a description of herself and can weigh it from an outside position (or from a position within the self, which is displaced temporally and spatially from the speaker in the text).

I seem to have diverged from my anxiety about the apparent absence of an audience for these poems, but what I want to suggest is that there is in fact a problem with Bakhtin's original assignation of discursive homogeneity in poetry. To begin with, this assumes that the self is somehow capable of operating independently of the language(s) spoken in its historical field, or indeed that the self is a unified and coherent entity in full control of its own meanings. What I have been suggesting about Dickinson's dependence on definitions, which Dickinson is clearly uncomfortable with (as well as the disparate lyric selves exhibited in the fascicles), complicates that. Second, though Bakhtin does not himself say this, my own misgivings about nonpublication as a deliberate act of contemptuous silence in the face of social and historical dialects is based on the hypothesis that dialogism is a *willed* or *intended* strategy when in effect it can be accidental. In other words, a poem does not have to be written with the purpose of dramatizing or reflecting heteroglossia in order to be polyphonic. Dickinson's graphic suspension of words in quotation marks has the effect of multiplying the words' voices, creating a series of ideological echoes, and therefore alerting us to the complex, competitive, and many-leveled world of objective social reality, even if that was never her purpose. When Bakhtin writes that the *"plurality of independent and unmerged voices and consciousnesses and the genuine polyphony of full-valued voices are in fact characteristics of Dostoevsky's novels"* it feels legitimate to substitute Dickinson's poetry at the end of that sentence and still retain the integrity and accuracy of the original insight.[22]

There is another point worth making here. Not all dialogue takes place under the conditions of equality, and it is not always and everywhere conducted between individuals. A poem like P#320A (J#258), "There's a certain Slant of light," describes an ostensibly neutral (because natural) encounter between a single speaker and sunlight on a winter landscape, but even such an apparently private event is saturated with a particular kind of residual nineteenth-century Christian ideology to such an extent that it comes to be associated in the speaker's mind with oppression and the threat of death. The speaker is powerless to resist the chain of associations set in motion by the light, an internalized logic that has nothing to do with the intrinsic properties of light in itself.

There's a certain Slant of light,
Winter Afternoons –
That oppresses, like the Heft
Of Cathedral Tunes –

Heavenly Hurt, it gives us –
We can find no scar,
But internal difference,
Where the Meanings, are –

None may teach it – Any –
'Tis the Seal Despair –
An imperial affliction
Sent us of the Air –

When it comes, the Landscape listens –
Shadows – hold their breath –
When it goes, 'tis like the Distance
On the look of Death –

The sight of the sun's rays piercing through the winter gloom and illuminating the landscape below is hardly an uncommon one. What is unusual, however, is the substitution of this phenomenon with the unfamiliar and uncertain simile at the close, where its departure is compared with death. The equation of death and a landscape vacated by light may be brought about by the accident of verbal associations, by the double meaning of the word "light," which is not only that which shines, but also that which is of little weight, the opposite of heavy. The developing metaphors of "light," "oppresses," and "Heft" all have a logic that is more than accidental, however. As other critics have pointed out, the poem is concerned with things other than the natural—with the institutions of church and state, for example. There is a discourse of violence that is also linked to these institutions—death as punishment for infraction by both religion and government. This is anything but the simple dramatization of a single speaker's meeting with the alterity of nature, for that would make the poem free of ideological or historical context—the product of a private lyric consciousness taking an immaterial being as its subject. Instead, the poem stages an encounter of a very specific kind, between the present, particular apprehension of the light by a historically situated speaker who has been given to understand that it embodies a very definite spiritual reality. The event itself takes place in nature not because it is ahistorical, but because it confronts the naturalization of ideologies in and by society. The poem may be situated in a natural landscape, in other words, but it is concerned with how even such a traditionally neutral territory is saturated with ideology, and even determined by it. Light cannot be experienced without encountering its social significance, the meaning of "light" as it has been formulated over a long period. What the light traditionally represents, of course, is divinity, and it is with this tradition of meaning, this conventional sense, that the poem deals.

Words are signs for the objects in the world around us. But those signs are not neutral—they carry with them all kinds of cultural baggage. In this instance, the speaker has been taught to associate light with divinity, and it is the literalness of this vision that results in the moods of deflation and despair with which the poem ends. That God fails to reveal his presence, or instigate that knowledge of his existence known as grace, must mean that the speaker is punished for a crime that is so taken for granted that it is left unstated: original sin, or the inherited guilt of Adamic transgression, is one obvious possibility. The spiritual dereliction experienced by the speaker can only happen if there were some sort of spiritual expectation established in the first place: the correlation of light and death in the speaker's mind is a result of fear—not having experienced the expected conversion, the speaker believes herself to be unregenerate, and therefore excluded from immortality. The disappearance of the light indicates the withdrawal or withholding of favor, and the trauma concomitant with this necessary equation is developed through a corresponding imagery of retributive violence ("Hurt," "scar," "affliction") and subordination ("Heft," "oppresses").[23]

This encounter with a natural experience that produces an unnatural response is a comment about the social formation of thought, and how this formation is internalized to such an extent that it works almost invisibly within us, mediating our responses to events and to people. Perhaps this is precisely one of the reasons why the voice of the poem remains plural. Caught unawares, the speaker finds her- or himself responding in a predetermined way to experience, and therefore becomes conscious that she or he is not always and everywhere a free-thinking subject in control of her or his own meanings, but someone who is restricted by unwritten assumptions that are imposed upon her or him by society, and therefore shared, communal, nonindividual. The point of describing a landscape that actively responds to the appearance of light (it "listens" while "Shadows – hold their breath") is that nature itself is activated, or constituted, through discourse. There is no site that is free of the signs that we have for it, and these signs are inherited, imposed, inflicted. The light may not speak, but it does not have to, for it is already spoken for. Indeed, any kind of communion between nature and the speaker(s) is blocked because of this: instead, there is a dialogue with socially assigned meanings.

In many ways, the poem is a remarkably dispassionate investigation of how the equation of light with death ever happened in the first place. From nature to church, through the self and back again to nature, the poem traces the origins of that equation. If we take "light" not just as a self-conscious Christian metaphor but as a cleverly manipulated metonym (the light standing for the sun, the sun standing for the Son, the Son standing for resurrection), then we can see Dickinson peering through the layers of sense in order to see just how deeply and pervasively language is saturated with previously inscribed meanings. The reference to the cathedral in particular situates the speaker's response very precisely in the restrictive codes and practices of the church. Cathedral tunes are accompanied by the singing of hymns, which are in themselves collective and socially approved expressions of faith, the mass organization and communication of sanctioned belief. These hymns are therefore linked to the function of the church service itself and to religion more generally. They are carriers of value, formal instruments of control or coercion. In Althusserian terms, religion is an ideological state apparatus that exists in a relationship of mutual dependency and support with a repressive state apparatus such as the law. Though apparently descriptive, the poem therefore describes the hidden processes at work in the terms of any description, the subjectivization of external media of oppression—what Dickinson refers to as "internal difference."

Within the parameters of the poem there is a struggle for control over the potential significances of the light, its appearance in the world, and the history of its meanings. The poem becomes the site for an encounter between the self and outside voices, which attempt to impose their meanings upon her. At the same time, the language of punishment in the poem reminds us that discourse is not always a genteel activity, the "turn-taking exchange of ideas between individuals," but that it can instead take the form of coercion and torture. "She dealt her pretty words like Blades" begins the speaker of P#458A (J#479), "And every One unbared a Nerve /

Or wantoned with a Bone." In a letter to Louise and Frances Norcross, Dickinson writes, "What is that instructs a hand lightly created, to impel shapes to eyes at a distance, which for them have the whole area of life or of death? Yet not a pencil in the street but has this awful power, though nobody arrests it."[24] A glance at the list of first lines at the back of Ralph Franklin's 1998 edition of *The Poems of Emily Dickinson* shows that many of them describe scenes of internalized conflict and opposition in a discourse of extreme violence. If this is pugilism, then the Marquis of Queensberry rules do not apply.

If one looks at the list of Dickinson's correspondents, one is struck by how their lives reflect the nineteenth-century division of the spheres: the women are (for the most part) the invisible daughters, mothers, sisters, and wives of more famous men, while the men themselves are often significant and influential public figures. The women write private letters to each other, while the men have their letters and views printed in the newspapers. Despite its profession of equality, America was still a country without a level playing field. Perhaps this might explain the apparent paradox alluded to earlier of a dialogic poet who published next to nothing (in the conventional sense by which publication is equated with print). Because a complex of extraliterary constraints prevented her from public dialogue, Dickinson pursued certain arguments in her poetry instead. The paradox may also be the explanation. For if dialogue does not always occur in a structure of equality, those inequalities must be performed and addressed internally. This is why Dickinson's lyrics can dramatize such urgency and force, and yet remain largely unread. In that sense, they are what Vincent Crapanzano usefully calls "*shadow dialogue* . . . those dialogues that one partner to the primary dialogue has with an interlocutor, real or imaginary, who is not present at the primary dialogue. Such dialogues are 'silent,' 'mental,' 'quasi-articulate,' 'beneath consciousness' though capable, at least in part, of becoming conversation."[25]

It is possible to argue that Dickinson's correspondents who might have been in a position to have her published—I am thinking here of Samuel Bowles, Josiah Holland, and Thomas Wentworth Higginson—let her down because they were unable to accept precisely this linguistic practice, which differed so much from the conventional verse of the day. Between them, it should be recalled, these three men represented a good part of the institution of literary culture in Massachusetts: Bowles published poetry daily in the *Springfield Republican*, but printed only four of her poems, and either altered them or did not prevent them from being altered; in the first issue of *Scribner's Monthly,* Holland felt able to publish a fifteen-page comic morality poem in rhyming couplets with anapestic tetrameter on the rescue of the marriage of "Jeremy Train," but was reported as saying in the same year (1870) that he had "some poems of [Dickinson's] under consideration for publication—but they really are not suitable . . .";[26] and, judging by the reflection of her replies to his letters, Higginson was clearly worried by the lack of formal correctness in the poems. Susan Dickinson seems to have tried to help her sister-in-law publish in the early sixties, but then gave up, partly because she was busy with her own life (and that of her husband and children), partly because poems that she did submit on Dickinson's behalf (but not necessarily with her knowledge) were changed, and partly (it has been suggested) because she may have come to realize (either singly or together with the poet herself) that Dickinson's poetry was so distinct that the conventions of print culture could never properly or adequately represent it. Her daughter Martha Dickinson Bianchi was quite happy to allow them to be altered and prepared for print, which would suggest that she was ignorant of her mother's opinions, that she disagreed with them, that she accepted compromises in order to have them published, or that her mother never objected to the demands of printers to the extent that contemporary critics have suggested. Mabel Loomis Todd tried and succeeded, but at a cost: she too altered the meter, rhyme, syntax, and typographical characteristics of the poems in order to make them conform to her own and the public judgment of what good poetry should sound and look like on the page.

A part of the Emily Dickinson exhibition in the special collections of the Jones Library in Amherst records how Todd (in the 1896 edition) altered P#1029A (J#1020), "I had a daily Bliss," from a nontitled two-stanza poem of five and six lines respectively to one with two quatrains, a title ("Lost Joy"), and a sequence of changes to the capitalization, punctuation, and word choice. The exhibition points out how "Hight" of line seven became the "crag" of line five (presumably on the grounds that crag sounded more poetic, and Dickinson did herself use "crag" four time elsewhere), "Increased" in line nine became "Enlarged" in line seven (admittedly listed as an alternative on the original manuscript), and the last line replaced "I learned to estimate" with "I learned its sweetness right" (for the purpose of rhyme, but without the slightest precedent in Dickinson's manuscript or work). Surely what we see here is the imposition of what Bakhtin termed "an officially recognized literary language" onto an unstable, dialogic text:

Unitary language constitutes the theoretical expression of the historical processes of linguistic unification and centralization, an expression of the centripetal forces of language. A unitary language is not something given [*dan*] but is always in essence posited [*zadan*]—and at every moment of its linguistic life it is opposed to the realities of heteroglossia. But at the same time it makes its real presence felt as a force for overcoming this heteroglossia, imposing specific limits to it, guaranteeing a certain maximum of mutual understanding and crystalizing into a real, though still relative, unity—the unity of the reigning conversational (everyday) and literary language, "correct language."[27]

The history of Dickinson's publication would therefore appear to indicate the inequality that exists between the institutional voices of normalization and those of the margin. There are different levels of inequality, however, which is why I want to step back slightly at this point and ask if by identifying Dickinson as disempowered we are allowed to make all kinds of ahistorical generalizations about the sociopolitical position evinced by her poetry. Take as an example Paul Crumbley's claim that the early, regularized editions of Dickinson's poetry "are extremely useful both in clarifying her reasons for not publishing and in isolating the dominant discourse she sought to dismantle."[28] Crumbley's supposition that all printings of Dickinson's work would have regularized her poetry seems suspect to me, given that publishers have demonstrated typographic and editorial flexibility with other writers. It is possible, however, that the particular kinds of high-cultural publishing institutions or avenues Dickinson would have preferred may not have fully appreciated her talents, but this is not the same as saying that every publisher in the United States would have rejected her terms outright. Not publishing, in other words, may have been just as much a matter of choice as necessity. (It seems to me for instance that the dialogic potential of Dickinson's poetry is—or should have been—at its greatest in their newspaper publication, for newspapers are inevitably placed into alien discursive territories and derive new meanings because of that.) And again, I have to admit to some difficulty with the idea that Dickinson's private acts had a public dimension to them, that they constituted a deliberate project of destabilizing social and political discourses. There is so little evidence of an interest in political affairs in Dickinson's letters that it is unlikely a wider political engagement would have manifested itself at the linguistic or generic levels. On the contrary, direct comments on public events (presidential campaigns, her father's political career, hangings) are sporadic and tend to dismiss their seriousness. Finally, one wonders to what extent Dickinson could have dismantled any kind of discourse if she herself decided to publish only through letters and notes. True, her poems may potentially have discomfited the received certainties of the largely middle-class readers who were her correspondents, but there is very little evidence that this was the case (as there is for example with Gerard Manley Hopkins): some of her recipients thought her weird, but most were delighted and even honored to receive such original work. If this was heteroglossia, many of her contemporaries were remarkably blind to its deviant effects. It is even possible to say that the originality of the language may have disabled whatever unconventional implications her words may be constructed as having had.

Because of Dickinson's noncontribution to her literary field, one is drawn into making what may well be nonhistorical generalizations about her—such as claiming that she was a dialogic poet in Bakhtin's sense of that word. One wonders if seeing her as the victim of forces of normalization is equally ahistorical—a retrospective insertion of a writer into a cultural environment she ignored in order to construct a sentimental vision of herself as an imprisoned and oppositional voice (what Dobson calls "a dynamic of articulation directly in opposition to that of her female contemporaries").[29] In a sense, this is inevitable: one reads Dickinson on her own terms, forced to approach her poetry out of context because she herself appears to have removed it from most contexts. Wondering who is to blame for this situation is like pondering the originality of her style: Did she write the way she did because she was unpublished, or was she unpublished because she wrote the way she did? That Dickinson was a victim of unwarranted editorial interference seems clear. But it is not at all clear that her twentieth-century appearance in nineteenth-century American literature necessarily makes her the linguistic wing of political liberalism. Unlike the work of Harriet Beecher Stowe, Rebecca Harding Davis, and Helen Hunt Jackson (which she read and admired), her writing is more attentive to craft and finish—the purely formal, self-referring aspects— than to issues. She works at some remove from the world of politics: slavery (to take one example) is not a particular set of economic relations affecting historically specific individuals of color, but a metaphor for her position as a woman writer. In some senses, she seems to inhabit what Raymond Williams would call both *residual* and *emergent* conceptions of the artist (which seems historically credible given that she was born in the first third of the century and died in the last), for on the one hand she is the amateur gentlewoman writer of handwritten and unpublished manuscripts, which are circulated privately as gifts among people of her own ethnic and class background, but on the other she is the producer of finely wrought aesthetic objects, for whom poetry (and not marriage or child-bearing or teaching or reforming) was a serious vocation, even a career, as much as (if not more than) a leisured pastime. Nonetheless, it would be a mistake to see her pieces as self-contained, even if they do not appear to be obviously political or social. They are speech acts, and not actions, but they register and respond to the world around them.

It seems to me that Dickinson's style of writing draws attention mostly to itself, that enclosing instances of conventional usage within her poems is part of a strategic conferral of distinction upon herself. This is poetical, though it also has sociopolitical overtones: it is a way of highlighting her superiority, her utter difference from anything else then in production and circulation. It is remarkable how so many of Dickinson's poems begin like one-line newspaper advertisements: "Dare you see a soul 'at the white heat'?"; "Perhaps you'd like to buy a flower?"; "A letter is a joy of earth"; "A word made flesh is seldom"; "Would you like summer?" The use of imported words is part of a competitive instinct: they are markers by which to measure the effortless preeminence of her own performances. Normative definitions become the milestones of her genius. She uses other words not to admit other views, but to lampoon the ordinary. Martha Nell Smith was right when she wrote that Dickinson was a cartoonist, but not because of her doodles: Dickinson belongs to a tradition of writers who use caricature as an indirect means of defining their own distinction and achievement.

Any portrait of Dickinson as disruptive transgressor or silenced victim is likely to oversimplify the more complex reality of her social situation as a woman of means who did not behave like a conventional woman of means. It emphasizes her as a critical voice whose contemporary political correlative would be radical dissidence. To read her poetry this way is to place gender over certain aspects of her socioeconomic background, and the result must always be a partial understanding of the writing. I want to bring this chapter to an end by looking briefly at Dickinson's use of madness as a trope for her opposition to, and perhaps even her oppression by, society. For madness is writing from the margins, using language to contest received meanings and binary oppositions. "Insanity to the sane seems so unnecessary – but I am only one, and they are 'four and forty,' which little affair of numbers leaves me impotent," Dickinson wrote in a letter to Kate Anthon in late 1859.[30] The remark is useful inasmuch as it suggests madness as a kind of metaphor for a perspective at odds with that of the majority: it is a shorthand term for a point of view that is resistant, unstable, fluid. In my view, it is typical of a kind of hyperbolic or extremist strategy of self-valorization in Dickinson: she diagnoses herself as mad in order to underline a sense of her uniqueness. It is a form of self-aggrandisement, in other words, a raising of the self to an heroic status:

Much Madness is divinest Sense –
To a discerning Eye –
Much Sense – the starkest Madness –
'Tis the Majority
In this, as all, prevail –
Assent – and you are sane –
Demur – you're straightway dangerous –
And handled with a Chain –

Division 3 starkest |
P#620A (J#435)

In *Madness and Civilization* Michel Foucault wrote that "unreason" was one of the ways by which "reason" could be differentially calculated: Dickinson seems to reverse that hierarchy.[31] To begin with, reason and unreason are understood in the poem only in the sense that they are opposite to each other: they are both undefined, reified, abstract (this vagueness is quite common for Dickinson). Gradually, however, we come to understand that sanity involves "assent,"—that it involves some act of compliance or complicity. If one were to extrapolate from this, one would say that "sanity" probably stands for those unspoken agreements between people at a given time and place about the meaning of society. Further precision is difficult, and this is Dickinson's genius: although there is nothing in her life or writing or economic background to suggest that she would have sympathized with, say, the plight of striking workers, nonetheless the poem's oblique definition of insanity as any act of social dissent leaves open room for the piece to be read as communicating the plight of any suppressed group or minority—except that the poem was never published in any form, not by letter, or note, or in the kind of cheap edition that might have made it available for suppressed groups or individuals to read and appropriate for their own uses. The writer's decision not to give the poem a wider distribution would appear to segregate its meaning. The material circumstances of its nonappearance in the world, its preservation within the folds of a fascicle discovered only after her death, throws some light on the extent to which Dickinson was willing to engage publicly with political systems. It suggests that her speaker's opposition to society is a complicated one that reflects both a sense of privilege and a desire not to have that privilege compromised.

The speaker in this poem belongs to a category of people whose relation to society is a tense one, who exist *within* society as its potential victim but at the same time are *outside* it and therefore able to contest its definitions. We have come full circle here, for madness is the exact equivalent of putting words in quotation marks, shaking off their conventional meanings, and standing at a distance from the world. Dickinson deploys terms related to mental illness not as symptoms of disorder, but as a rhetorical device with which to communicate her sense of herself as a Monarch of Perception[32]—albeit a monarch forced to live in a world where her right to the throne is clearly disputed, contentious. "Sense" carries within it its Austean opposite, sensitivity, and the association of madness with discernment suggests that the "insane" are in fact an intellectual elite who possess faculties of insight and understanding which are beyond the comprehension of ordinary men and women. The remark in the letter to Kate Anthon and the poem have this much in common: both speakers align themselves with insanity as a concept, but they write from outside, rather than from within, the condition of madness. For madness does not make sense, cannot make itself understood: the paradox of both letter and poem is that they are *about* madness but that they are not mad in themselves. In fact, they are both very sane: it is true that they are complicated, that they appear to challenge "conventional" logic and understanding, but they are not confused in any way. The systematic use of paradox in the poem for instance demands a close, almost classical, attention to verbal and rational detail. It seems to me that the poem is very carefully argued, and it depends for its success on the application of logic, albeit logic employed in the service of overturning "traditional" sense. Judging by this poem, there is a form of madness in Emily Dickinson's writing that is rhetorical, not pathological. The latter is a clinically defined condition, with a variety of treatments, the former a kind of subject position, madness deployed as the symbol of a special kind of knowledge or perspective that is associated with heightened emotional sensitivity and imaginative capacity.

The deployment of madness as a trope in Dickinson's poetry can be understood as an expression of her desperation as an unusual woman in patriarchal society. But that does not mean that she saw herself only as a victim, actual or potential. On the contrary, insanity cuts both ways: the speaker in the poem is both victim and tragic victor, a kind of epic heroine in defeat, just as in the letter which links "impotence" or powerlessness metaphorically to both insanity and singularity. Dickinson uses insanity as a code for a kind of esoteric knowledge that is unavailable to others, as well as a signal of her sense that this differential knowledge placed her at odds with society. It marks her off as distinctive, unusual, and remarkable, but also as potentially vulnerable. There is no reason to dismiss these pronouncements: they exist at one level as genuine responses to specific and potentially threatening developments within society as a whole, but they can also be related to a philosophical tradition in ways that tend just as much toward the literary as the literal.

For madness in literature has often been understood as a kind of wisdom at odds with general experience. In societies defined as primitive and in certain religious movements, both ancient and modern, the individual seen as mad was thought to be possessed by divinity and thus given access to a higher order of understanding. For Plato, frenzy was an enabling condition, which brought inspiration in music and poetry, while Socrates said that "frenzy, provided it comes as the gift of heaven, is the channel by which we receive the greatest blessings."[33] More recently, Boswell wrote that "[Samuel] Johnson, who was blest with all the powers of genius and understanding in a degree far above the ordinary state of human nature, was at the same time visited with a disorder so afflictive, that they who know it by dire experience, will not envy his exalted endowments."[34] In the nineteenth century, this link between sensitivity to suffering and the production of great art was developed into the melancholic hero in the writings of Romantic philosophers and poets, among them Keats, in "Ode on Melancholy":

Ay, in the very temple of Delight
Veil'd Melancholy has her sovran shrine,
Though seen of none save him whose strenuous tongue
Can burst Joy's grape against his palate fine; . . .

These lines are representative inasmuch as they suggest that "Melancholy" was both an affliction and a badge of honor. Those who felt great sadness were also those best able to experience great joy. Extremes of mental indisposition were a sign of an acute openness and sensitivity, like Shelley's consciousness that faints even as it imagines flowers. Poetic inspiration, too, is sometimes figured as a form of madness, and Keats's image of extreme emotional states being a kind of intoxication (the grape of joy suggesting the grape that brings joy, alcohol) suggests that by the nineteenth century there was an established literary tradition that saw drunkenness, madness, and creativity as parts of a continuum. In "The Poet" (1841) Ralph Waldo Emerson discusses the idea that poets gravitate naturally to artificial stimulants as a way of escaping the confines of the real:

This is the reason why bards love wine, mead, narcotics, coffee, tea, opium, the fumes of sandal-wood and tobacco, or whatever other species of animal exhilaration. All men avail themselves of such means as they can, to add this extraordinary power to their normal powers; and to this end they prize conversation, music, pictures, sculpture, dancing, theatres, travelling, war, mobs, fires, gaming, politics, or love, or science, or animal intoxication, which are several coarser or finer quasi-mechanical substitutes for the true nectar, which is the ravishment of the intellect by coming nearer to the fact. These are auxiliaries to the centrifugal tendency of a man, to his passage out into free space, and they help him to escape the custody of that body in which he is pent up, and of that jail-yard of individual relations in which he is enclosed.[35]

In 1844, three years after "The Poet" was published, and following the death of Dickinson's friend Sophia Holland, Emily Dickinson's parents were sufficiently worried about her mental health to send her off for a month or so with her aunt Lavinia Norcross in Boston and her uncle William Dickinson in Worcester. Edward wrote to her, on 4 June: "I want to have you see the Lunatic Hospital, & other interesting places in Worcester, now you are there."[36] (He had made a similar recommendation to his wife in the autumn of 1835, when she made an extended visit to Boston for rest and recuperation: he urged her to see the hospital for the insane, perhaps the one in Charlestown.) Later, Edward begged Dickinson not to read books "because," as she explained to Higginson, "he fears they joggle the Mind."[37] The point is that "madness" is one word with many very different explanations. With Dickinson, it can be seen as a clinical condition, an indication of her dissatisfaction with the constraints placed on women's behavior in the nineteenth century, in addition to a rhetorical position by which she defined her distance from, and superiority to, the society she lived in. For instance, when she mentions the emotionally charged "Chain" in the last line of "Much Madness is divinest Sense," one acknowledges the very real dangers of being incarcerated on the grounds of *clinical* abnormality for any young woman whose behavior was seen as deviating from *cultural* norms of female comportment, as well as the oppressive nature of social convention and consensus, which marginalize those who are different in some way. But one recognizes also the criticism of a linear mode of thought and language, where one idea is connected to another in a way that Dickinson compares to the links of a chain, and by extension a kind of entrapment, a means of confinement.

Heteroglossia is not a disease, but neither is it necessarily a fully willed condition. That sense can be understood as madness, and madness the greatest sense, tells us not only of an individual's relation to society, but of social relations generally as these are perceived by that individual in history. The transgression of limits is as much a feature of the age as a characteristic of the poetry, as Marx and Engels pointed out in 1848:

Constant revolutionizing of production, uninterrupted disturbance of all social conditions, everlasting uncertainty and agitation distinguish the bourgeois epoch from all earlier ones. All fixed, fast-frozen relations, with their train of ancient and venerable prejudices and opinions, are swept away, all new-formed ones become antiquated before they can ossify. All that is solid melts into air.[38]

When Paul Crumbley argues in *Inflections of the Pen* that Dickinson's exploration of what it is to be (among others) a wife, a daughter, a nun, a lover, a queen, a seamstress, a dying woman, and a corpse is equivalent to the dialogic novel, he overlooks historical pressures other than the creative impulse that might have enforced such a condition. He also ignores the extent to which our relations with other individuals and institutions within society often cause us to act out certain social roles and positions. For as Terry Eagleton reminds us, there "is no social reality without its admixture of feigning, mask, performance, delusion, just as there is no sign which cannot be used to deceive. Being yourself always involves a degree of play-acting."[39] And for any woman writer in nineteenth-century American society, using the word "I" necessarily involved an engagement with conflicting definitions of women, women's roles, women writers, and women's writings. If it can be said that Emily Dickinson incorporated contemporaneous discourses into the lyric selves of her poetry, it is because at one level she did not have a choice. Her poems therefore dramatize socially assigned personalities as much as they perform a singularly ludic authorial identity (though this does not mean that the "I" in Dickinson's poetry is consistently a third-person pronoun). Emily Dickinson does not speak all of her own poems, then, for her needs, responses, and preoccupations intersect with the selves made available to, and by, her meeting with history.

It is misleading to think that Dickinson would have wanted to introduce alien voices and perspectives into her poetry on conditions of equality: sometimes she supposed them inferior to her own, sometimes not. And although her poetry as a whole contains sufficient diversity of independent opinion to make it dialogic, there are nevertheless an equal number of single poems that seem to me to be monologic, that respond to verbal histories by attempting to suppress them. Words in quotation marks are fault lines, verbal fissures, areas of weakness where contending forces collide over the control of meaning within society, but they are not always admitted to her lyric premises on the same condition.[40] Such fault lines are the sites of innumerable ideological struggles that reveal all language to be enmeshed in conflicting social determinations and historically contested definitions. The precise social coordinates of Dickinson's pronouncements are difficult to chart, but they must not be understood simplistically as recording either political radicalism or social conservatism. There are signs of both. The exact range of Dickinson's social and political allegiances is complex and shifting, depending on what strata of society she can be said to be in relation to at any given point within a poem. Her writing as a whole is of course infinitely more sophisticated than any crude political paraphrase can ever admit—though it has to be recognized that not all the utterances are equally nuanced. The poem on madness, to take a final example, reveals a highly productive tension between the speaker's confidence in her own originality and the continuing knowledge that this confidence is held to be suspect by others who have greater power. This position seems to me to be closest to that of the nineteenth-century intelligentsia, standing outside society in opposition to its conventions, existing nonetheless in a position of economic privilege within it, and yet removed from the real centers of political power. No matter how much Dickinson sought to claim a patent on her language, she inevitably includes an alternative network of discursive possibilities. The result is a diversity of voices, which includes preferences different from, and even opposite to, her monarchy of perception.

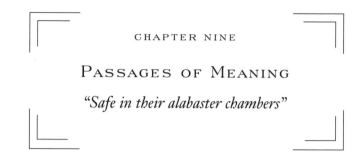

CHAPTER NINE

PASSAGES OF MEANING

"Safe in their alabaster chambers"

IN this final chapter I will look more closely at issues raised in previous chapters and put them into critical practice with reading a poem that combines speculation about its contexts with a sensitivity to its verbal nuances. I will be concerned with Dickinson's relations to history, her preoccupation with her own home-based assault on a posthumous literary immortality, the interdependency of her individual lyrics; and the status of her manuscripts. The poem I have chosen to look at is a personal favorite, and one that has received a great deal of critical scrutiny, most extensively and brilliantly in Martha Nell Smith's landmark *Rowing in Eden: Rereading Emily Dickinson.*[1] What is useful about the poem is that it exists (in manuscript form) in a number of related, and yet subtly different, versions. The truth, as Smith points out, is that P#124 (J#216) "Safe in their alabaster chambers" is more than a single remarkable poem; it is a series of them (Franklin thinks six or seven, one or two of which are lost), and any credible reading needs to take all of these into account, if not literally by offering an interpretation of each, at least by establishing the grounds for choosing one variant in front of the others. This is a poem (for the sake of convenience, I will continue to operate with the singular) that can be approached in many ways. Read in its sequence of composition, it can tell us many things about what goals Dickinson had in mind when she revised images or thought of new ones. In addition, versions of the poem are recorded singly (P#124C) and as a cluster of alternatives

(P#124B and P#124E) in two different fascicles (the sixth and tenth, respectively). One could legitimately attend to these in the setting of their appearances both within those particular miscellanies and in the order of the manuscript anthologies as a whole. It would seem to me, however, that the different fascicle placements of the poem's variants suggest at least the possibility that it can function equally well in a variety of structural and semantic circumstances, and as a consequence that a poem and its variants existed quite adequately for Dickinson as a unit of meaning in itself, or as units of meaning that operated with changing horizons of meaning.

It was Smith who most seriously advanced the theory that "Safe in their alabaster chambers" could be read in the context of an epistolary exchange about its second stanza variants between Dickinson and her sister-in-law, Susan. As I understand it, Smith's groundbreaking work changed the landscape of Dickinson scholarship in arguing that the correspondence between the two women functioned as a kind of poetry workshop for both, and that Dickinson was therefore not as remote a writer as historical representations of her would have us believe. Smith has forged a deserved reputation as perhaps the leading Dickinson critic of our day, and one applauds her work for its informed and judicious revision of our understanding both of Dickinson's writing and of Susan's contribution to it. At the time of writing, I have not had the opportunity to review Smith's latest project, *Open Me Carefully: Emily Dickinson's Intimate Letters to Susan Huntington Dickinson* (edited with Ellen Louise Hart), so while I have no hesitation in accepting the idea that Susan was an important reader, supporter, and source of inspiration, I still have some misgivings about the description of her as an active collaborator. As I contend later in this chapter, Dickinson withheld one of the stanza variants from Susan and seems possibly (and, if so, rightly, in my opinion) to have disagreed about which version of the poem was the best (Susan thought that the first stanza was self-sufficient: Dickinson tried different permutations with a second). There is no suggestion in other correspondence that Dickinson ever seriously thought of altering a poem at Susan's request again (though she was often prepared to alter a poem in order to make it suit Susan better). In addition, basing the implication of mutual creative activity on the evidence of Dickinson's willingness to engage positively in and to act upon an exchange of views on one poem is complicated by the correspondence itself, which seems to me to be highly ambivalent at one point. Nonetheless, even if some of Smith's conclusions seem questionable to me, they are based on impeccable scholarship and a profound desire not only to contest stereotypes about Dickinson but also to see justice done in the case of the much maligned Susan. And although the writing itself is Smith's primary point of focus, she does at least move the discussion about the poem's significance into its biographical and epistolary contexts, often with stunning results.

The advantage of interpreting "Safe in their alabaster chambers" as part of a sequence of other poems in a fascicle or fascicles, or indeed as part of the sequence of its own variants, is that the frontier of any poem's significance is extended, so that it becomes part of a network of Dickinson's texts, which comment on and combine with each other in ways the collected editions of her poetry do not make possible. The potential danger in this approach, I am persuaded, is that it encourages an inward-looking reading attentive only to the minutiae of technique and language, a segregated area where poems play off against each other in an endless shimmer of possible readings, as Smith suggests: "Offering itself in various manifestations, the lyric is more fascinating poetically, for scrutinized intertextually each version engages the reader in many more ways than either might alone."[2]

While tentatively concurring with this statement, I also worry that such an approach might decontextualize Dickinson's writings, so that they will once again be seen as the equivalent of the figure on the T-shirt I mentioned in my introduction; self-enclosed, self-referential, self-important, and capable of generating myriad readings irrespective of the worlds and voices outside the poem's frame.

Accordingly, P#124 (A, B, C, D, E, F, and G as Franklin identifies it) might serve as a practical test case for anyone attempting to relate Dickinson to larger cultural, political, social, and linguistic contexts.[3] To generalize from one particular is always dangerous, but P#124 is not only a useful and not entirely extreme example of how the simultaneous existence of numerous forms of the "same" work can become more intriguing and interesting for readers; in addition it illustrates the challenges and opportunities, the limits and possibilities that Dickinson's poetry collectively offers.

For the purposes of discussion I therefore transcribe the poem as fully as the exigencies of print allow. The first version (P#124A in the Franklin variorum sequence), based on a lost manuscript sent to Susan Dickinson, follows the edition of the poem published in the *Springfield Daily Republican* on 1 March 1862, where it was entitled "The Sleeping" and included a postscript, "*Pelham Hill, June,* 1861." The second (P#124B), derives from the earliest extant holograph, which is copied into Fascicle 6. The third and fourth (P#124C & P#124D) are versions included in an exchange of letters with Susan Dickinson, where Emily supplied alternatives or new suggestions for the second stanza. The fifth (P#124E) offers a complete record of the new second stanzas, and was copied into Fascicle 10.[4] The sixth (P#124F), which I will discuss later, was enclosed in a letter to Thomas Wentworth Higginson. Finally, there is a seventh transcript (P#124G), which I will not discuss because it was not recorded by Dickinson herself and because Franklin suggests that it was "recalled, unreliably, from memory."[5]

Safe in their alabaster chambers,
Untouched by morning,
And untouched by noon,
Sleep the meek members of the Resurrection,
Rafter of satin, and roof of stone.

Light laughs the breeze
In her castle above them,
Babbles the bee in a stolid ear,
Pipe the sweet birds in ignorant cadence:
Ah! what sagacity perished here!

Emendation 3, 5, 8, 10] *indented* 9 cadence] cadences
P#124A

Safe in their Alabaster Chambers –
Untouched by morning
And untouched by noon –
Sleep the meek members of the Resurrection –
Rafter of satin,
And Roof of stone.

Light laughs the breeze
In her Castle above them –
Babbles the Bee in a stolid Ear,
Pipe the sweet Birds in ignorant cadence –
Ah, what sagacity perished here!

P#124B[6]

Safe in their Alabaster Chambers,
Untouched by morning –
And untouched by noon –
Lie the meek members of the Resurrection –
Rafter of satin – and Roof of stone –

Grand go the Years – in the Crescent – above them –
Worlds scoop their Arcs –
And Firmaments – row –
Diadems – drop – and Doges – surrender –
Soundless as dots – on a Disc of snow –

Division 4 of | 5 Roof of | 6 in the | 9 Doges – | 10 a |
P#124C

Springs – shake the Sills –
But – the Echoes – stiffen –
Hoar – is the Window – and – numb – the Door –
Tribes of Eclipse – in Tents of Marble –
Staples of Ages – have buckled – there –

Division 3 and | 4 Tents | 5 have |
P#124D

Safe in their Alabaster chambers –
Untouched by Morning –
And untouched by Noon –
Lie the meek members of the Resurrection –
Rafter of Satin – and Roof of Stone!

Grand go the Years – in the Crescent – above them –
Worlds scoop their Arcs –
And Firmaments – row –
Diadems – drop – and Doges – surrender –
Soundless as dots – on a Disc of snow –

Springs – shake the sills –
But – the Echoes – stiffen –
Hoar – is the window –
And – numb – the door –
Tribes – of Eclipse – in Tents – of Marble –
Staples – of Ages – have buckled – there –

•

Springs – shake the seals –
But the silence – stiffens –
Frosts unhook – in the Northern Zones –
Icicles – crawl from polar Caverns –
Midnight in Marble –
Refutes – the Suns –

Division 1 Alabaster | 4 of | 6 in the | 9 Doges – | 10 a | *alt* 6–10 window–|| *alt* 6–10
Tents – | *alt* 6–10 have | *alt* 6–10 in the | *alt* 6–10 polar |
P#124E[7]

As I previously remarked, when a version of the poem first appeared in typographic form in *Springfield Daily Republican,* it was unsigned, but printed directly beneath it were the words "*Pelham Hill, June,* 1861." I find this postscript intriguing for all sorts of reasons, not least because it is a rare instance of contextual information, and therefore worth investigating in itself. Although it is always possible that the information derived directly from Dickinson, this would seem unlikely, given that she did not as a rule attach dates or places to a poem, and that the date assigned is in fact wrong: the first version of the poem was written in 1859. There is another possibility: that the date was inserted by Samuel Bowles, who was a friend of Austin, Emily, and Susan and often went on excursions with them to Pelham. But it was not normal practice for the *Republican* to add this kind of information, and Bowles himself would have had no reason for doing so (there are no references in his letters to his attending any social occasion there during June 1861). The information might then have been supplied by Susan; it was almost certainly she who supplied Bowles with the manuscript on which the poem is based. By 1861 there were a number of variants of the poem available, and it is interesting that *Republican* printed the first version—the one that Susan seems to have preferred. This was not Dickinson's favorite, judging by the several variants that were recorded in Fascicle 10 and by the different version that she sent to Higginson. To be precise: Susan preferred the first stanza alone, but by 1861 would also have been acquainted with three alternatives for the second stanza. In all probability it was she and not Emily who made the choice of using the first version. When Dickinson recorded variants in P#124E, in the tenth fascicle, she discarded version A completely.

Now, just because Dickinson made no objection either to the published poem or to its glossary in her letters does not necessarily mean that she approved of either as they were presented in the *Republican*. Dickinson withheld one version of the poem from Susan (the fourth version of the second stanza that is recorded in P#124E), and she chose the second version of the second stanza ("Grand go the Years") in the copy of the poem she sent to Higginson in 1862 (P#124F). This information complicates the portrait presented by Martha Nell Smith in *Rowing in Eden* of Susan and Emily working in tandem on this poem. It suggests that Susan and Emily had different preferences when it came to the poem (or that Susan had one preference where Dickinson, typically, had several), and that it was Susan's decision to publish the earlier version that she preferred, with a postscript she supplied to give it an extra dimension of significance that related in some way to her own life or state of mind at this time. In the same year, then, "Safe in their alabaster chambers" was published twice: once (P#124A) in the *Republican* by Susan, and once (P#124F, essentially a copy of P#124C, which Susan knew about) by Dickinson herself in her correspondence with Higginson. Emily's having sent that version suggests either that Dickinson wanted Higginson to read the one she preferred or that she hoped that he would take a position himself as to which of the two publications he liked best.

I am not trying to raise again the old story of a rift between Dickinson and her sister-in-law so much as I am advancing the view that these two women operated independently of each other's wishes with regard to the various publications of the poem, and that they were not quite as united in their opinions as Smith implies. If Susan did supply the postscript, however, she must have known that Emily would read it eventually and Susan's including it therefore indicates both her confidence in Dickinson's approval and the level of intimacy they shared, for it must have referred to something that they both associated with Pelham in June of that (or an earlier) year: consequently, it functioned as some kind of oblique code, either between them, or between Emily, Susan, and Bowles, or between Emily, Susan, Bowles, and Austin. The postscript could be read by the initiated for its private significance, but would also carry a more neutral or less personal meaning for the general reader. This suggests that the poem took as its starting point an event, or a sequence of thoughts anticipating an event, that was connected in some way with the time and place recorded in the postscript. Such a paradigm of simultaneously restricted and inclusive meanings is, of course, not untypical of this writer's work as a whole.

Pelham Hill was associated at least in part with Susan, who often organized outings and picnics there, but because Susan was in confinement in June and July 1861, it seems unlikely that the postscript refers to an actual excursion. (One accepts the possibility, however, that the date may have been a compositor's error, or that it represented the anniversary of something important associated with Pelham, where Austin and Susan owned property.) Edward (Ned) Dickinson, the male heir to the Dickinson estate, was born on 19 June almost five years after Austin and Susan were married on 1 July 1856, thereby (it was thought) ensuring the succession of the family name. Now, it is true that the first version of the poem has been dated before 1861, but even so, there is a sense in which the 1859 poem and the 1861 postscript can still be understood as converging, both having some common source in the psychological dynamics accompanying changes in a family's history. It has been speculated that there may have been some anxiety on the part of (the senior) Edward Dickinson about the failure of his son to produce an heir before 1861, but the poem seems to indicate that the initial years following Susan's marriage occasioned conflicting impulses in Emily herself. With the completion of the Evergreens, the expectation of a child, and the early success of Austin and Susan as a social couple, Dickinson may have felt that the primary site of the family dynasty had shifted, and that those living in the Homestead were in the process of being left behind: although the poem's opposition between the living and the dead can be rendered graphically as a vertical hierarchy of those above and below the ground, it can be also be understood less literally as horizontal and generational division between the Dickinson houses. The difference between the stanzas is the difference between the stillness and darkness of the ancestral mansion, and the liveliness and promise of the Evergreens next door. This is not to say that Dickinson herself felt excluded from that jollity or was in any way opposed to it, but it is to admit that she might have been aware of her own biological or dynastic redundancy. The description of the dead as living in a state of suspended animation has a particular force when one realizes that it may refer to the living but childless daughter(s) of the patriarchal line. Although composed before 1861, the aggregate of feelings that the poem dramatizes (and that Susan, Dickinson's intimate friend, may well have known about) would have existed latently before Ned's actual birth: though it might appear selfish or morbid to twentieth-century readers, it was often the case that parents, relatives, and friends reflected on their own mortality when they were close to a newly married couple who expected to have children. The addition of the date in the *Republican*, whether deliberate or accidental, strengthens the sense that the poem addresses anxieties occasioned and then consolidated by the promise and subsequent realization of a male child's birth. *"Pelham Hill, June, 1861"* could have been Susan's way of saying in 1862 that she had felt the same way in 1861 that Emily did in 1859.

Nevertheless, although the origin of this poem could possibly have been private, the responses to birth and death that it enacts are fairly universal, and the poem does have a public aspect. Given Dickinson's concern with privacy (and Susan's later concern to protect that privacy), one does not rule out the strong possibility that the postscript in the *Republican*, functioned as a kind of decoy, leading readers *away* from an understanding of the poem as a personal document rather than toward such an approach (giving it an occasional significance associated with a public event of that time, in other words, and therefore masking its emotional origins). But it may not be a decoy either: there is a reasonable argument for saying that the text is the end product of a series of thoughts occasioned by one or more visit to Pelham, one of the oldest settlements in western Massachusetts, and a favorite site for locals and visitors (Samuel Bowles often went up there for the view). Pelham was in the public eye in June 1861, as it prepared for a major event, an Independence Day celebration and the dedication of the new Pelham Springs Hotel (a combined health spa and hotel), the latter to be opened by Dr. Sornberger. In late June, the *Hampshire and Franklin Express* had articles announcing that a brass band would be there, Professor Seelye would give an oration, Charles Sweetser would deliver a poem, and a special cannon would be cast to give the salutes. Little was being planned for Independence Day in Amherst that year, and it was therefore suggested Amherst people go up to Pelham.

So it is possible that the postscript is drawing attention not to a private set of references but to historical or social or doctrinal ones. First occupied by Scottish Presbyterians, Pelham was the center for Shays' Rebellion from 1786 to 87 and its Congregational meetinghouse (on Pelham Heights) was erected in 1839.[8] However, it is perhaps not so much the white meetinghouse (might this have been one of the chambers at the back of the poet's mind?) as it was the burial ground that lies behind it that is of interest, for it also seems reasonable that, because of its elevated position, this was the place where the poem began. Today, the cemetery looks as old as it is: though the gravestones are neatly arranged, they are in various stages of erosion and stick out from the ground in all kinds of shapes and at odd angles. Though there is nothing today that resembles an aboveground "Alabaster Chamber," there are several headstones of Vermont marble (the others are mainly granite and sandstone), among them one inscribed "In Memory of / Mrs Margret / Peebles wife of Mr. Patrick / Peebles / Who died Febry 12 / 1794 in the 74th / year of her / age." The marble is worn, and soft to the touch, and it was perhaps this quality of softness that reminded Dickinson of alabaster, which, although easy to carve, chips and crumbles easily. "True alabaster is a form of gypsum, the chalky material used to make plaster of paris and sheetrock;" and it is a cousin of marble (for which it is sometimes mistaken), though it does not have quite the same pedigree: marble is monumental, while alabaster (especially in the nineteenth century) was more often employed as an imitation.[9] Though Smith is correct in asserting that alabaster is a biblical stone, she overlooks that it is also one with fairly precise social and geological associations: it is not worth as much as and is less durable than many other raw materials.

Nothing in the cemetery looks like an *above-surface* chamber, but there are three graves adjacent to each other that have granite table-stones: these are possibly the originals for the image of the "Roof of stone." Dickinson would also have been interested by the legend on one of these, which says: "READER / It's dreadful to behold / the seting sun / and night approaching / 'ere your work is done / Mr George Cowan / Oct. 28th 1765 / aged 69 years." The cliché of death-as-night is recovered (and ironized) in the poem's image of the dead sleepers, and the graveyard's folk-art images of skulls-faces with wings attached also find their response in the reference to bees in the second version of the last stanza. Puritan gravestone iconography progressed from a death's head in the seventeenth century to an angel's face in the period between 1740 and 1760, which is roughly consistent with the three gravestones at Pelham, and corresponds to a move away from an emphasis on mortality (or on a struggle between death and the soul) to a more positive view of resurrection's possibilities (with the soul being released from the body by death and rising toward Heaven).[10] Dickinson's own imagery can be seen as a commentary on such iconic practices, as well as a complication of their messages.

This is one of "a few Dickinson poems which use the iconography of the stones" in graveyards, as Thomas A. Zaniello argues.[11] Zaniello quotes two poems of this subgenre, P#1453C (J#1396), "She laid her docile Crescent down," and P#210A (J#182), "If I shouldn't be alive." Franklin, in his notes to P#1453 shows how this iconographic engagement was almost literal in the second version of the poem (B), sent to Elizabeth Holland, which included two newspaper clipping affixed to the paper: "at the left a star and crescent (unidentified source), at the right tombstones leaning against each other (from the *Hampshire and Franklin Express*, 12 December 1856)."[12] Zaniello fails to comment in detail on correspondences between mortuary folk art and the earlier of these two poems, P#210A (as Franklin reproduces it):

If I should'nt be alive
When the Robins come,
Give the one in Red Cravat,
A Memorial crumb –

If I could'nt thank you,
Being fast asleep,
You will know I'm trying
With my Granite lip!

Although most scholars have tried to see the "Granite lip" as the gravestone itself (a kind of Whitmanesque tongue), it is possible to be more accurate and to suggest that the poet has in mind one of the winged angel faces which were commonly carved on stones in the eighteenth century and often featured "mouth-marks" to convey a particular thought or feeling—the frown to remind the viewer of her or his own mortality, for example, or the smile that reassured the viewer of the promise of resurrection. Dickinson's poem features a typical interplay between the living, winged creature of the bird and the inscription of another kind of winged creature representing the desire for immortality. The two images comment on each other, not in any simplistic way, but in a dynamic and restless revision of the values and perspectives they each embody. And as Zaniello goes on to suggest about Hawthorne, there is also a degree of metafiction here, for Dickinson's sophisticated elegiac form comments on the limitations of popular icons for death: the granite lip cannot express its gratitude because the genre, technology, and medium of gravestones did not lend themselves to a nuanced emotional response to the subject of death. Dickinson plays with those limitations in her poem, and with the impossibility of posthumous speech generally (except in fictional form), but adds more depth and variety to the perspectives available on the possibility of posthumous survival. Elegies, it should be recalled, where often carved on grave markers in ancient Greece, and at some level Dickinson's elegist negotiates with the imagery of gravestones in Massachusetts, and with the values that underpin them.

For example, one of the beliefs that P#124 dramatizes at a number of removes is that of soul-sleep, or psychopannychy, defined in the *OED* as "the state in which (according to some) the soul sleeps between death and the day of judgement." Calvin and John Donne both "preferred the metaphor of an extended slumber between the particular and the final judgement," while the majority of New England theologians dismissed the idea of the soul's unconsciousness after death, and Dickinson's first stanza engages in important ways with these doctrines.[13] The suspense reported in the poem is informed by descriptions such as the one in 1 Corinthians 15.52–54, where it is said that the dead shall be raised incorruptible.[14] An assiduous and careful reader of the Bible, Dickinson might also have been thinking of passages such as the following in 1 Thessalonians 4.13–14:

But I would not have you to be ignorant, brethren, concerning them which are asleep, that ye sorrow not, even as others which have no hope.
For if we believe that Jesus died and rose again, even so them also which sleep in Jesus will God bring with him.

Perhaps it is not only the unquestioning acceptance that such passages are literally true but also the elect's taking for granted that such passages apply exclusively to them that allows for the poem to be read as satire, though in other poems (such as P#804D [J#760], "Ample make this Bed"), there is no such marked ironic detachment, and death is accepted as the slumber that not only precedes but also postpones and defers the Second Coming. Indeed, it is possible to argue that such suspension becomes a convenient poetic device for Dickinson, providing a space whereby a kind of life after death could be imagined without entailing commitment to, or certainty of, its existence.

As I said before, not all theologians accepted the idea of there being an interval between death and the resurrection or damnation of the soul: the heirs of Jonathan Edwards, as Barton Levi St. Armand puts it, saw death as "the terrible call to judgement."[15] Indeed, the Bible makes a similar distinction between those who will sleep and wake, and those who will not arise. For example, in 1 Corinthians 15.16–18:

> For if the dead rise not, then is not Christ raised:
> And if Christ be not raised, your faith *is* vain; ye are yet in your sins.
> Then they also which are fallen asleep in Christ are perished.

The note of doubt struck here reverberates in Dickinson's poem: it is not certain if the chosen are as destined for Heaven as they might have believed, nor is it at all clear that the investment of humility can be rewarded in any way. If sleep is the time of dreams, then Heaven and the prospect of eternal reward may be just other illusions. According to the evidence of the senses as they are reported in the poem, it is life at its most pagan and primitive that continues after death, and not the souls of the faithful.

Another possibility for the hostility shown by this first version is that this is one of Dickinson's antidemocratic verses, a slap in the face for those (self-appointed or economically disadvantaged) "meek" and humble members of society who believe that their present suffering will be rewarded posthumously. Such anti-egalitarian statements are not out of place in Dickinson's work: they communicate a political disdain, which occasionally and not unexpectedly emerges from her own privileged socioeconomic position. It is unlikely that any exploited element in society could afford such mortuary grandeur: the extravagant architecture of the tombs suggests that this posthumous population was once comparatively wealthy, and therefore the reference to "meek" must be seen as ironic. In fact, the poem can be seen as a proto-Riffaterrian reworking of Christ's Sermon on the Mount, and the phrase "Blessed are the meek: for they shall inherit the earth" (Matthew 5.5) in particular: the irony is both that the dead do not appear to have been very meek either before or after their passing and that the earth is *all* that they inherit (not the world after the Second Coming, but the ground in which they lie is their reward). However, in the second version of the poem, it is death's indifference to status or skill that the speaker finds disturbing: given Dickinson's preoccupation with aristocracy and royalty, those images that connote the dissolution of wealth, excellence, and power (and its figurative equivalents) all possess personal and potentially terrifying implications.

What is clear, however, is that the first versions of the poem (124A and 124B) close by putting a safe distance between the speaker and that which is spoken about: the tone is comic, as if the scene described had no serious or direct implications for the person doing the describing. The vitality and musicality of the birds and bees are in marked contrast to the silence of the sleeping dead, and nature in general seems not only indifferent to them but even actively dismissive (or dismissive by the actions of its parts): instead of the cycle of birth, life, death, and resurrection, which the references to "morning" and "noon" gesture toward, there is only the literal bustle and activity of morning and noon during the spring and summer seasons. The music produced by nature is also imitated to some extent by the music of the poem itself, for there are many instances of near alliteration (meek members; Resurrection, Rafter, roof/Roof; satin, stone), and assonance (Safe, chambers/Chambers; noon, roof/Roof).[16] In addition, the speaker would appear to share and to applaud nature's propensity for satire: the exclamation mark at the end of the second stanza can signify some private joke or amusement, a subsequent and similar echo of that coined by the breeze and by the local fauna (thought it can additionally function as an indicator of surprise, perhaps even mystification of some kind).

A series of ironic contrasts operates within the poem and provides its framework. For example, if we chart religious aspiration graphically as an upward movement toward Heaven, we can see that a kind of reversal takes place instead: the breeze, insects, and bird life occupy the space that the sleepers below ground aspire to.[17] Of course, it can be argued that it is not the world of nature that the faithful desire, but nevertheless there is a playful inversion at work here that situates believers beneath (and not above) the world they renounced during their lifetimes, but from which they have not been entirely freed by death. This lucid, almost burlesque impulse is continued in the opposition of ignorance and knowledge, which surfaces in the second stanza, for in spite of nature's lack of self-awareness, and despite the reserves of knowledge acquired by the dead, it is the physical world rather than its spiritual counterpart that continues to exist. This is a world almost literally, but comically, turned upside-down: the wise rulers and preachers become mute, impotent idiots, while the unruly fools of nature become overseers and survivors. The penultimate line even ascribes ignorance ambiguously: is it the birdsong that is unintelligent, or is it the listeners who have become stupefied (being asleep, or dead, they are evidently incapable of thought or response)? The final line repeats this ambiguity, for it can be understood as a translation of the birdsong, or as the speaker's final satiric observation: in any case, it tends to blur, and thus to merge, the sardonic voices in the poem.

This element of laughter is important in the poem, for it suggests distance and mockery—the distance that comes with indifference, as well as mockery directed at both the sleepers and the official truth their tombs embody. Mikhail Bakhtin is useful here:

> The serious aspects of class culture are official and authoritarian; they are combined with violence, prohibitions, limitations and always contain an element of fear and of intimidation. These elements prevailed in the Middle Ages. Laughter, on the contrary, overcomes fear, for it knows no inhibitions, no limitations. Its idiom is never used by violence and authority.[18]

The basic contrast in the poem, between the religious dead and the living wilderness, can be extended into a broader opposition between the institutions of established doctrinal worship and the liberated, energetic experiences made available by nature. There is an almost carnivalesque quality to the laughter of the breeze, birds, and bee (it may well be that this spirit of carnival led Dickinson to Venice, famous for its masked processions, in the "C" version of the poem), and it is clear that humor in the poem functions in an adversarial relationship to the literalist (and literal) inertia of the orthodox: as Bakhtin puts it, "Laughter purifies the consciousness of men from false seriousness, from dogmatism, from all confusing emotions."[19] What the speaker can be said to be attacking, therefore, are the paralyzing, enervating effects of spiritual conformity, the stunned submission of the faithful to religious discourses of transcendence and immortality. In particular, the rejection of the body ("Untouched" is repeated in the opening three lines) for a promise of everlasting reward in a nonmaterial afterlife is contrasted with the birds and the bee, associated with sexual activity not only in popular culture generally but in Dickinson's erotic poetry in particular. Whereas the breeze is clearly female, the sleepers are curiously ungendered and sexless. The dynamic, Dionysian performances which are potential within nature everywhere mock the doctrine of a deferred eternity for those who prefer passively to lie and wait. Authority is taunted, hierarchies are turned on their heads, fixed positions are reversed. Similarly, the noises of the world exist in contrast to the silence of death: not for the first time in her work, Dickinson posits a contrast between the Word and the wor(l)d, between the allied forces of nature and poetry and the perceived failures of theology. The tumult of heteroglossia triumphs (however briefly) over the attempt to hush and deny its dialects—though exactly where Dickinson stands in relation to this heteroglossia is difficult to say.[20]

The third (C) version of the poem, believed by Franklin to have been written some two years later, in 1861, collapses the distinction and the distance between speaker and subject, so that it effectively becomes a quite different work. In particular, this variant poem intensifies (to my ear) the deployment of sounds in the last two lines, especially the vowels (drop, Doges, Soundless, dots, on, of, snow) and initial consonants (Diadems, drop, Doges, dots, Disc; surrender, Soundless, snow): the practice is not different from the first version, but the message would appear to be. At one level, the repetition of sounds becomes a mimetic device, a layering of similar auditory entities, which verbally mirrors the layering of flakes in a snow shower. At another level, the poem itself is suddenly, frighteningly foregrounded: like the snow flakes they describe, the words lie cold and silent on the page, and the speaker is reminded that sounds must be enunciated in order to be heard and to live on after their inscription. This self-conscious reading is prompted by the indistinctness of the references to the "dot" and the "Disc of snow," both of which can suggest aspects of writing (punctuation, for instance, as well as the blank page itself) as it is graphically rendered: having admitted that, one concedes the possibility that, although Franklin's transcription of the poem seems perfectly adequate to Dickinson's practices, many twentieth-century readers will find that it regularizes the line sequence and therefore loses the formal disintegration, the meandering and disorientation, which might appear to accompany the contents of this most self-conscious of poems. Of course, if the unit of meaning was the *spoken* poem, then there would be even more tension between the speaker and the silence of the dead.

In other words, the poem becomes implicated in the scene it describes. If the Christian promise that death is merely a sleep that precedes everlasting life is an illusion (a possibility made more explicit by a change of verb in the "C" version from "Sleep" to the more explicitly ambiguous "Lie"), what then becomes of the belief that poetry confers a kind of immortality on its writer? What if, the poem might appear to ask, all of this creative enterprise (this fiction or lie) remains soundless as the marks on a page, which lie unseen and unheard in an unknown place? If the world is indifferent to the Christian dead, why should it behave any differently to the deceased ranks of the literary? What is interesting about such questions is that they are answered much more positively elsewhere: in P#448A (J#449), "I died for Beauty – but was scarce," poetry offers the relatively unproblematic possibility of a kind of life beyond death, the continued presence of relived speech long after the living presence of the speaker has ended. But nineteenth-century immortality may be said to depend on the truth of the resurrection for its credibility: to doubt the one is by implication to doubt the validity of the other. With this in mind the poem can be situated historically between competing institutions of transcendence, the religious, and the literary-poetic, with the demise of one undermining the promises and premises of the other.[21]

What Ralph Franklin calls Dickinson's C version of the poem is therefore a critical as well as a creative reworking of the first, not in the obvious sense that it revises or in the debatable sense that it improves on it, but in that it consciously questions some of the speaker's assumptions in that first attempt. For example, the C version would seem to embrace a wider view of death as a potential threat to *classes* and *empires* in addition to religious hierarchies: "Diadems" and "Doges" are also implicated this time around (emblematic of wealth and power). The reference to the military defeat of Venice at the end of the eighteenth century is an interesting one, and may be seen as an example of Dickinson's use of historical materials under the restricted conditions of temporal and spatial distance. And yet, there are oblique implications for nineteenth-century America as well. When Pennsylvania and New Jersey established their constitutions, they looked to Venice's government as a model.[22] More significant, nineteenth-century America justified territorial aggression and expansion with the claim of a Manifest Destiny; Venice, the supposed burial place of Saint Mark, took the presence of the evangelist's body in the city as a heavenly guarantee of its special destiny (many of its early wars were also fought with westward expansion in mind). Known for its commitment to justice, liberty, and peace, Venice dominated the seas for centuries but fell to the victorious armies of Napoleon in 1797: as Frederick Lane has pointed out, the sea was an early and important source of wealth and power for both republics (and in addition, both began as dependents: Venice as a part of the Byzantine empire, America as an English colony).[23] As a piece of political iconography, Dickinson's reference to the death of the doge has oblique implications for America's quasi-messianic sense of its own significance.

The question to be asked, is what kind of political agenda (if any) the poem's iconoclasm might conceivably serve? It can be argued, as indeed I have, that the first poem subjects hierarchy to radical critique, but this is a very apolitical overthrow: the religious elite are displaced and replaced by figures from nature, a gesture that defuses or disguises the potential element of social radicalism. Even the laughter can be understood as a form of release, a temporary suspension of the inevitable, a nonideological gesture of defiance. As Bakhtin asks in *Rabelais and His World*, "Is there upon earth a more potent means than laughter to resist the mockeries of the world and of fate?"[24] A different kind of hierarchy is set up: the religious establishment might be gotten rid of, but the hierarchical impulse still remains (nature has assumed supremacy). At any rate, those variants of the poem (A and B) represent a flight from doctrine and from the perceived ephemerality of received forms of cultural knowledge (the "sagacity" of the final line in both). The writer's reference to the castle in the second line of the second stanza, first versions, may suggest that nature represents an alternative site of stability and order in the nineteenth century. Ironically, given that the dead have once aspired to the condition of immortality, the poems appear to argue that natural values are eternal, unchanging, and uncorrupted by ideology, which is temporal and temporary.

All of this may represent a rejection of history, the redundancy of the political, which is in itself a deeply conservative reflex. There is something of this in Dickinson's reaction to the Washington Monument which I quoted in the introduction: she seems, on the evidence of the setting at least, to accept Washington's superiority as natural, not as (very literally) constructed. What is interesting about the C version of the poem, however, is the crisis of representation brought about by the failure of authority embodied by the sleeping dead. The promised afterlife has not materialized. Moreover, the millennialist vision shared by the early church fathers has not come about either: instead of Heaven on earth, the last year of the 1850s presages only the fragmentation and dissolution of that vision. All of this has implications for the writing of poetry, which—perhaps more than prose—aspires to the condition of monumentality. Whereas the first version of the poem contrasts the unsuccessful attempt to endure, to achieve fixity through fixed forms, and the free, fluid, and playful patterns of nature, the third version appears to erase this escape route by switching attention in the second stanza to a historical scene. For Dickinson, of course, the fall of Doge Manin is as soundless as the fall of snow because, as Jane Donahue Eberwein points out, Dickinson read about in the *Springfield Republican* and did not directly experience it.[25] It is this distance (temporal and spatial) between events and their expression that, I am persuaded, causes the poem to gaze inward. For what experience(s) does poetry make available if it is mute, page bound rather than uttered? How can these thoughts be transferred to the reader when the writer herself is not there to authorize them?

As I have suggested, the 1859 copies are more obviously satirical, as they contrast the passivity of the "meek members of the Resurrection," with the activity of the natural world above them. Whatever social or religious pretensions the dead may once have entertained are undermined by the freedoms and superiority of the living. By contrast, the 1861 version is more muted and solemn in its treatment because it is less carefree about the nature of death, which is seen as relentless and pervasive as snow. And the cosmic view supersedes the comic one: there is more mystery, more puzzling at the fate and function of the deceased than there was before. The speaker of the first poems almost supposes an escape from the implications of his or her satire, but, in the third, the joke is a little bleaker and blacker: the satire is still there, but the toning down of the narrative voice suggests that it is at everyone's expense. No one escapes: the gradual breakdown of substance is also the reduction of everyone and everything substantial. In choosing between the various copies, therefore, we need to be aware that we are choosing between texts with subtle divergences in the treatment of their subject.

It is even possible that a measure of contrast is offered between the previously satirized members of the exclusive club of the resurrection and the doges; there is an element of permanence about the condition of the former that is opposed by the transitoriness of the latter. The world passes (Margaret Fuller Ossoli described Venice as "a fit asylum for the dynasties of the Past");[26] events, empires, and emperors change; the faithful endure, almost suspended between life and death, this world and the next. This possibility has the effect of returning our attention to the first copies of the poem: What if the bees and birds are the true objects of the poem's humor, for their joy is a result of their inability to think, to distinguish between tenses and times, and therefore to conceive of their own mortality?

The sequence of the trial variants is interesting not least because it shows what Dickinson does to history. In the first versions (A and B), there are no specific historical references, though within the context of a postcolonial American literary tradition, the poem can be represented as satirizing either the original Puritan fathers (and their millenialist program) or the pious members of the Amherst church, including the poet's own father and extended family, who converted to Christianity in successive waves of religious enthusiasm during the nineteenth century.[27] In the third version, historical events and characters are alluded to generally, but are seen as subject to, and subsumed by, vast and indifferent forces whose motivation, function, and purpose are all inexplicable, and this is made all the more forceful by the second line of the second stanza: we know it means something, but exactly how that meaning can be rendered in language is extremely difficult, both for critics and, presumably, for the writer herself. In this reading, identity, status, and achievement are all insignificant when compared to the majestic powers of nature and time. History, and by implication all human activity, is rendered vulnerable and perhaps even void: the poem enunciates the same kind of nihilistic paralysis found in P#291A (J#311), "It sifts from Leaden Sieves," where snow also acts as a metaphor for the accumulative effects of time.[28] (A different gloss on the poem is provided in a letter to Elizabeth Holland in 1880, [L#678], where Dickinson writes that the snow "is so white and sudden it seems almost like a Change of Heart – though I dont mean a 'Conversion' – I mean a Revolution.")[29] It is not at all clear if the speaker is exempt from this process of time by virtue of her ability to see that the vanities of the world are temporary and of no lasting value, though it is possible to argue that the speaker's self-consciousness (she describes in language the limitations of all enterprise, including the linguistic) separates her from the sleepers in that quiet earth and marks her off as different. The satirical element still remains, though, for comparing members of the elect to a political or class-based hierarchy ironically opposes their own religious rationale, but the distance between the person doing the satirizing and the people being satirized is not as wide as it was in the first version of the poem.

Or is it? The self-conscious interpretation of the C text I propose takes it for granted that literature must be implicated in death's erosion of matter. But that may not be the case. It is also possible that the poem proposes a reversal of hierarchies similar to that encountered in the first copies: the kind of historical, religious, or material achievement that are marked by posthumous memorials are mute in comparison with writing's ability to confer speech on the dead, whereas the poet lives on in the minds and mouths of her readers long after she herself has died. History is opposed by story, religious with literary immortality. In this version, the silence of the dead is an index of their failure to establish anything other than a monumental immortality; whether the writer of their epitaph incurs a similar fate is open to question. In a sense, this dilemma is similar to that in Shelley's "Ozymandias": does the disappearance of that massive monument mean that all human activity and endeavor is hopeless? Or can the poem (as John Donne suggests in "The Canonization") function as a cornerstone of eternity? Here too, the poem may be said to establish a distinction between those who are concerned with achieving a material power and recognition, which is ultimately transient, and those (such as poets) who deal with universal, abstract matters and who continue to matter long after their own deaths.

The single reference to a historical actuality (the doge of Venice and his overthrow by Napoleon) is removed in Franklin's next, D, version of Dickinson's second stanza: the cosmic element is further foregrounded, and the references to historical events are replaced with meteorological ones. Again, we can trace Dickinson's mind playing with the possibilities offered by the last few lines of the previous versions: the initial image of snow is developed into a broader preoccupation with freezing and rigidity, qualities that evoke not only rigor mortis but perhaps more generally the inflexibility of religious dogmatism, the original severity of New England Puritanism as it was perceived by later writers like Dickinson, Hawthorne, and Melville. The effect of concentrating on climactic (rather than historical, economic, or social) conditions is to make the poem more abstract and less confined to a particular time and place. This commitment to nonspecificity can be explained in terms of Dickinson's own project of trying to ensure that her poetry outlived its maker: writing to Susan Dickinson about this third of the stanzaic variants, Dickinson implied as much by hoping that she could "make you and Austin – proud – sometime – a great way off."[30]

But this nonspecificity can also be understood as an attempt at stimulating an emotion or sensation equivalent to that which made the poem necessary in the beginning (and one wonders, incidentally, what implications such an affective view of poetry might have for twentieth-century reading practices that attend so intensely to the word as a unit of meaning, and not to the poem as the detonator of an essentially nonverbal experience).

Susan Dickinson is rightly given credit for what is a "remarkably perceptive" criticism of the poem:

> I am not suited dear Emily with the second verse – It is remarkable as
> the chain lightening that blinds us hot nights in the Southern sky but
> it does not go with the ghostly glimmer of the first verse as well as the
> other one – It just occurs to me that the first verse is complete in itself
> it needs no other, and can't be coupled – Strange things always go
> alone – as there is only one Gabriel and one Sun – You never made a
> peer for that verse, and I *guess* you[r] kingdom doesn't hold one – I al-
> ways go to the fire and get warm after thinking of it, but I never *can*
> again.[31]

Though it is easy to overlook the double-edge potential in statements like
"You never made a peer for that verse, and I *guess* you[r] kingdom doesn't
hold one," and in Dickinson's own reply to Susan's comments, which states
that "Your praise is good – to me – because I *know* it *knows* – and *suppose* it
means – ." There is some ambiguity here, but there is also precision: Dickinson distinguishes between her confidence in Susan's capacities as an interpretive editor ("I *know* it *knows*"), and the uncertain motivation for such
criticism ("*suppose* it *means*"). Such remarks are, like many of Dickinson's
poems, intriguing for what they imply but do not directly state, and they
are of interest because they offer us something we do not otherwise have:
an indication of how Dickinson might have functioned in an editorial relationship where there was mutual respect, appreciation, and understanding.

As I have written before, Smith in *Rowing in Eden: Rereading Emily Dickinson* has a long discussion of this poem (and the correspondence it occasioned between the writer and her sister-in-law) in which she promotes
Susan as critic, editor, and audience, prompting Dickinson to new varia-
tions on the same theme. In her reading of this poem and its trial verses,
Smith stresses the multitude of interpretations made available by all the
experimental stanzas, and intriguingly proposes each one of the four alternatives as possible critiques of Victorian attitudes to female sexuality. According to her, the dead are wives who are "pure in a dutiful sexuality,
untainted by lust or passionate desire."[32] Smith's remarks can be developed
further in the direction of a reading that conflates gender and literary issues, for there is no doubt that the last two of the four variants for the
second stanza employ a vocabulary closer to the domestic, and thus to the

feminine sphere as it was defined conventionally by nineteenth-century American society. Alabaster itself was used for domestic as well as mortuary purposes: in the Evergreens, for example, there are decorative alabaster objects dating from the latter half of the nineteenth century, which shows how fashionable these were among the middle classes in particular.[33] Brita Lindberg-Seyersted was the first to maintain that the first stanza contains within itself the potential for such a gender-related reading: "The metaphors for the coffin-grave are made up of terms from more than one vocabulary: the domestic connotations of 'chambers,' 'Rafter,' and 'Roof' combine with the terms of mineralogy. 'Satin' belongs to a more specifically feminine branch of domesticity."[34]

There is a sense of imagistic osmosis here: the C version may appear to contain more references to males than to females, but it should be remembered that Venice in the nineteenth century was conceived of as female and given names like "La Serenissima" and "The Pearl of the Adriatic." However, my own sense of this is that although the identification of the dead with women does not necessarily increase as the sequence progresses, it does become a more explicit concern in the penultimate revision. Note for instance the clothing associations of the word "buckle": in *Seven Types of Ambiguity*, William Empson has a section on Hopkin's "Windhover" in which he writes: *Buckle* admits of two tenses and two meanings: "they do buckle here," or "come, and buckle yourself here"; *Buckle* like a military belt, for the discipline of heroic action, and *Buckle* like a bicycle wheel, "make useless, distorted, and incapable of its natural motion."[35]

Mention is made, as Smith also notices, of "Sills," "Window," "Door," and "Tents," all of which can be associated with home and the woman's accepted sphere of industry (though it seems to me that the force of Dickinson's capitalization, here as elsewhere, is to lift the word out of its literal and into a figurative context, or at least to occasion a dynamic between a depicted scene of death and the domestic terms of the description). There is as well a reference to "Tribes," and therefore to procreation. Again, the concern with language (or nonlanguage) which is thematically consistent in all the variants is pursued: instead of sounds, there are "Echoes," or the ghosts of sounds, and "numb[ness]," a desensitized state that not only approximates death but is close in sound to "dumb[ness]" or the muteness that is at once caused by death and something other or more than it. For muteness can be a muzzling as well as a medically defined condition, and echoing can be seen as a woman's dutiful reflex, emptily repeating what husbands, brothers, and fathers pronounce upon. Clearly, this has a literary analogue: if women's options are confined to the home, defined as silent muse, housewife, or the subject of domestic fiction, then what awaits them for a reward are elegies such as this one, rather than lyrics bodying forth the full possibilities of identity and language. This is as close to a radical feminist position as Dickinson will allow herself, and in truth it emerges from a psychological as much as a political imperative—the fear of becoming a nameless, faceless nonbeing whose importance is ultimately related in terms of her biological function.

In the next variant (that is, the fourth major variation of the second stanza that is recorded in the "E" copy), Dickinson once more takes up the issue of speechlessness by changing "Echoes" in line two to "silence." The change from "sills" to "seals" is perhaps more than a shift of location from deserted home to frozen landscape: it can also be understood as a familiar attempt to defamiliarize, to make the poem more evocative and less specific. In fact, "seals" recalls the use of the same word (this time a verb, not a noun) by Wordsworth in one of the Lucy poems, "A slumber did my Spirit Seal." In poem and title, "Seal" possesses a similar ambiguity, since it signifies both a perceived mark of approval and a dangerous closure to the reality of time. Indeed, there are further parallels between Dickinson's variant and Wordsworth's poem: in both, the speakers report death in a kind of detached, neutral tone that implies shock, bewilderment—and perhaps lack of comprehension. In addition, both suggest the continuing and mysterious movement of a universe indifferent to human beings and to their feelings for and toward each other. The implication seems to be that humanity does not exist outside nature, but is caught up in its process. The world observes laws that are relentless, even irresistible, and that operate independently of human concerns.

This third major variant of the second stanza invites us to consider the content of the original (A and B) versions, which are very different in spirit. Gone are the carnivalesque noise and movement, which mock the dead, and in their place is the slow, gradual disengagement of spring from winter, when glaciers crumble and icicles begin to melt. As critics like Smith have already pointed out, there is a potentially sexual charge to some of these lines: although the stiffness of the silence needs no paraphrase, the unhooking of the frost seems akin to a loosening of constrictive clothing, and spring shakes the dead (or the graves, which are substituted for them) in the way that a lover will attempt to waken a sleeping partner. A warm, fluid physicality is set against the rigid and unyielding nature of the dead. But this eroticism, if it exists, is muted compared to the frank celebration of corporeality in the first version, and here the focus is more on escape, the act of organic resurrection seeming to displace and even (again) deny the human aspiration for immortality. Like Lazarus, the earth awakes with painful sluggishness, and almost with reluctance. Crucially, however, the natural is still described in human terms: the animation of nonanimate elements such as seasons, frosts, and icicles can function doubly, indicating both a physical rebirth, which mocks the possibility of a spiritual one, and a paradigm, which human beings must necessarily aspire to (the pattern of yearly renewal inspiring the hope of life after death even in the face of resurrection's apparent absurdity).

The verb "hook" can have several implications, including "catch," "capture," or "secure": unhooking is therefore a kind of release not only from the imprisonment by winter, but perhaps more generally from the state of mind represented by the dead, whose "stiffness" suggests their stern inflexibility, perhaps even their disdain. The verb "Refutes" connotes a kind of pride bordering on arrogance, while "Marble" hints at a similar vanity that stands in opposition to the supposed status of "meek members of the Resurrection." Finally, there is a standard pun in the last line that implies not only that the dead are unable to respond to nature (their darkness standing in opposition to the daylight of suns), but that this inability further hints at the impossibility of their aspirations for rebirth: Dickinson, and writers before her (Taylor most notably), often punned on "sun" as "son" (or Christ, Son of Man), and the failure of the dead to react in any way to the sun (or even to *want* to react) suggests that their convictions are either misplaced or bankrupt. Perhaps there is even a reference to the summer solstice here, which would link this version of the second stanza with the first version ("Light laughs the breeze"): the sun in the air at midnight signifies the brief triumph of a pagan god, while within the graves nothing stirs and all is darkness.

Any single Dickinson poem can be approached in a variety of ways—and these are not necessarily mutually exclusive. To begin with, each poem (with or without its variants) exists potentially as a sufficient unit of meaning: the separate but related versions of "Safe in their alabaster chambers" (as they are listed in the Franklin edition) contain within themselves the kinds of linguistic resources and dialectic tensions that I see as operating generally in many of Dickinson's best poems. Indeed, one could go so far as to suggest that this particular indeterminacy can be understood as an identifying characteristic—Dickinson's style or poetic signature—and even as a possible criterion of excellence, a means of indicating which were the most effective and successful poems. In putting forward this argument, I do not propose to have discovered a poetic that can apply to every example of her work, but I try instead to trace some of the reasons for the interpretational multiplicity that I and others allege to be made available by Dickinson's poems.

A poem also derives some of its significance from the manner, time, and place of its first appearance (or nonappearance), and "Safe in their alabaster chambers" is no exception, for all the complexity of its various times and media of publication. A further copy of the poem was sent to Higginson as well, and the choice of the C version might suggest that the writer had decided that this was the best one (or decided at that time that it was the one she liked best, or that it was the one most likely to please Higginson). It is interesting that this version (which I have transcribed from a photostat at the Boston Public Library, but which is represented in the Franklin edition as P#124F) is also the most experimental in terms of line arrangement and word division, if one takes seriously (as I certainly do not in this instance) the suggestion that these are intentional and not accidental features:

Safe in their Alabast-
ter Chambers –
Untouched by Morning –
And untouched by noon –
Sleep the meek mem-
bers of the Resurrection –
Rafter of Satin and
Roof of Stone –

Grand go the Years,
In the Crescent above
them –
Worlds scoop their Arcs –
And Firmaments – row – [page break]
Diadems – drop –
And Doges – surrender –
Soundless as Dots,
On a Disc of Snow.[36]

The inclusion of this, with three other poems (P#204B [J#318], "I'll tell you how the Sun rose – ; P#304B [J#319], "The nearest Dream recedes – unrealized – "; and P#282A [J#320], "We play at Paste": a variant of "I'll tell you how the Sun rose – " is also included in Fascicle 10 with "Safe in their Alabaster chambers") provides us with further environments within which the poem can be read—both that of the poet's correspondence with Higginson and as a poetic cluster in themselves. Still another context of interpretation for the poem would exist at the levels of its various material inscriptions. Fascicle 6 has an additional sixteen poems, transcribed about 1859 on four sheets of cream stationery, lightly ruled, and "embossed PAR-SONS PAPER Co. within a decorated vertical oval."[37] The paper measures approximately 19.9 centimeters in length and 12.3 centimeters in breadth (roughly 7½by 5 inches). Written on five sheets of paper, "cream with a blue rule, and not embossed" or watermarked, Fascicle 10 contains twenty-two poems in total (including P#247A, [J#233], "The Lamp – burns sure – within"), and was probably assembled around 1860 or 1861. The sheet on which the poem is recorded measures 20.6 by 13 centimeters (or 8.8 by 5.8 inches). The first four words of the opening line ("Safe in their Alabaster") measure about 7.4 centimeters in Fascicle 6 (and the spaces between the words are about 4 millimeters), while they take up 9 centime-ters in Fascicle 10 (and the space between them increases to about 7 milli-meters): Dickinson also allows herself slightly more space on the left-hand side of the margin in Fascicle 10. I list these facts and figures because in the version of the poem in Fascicle 6, the first line fits together as one ("Safe in their Alabaster"), while in Fascicle 10, the same phrase is ar-ranged over two lines, "Safe in their Alabaster / chambers." In the sixth fascicle, the first stanza contains six lines, in the tenth fascicle it extends to eight.

Safe in their Alabaster Chambers –
Untouched by morning
And untouched by noon –
Sleep the meek members of the Resurrection –
Rafter of satin,
And Roof of stone.

(P#124B, Fascicle 6)

Safe in their Alabaster
chambers –

Untouched by Morning –
And untouched by Noon –
Lie the meek members of
the Resurrection –
Rafter of Satin – and Roof
of Stone!

(P#124E, Fascicle 10. [Franklin fails to record the division after Roof.])

After "Alabaster" in (P#124E), about 2.4 centimeters of space remain after the end of that word to the right-hand edge of the page, while the word "chambers" takes up approximately 3 centimeters (with the dash, 3.5). Clearly, the run-on could be because Dickinson realized she didn't have enough room. In addition, she leaves roughly eight centimeters of space after "chambers," which suggests either a deliberate visual and semantic isolation of the word, or an indication that it belongs to the line that preceded it: much the same can be said of the word "Resurrection" (and its subsequent dash) in the sixth line, where there is about 5.3 centimeters of unused space available, and "Stone!" in the eight line, where there is about 7.3 centimeters of space. In the three-volume variorum edition of 1955, and in the one-volume *Complete Poems*, Johnson transcribed this stanza as five lines; Franklin does the same in his 1998 variorum. A modern editor of the manuscript school (I am persuaded) would allow them to stand as eight.[38] But there is nothing on the page to suggest that Johnson and Franklin were wrong to do what they did: on the contrary, the evidence of the blank spaces can be exploited legitimately to support their conclusions. Although the differences between the versions of the poems recorded in the fascicles might prompt one to speculate on the degree to which the line arrangements can be described as significant, they are probably due to the arbitrary relationship of the handwriting and the physical space on the page. In this context, it is also interesting that the dashes in the sixth fascicle (P#124B) version are more irregular in shape than those in the tenth fascicle (P#124E), which are fairly uniform: this seems to interrupt and perhaps even to reverse the contemporary assumption that Dickinson became *more* attentive to the visual potential of the inscribed work about the time of the ninth fascicle. But it is dangerous to attempt to superimpose any kind of narrative on Dickinson's poetry: the regular dashes of the tenth fascicle "Safe in their Alabaster chambers" simply make it more difficult to arrive at a coherent and consistent picture of the deliberateness of chirographic practices. There are many gaps in the recoverable evidence about the use of the dash, and some apparent contradictions such as this one. These inconsistencies may mean that Dickinson abandoned experimenting with the dash around this time (to take it up again later); or that it was important to her (as it was not when she wrote the sixth) that this particular notebook be transcribed as neatly and legibly as possible; or (most radically) that there never was such a thing as dash experimentation.

What are the social and political meanings of such manuscript transmission? In the seventeenth century, circulation of handwritten poems and miscellanies would not have been unusual among a certain class of gentlemen writer. Even in Dickinson's time, this kind of circulation was essentially elitist—although one might argue about whether the elitism was primarily sociopolitical (trying to ensure that one's poems circulated among, and helped to bond, members of one's own class) or literary (trying to ensure that those who read the work would have the education and training properly to appreciate and respond to its subjects), or indeed whether these can be separated.[39] Dickinson's style may be seen as a kind of aesthetic contraception, ensuring that only readers of a certain kind could approach her work. It may also be that, as a woman who appeared ambivalent (or selective) about society generally, she found manuscripts a more congenial form of publication, though it also seems plausible that the kind of alternative publication Dickinson engaged in enabled her to preserve a sense of social superiority that was important to her. At the same time, it provided her with a sense of artistic dignity, integrity, and self-worth, which ordinary print, with its standardization of punctuation and language, may not have afforded. Again, it is hard to say if the motivation for rejecting print as a medium is social or aesthetic or gender related: perhaps it is all three.

A poem has a variety of contexts and among the most important are the historical ones. It is always tempting to say that, like the larger body of poetry, a lyric poem doesn't have a wider historical significance: but sometimes there are very specific historical circumstances and conditions that add value and depth to our understanding of a poem's imagery. The work of Daniel Lombardo, the curator of special collections at the Jones Library, is especially useful in this respect—and particularly for those of us who live outside Amherst and America—because the photographs and stories Lombardo records about the town Dickinson lived in often provide fascinating insights into Dickinson's poetry. For instance, in his latest collection, *Images of America: Amherst and Hadley*, he includes the 1905 photograph of a blacksmith and tells us that "for less money than a skilled carpenter or mason could make, the blacksmith suffered extreme heat, noise, and dangerous kicks from his clients."[40] (Although this photograph postdates Dickinson's poem, Lombardo's description of the work itself is useful.) Neither the photograph and text nor the book as a whole take Dickinson as their primary agenda, and yet the comments do remind us that blacksmiths were common in the poet's day, and therefore part of the store of images and phrases which she had to draw on for her own habits of self-definition and exploration through poetry.

> In an age when most transportation still depended on horses, no community could function without at least one blacksmith. Horses pulled farm wagons and family buggies. They hauled heavy freight to and from factories, ware-houses, depots and wharves. Many stores owned single-horse delivery wagons (often with business advertisements painted on the sides), and all sorts of delivery services—such as ice and coal—used wagons and carts. . . . Blacksmiths had to keep this necessary motive power well shod. . . . In addition to shoeing horses, mules, and oxen, they repaired wagons and, in agricultural towns, sharpened plows and other farming implements. Small towns sometimes offered good blacksmiths free town lots as incentive for them to settle in the community.[41]

Such knowledge, I am persuaded, helps to counteract the understandable tendency of readers to see the occasions of Dickinson's poetry as exclusively philosophical, or religious, or emotional. Her images and words derive much of their charge from their wider social contexts. In understanding P#401C (J#365), "Dare you see a Soul at the 'White Heat'?," for example, it is perhaps useful to know that Perez Dickinson, Samuel Fowler Dickinson's brother, was a blacksmith, a farmer, and a mill owner, and that (in 1869, seven years after that poem's estimated date of composition), there were seven blacksmiths working in Amherst (one on Main Street and another near the depot, and therefore within Dickinson's immediate geographical vicinity), and that the *Hampshire and Franklin Gazette* often reported on the rapid turnover and changes of location of blacksmiths.[42]

Dare you see a Soul at the "White Heat"?
Then crouch within the door –

Red – is the Fire's common tint –
But when the quickened Ore

Has sated Flame's conditions –
She quivers from the Forge
Without a color, but the Light
Of unannointed Blaze –

Least Village, boasts it's Blacksmith –
Whose Anvil's even ring
Stands symbol for the finer Forge
That soundless tugs – within –

Refining these impatient Ores
With Hammer, and with Blaze
Until the designated Light
Repudiate the Forge –

4 quickened] vivid 5 sated] vanquished 6 She] it

Division 1 the | 9 Blacksmith] Black- | smith 12 within – ||

Blacksmiths advertised their wares and innovations in the Amherst newspapers and in the town directory: their failures were indicated by stories
about auctions (in the former) and by their intermittent disappearances
(recorded in the latter). Dickinson's poem is partly an act of self-promotion
and partly a challenge (both to blacksmiths and to readers): she imagines
herself as the fashioner of something much more necessary and lasting
than objects of utility and trade (she may also be responding to the ephemerality of some blacksmiths, not all of whom were sufficiently skilled or
fortunate enough to stay employed for long periods of time). There are
additional class aspects: the careful distinction between "common" and
"finer," as well as the double act of renunciation ("Light" from the "Forge"
of the poem, and the scene of the poem from real forges and blacksmiths)
and the fairly typical hierarchies of mental and manual forms of labor (nowhere more apparent than in the wonderful sleight of hand in the third
stanza, which points out the very real need for blacksmiths and then immediately converts them into ciphers of a superior spiritual manufacture).
The designation and differentiation of color (there is a clear progression

from red through black to white) potentially echoes nineteenth-century "scientific" discourses of racist supremacy, though since they refer to the procedure by which metals are shaped and made durable, this may very well be accidental (though one wonders incidentally how a champion of manuscript turnovers might respond to the potential pun made available in "Least Village boasts it's Black"). One detects a sense of competition too, a need to feel needed (masked, though, by the speaker's insertion of herself into an invented narrative of indispensability in the third stanza and by the assertiveness of the first line), as well as an urge to transform energies (thoughts, words, desires) into objects of substance and permanent value (poems, souls). Although I have commented earlier on poems that appeared to dismiss the significance of a poem's making (P#247A [J#233], "The Lamp burns sure – within," and P#930A [J#883], "The Poets light but Lamps") I believe that this one has been constructed as reversing that impulse, almost inviting the reader to watch the poem as it is being composed (albeit after it is written). In this instance, choosing a manuscript version of the poem would appear to make better sense, because it takes as its subject the restless forces of inspiration: with print, what we get is a finished product rather than the original scene and process of production, and in a sense a printed text readjusts the balance of the poem's concerns in favor of the last three lines (which deal with what has already left the forge). Whether or not a printed version seriously distorts the poem, as Paul Crumbley argues eloquently in *Inflections of the Pen*, is another question: the autograph version clearly has merits because it reproduces textually the animation it describes, but there is a sense in which seeing the poem in manuscript actually closes down the meaning and makes it more self-referential (or suggests a formal correlation between the conditioning of the forge and the regularization of print).[43] Dickinson herself, when she sent a copy of the poem to Higginson (in November 1880), entitled it "Cupid's Sermon," which suggests how different her purposes might have been from ours.[44] And though Crumbley contrasts the efforts of the blacksmith-wordsmith "to create a poem that effaces the stages of its creation" and argues that this "is at odds with the manuscript Dickinson left," it does seem allowable that the poem (even in manuscript form) can never fully perform the process of its own creation when it has already been written: it can only re-create, reconstruct, represent.[45] We arrive at the site of manufacture, as it were, only to witness a working model of former manufacturing practices: the poem is its own museum, and by the time we get to it, the originating light has left. Indeed, with

"The Lamp burns sure – within" and "The Poets light but Lamps," a different view of the poetic process is implied, one that does in fact emphasize the independence of the finished product from the process of its construction. A printed version of "Dare you see a Soul at the 'White Heat'?" more effectively enacts the inevitable distance between the scene of writing and the completed object.

If the recoverable evidence of Dickinson's attitudes to the scene of writing is conflicting (as I think it might be), we need to acknowledge that Dickinson may have operated with more than one view of literary performance and that she was interested in both the course of writing and its presentation as a completed object. In his book *Identity and Relationship*, Jeremy Hawthorn quotes a passage from Marx that has interesting implications for exactly these kinds of issues:

> it is generally by their imperfections as products, that the means of production in any process assert themselves in the character of products. A blunt knife or weak thread forcibly remind us of Mr. A., the cutler, or Mr. B., the spinner. In the finished product the labour by means of which it has acquired its useful qualities is not palpable, has apparently vanished.[46]

What we are seeing in these poems are responses to the complexities of the industrial and manufacturing method of production as they impinge on and inform the arena of creative expression and transmission. Since Dickinson did not publish in the conventional sense, it can be said that it is precisely this aspect of "imperfection" that sends us back to their "means of production." But in "The Lamp burns sure – within" and "The Poets light but Lamps" the law of invisibility Marx describes seems more pertinent: the labor by which this small object of illumination (lamp and poem) functions has vanished, and the speakers of the poems seem to accept this (which is not to say that their creator does).[47] Taken together, the three poems might be seen as dramatizing differing literary theories, all in ways that can usefully be related to larger social issues.

In chapter 6, I mentioned "Dare you see a Soul at the 'White Heat'?" as one of the eighteen poems that make up Fascicle 20, and suggested that it would be worthwhile to look at Dickinson's manufacture of hand-bound volumes as an extension of the alienation that might lie under the surface of her poem: her private volumes exist in opposition to the anthologies of literature produced in greater numbers during the second half of the nineteenth century. The poem's promotion of a single, anonymous speaker above the very public blacksmith mirrors the writer's own dedication to the privatization of poetry, the pursuit of the single author against the multiple (or magazine) author. This privileging has very clear class correlatives, though they may not fully explain Dickinson's reasons for writing and publishing as she did.

The fascicle placement of "Dare you see a Soul at the 'White Heat'?" results in patterns of theme and imagery that link the poem to others in the collection but also subtly highlights their differences. This poem is typical, for instance, in that it begins with a reference to a door, which echoes the "door" of P#405A (J#366), "Although I put away his life" (the tenth in the sequence), and the "gate" of the second poem, P#397A (J#1761), "A train went through a burial gate," but it is atypical because here the door is open whereas many of the other entrances in the same fascicle (for example, the "Door" in the last stanza of P#407A [J#670], "One need not be a Chamber – to be Haunted," and in the first stanza of P#409A [J#303], "The Soul selects her own Society") are closed. The poem characteristically employs color and brilliance as a structural trope in the same way as P#411A (J#528), "Mine – by the Right of the White Election!" Another shared detail is the reference to an experience so intensely overwhelming that it can only be compared to an act of force or violence: here, the transformation the poem describes is akin to the burning and shaping of raw materials into tools and utensils. The "Hammers" of the third poem in the series, P#398A (J#364), "The Morning after Wo," become the "Hammer" of this, the sixth poem, and both allude to the crucifixion, but both draw very different conclusions: P#398A seems to suggest that death opens up a gap between physical creation and its biblical explanation (a gap that widens to an abyss in P#399A [J#524], "Departed – to the Judgement," where death is followed by two worlds dispersing), whereas "Dare you see a Soul at the 'White Heat'?" is potentially more conventional—death and suffering are agents of transcendence and release the soul from the body. The trouble with such a reading (which at one level is entirely valid) is that it makes the poem rather static, for the second stanza then becomes a simple reiteration of the first—and a redundant one at that. That would make the poem a kind of exercise in the Puritan plain style explicating metaphor, controlling and regulating its implications. In fact, the effect of the second stanza seems to be exactly the reverse: it unsettles the established meanings (those that would be informed by the traditional Christian association of light with divinity) and suggests the possibility of other approaches to transcendence—that of poetry, for example, or love.

The poem's preoccupation with whiteness clearly relates it to the one immediately preceding it in the sequence, P#400A (J#525) "I think the Hemlock likes to stand," a curious poem that attempts to reattach scriptural explanations of creation to natural phenomena: in this instance, the tree of the titular first line is seen as a kind of solitary figure who renounces the world and thrives on privation (like a prophet in the wilderness or in the desert, the speaker suggests). It is difficult to see if Dickinson is attempting to displace the Bible or to graft its meanings back onto the known (thus harmonizing human activities and emotional needs with those of nature), but what *is* clear is that "Dare you see a Soul at the 'White Heat?' " reverses the preponderance of icy images (there are references to Lapland, Norway, and Russia) and concentrates on intense heat instead (though both are linked by improvising on a similar theme of whiteness), perhaps corroborating Martha O'Keefe's belief that Dickinson composed in pairs of opposites.⁴⁸48 Jane Donahue Eberwein also notices the difference:

> Her juxtaposition of "I think the Hemlock likes to stand" ([J]#525) with "Dare you see a Soul at the 'White Heat?' "([J]#365) offers a sharp contrast. The hemlock—black, massive, nobly drooping tree that she identifies with northern climates and races (such as her own)—finds the complement of its dark power in the snow because, she says, it satisfies "An instinct for the Hoar, the Bald." In some moods, anyway, Dickinson too shared this craving that satisfied her awe with its austerity; and she may have complemented the blackness of her tragic moods with Lapland's chill pallor.⁴⁹

If this procedure for reading poems according to their placement in a fascicle works for J#365, it is certainly true for P#124, "Safe in their alabaster chambers" and suggests that many of Dickinson's poems also exist in other environments, outside the biographical, literary, and social frame of her relationship to Susan and other intimates. The change of media from epistolary exchange to manuscript volume also involves a potential shift of audience or context. As I have already written, versions of the poem appeared separately in Fascicles 6 (the first version with the second stanza beginning "Light laughs the breeze") and 10 (the second, third, and fourth versions of the second stanza). Fascicle 6 has an additional sixteen poems, and Fascicle 10 has a total of twenty-two—including the poem discussed earlier, P#247A "The Lamp burns sure – within." What difference, if any, does the placement of the poem in these separate environments entail for our reading?

In the sixth fascicle, "Safe in their Alabaster Chambers" has a disruptive effect, for most of the other poems in the collection deal very conventionally with the subject of death: the seventh poem (P#142A [J#129], "Cocoon above! Cocoon below!"), for instance, sees Dickinson borrowing from Edward Hitchcock's *Religious Lectures on Peculiar Phenomena in the Four Seasons* and—perhaps—from an illustration entitled "Emblems of the Resurrection," in comparing a butterfly emerging from its cocoon with a man's escape from the tomb (the word "Escape" provides the starting point for a similar meditation in the ninth poem of the sequence, P#144B [J#77], "I never hear the word 'Escape' ").[50] The imagery of flowers links it to others in the sequence: the second for instance (P#137B [J#74], "A lady red – amid the Hill") uses the coming of flowers as the first intimation of spring, and therefore of immortality, while the fifteenth (P#127A [J#133], "As children bid the Guest 'Good Night' ") shows Dickinson's thoroughly domesticating nature by describing plants as children who go reluctantly to bed but wake happily in the morning. The sleepers of "Safe in their alabaster chambers," by contrast, are much less sentimentalized: they give expression to an impulse that mocks the solemnity of middle- and upper-class death rituals and the piety of P#127A, though their usage is closer to that of P#141B [J#75], "She died at play," where the sudden death of the subject, who sinks "as gaily as a Turk / Opon a Couch of flowers," hides a measure of terror at death's random and mysterious intrusions: both may be seen as examples of what Gary Lee Stonum calls the Dickinson sublime.

The absorbing thing about "Safe in their alabaster chambers" is that it exists in several contexts—that of its fascicle placement, and that of Susan's relationship with Emily: privileging a single transcription of the poem can therefore make it easier to assimilate into a theoretical narrative of one's own making. This procedure is a valuable reminder of how editorial considerations can determine critical readings, and of how a critical perspective can be advanced by textual choices. What are the implications for the supposed narrative of the fascicles that many of the poems also appeared elsewhere (of the seventeen in Fascicle 6, for instance, fully eleven were sent to Susan)? By extension, what (if anything) are the consequences for the writerly relationship between Susan and Emily that Susan was sent eleven of the poems and not the full seventeen? My own approach is not immune to the prejudices I describe. What are the repercussions for a historical perspective on the poems to know that they were withdrawn from a fuller circulation in, and engagement with, public discourses? The political reading that I offered as a possibility for the first versions of the poem (those with "Light laughs the breeze" as their second stanza), for instance, does not seem immediately relevant to the tone or theme of the sixth fascicle, which deals with questions of spirituality and treats the subject of death in a positive but socially nonspecific manner. Even then, however, one could focus on the recurrent imagery of anonymous courage in the face of death, and especially on the references to soldiers (in P#136B [J#73], "Who never lost, are unprepared," the first in the fascicle; in P#138A [J#126], "To fight aloud, is very brave," the third; and in P#144B [J#77], the ninth), which are quite clearly related to political fears about the Civil War and the dissolution of the Union (the fascicle is estimated to have been collated in 1859). In light of that historical sense, my reading might be justified and related to others because it reflects a fear of political unrest that can be associated with more abstract feelings of transience and insubstantiality. The political climate can be seen as disrupting the apparent Christian narrative of the fascicle because the image that the nineteenth-century United States had of itself as an empire is bound up so indelibly with Puritan ideas of the City upon the Hill: if that project were to fail, then perhaps the role the individual American had in God's plans would be similarly weakened.

Of course, the fact that one approach to the poem may run counter to its significance as a structural element of a fascicle does not necessarily invalidate that reading, and the point to make is that Dickinson's own editorial narratives (or those she constructed for Susan Dickinson and Higginson) need not be seen as being definitive, no matter how much valuable information they yield about their meanings: the poems create their own contexts, and anyone with a copy of the Variorum edition and Rosenbaum's *Concordance* can come up with other constellations of meaning that would be equally valid and enlightening. One cannot insist that any reading of a single poem take into account the various occasions and genres of its publication and reception (although such an insistence may be the direction Dickinson scholarship is presently taking), because such a tendency privileges certain contexts over others and overdetermines texts that in many instances seem to insist on their own emancipation from a multitude of defining circumstances. And yet, the advantage of such approaches, no matter how text based they might seem, is that they actually reach outside and beyond the text to the people in Dickinson's life and letters: they succeed in *humanizing* her poetry in ways that help to correct the legacy of inaccurate or impressionistic versions of her withdrawal from nineteenth-century society. There are two ways of looking at this: on the one hand, one can criticize such efforts because they open up Dickinson's world only slightly in order to admit a few close friends and family members, and on the other hand, one can celebrate the fact that the closed door, which often accompanies our image of Dickinson, has begun to open slightly wider than before.

Every day for almost a year, in all kinds of inner and outer weather, I sat in the Special Collections Room at the Jones Library in Amherst from ten in the morning until five in the early evening and wrote about Emily Dickinson. Each day too, I watched a succession of visitors who came either to view the permanent exhibition on Dickinson's life or to browse through the archives in search of family genealogies and local history. The people who go there are not usually specialists or scholars: they tend to be divided between fans and enthusiasts fascinated by Dickinson and the students, town professionals, and retired individuals who require information about people, places, and events of previous years. What unites them is an involvement with the experiences of the past and a commitment to know more about, and to preserve what is meaningful from, those experiences. This book emerged from a similar combination of interests: as well as reading the poetry (in autograph and typographic forms), I have spent a long time looking at nineteenth-century maps of Amherst, tax records, copies of the census, account books, and ledgers from the Hampshire Agricultural Society, records of the Amherst and Belchertown Railroad Company, pages of the *Hampshire and Franklin Express* (on microfiche), Amherst business directories, family genealogies, and documents recording the purchase and sale of property owned by the Dickinsons at the Hampshire County Registry of Deeds at Northampton, in order to reconstruct for myself the world that Emily Dickinson looked out on from the four south- and west-facing windows of the second-story bedroom in the Main Street Homestead where she wrote from 1855 to 1886. What she left out I have tried to include in my research; what she took for granted, I have tried to reconstruct—not in order to oppose her but to attempt to understand the fuller complexity of her reasons for omitting and presupposing some things rather than others.

Emily Dickinson wrote in an age of increased migration and spiraling immigration: around 60,000 people came to America in the decade in which she was born, a number that increased to 1,700,000 in the 1840s and to 2,600,000 in the 1850s.[51] The trajectories of a Dickinson life were sometimes mapped out by such accidents: because he needed to acquire a profession, Dickinson's brother briefly taught the children of Irish immigrants in Boston, but he entered the law instead, found an outlet for his interest in culture and nature by collecting art and planting trees, and embraced a private politics of reaction, which is occasionally shown in his correspondence. Dickinson's own preoccupation with home and family suggests an anxiety about both that is partly informed by the social and political realities of her day. Society was under pressure: assimilation and relocation of Native Americans revealed some of the more widespread fears at the heart of American politics at that time (it has been said that "The Soul Selects her own Society" is a classic expression of a domestic policy that reacts to the foreign by closing its doors). As people pushed westward and southward into "new" territories that had been occupied by Native Americans for centuries, warfare broke out on a number of fronts: in 1862, one of the peak years of Dickinson's creative enterprise, thirty-eight Dakota Sioux were hanged in the largest mass execution in U.S. history. These years were also the period of agitation by women for rights, votes, and increased access to public spheres of influence: the landmark Women's Rights Convention was held at Seneca Falls, New York, in 1848 and a national convention was held there in 1850. At the same time, the nation's expanding economic and industrial capacities, together with the growth and ethnic diversification of the workforce, consolidated differences and unsettled relations between the laboring, propertied, and capitalist classes. There was increasing unrest and violent confrontation: in 1877, a strike that began as a protest by railroad workers against wage reductions in Baltimore and Ohio spread east and west to other cities and there were riots.[52] Several members of the Mollie Maguires, a secret organization of Irish miners in Pennsylvania, were hanged between June 1877 and January 1879.

As Joanne Dobson and a number of other scholars have pointed out,[53] these details are almost completely absent in Dickinson's poems, and when they appear in the letters, they are often the occasion for some private witticism, as in this letter to Elizabeth Holland in early January 1879: "I am glad you are not hung – like the "Mollie Maguires," tho' doubtless heinous as themselves – in a sweet way."[54]

The minutiae of nineteenth-century life, the stories that made the newspapers that Emily and Vinnie read to each other, rarely appear directly in Dickinson's poetry. And yet they are ambiguously present. For instance, in early June 1864, Dickinson sent Higginson (then in the south with his regiment) a copy of the first stanza of P#820A [J#827], where she claimed that "The only New I know / Is Bulletins all day / From immortality," and there is a tension between the meaning prompted by the placement of these lines in a letter to a participant in the Civil War (Dickinson read of constant casualties in the newspapers) and the implication that, despite the war, the only news worth attending to was the "simple News that Nature told" (P#519A [J#441]). There are power struggles within power struggles here (North and South, public soldier and private poet, man of society and asocial woman) that remind us that politics and history do not have the theater of their performances only in Washington and in war.

Who knows for certain what contests are enacted in the verbal spaces of references to "market" and "markets" (three times), "scaffolds" (three times),[55] "wampum" (once, in P#140B, J#128), "scalp[ing]" (twice), and in the absence of any reference to African Americans, Native Americans, Chinese, Irish, immigrants, and laborers? My work is an attempt to direct attention to these absences, and to ask why they occur. To some extent, this is explicable in the sense that western Massachusetts in general and Amherst in particular were not major urban centers of industrial, ethnic, and class conflict—though Dickinson did keep up with these events through the newspapers (and through their local manifestations). Nevertheless, I have tried (to repeat an earlier formulation) to show that Dickinson could live at home and live at home in history too. Indeed, I hope to have proved that her preoccupation with home can also be understood as dramatizing an acute sensitivity to socioeconomic shifts and instability during the nineteenth century. Her isolationist practices can be further contextualized historically—as an accident of demographic changes, an improved infrastructure of transportation, and a westward movement that led to numerical discrepancies between men and women; they could be looked on as a singular equivalent to social experiments in alternative living such as the Shaker 'Families' at nearby Hancock Village, the Oneida movement associated with John Humphrey Noyes in upstate New York, or the short-lived Northampton Association of Education and Industry, a community founded in 1842 that had almost 250 members during its four and a half years of existence (Northampton is approximately seven miles from Amherst center).[56] Dickinson's withdrawal was more sustained and successful than those of Henry David Thoreau; Nathaniel Hawthorne at the Brook Farm community in West Roxbury; and Bronson Alcott at the Fruitlands community in the town of Harvard (all in Massachusetts), partly because she lived alone in the utopian society of her own family (the Dickinsons had a very keen sense of their own specialness and of their role within this extended "unit of meaning"). There are very profound differences between Dickinson's removal and those of thousands of other Americans who formed their own ideal communities (most notably in the commitment of the latter to specifically *social* reform and progress), although what lies behind both kinds of enforced isolation is a shared dissatisfaction with American society. The more important point, however, is that the coordinates of Dickinson's life can be seen as a part of larger social patterns, and not apart from them. The response to this dissatisfaction may have been very different, but the first impulse was, I suspect, very similar. Emily Dickinson had her own separate reasons for staying at home, forming select allegiances, and promoting a self-image of one set apart from "mainstream" society (an image Susan Dickinson also perpetuates in her *Springfield Republican* obituary of 18 May 1886).[57] We can respect the integrity of those reasons and take them seriously, but we do not need to accept literally or even reenact her figurative and self-conscious privatization of the literary self (or her privatization by succeeding generations of readers and commentators).

Connections among Dickinson, her family, and her friends are important as ways of understanding her poetic engagements, but so too is information about the neighborhood she lived in, the ideological networks she inhabited, and the "world" outside—which was hardly the static one that has often been described. Opening doors that have long appeared to be closed in her poetry (and to a lesser extent in her life) can, I am persuaded, yield crucial information about the fluidity, complexity, and even the contradictions of her literary dialogue with the often conflicting and contested *worlds* of nineteenth-century politics, economics, religion, and culture in Amherst, Massachusetts, New England, and the United States. This historicist approach can also be extended to Dickinson's aesthetics: despite the insistence of this critical moment that what Dickinson sought in her life and in her manuscripts was openness, fluidity, and the democratic participation of the reader in the construction of textual significance, it may well be that her poetic withdrawal also reflects a need to negotiate with the opposite qualities of stability, closure, and control, and that her relationship with an audience was as ambivalent and even conservative as her political allegiances (never directly stated) may have been. Who is to say that her refusal to print was not an attempt at controlling the means of her own production and directing not only how the reader was to react but also which readers would be given the opportunity to do so, and under what circumstances? And how are we to know that we belong to that circle of readers, as many critics so effortlessly suppose?[58] Perhaps the alleged indeterminacy of the poetry is not a strategic reaction against the monolithic society of political caricature that denied her access to its cultural institutions, but rather a reflection of wider historical struggles and processes of change. It would be wrong for us to continue believing that Dickinson and her times were permanently and irrevocably opposed, even as it is evident from the circumstances of her life that she could not easily coexist with its practices and traditions.

To return full circle: this book begins and ends with poems that manipulate funerary imagery in part to make oblique statements about the self. Throughout, I have argued that historical contexts provide us with difficult but necessary approaches to understanding Dickinson's writing and its subjects, forms of inscription, collation, and distribution. As evidence for "Safe in their alabaster chambers," I suggested that the postscript that accompanied the printed *Republican* version offered us a wealth of contextual information that none of Dickinson's other poems do. This detail led me, among other places, to trace the poem's composition to a burial ground behind a Congregational meetinghouse on Pelham Heights. But as Al Habegger reminds me, the Pelham *Town History* lists eleven "Old Burial Places" in total, most of which were family plots, and some of which were quite elaborate and pompous. Habegger points out (in private correspondence) that Adam Johnson, a "liberal donor to Amherst College," was buried in 1823 at the west burying ground, "located on a hillock which commands a magnificent view down the valley westward." Trustees erected a white marble slab, which may be among the sources for Dickinson's alabaster chambers. The point to be made is that exploring aspects of the complex historical forces and shifting set of social relations in which Dickinson's manuscripts are ambiguously embedded is by no means a way of closing down the meanings of those poems. History offers many paths to the doors and windows of the Monarch of Perception's poetry, and there are many more that have not yet been traveled: it's time to try them.

NOTES

Introduction

1. For a different understanding of "publication" see Martha Nell Smith, *Rowing in Eden: Rereading Emily Dickinson* (Austin: University of Texas Press, 1992).

2. The T-shirt is made by Largely Literary Designs, of Chapel Hill, North Carolina, and is based on an original caricature by Steven Cragg.

3. See for instance Barton Levi St. Armand, *Emily Dickinson and Her Culture: The Soul's Society* (Cambridge: Cambridge University Press, 1984); Beth Maclay Doriani, *Emily Dickinson, Daughter of Prophecy* (Amherst: University of Massachusetts Press, 1996); Smith, *Rowing in Eden*.

4. My thanks to Gregory Farmer, director of the Martha Dickinson Bianchi Trust for the restoration of the Evergreens, for this information, conveyed to me in an e-mail message of Tuesday, 3 March 1998.

5. Quoted in Jane Holtz Kay, *Lost Boston* (Boston: Houghton Mifflin, 1980), 130. The figures for the Bunker Hill Monument are taken from the same source.

6. Richard B. Sewall, *The Life of Emily Dickinson* (New York: Farrar, Straus and Giroux, 1974), 1: xxi.

7. They are listed in *A Popular Guide to the Public Buildings and Museums of Amherst College* (Amherst, 1875).

8. Amherst Academy, a three-story brick preparatory school attended by Emily and Lavinia, was built in 1814. Johnson Chapel was completed in 1827; the present College Hall in 1829; Amherst College president's house in 1834–35; the First Baptist Church in 1835; Cook's block on the corner of Main and Pleasant Streets in 1838–39; the railroad station in 1853; Morgan Hall in 1852–53; Grace Episcopal Church in 1865–66; and the First Congregational Church in 1867. In terms of private residences, the Dickinson Homestead was begun in 1813 and renovated in 1855; the Snell House in 1820; the Edward Hitchcock House in 1828; the Helen Hunt Jackson House in 1830; the Fisher House in 1830 (Emily attended a school there in 1837); the Sweetser House in 1832; Eugene Field House in 1839; the Egbert Perry House in 1855; the Evergreens (next door to the Edward Dickinson Homestead) in 1856; the Leonard M. Hills and the Henry Hills houses in 1862; and the Henry Goodell House in 1875. This selective list was taken from http://www-astro.phast.umass.edu/local/amherst/walking_tour/, March 11, 1998.

9. L#179, to Mrs. J. G. Holland, 18 March 1855, in *The Letters of Emily Dickinson*, ed. Thomas Johnson and Theodora Ward (Cambridge: Harvard University Press, Belknap Press, 1958), 2:319.

10. Robert H. Byer, "Words, Monuments, Beholders: The Visual Arts in Haw-thorne's *The Marble Faun*," in *American Iconology: New Approaches to Nineteenth-Century Art and Literature*, ed. David C. Miller (New Haven: Yale University Press, 1993), 164 and passim.

11. Henry Merrill (of New York), executor of the estate of his mother Orinda Merrill, sold her homestead and four acres of land on the east of the Common for four thousand dollars to Edward Dickinson. The sale took place by public auction on 7 February 1863 and was ordered by the Court of Probate at Amherst on 13 January (Book 210, p. 226). Henry Merrill then paid four thousand dollars for the same tenement and land, on 18 February 1863. The deed was witnessed by Austin, Edward, Emily, and Emily E. Dickinson. Registry of Deeds for Hampshire County, Northampton Massachusetts, Book 210, p. 155.

12. James R. Guthrie, *Emily Dickinson's Vision: Illness and Identity in Her Poetry* (Gainesville: University of Florida Press, 1998), 93.

13. For more on the theory of the field, see Pierre Bourdieu, *Distinction: A Social Critique of the Judgment of Taste*, trans. Richard Nice (London: Routledge, 1984).

14. My thanks again to Gregory Farmer for this information.

15. Marilyn R. Chambers, *Dwelling in the Text: Houses in American Fiction* (Berkeley: University of California Press, 1991), 3.

16. Martha Dickinson Bianchi, *Emily Dickinson Face to Face* (Boston: Houghton Mifflin, 1932), 49.

17. S. V. "Stone, Lucy," in *Britannica Online*. http://www.eb.com:180/cgi-bin/g?DocF'micro/567/73.html. Accessed 17 March 1998.

18. Paul Foot, *Red Shelley* (London: Bookmarks, 1984).

CHAPTER ONE   *The Train, the Father, His Daughter, and Her Poem*

The poetry epigraph with which I begin this chapter is an edited version of the first line and last three of "I like to see it – lap the Miles." I want to draw attention to the tension between movement and stasis in the poem and to the speaker's role as witness, not traveler.

1. *The Journals and Miscellaneous Notebooks of Ralph Waldo Emerson*, ed. William H. Gilman et al. (Cambridge: Harvard University Press, 1960–), 7:268.

2. Such as the Roper Repeating Rifle and Shotgun Works, which opened in 1866 and closed in 1869. Its factory was situated near the railroad. See the *Amherst Record*, 18 December 1905.

3. Daniel Lombardo, "Edward Dickinson and the Amherst and Belchertown Railroad: A Lost Letter," *Historical Journal of Massachusetts* 12, no. 1 (1984): 34. According to the federal census, the population of Amherst increased from 3,057 in 1850 to 4,298 in 1880. Springfield, by contrast, jumped from 11,766 to 33,340 during the same period. See Hilda H. Golden, *Immigrant and Native Families: The Impact of Immigration on the Demographic Transformation of Western Massachusetts, 1850 to 1900* (Lanham, Md.: University Press of America, 1994), 19.

4. Lombardo, "Edward Dickinson and the Amherst and Belchertown Railroad," 34.

5. See the *Springfield Sunday Union and Republican*, 24 December 1944, 3D, where charges of high-speed competition on the part of neighboring towns are made by Stetson Conn, a professor from Amherst College.

6. Quoted in Millicent Todd Bingham, *Emily Dickinson's Home: Letters of Edward Dickinson and His Family* (New York: Harper and Brothers, 1955), 219. Ebeneezer is the name of the stone that Samuel erected to commemorate his victory over the Philistines (1 Sm. 7.12).

7. The dates are taken from Alycia Cathryn, Regan, "An Untold Story: Irish and Irish-Americans in Amherst 1850–1920" (honors thesis, Amherst College, 1994). My thanks to Dan Lombardo, curator of the special collections at the Jones Library, for first introducing me to this text.

8. L#127, to Austin Dickinson, 13 June 1853, in *The Letters of Emily Dickinson*, ed. Thomas Johnson and Theodora Ward (Cambridge: Harvard University Press, Belknap Press, 1958), 1:254.

9. See, for example, the statue by Horatio Greenough entitled *Rescue Group*, where a semi-naked Native American is prevented from using a tomahawk on a cowering mother and infant by a larger, clothed male of European ancestry. It has been pointed out that the larger figure (representing the New American) is wearing what looks like a Roman helmet. See also the so-called Indian-hating chapters of Herman Melville's *The Confidence-Man*, where the associations between Manifest Destiny and the Roman Empire are ironically considered. Interestingly, the *Franklin and Hampshire Express* of Friday, 17 June 1853, includes a report date taken from the *New London Chronicle* on the same event, where the day was described "as fine a one as even Italy could ever boast of." Dickinson's letter is dated June 13, though it is possible that her father may have received a copy of the *Chronicle* edition before that. At any rate, she was not the only one whose thoughts journeyed to Italy on that day. And in Jay Leyda, *The Years and Hours of Emily Dickinson* (New Haven: Yale University Press, 1960), 1:340, Dickinson is quoted as saying in a letter dated 27 April 1856 to John L. Graves that the "skies [are] fairer far than Italy."

10. See also the version of the poem that appears in R. W. Franklin, *The Manuscript Books of Emily Dickinson* (Cambridge: Harvard University Press, Belknap Press, 1981), 1:414.

11. Wolfgang Schivelbusch, *The Railway Journey: The Industrialization of Time and Space in the Nineteenth Century* (Berkeley: University of California Press, 1977), 98. My discussion of differences between American and English rail routes is based on Schivelbusch's chapter "The American Railroad." My thanks to Jonathan Morse, professor of English at the University of Hawaii, who first directed my attention to this book.

12. Charles Anderson, in his powerful reading of the poem (one of the few to take it seriously), notes that "there are no passengers or freight on the train, and no meaningful route." See his *Emily Dickinson's Poetry: Stairway to Surprise* (New York: Holt, Rinehart and Winston, 1960), 16.

13. Karl Marx and Frederick Engels, *On Literature and Art* (Moscow: Progress, 1976), 296–97.

14. Leo Marx records a phrase from "The Poetry of Discovery" which appeared in *Scientific American* in 1849: "inventions are the poetry of physical science, and inventors are the poets." There should be a stronger element of conflict between the poet and "the mechanic arts" than is actually apparent (to me)— though the imagery expresses an oblique anxiety, and the reason for this (I suspect) is that the point of the poem is the victory her father achieved by harnessing the forces of capital and technological progress. He has brought the new machine home. See *The Machine in the Garden: Technology and the Pastoral Ideal in America* (Oxford: Oxford University Press, 1964), 200.

15. David T. Porter, *Dickinson, the Modern Idiom* (Cambridge: Harvard University Press, 1981), 40; Anderson, *Emily Dickinson's Poetry*, 15–16.

16. This condescension is echoed by William Freedman in his interpretation of the poem in "Dickinson's 'I like to see it lap the miles,'" *The Explicator* 40, no. 3 (spring 1982), where he describes (with no apparent sense of irony) "a poetry . . . that looks with supercilious disdain at mere 'shanties . . .' the shoddy, representable world it passes alongside, but which, like conventional form, cannot define or intimidate it" (31).

17. A good illustration of this is provided by a contemporary picture of a stage-coach stopping to let a locomotive pass: the driver and even the passengers on the coach are fully visible, while the engine driver and train passengers are largely obscured. See Ronald Dale, Karr, *Lost Railways of New England* (Pepperell, Mass: Branch Line Press, 1989), 37.

18. Michael T. Gilmore, *American Romanticism and the Marketplace* (Chicago: University of Chicago Press, 1985), 16.

19. My thanks to Jeremy and Bjørg Hawthorn for giving me the opportunity to witness the habits and whims of their cat, Mia, at close quarters. Of course, Jonathan Arac also mentions the "banal naturalization of the machine as a pussycat" (*Critical Genealogies: Historical Situations for Postmodern Literary Studies* [New York: Columbia University Press, 1989], 212). Rather than seeing this naturalization as banal, however, I read it as a disguised but determined attempt to regulate the forces of nineteenth-century industrial capitalism within an occasionally patronizing and often patrician discourse.

20. W. B. Adams, *English Pleasure Carriages* (London, 1837), quoted in Schivelbusch, *The Railway Journey*, 13.

21. From April 1846 to January of the following year, a series of chapters appeared in the *Hampshire and Franklin Express* drawing this conclusion. Because the *Express* (as its name might suggest) was established as a promotional organ for the Amherst and Belchertown Railroad, the source is not unbiased. But other commentators suggest that the new rail lines offered transportation that was as much as a third times cheaper than horse-drawn wagons. See Jensen, Oliver, *The American Heritage History of Railroads in America* (New York: American Heritage, 1975), 32.

22. The evidence on Dickinson's antipathy for cats seems contradictory: al-

though Martha Dickinson Bianchi notes an incident where her aunt tried to of-fload some kittens, there are references in letters that seem to express a fondness for them. Perhaps it was the quantity, rather than the species, that annoyed her from time to time. See Bianchi, *Emily Dickinson Face to Face* (Boston: Houghton Mifflin, 1932), 7, 203.

23. George Frisbie Whicher, *This Was a Poet: A Critical Biography of Emily Dickinson* (1938; reprint, Ann Arbor: University of Michigan Press, 1957), 27; Martha Dickinson Bianchi, *The Life and Letters of Emily Dickinson* (Boston: Houghton Mifflin, 1924), 8; Cynthia Griffin Wolff, *Emily Dickinson* (New York: Knopf, 1986), 33. Although I have looked through the pages of the *Hampshire and Franklin Express* (which listed premiums awarded to the best and fastest horses at the East Hampshire Agricultural Society annual fairs), I can find no evidence to support the assertion that Edward Dickinson owned the fastest horse in either the county or the town: the truth, as Bianchi suggests, is probably that he *wanted* to own the quickest one.

24. Bianchi, *Life and Letters*, 41.

25. Edward Dickinson, along with Alfred Burke and Luke Sweetser, are mentioned in the act by which the East Hampshire Agricultural Society was made into a corporation "for the encouragement of Agriculture and Mechanic Arts by Premiums." At that time Dickinson was on the executive committee, and in 1852, was elected vice president.

26. "Secretary's Book of the East Hampshire Agricultural Society" (1850–1881), 1:53. The book is kept in the special collections of the Jones Library at Amherst, where Daniel Lombardo kindly brought it to my attention.

27. See the *Hampshire and Franklin Express* for Friday, December 12, 1862.

28. Bianchi, *Emily Dickinson Face to Face*, 129–30.

29. In the tax returns of 1863, Edward was recorded as having two horses and two carriages at a combined value of $500, which was $100 more than his professional income for that year. In 1864, the horses alone were valued at $400, and the carriages at $250. By 1867, the horses were worth $450 and the carriages, $300. During the same year, L. M. Hills, the wealthy manufacturer, owned four horses, but they were priced at $500 dollars (or $125 each, as opposed to Edward's $200 animals), and his two carriages only at $200. Edward Hitchcock meanwhile had only one horse, worth $75, and one carriage valued at $100.

30. Quoted in Schivelbusch, *The Railway Journey*, 5.

31. W. S. Tyler, *The History of Amherst College during Its First Half Century, 1821–1871* (Springfield, Mass: Clark W. Bryan, 1873), 121.

32. Quoted in Polly Longsworth, *Austin and Mabel: The Amherst Affair and Love Letters of Austin Dickinson and Mabel Loomis Todd* (New York: Farrar, Straus and Giroux, 1984), 122–23.

33. The quotation is from "The Poet" in Emerson, *Essays: Second Series* (Boston: Houghton Mifflin, 1892), 23–24. A more extended quotation which includes these lines forms part of Mario D'Avanzo's article, "Explications of Single Poems: J#585, 'I like to see it lap the Miles,'" *Emily Dickinson Bulletin* 31 (1977): 59–61, which argues that "I like to see it lap the Miles" is Dickinson's answer to

Emerson's challenge to the poet to find a "place for the railway." He presents a case for a more inclusive attitude to the train on Dickinson's part, an attitude I can find no support for.

34. L#72, to Austin Dickinson, 6 February 1852, *Letters of Emily Dickinson*, 1:173.

35. Quoted in Thelma M. Kistler, *The Rise of Railroads in the Connecticut River Valley*, Smith College Studies in History, vol. 23, no. 4 (Northampton, Mass: Department of History, Smith College, 1938), 74.

36 .L#123, to Austin Dickinson, 16 May 1853, *Letters of Emily Dickinson*, 1:250.

37. L#140, to Austin Dickinson, 10 November 1853, ibid., 269.

38. Karl Marx and Frederick Engels, *On Literature and Art* (Moscow: Progress, 1976), 41.

39. Elias Nason, *A Gazetteer of the State of Massachusetts* (Boston: B. B. Russell, 1874), 32.

40. Noah Webster, quoted in Leo Marx, *The Machine in the Garden*, 210–11.

41. Bianchi, *Life and Letters*, 16.

42. The physical resemblances between the (presumably wooden) Dickinson barn and the (brick) railroad station (built, but probably not designed, by Robert Cutler) are fairly remote: both had two wings (unevenly matched in the case of the barn) and a central section (the barn's being much bigger than its own wings), as well as a cupola (possibly decorative in the case of the depot, but used for ventilation purposes on the barn). My comparison is based on the photograph of the depot in Paul F. Norton, *Amherst: A Guide to Its Architecture* (Amherst: Amherst Historical Society, 1975), 40, and on the illustration (plate 2) of the barn in Guy Leighton, "The Emily Dickinson Homestead: A Historical Study of Its Setting with Recommendations for Preservation and Restoration" (MLA thesis, Department of Landscape Architecture and Regional Planning, University of Massachusetts, 1978), 38.

43. The quotation from the *Republican* is taken from Leyda, *Years and Hours*, 2:46. On page 71 he quotes a very similar passage to that in the *Express* of 12 December which appeared in the *Republican* of 13 December: "The locomotive on the Amherst, Belchertown, and Palmer railroad, formerly known as the 'Amherst,' has been thoroughly renovated at the machine shop, and reappears as the 'Edward Dickinson'—worthily named after the president of the road."

44. J. R. Greene, *The Mass. Central: Quabbin's Phantom Railroad* (Athol, Mass.: Athol Press, 1996), 44. More than seventy years old, Edward had consented to be nominated for yet another term to the Massachusetts legislature in order to look after the interests of the Massachusetts Central Railroad. As the *Amherst Record* notes, Austin was also to become involved with the Massachusetts Central. In the issue of Wednesday, 3 April 1878, on page 5, it says, "At the meeting of the stockholders of the Massachusetts Central Railroad in Boston, today, the following new directors were chosen: W. A. Dickinson, Esq., Luke Lyman, Thomas C. Durant, William Cartright [*sic*]." Lyman was from Northampton, and both Milton Courtwright and Thomas Durant from New York (see Greene,

Mass. Central, 54.). Although the *Record* does not state explicitly that this was Austin, it was an Amherst paper, which would make it seem as if some local interest was being reflected in the report. The *Amherst Directory* for 1879 lists three William Dickinson's, but only two have the initials W. A.: one is a farmer, the other (Austin) is an attorney. It would therefore seem as if Austin was the person referred to in the report, especially since the honorary title of Squire was commonly added to the names of men who were justices of the peace (like Austin, and like his father, Edward, and his grandfather Samuel Fowler, before him). See *Directory and Business Advertiser of the Town of Amherst Combined with a Directory of Hadley* (Amherst, Mass.: McCloud & Williams, 1879), 33. There is no directory for 1878.

45. L#360, to Louise Norcross, spring 1871, *Letters of Emily Dickinson*, 2:486.

46. Lombardo, "Edward Dickinson and the Amherst and Belchertown Railroad," 42; George R. Taylor, "The Rise and the Decline of Manufactures and Other Matters," in *Essays on Amherst's History*, ed. Theodore Greene (Amherst: Vista Press, 1978), 77.

47. Stanley King, *A History of the Endowment of Amherst College* (Amherst, Mass.: Amherst College, 1950), 56.

48. Of course, the stated value of the shares is fairly meaningless unless one knows how many shares Edward owned (there are no details given in the tax records for 1859 and 1862) and their original cost, but at least he did not have to sell his own property in order to pay off any losses he might have incurred. According to a photocopy of a certificate owned by Henry P. Haven—a share in the Amherst, Belchertown and Palmer Railroad Company—one share was worth one hundred dollars at par value, but this information does not correspond to Edward's shares, which were purchased much earlier. The tax records of Amherst, which are housed in the special collections of the Jones Library, show that Edward retained his house, a barn, the Matthews' house, the land around these buildings (as well as the ninety-two acres at the front of the family home), and assorted horses, cows, swine, and carriages, until his death in 1874.

49. R. E. Lowrey, " 'Boanerges': An Encomium for Edward Dickinson," *Arizona Quarterly* 26 (spring 1970): 54–58. As I have, Lowrey mentions the fact that Edward was president of the Amherst and Belchertown Railroad and that a locomotive was named after him, and goes on to argue that the poem may be a literal glorification of the attributes of a locomotive and a tribute to Dickinson's father. My reading implies a more unstable correspondence, and a social or ideological triumph on Edward's part more than a personal one.

50. Regan, "An Untold Story," 28–29. Regan also mentions that another railroad company, the Northampton and Amherst, was incorporated in 1867 and absorbed by the Central Massachusetts in 1869. By 1878 there were two rail lines running through Amherst. Early maps showing the second route in 1873 reflect the fact that a line had been designed and approved, but not yet built (a financial panic in that year delayed its implementation). I am indebted once again to my friend Daniel Lombardo at the Jones Library for bringing my attention to the excellent Sanborn Fire Insurance maps for the City of Amherst (published on

microfilm by Chadwyck-Healey, Inc), from which this information is partly derived.

51. L#128, to Austin Dickinson, 19 June 1853, *Letters of Emily Dickinson*, 1:257.

52. Robert Doherty, *Society and Power: Five New England Towns, 1800–1860* (Amherst: University of Massachusetts Press, 1977), 21.

53. Quoted in Richard B. Sewall, *The Life of Emily Dickinson* (New York: Farrar, Straus and Giroux, 1974), 2:566.

54. The average is calculated by adding the number of students (both graduates and nongraduates) from the classes of 1862, 1863, 1864, and 1865. They amount to approximately 302 persons. See the *Amherst College Biographical Record of the Graduates and Non-Graduates of the Classes of 1822–1962 Inclusive* (Amherst: Trustees of Amherst College, 1963), 101–20.

55. An entry in Austin Dickinson's diary for Saturday, 15 May (the day Emily died) mentions the sound of the whistles at six. The *Amherst Record* for Wednesday, 12 May, gives the timetable for (what was by then) the New London Northern Railroad, but there is no train listed as arriving or departing at that time: it therefore appears more probable that it was the factory whistle that Austin heard.

56. A typical example would be the *Hampshire and Franklin Express* piece in the edition of 8 July 1853, which told of how a group of passengers traveling from Springfield to Amherst via Palmer were drawing near the station at Palmer only to see the train leave without them. The directors of the railroad informed the newspaper that the conductor had ignored orders. Although there were other stories of missed connections, and even of a man who managed to catch a train in the Dickinson meadow that was carrying his wife and had set off without him, the service seems to have been largely reliable. See David W. Sargeant Jr., "The Railroad Mania in Amherst," *Bulletin of the Railway and Locomotive Historical Society*, no. 47 (Boston: Railway and Locomotive Historical Society, Harvard Business School, 1938), 24–25.

57. Arac, *Critical Genealogies*, 199.

58. After the train came to Amherst, Dickinson would have traveled to Palmer, and then taken the Boston and Worcester line (in operation from 1834 to 1867, when it became the Boston and Albany) through Worcester. Before that, she would have taken the coach (or been driven by her father in the family carriage) to either Palmer or Springfield, and then via the Western Railroad (in operation from 1839 onward). See Ronald Dale Karr, *The Rail Lines of Southern New England: A Handbook of Railroad History* (Pepperell, Mass.: Branch Line Press, 1995), 277–80.

59. Even if she (somehow) did not manage to see this smoke—because of poor eyesight, for example, or because of the circumstances of her life, she could not avoid reading about the effects of modernization: there were reports of railroad disasters, industrial accidents, factory deaths, strikes, and the pitiful living conditions of the poor in a number of editions of the *Hampshire and Franklin Express*.

60. My sincere thanks to Daniel Lombardo for his help in clarifying this issue of brick chimneys on mills powered by water, and for his detailed comments on

an earlier version of this chapter. Needless to say, errors of historical accuracy are entirely my own.

61. These figures are taken from Golden, *Immigrant and Native Families*, 193–95. Nason's *Gazetteer of the State of Massachusetts* lists (pp. 268–69), a mix of German, French Canadian, and Irish immigrants (who lived, appropriately enough, in a section called Ireland Parish). He includes fourteen paper-mills, three cotton factories, three woolen mills, two thread mills, and a machine works employing more than five thousand operatives.

62. Golden, *Immigrant and Native Families*, 195.

63. Berthoff quoted in Doherty, *Society and Power*, 4.

64. Arac, *Critical Genealogies*, 212.

65. Daniel Lombardo, *A Hedge Away: The Other Side of Emily Dickinson's Amherst* (Northampton, Mass.: Daily Hampshire Gazette, 1997), 131. Work on Grace Episcopal Church began in 1865, but the bell tower in which the clock was set was not erected until 1868. The dates are not immediately relevant to the poem, therefore, though my general point (I hope) is.

66. Schivelbusch, *The Railway Journey*, 44.

67. Alan Trachtenberg, Introduction, in ibid., xiii.

68. Tyler, *History of Amherst College during Its First Half Century, 1821–1871*, 491.

69. Schivelbusch, *The Railway Journey*, 44.

70. Sargeant, "The Railroad Mania in Amherst," 20.

71. For a detailed view of the railroad's impact on the Amherst economy, see Stephen A. Aron, "The Minds of Hands: Working People of Amherst in the Mid-Nineteenth Century" (honors thesis, Amherst College, 1982).

72. The fantasy that the train (or what it represents) can be governed surely aligns the speaker with the governing classes: for the laboring classes, the opposite is almost the case—the train seems stoppable but is always in danger of becoming uncontrollable. On Tuesday, 8 May 1862 (the conjectured year of the poem's composition), sixteen-year-old Thomas Darrigan, a fireman employed by the Amherst, Belchertown and Palmer Railroad Company, was shackling freight cars at the Amherst yards when they moved and he was crushed so severely that he died shortly afterward. See the *Hampshire and Franklin Express* of 11 May 1862, p. 1.

73. Karl Mannheim, *Ideology and Utopia: An Introduction to the Sociology of Knowledge*, trans. Louis Wirth and Edward Shils (1936; reprint, San Diego: Harcourt Brace Jovanovich, 1985), 9.

74. My thanks to Jeremy Hawthorn, chair of the English department of the Norwegian University of Science and Technology at Trondheim, who read this chapter in various guises and made a number of helpful suggestions, among them this comparison between Dickinson's poem and the works of Shelley and Blake. His support and advice were invaluable.

75. I hasten to add that I do not in any way align myself with the statement of Yvor Winters, made in "Emily Dickinson and the Limits of Judgement" (*Emily Dickinson: A Collection of Critical Views*, ed. Richard B. Sewall [Englewood Cliffs, N.J.: Prentice-Hall, 1963]) that the "poem is abominable; and the quality of silly

playfulness which renders it abominable is diffused more or less perceptibly throughout her work" (29). I think, on the contrary, that Dickinson's playfulness is profound (and I argued so in my Ph.D. dissertation, "Emily Dickinson and the Limits and Possibilities of Critical Judgment" [Trinity College, Dublin, 1990]). I also do not think the poem is abominable, aesthetically or politically. It is an important cultural document that attempts to mediate historically contemporary and complex social forces and energies. Although it may (in my view) fail to control those energies, this does not imply an intellectual deficiency on the part of Dickinson.

76. Anderson, *Emily Dickinson's Poetry*, 15–16.

CHAPTER TWO   *"Homeless at Home"*

1. Adrienne Rich, *On Lies, Secrets, and Silences: Selected Prose 1966–1978* (New York: W. W. Norton, 1979), 158; Randall Jarrell, *Poetry and the Age* (New York: Vintage Books, 1953), 101.

2. J. Ritchie Garrison, *Landscape and Material Life in Franklin County, Massachusetts, 1770–1860* (Knoxville: University of Tennessee Press, 1991), 161.

3. Edward Dickinson, "Report of the Committee on the State of the (Cattle) Show Generally," *Hampshire Gazette*, 26 October 1837. Quoted in Jay Leyda, *The Years and Hours of Emily Dickinson* (New Haven: Yale University Press, 1960), 1:34.

4. Jonathan Arac, *Commissioned Spirits: The Shaping of Social Motion in Dickens, Carlyle, Melville, and Hawthorne* (New Brunswick, N.J.: Rutgers University Press, 1979), 5–16.

5. It is also, in a related way, a fear of illegality—that one is an intruder in another person's house. In a similar way, the heroine of the Gothic novel often "feared [that] her monetary or biological heritage was in some uncontrollable way tainted." See Daneen Wardrop, *Emily Dickinson's Gothic: Goblin with a Gauge* (Iowa City: University of Iowa Press, 1996), xii.

6. Martha Dickinson Bianchi, *The Life and Letters of Emily Dickinson* (Boston: Houghton Mifflin, 1924), 42.

7. *Collier's Encyclopedia* (New York: P. F. Collier, 1993), 12:46.

8. Walter Benn Michaels, *The Gold Standard and the Logic of Naturalism* (Berkeley: University of California Press, 1987), 89.

9. See Wardrop, *Emily Dickinson's Gothic*, esp. 21–22.

10. *An American Dictionary of the English Language* (1844), s. v. "specter."

11. Christopher Clark, *The Roots of Rural Capitalism: Western Massachusetts 1780–1860* (Ithaca: Cornell University Press, 1990), 219.

12. Ibid., 200.

13. Barton Levi St. Armand, *Emily Dickinson and Her Culture: The Soul's Society* (Cambridge: Cambridge University Press, 1984), 308. As administrator of the Edward Dickinson estate, Lavinia signed for fifty shares in Michigan Barrel Stock, seventy shares in the Holyoke Water Power Company, one share Central

Mass. common stock, thirty shares Union Pacific Stock, four shares in the Citizens Bank of Wichita, Kansas, as well two thousand dollars worth of bonds and a number of notes and securities. See Hampshire County Probate Court, Case #5799. I cite the microfiche records at the Jones Library, Amherst.

14. On 24 April 1863, Harriet P. Mack quit all rights to the house formerly owned by her deceased husband David Mack Jr. after receiving a final payment of $4,000 from Edward Dickinson. Hampshire County Probate Court, Registry of Deeds, book 212, p. 37.

15. L#52, to Austin Dickinson, 23 September 1851, *The Letters of Emily Dickinson*, ed. Thomas Johnson and Theodora Ward (Cambridge: Harvard University Press, Belknap Press, 1958), 1:134–35.

16. Jean McClure Mudge, *Emily Dickinson and the Image of Home* (Amherst: University of Massachusetts Press, 1975), 26.

17. Helen McNeil, *Emily Dickinson* (London, Virago Press, 1985), 112, 113.

18. L#281, to Louise and Frances Norcross, late May 1863, *Letters of Emily Dickinson*, 2:424.

19. *Random House Dictionary of the English Language*, s. v. "booger." My thanks to James Smith, town engineer for Amherst, who confirmed during a telephone conversation that there was no municipal or private supply of gas to the Dickinson household at this time.

20. *Letters of Emily Dickinson*, PF 21, 3:914.

21. Arac, *Commissioned Spirits*, 126–27.

22. L#58, to Austin Dickinson, 17 October 1851, *Letters of Emily Dickinson*, 1:148.

23. Wardrop, *Emily Dickinson's Gothic*, 25.

24. L#52, to Austin Dickinson, 23 September 1851, *Letters of Emily Dickinson*, 1:133.

25. See Johnson's notes to L#52, ibid., 1:136.

26. Thelma M. Kistler, *The Rise of Railroads in the Connecticut River Valley*, Smith College Studies in History, vol. 23, no. 4 (Northampton, Mass.: Department of History, Smith College, 1938), 29–31.

27. Alan Trachtenberg, Introduction to Wolfgang Schivelbusch, *The Railway Journey: The Industrialization of Time and Space in the Nineteenth Century* (Berkeley: University of California Press, 1977), xiv.

28. Daniel E. Sutherland, *The Expansion of Everyday Life, 1860–1876* (New York: Harper and Row, 1989), 180.

29. Schivelbusch, *The Railway Journey*, 113–23.

30. Robert Doherty, *Society and Power: Five New England Towns 1800–1860* (Amherst: University of Massachusetts Press, 1977), 3.

31. L#43, to Austin Dickinson, 15 June 1851, *Letters of Emily Dickinson*, 1:113.

32. Betsy Erkkila, "Emily Dickinson and Class," *American Literary History* 4, no. 1 (Spring 1992): 9. I am indebted to Aífe Murray for drawing my attention to this article during our e-mail correspondence of 1996. For the meaning of "going up," see Eric Partridge, *A Dictionary of Slang and Unconventional English*,

7th ed. (New York: Macmillan, 1978), 337, where it is defined as "To be ruined, financially, socially, or politically." There are other ways to read the phrase, though not all of the meanings may be recoverable.

33. Mary P. Ryan, *The Empire of the Mother: American Writing about Domesticity, 1830 to 1860*, Women and History, no. 2–3 (New York: Institute for Research in History and Haworth Press, 1982), 101.

34. Richard Brodhead, *Cultures of Letters: Scenes of Reading and Writing in Nineteenth-Century America* (Chicago: University of Chicago Press, 1993), 18–27. The phrase "bodily correction" is his.

35. Edward Carpenter and Charles Morehouse, *History of the Town of Amherst, Massachusetts* (Amherst: Carpenter & Morehouse, 1896), 270.

36. Minutes from a meeting of the trustees of the Amherst Academy (including Edward Dickinson) on 6 September 1838 note the acceptance of the following bylaw (Article 10): "Punishments shall be either private or public admonition, or degradation, to be inflicted at the discretion of the Preceptor . . ." (cited in Leyda, *Years and Hours*, 1:51).

37. Lucius Boltwood, Diary (1844), pp. 42–43, Special Collections, Jones Library, Amherst, Massachusetts. Born in 1825, Boltwood was a teacher, Congregational clergyman, historian, and genealogist. His father, Lucius, studied law under Samuel Fowler Dickinson, was sympathetic to the Whig Party and secretary to Amherst College from 1828 to 1850. Lucius Manlius and Austin were contemporaries with similar backgrounds and corresponding political views. See James Avery Smith, *Families of Amherst, Massachusetts* (Amherst, 1984), vol. 1 (A-Di), 80.

38. I am grateful to Gary Lee Stonum of Case Western Reserve University for trying to warn me against the dangers of simplifying cultural politics along strictly left-right lines.

39. *The Boston Directory for the Year 1851* (Boston: George Adams, 1851), 14–15.

40. Doherty, *Society and Power*, 5.

41. Ibid., 7.

42. The information here is taken from Cynthia Griffin Wolff, *Emily Dickinson* (New York: Knopf, 1986), 545. The list I have drawn up does not include the offices Edward held locally, which included "justice of the peace, fire warden, town-meeting moderator, member of the Town Tomb Committee, Town Hall Committee, High School Committee, and a committee to consider annexations of Pelham, highway surveyor . . ." (545–46).

43. Polly Longsworth, "The Growth of Civic Consciousness," *Essays on Amherst's History*, ed. Theodore Greene (Amherst: Vista Press, 1978), 149.

44. L#141, to Austin Dickinson, 14 November 1853, *Letters of Emily Dickinson*, 1:270.

45. L#52, to Austin Dickinson, 23 September 1851, ibid., 1:132.

46. L#59, to Austin Dickinson, 25 October 1851, ibid., 1:150–51.

47. Quoted in Ryan, *Empire of the Mother*, 111. The original quotation is from *The Lily* 7 (August, 1855): 110.

48. From W. S. Tyler's diary for 4 July 1879. Quoted in Leyda, *Years and Hours*, 2:311. The dates of the fires are all taken from entries in Leyda's book.

49. Clark, *Roots of Rural Capitalism*, 202.

50. Stephen Aron, "The Minds of Hands: Working People of Amherst in the Mid-Nineteenth Century" (honors thesis, Amherst College, 1982), 39, 36, 40, 42.

51. Edward Dickinson's tax returns are stored in Special Collections, Jones Library.

52. L#16, to Austin Dickinson, 21 October 1847, *Letters of Emily Dickinson*, 1:48–49.

53. W. S. Tyler, *History of Amherst College during Its First Half Century, 1821–1871* (Springfield, Mass.: Clark W. Bryan, 1873), 121.

54. Leyda, *Years and Hours*, 1:44.

55. L#145, to Austin Dickinson, 20 December 1853, *Letters of Emily Dickinson*, 1:275.

56. Doherty gives a short synopsis of Rothman, *Discovery of the Asylum in America*, in *Society and Power*, 4.

57. The old wooden building was moved to Pleasant Street, it is thought, and probably still stood when Edward Dickinson moved his family to a spot just across the road in 1840.

58. Guy Leighton, "The Emily Dickinson Homestead: A Historical Study of Its Setting with Recommendations for Preservation and Restoration" (MLA thesis, Department of Landscape Architecture and Regional Planning, University of Massachusetts, 1978), 20. This is a relatively unknown overview of the history of the Homestead and its grounds.

59. Mudge, *Emily Dickinson and the Image of Home*, 84.

60. Jean Merrill Balderston, *The Edward Dickinsons of Amherst: A Family Analysis* (Ann Arbor, Mich.: University Microfilms, 1969), 91.

61. J. Ritchie Garrison, *Landscape and Material Life in Franklin County, Massachusetts, 1770–1860* (Knoxville: University of Tennessee Press, 1991), 154.

62. Leighton, "The Emily Dickinson Homestead," 20. Leighton also notes on the same page that the "substantial, Federal-style house, which comprises the central rectangle of the house today, follows quite closely a design in *The Country Builder's Assistant* by Asher Benjamin (Greenfield, Mass., 1805), a popular pattern book of the era." John J. G. Blumensen, in *Identifying American Architecture: A Pictorial Guide to Styles and Terms, 1600–1945* (Nashville: American Association for State and Local History, 1977), 21, confirms that an "elliptical fan light" is typical of the Federal style. See also John Poppeliers, S. Allen Chambers, and Nancy B. Schwartz, *What Style Is It?* (Washington, D.C.: Preservation Press, 1977), 12–13. Marcus Whiffen also states that "the semi-elliptical fanlight" is typical of the Adam (or Federal) style. See *American Architecture since 1780: A Guide to the Styles* (Cambridge: M.I.T. Press, 1969), 23.

63. Tara L. Gleason, "The Architectural History of the Dickinson Homestead: The Evolution of a Home" (Junior Paper, Amherst College, 1992).

64. Hampshire County Probate Court, Registry of Deeds, book 53, p. 642.

Born on 29 October 1769, Oliver Smith was the son of Oliver and Elizabeth (Eastman) Smith of Hadley, and he was Samuel Fowler Dickinson's brother-in-law. He married Samuel's sister Anna (daughter of Nathan and Esther [Fowler] Dickinson) on 11 June 1806. He died on 13 August 1851, Anna on 15 November 1867.

65. Hampshire County Probate Court, Registry of Deeds, book 58, pp. 561–63. For more information about Nathan, see Elinor V. Smith, *Descendants of Nathan Dickinson* (Amherst: Dickinson Family Association, 1978), 207. The existence of this document was first brought to my attention to Al Habegger, formerly of the University of Kansas.

66. The quotation is from the deed of sale drawn up by Leland and Dickinson on 30 March 1830, and recorded at Hampshire County Probate Court, Registry of Deeds, book 63, p. 422. Copies of this document are also stored in the Special Collections of the Jones Library, Amherst.

67. The document, witnessed by Edward on 30 March and by Samuel F. Dickinson on 3 April, is contained in Hampshire County Probate Court, Registry of Deeds, book 63, page 423. It reads (in part) "Provided nevertheless, that if the said Edward his heirs, Executors or Administrators, pay to the said Leland & Dickinson their heirs, Executors Administrators or Assigns, the sum of Eleven Hundred Dollars in Manner, following that is to say, Five Hundred Dollars in three years from & after the first day of April next & six hundred dollars in five years from and after the said first day of April next with interest annually on said sum, then this Deed . . . given by the said Edward to the said Leland & Dickinson to pay the same sums at the times aforesaid shall be void otherwise shall remain in full force."

68. Wolff, *Emily Dickinson*, 29–30.

69. Hampshire County Probate Court, Registry of Deeds, book 71, p. 89. On the same day, Edward paid Solomon Eastman five hundred dollars for "a certain piece of land lying in said Amherst, being the west part of said Edward's homelot, which was conveyed by said Edward to said Eastman by his deed of July 23, 1831." The deed is in book 71, p. 88. Clearly, Edward needed to raise cash in 1831, albeit by selling his land to someone he hoped he could trust. But after selling out to Leland and Dickinson, he may have wanted to retain a portion of the family land as security against his return. The Evergreens would eventually be built on this plot.

70. Hampshire County Probate Court, Registry of Deeds, book 160, pp. 466–67: "Know all men by these presents, that I Samuel E. Mack of the City of Cincinnati . . . in consideration of six thousand dollars paid by Edward Dickinson of Amherst . . . the receipt whereof is hereby acknowledged, do hereby give, grant, bargain, sell and convey unto the said Dickinson, the homestead in said Amherst, where my late father David Mack Esq, now deceased, resided. . . ."

71. Mudge, *Emily Dickinson and the Image of Home*, 84. The "cupola was designed by the Northampton architect, William F. Pratt, who was later to design many of the homes on Main Street. . . ." It "closely follows examples in Alexan-

der Jackson Downing's books . . ." (Leighton, "The Emily Dickinson Homestead," 27).

72. Garrison, *Landscape and Material Life,* 179. Garrison later describes how "Italianate house forms first emerged in the late 1840s and early 1850s . . ." (183). The Evergreens, built in the style of an Italian villa, was constructed in 1855.

73. The quotation is from Leighton, "The Emily Dickinson Homestead," 30.

74. See Roger W. Moss, *Century of Color: Exterior Decoration for American Buildings, 1820–1920* (New York: American Life Foundation, 1981), for a history of changing theories of taste during this era. See also Edgar de N. Mayhew, and Minor Myers, Jr., *A Documentary History of American Interiors: From the Colonial Era to 1915* (New York: Charles Scribner's Sons, 1980), 140–44, for a discussion of choosing colors for inside walls. The color chosen would have been influenced by the theories of Downing, and therefore reflected a sensitivity to, and knowledge of, prevailing fashions.

75. The Evergreens was designed "by William F. Pratt in the popular Italianate style" (Leighton, "The Emily Dickinson Homestead," 31). My thanks to Gregory Farmer, of Museum Resource Consultants, who is responsible for supervising the restoration of the Evergreens. In a telephone conversation of 13 December 1996, he discussed the results of a chemical analysis done on the exterior walls of the Austin and Susan Dickinson residence, which showed that the house had originally been painted a buff color.

76. The quotation is from the *Hampshire and Franklin Express,* 20 April 1855, p. 2. Leyda includes the same quotation in *Years and Hours,* 1:331.

77. Henrietta Robins Mack Eliot to Grace Eliot, January 1915, Special Collections, Jones Library, Amherst. Henrietta, born on 12 June 1845, was the second (surviving) child of Samuel Ely Mack, and she married Thomas L. Eliot on 28 November 1864. Grace (born on 13 September 1876) was their fifth child. See Sophia Smith, and Charles E. Smith *Genealogical Records of the Descendants of David Mack to 1879* (Rutland, Vt.: Tuttle, 1879), 33–35.

78. Smith and Smith, *Genealogical Records,* 33.

79. Leyda, *Years and Hours,* 1:332.

80. Mrs. Elizabeth Hannum to her brother, 7 December 1855. Quoted in Leyda, *Years and Hours,* 1:339.

81. L#182, to Elizabeth Holland, about 20 January 1856, *Letters of Emily Dickinson,* 2:323–24.

82. Leyda, *Years and Hours,* 1:36–37.

83. Wolff, *Emily Dickinson,* 24–25.

84. See Mudge, "The House on Pleasant Street," *Emily Dickinson and the Image of Home,* 25–72. The advertisement in the *Express* of 23 November is quoted in Leyda, *Years and Hours,* 1:338.

85. For a psychological reading of the relationship between the Dickinson family and their houses, see Balderston, *The Edward Dickinsons of Amherst.* The chapter on the Mansion/Homestead is entitled "Repossession" (116–27).

86. Clark, *Roots of Western Capitalism,* 209, 213. My discussion of temperance

is based in part on Clark's sixth chapter, which includes a section on this subject and mentions Edward Dickinson and David Mack.

87. When I write "significant proportion," I am suggesting that these images are frequent enough to warrant being taken seriously, without claiming that a theory of economic determinism represents the best or only way to approach Dickinson's poetry.

88. Daniel Lombardo, "A Look Back: Financial Ruin," *Amherst Bulletin*, 12 December 1984, 43.

89. L#591, to Maria Whitney, early 1879 (?), *Letters of Emily Dickinson*, 2:634. The conjectured date is Johnson's, and a question mark indicates his uncertainty.

90. Mudge, *Emily Dickinson and the Image of Home*, 6.

91. In a letter to her mother, Lucretia Gunn Dickinson, from Brooklyn, dated 29 April 1838, occasioned by Samuel F. Dickinson's death, Catharine Dickinson Sweetser wrote, "It seems as if his depression of spirits caused his sickness which terminated his life. . . ." Quoted in Leyda, *Years and Hours*, 1:49–50. Catharine makes it clear that, in her mind, his children's failure to provide him with "a comfortable home in his old age" led to his premature death (ibid., 50). When Lucretia Dickinson died not long afterward, the same cause of death was suspected, for none of her children was willing to have her live with them for very long.

92. L#788, to James D. Clark, late 1882, *Letters of Emily Dickinson*, 3:751.

93. Johnson, *Letters of Emily Dickinson*, 2:332.

94. Erkkila ("Emily Dickinson and Class") is a notable exception. Jane Donahue Eberwein (in part) another. See Eberwein, *Dickinson: Strategies of Limitation* (Amherst: University of Massachusetts Press, 1985), 30–33.

95. The "pursuits and embarrassments" of Samuel Fowler Dickinson's career were followed also by the *New-England Inquirer*, and the public sale of his half of the house was advertised in the *Hampshire Gazette* in 1833. See also Leyda, *Years and Hours*, 1:19–20.

96. George, Eliot, *Middlemarch* (1871; reprint, Harmondsworth, England: Penguin Books, 1965), 47.

97. One political reading that does come to mind is Celia Catlett Anderson's "Deep Dyed Politics in Emily Dickinson's 'Revolution is the Pod,'" *Dickinson Studies* 49 (1984): 3–8, where Anderson suggests that the poem is a Hegelian reading of historical processes.

98. Gillian Brown, *Domestic Individualism: Imagining Self in Nineteenth-Century America* (Berkeley: University of California Press, 1990), 18.

99. Feminist critics advance gender as the primary reason for withdrawal, but this may not be the only reason, I suspect. Although nineteenth-century American women were citizens (as long as they weren't slaves or first-generation immigrants) without a vote, it did not follow that "they were not part of the political community." Women writers used literature as a means to influence public policy: Harriet Beecher Stowe is the best example, but Lydia Maria Child, Catharine Maria Sedgwick, and (most interestingly) Helen Hunt Jackson all used fiction as a forum for reform. Jackson was described by Emerson as America's

greatest living novelist and she was immensely popular, as well as being Dickinson's correspondent for many years and someone who urged her to publish. For a discussion of women and public life see Lois W. Banner, "Elizabeth Cady Stanton: Early Marriage and Feminist Revolution" in *Women's America: Refocusing the Past*, ed. Linda K. Kerber and Jane de Hart-Matthews, 2d ed. (New York: Oxford University Press, 1987), 201.

100. Perry Anderson, "Components of the National Culture," in *Student Power: Problems, Diagnosis, Action*, ed. Alexander Cockburn and Robin Blackburn (Harmondsworth, England: Penguin, 1969), 242.

101. Pierre Bourdieu, *Outline of a Theory of Practice* (Cambridge: Cambridge University Press, 1977), 197.

102. Richard B. Sewall, *The Life of Emily Dickinson* (New York: Farrar, Straus, and Giroux, 1974), 2:536. I am grateful to Jonathan Morse for reminding me in an e-mail with the subject-heading "Chapter" that "1854 was the year when Dickinson was overwhelmingly defeated in his bid for a second term in Congress for no other reason than his stubborn allegiance to the discredited and dying Whig Party, which was tearing itself apart over the issue of slavery. . . . And of course in 1860 Dickinson was to run for Lieutenant Governor from the Constitutional Union Party, which on the eve of the War was still trying to compromise the uncompromisable" (13 April 1996).

103. The phrase comes from Sewall's biography. Contrast this with Poe's reading of America as a house divided in "The Fall of the House of Usher." Of course, interpretations and intentions may not necessarily coincide.

104. L#368, to Thomas Wentworth Higginson, November 1871, *Letters of Emily Dickinson*, 2:491. The source for the "granite" quotation is Leyda, *Years and Hours*, 2:262. The "Pyramidal Nerve" is taken from P#1011A [J#1054], "Not to discover weakness is."

105. Polly Longsworth, *Austin and Mabel: The Amherst Affair and Love Letters of Austin Dickinson and Mabel Loomis Todd* (New York: Farrar, Straus and Giroux, 1984), 301. I am grateful again to Jonathan Morse, who first drew my attention to this (and my next extended) passage, and who sent me a copy of his paper, "Some of the Things We Mean When We Say 'New England,'" which also includes two of the three quotations I take from Longsworth's book.

106. Quoted in Longsworth, *Austin and Mabel*, 301, 300. Unlike Dickinson's speaker, though, Austin goes on to distinguish himself from "mules, and niggers, and dirt, and alligators and slovenliness. . . ." It is unfair to suggest that Emily would have shared these opinions or used the same terms, but it is fair to suggest that the sense of uniqueness that is expressed so often in her poems is linked to an inherited belief in the superiority of New Englanders to people of different ethnic, social, and even geographic backgrounds.

107. L#114, to Austin Dickinson, 8 April 1853, *Letters of Emily Dickinson*, 1:239.

108. Bianchi, *Emily Dickinson Face to Face*, 126–27.

109. L#118, to Austin Dickinson, 21 April 1853, *Letters of Emily Dickinson*, 1:245.

110. Bianchi, *Emily Dickinson Face to Face*, 126.

111. Balderston, *The Edward Dickinsons of Amherst*, 131.

112. L#165, to Austin Dickinson, early June 1854, *Letters of Emily Dickinson*, 2:296.

CHAPTER THREE *Housing Possibilities*

1. L#261 to Thomas Wentworth Higginson, 25 April 1862, in *The Letters of Emily Dickinson*, ed. Thomas Johnson and Theodora Ward (Cambridge: Harvard University Press, Belknap Press, 1958), 2:404–5. It is significant that Dickinson refers to Shakespeare as a writer of books, rather than as a dramatist; she therefore distinguishes between the man as artist and natural genius and as the creator of dramatic performances, which, in various forms, were immensely popular in nineteenth-century America. Her views on Shakespeare are therefore concordant with conservative literary opinions.

2. In the Dickinson household, there were subscriptions to *Springfield Republican, Hampshire and Franklin Express*, and the *Amherst Record*. All were papers of quality, though both Lavinia and Emily seem also to have enjoyed the more sensational items of interest. In addition, the family subscribed to *Harper's New Monthly Magazine* (mainly a collection of reprints from British publications), *Scribner's Monthly* and the *Atlantic Monthly*. See Jack L. Capps, *Emily Dickinson's Reading, 1836–1886* (Cambridge: Harvard University Press, 1966), 128–43.

3. Richard Sewall, *The Life of Emily Dickinson* (New York: Farrar, Straus and Giroux, 1974), 2:543.

4. The *Atlantic Monthly's* first appearance in 1857 marked a shift in power from New York to Boston, and from a radical to a (relatively) more conservative politico-literary platform, according to John Stafford in *The Literary Criticism of "Young America": A Study in the Relationship of Politics and Literature, 1837–1850* (Berkeley: University of California Press, 1952), 121–22.

5. Lawrence W. Levine, *Highbrow/Lowbrow: The Emergence of Cultural Hierarchy in America* (Cambridge: Harvard University Press, 1988), 213.

6. Peter Murphy points to a similar arrangement in Lord Byron's "triangular 'Gradus ad Parnassum,' " from his journal of November 1813. Byron places Walter Scott at the top of his pyramid and "The Many" at the bottom. For a reproduction of Byron's diagram, see Murphy's "Climbing Parnassus, & Falling Off," *At the Limits of Romanticism: Essays in Cultural, Feminist, and Materialist Criticism*, ed. Mary A. Favret and Nicola J. Watson (Bloomington: Indiana University Press, 1994), 41.

7. Lavinia Dickinson, quoted in Millicent Bingham Todd, *Emily Dickinson's Home: Letters of Edward Dickinson and His Family* (New York: Harper and Brothers, 1955), 413.

8. For a fuller discussion of these issues, see Stafford, *The Literary Criticism of "Young America,"* especially chapter 1, "Politics, Magazines, and Publishing."

9. The quotation is taken from Jones's article "Royal Authors" in *The United*

States Magazine and Democratic Review, 12 (April 1843): 392–400, and is quoted in Stafford, *The Literary Criticism of "Young America,"* 69.

10. Quoted in Stafford, *The Literary Criticism of "Young America,"* 58.

11. Ibid., 59.

12. L#165, to Austin Dickinson, early June 1854, *Letters of Emily Dickinson*, 2:296–97.

13. This precise formulation does not occur in either the Old or the New Testament, though there are plenty of passages that resemble it in spirit. "There be standing here, which shall not taste of death, till they see the Son of man coming in his Kingdom," is from Matthew 16.28, while death is "no more" in Revelation 21.4; death is "swallowed up" in Isaiah 25.8; death is either "destroyed" or "swallowed up" in 1 Corinthians 15.26 and 15.54; and death is "abolished" in 2 Timothy 1.10.

14. Pierre Bourdieu, "Flaubert's Point of View," in *Literature and Social Practice* ed. Phillippe Desan, Priscilla Parkhurst Ferguson, and Wendy Griswold (Chicago: University of Chicago Press, 1988), 225.

15. Dickinson expresses this idea directly in a letter to Dr. and Mrs. J. G. Holland, dated about 6 November 1858, where she writes "Ah! democratic Death! Grasping the proudest zinnia from my purple garden,- then deep to his bosom calling the serf's child!" (L#195, *Letters of Emily Dickinson*, 2:341). The language of feudal relations places the writer at a playful distance from what she is describing.

16. L#323, to Higginson, mid-July 1867, ibid., 2:457.

17. Levine, *Highbrow/Lowbrow*, 207–8.

18. Robert Doherty, *Society and Power: Five New England Towns, 1800–1860* (Amherst: University of Massachusetts Press, 1977), 40.

19. Levine, *Highbrow/Lowbrow*, 177.

20. Henry James's letter (to H. G. Wells) is quoted in Jeremy Hawthorn, *Cunning Passages: New Historicism, Cultural Materialism and Marxism in the Contemporary Literary Debate* (London: Arnold, 1996), 223.

21. Cristanne Miller, *Emily Dickinson: A Poet's Grammar* (Cambridge: Harvard University Press, 1987).

22. David T. Porter, *Dickinson, the Modern Idiom* (Cambridge, Mass.: Harvard University Press, 1981), 109, 112. Porter identifies the phrase "dance of tropes" as deriving from Harold Bloom.

23. See Bourdieu, "Flaubert's Point of View," 211–34, for an extended discussion of the argument that the writer is a dominated segment in a dominant class.

24. Betsy Erkkila, "Emily Dickinson and Class," *American Literary History* 4, no. 1 (spring 1992): 1–27.

25. Susan B. Warner's *The Wide, Wide World* (1850), for instance, sold 40,000 copies in its first year. Eventually 1,000,000 people would buy it. Maria Cummins's *The Lamplighter* (1854) sold 70,000 copies in its first year. For these figures, I am indebted to Michael T. Gilmore's *American Romanticism and the Marketplace* (Chicago: University of Chicago Press, 1985), 7.

26. Henry James, *A Portrait of a Lady* (1881; reprint, Toronto: Bantam Classics, 1983), ix.

27. Richard Brodhead, *Cultures of Letters: Scenes of Reading and Writing in Nineteenth-Century America* (Chicago: University of Chicago Press, 1993), 44. The discussion in this paragraph draws substantially on information provided by Brodhead and by Gilmore in *American Romanticism and the Marketplace*, 3–4.

28. *American Dictionary of the English Language*, (1844), s. v. "cedar." It is interesting that the pulpit in the First Congregational Church was made from a cedar log cut down in Lebanon by Daniel Bliss, the man who had married Emily Dickinson's childhood friend Abby Wood. The story is told in a pamphlet published by the First Church, entitled "Our Unique Pulpit: Made from Cedar and Olive Wood from Palestine. Transported by Camel and Boat from Mt. Lebanon. A Thrilling Story." Copies of this are in the special collections of the Jones Library, Amherst. There is a report of the shipment and carving of the log in the *Boston Sunday Herald*, 22 January 1961, sect. A.

29. James Ellis Humphrey, *Amherst Trees: An Aid to Their Study* (Amherst: Carpenter and Morehouse, 1892), 25.

30. For a description of the fence and the rule about the gates, see Martha Dickinson Bianchi, *Emily Dickinson Face to Face* (Boston: Houghton Mifflin, 1932), 4.

31. Julia M. Walker, "Emily Dickinson's Poetic of Private Liberation," *Dickinson Studies*, no. 45 (June 1983): 21.

32. For an investigation of both Mathers and specters, see Richard Slotkin, *Regeneration through Violence: The Mythology of the American Frontier, 1600–1860* (New York: Harper Perennial, 1996).

33. On the second page of the *Hampshire and Franklin Express* for 10 September 1858, there is an advertisement for "Bullard's panorama of New York," which included views of twelve miles of shipping and steamboats as well as thousands of people.

34. L#330, to Higginson, June 1869, *Letters of Emily Dickinson*, 2:460.

35. Terry Castle, "Phantasmagoria: Spectral Technology and the Metaphorics of Modern Reverie," *Critical Inquiry* 15, no. 1 (1988): 29.

36. The word "know" is used 230 times; "see," 146 times; "eyes," 88; "knew," 80 times; and "mind," 79 times. All these words point to a preoccupation with problems of perception that exist at the intellectual as well as at the visual level.

37. Karl Mannheim, *Ideology and Utopia: An Introduction to the Sociology of Knowledge*, 1936; reprint, trans. Louis Wirth and Edward Shils (San Diego: Harcourt Brace Jovanovich, 1985), 159, 161.

38. L#441, to Higginson, July 1875, *Letters of Emily Dickinson*, 2:542.

39. Bingham, *Emily Dickinson's Home*, 414.

40. Brodhead, *Cultures of Letters*, 31.

41. Northrop Frye, *Anatomy of Criticism: Four Essays* (Princeton: Princeton University Press, 1957), 271.

The title of this chapter is taken from a phrase used by Andrew Jackson Downing, a leading architect and horticulturalist of the nineteenth century, in "How to Popularize the Taste for Planting" (1852), quoted in David Schuyler, *Apostle of Taste: Andrew Jackson Downing, 1815–1852* (Baltimore: Johns Hopkins University Press, 1996), 117.

1. L. W. Goodell, *Catalogue of Choice Selected Flower Seeds and Bulbs for 1878* (Northampton: Gazette Publishing Co., 1878), 9.

2. L#823, to Mrs. J. Howard Sweetser, early May 1883, in *The Letters of Emily Dickinson*, ed. Thomas Johnson and Theodora Ward (Cambridge: Harvard University Press, Belknap Press, 1958), 3:775.

3. L. W. Goodell, Introduction, *Catalogue . . . for 1878* (inside front cover).

4. For a partial list of flowers grown in Dickinson's conservatory and in the family garden, see Guy Leighton, "The Emily Dickinson Homestead: A Historical Study of Its Setting with Recommendations for Preservation and Restoration" (MLA thesis, Department of Landscape Architecture and Regional Planning, University of Massachusetts, 1978), 90–91, 96.

5. Clark quoted in Ann Leighton, *American Gardens of the Nineteenth Century: "For Comfort and Affluence"* (Amherst: University of Massachusetts Press, 1987), 95.

6. *An American Dictionary of the English Language* (1844), s.v. "culture"; "cultivation." I am indebted to Jeremy Hawthorn at the Norwegian University of Science and Technology at Trondheim for making this point to me in comments on an earlier draft of this chapter.

7. The figure is given in Charles Johanningsmeier, "Sarah Orne Jewett and Mary E. Wilkins (Freeman): Two Shrewd Businesswomen in Search of New Markets," *New England Quarterly* 70, no. 1 (March 1997): 60.

8. Aimee E. Newell, " 'All Controversial Subjects Barred': Women's Leisure Activities in Amherst, Massachusetts, 1860–1890" (honors thesis, Amherst College, 1992), 17.

9. According to Daniel Lombardo the publications subscribed to included the *Observer, National Intelligencer, New England Farmer, Harper's Magazine, Springfield Republican, Boston Courier, Home Missionary, Congregational Quarterly, American Engineer Monthly, Greenfield Courier, Monthly Law Reporter, Youth's Companion, Boston Transcript,* and the *Round Table.* (*Tales of Amherst: A Look Back* [Amherst: Jones Library, Inc., 1986]), 101–2. Lombardo lists fourteen publications, as does the entry for Edward Dickinson in the "Periodicals and Newspaper Subscribers" for the 1860s, but writes that there were fifteen—on the grounds that the Dickinsons also received the *Hampshire and Franklin Express*. Figures for the average number of periodicals received per household, and how this related to the combined value of personal and real estate (according to the 1860 Census) and to the professional occupation of the primary wage earner are given in Newell, " 'All Controversial Subjects Barred,' " 19.

10. Johanningsmeier, "Sarah Orne Jewett and Mary E. Wilkins (Freeman)," 60.

11. Thomas Wentworth Higginson, "Letter to a Young Contributor," *Atlantic Monthly: A Magazine for Literature, Art, and Politics* 9 (April 1862): 401–11. The magazine was published by Ticknor and Fields, Boston.

12. The phrase is attributed, by Plutarch, to Sappho. It is quoted in Philip Knight, *Flower Poetics in Nineteenth-Century France* (Oxford: Clarendon Press, 1986), 6.

13. The issue of Dickinson's economic status is admittedly a complex one. She did not possess independent economic means, and indeed one of the many possible reasons for her withdrawal from the cultural world of her time, at least initially, may have been the difficulty of getting money for the kind of travel that would have been necessary for a provincial writer to gain access to the literary scene in Boston. Nevertheless, as long as her father lived (and even after his death), she was adequately provided for. Generally speaking, however, her correspondence does not touch on problems of economic dependency or class allegiance.

14. Jack Larkin, *The Reshaping of Everyday Life, 1790–1840* (New York: Harper and Row, 1987), 140. For a more detailed discussion of lamps, see Edgar de N. Mayhew, and Minor Myers Jr., *A Documentary History of American Interiors: From the Colonial Era to 1915* (New York: Charles Scribner's Sons, 1980), 137–38.

15. For a fuller analysis of heating in nineteenth-century New England, see Jane C. Nylander, *Our Own Snug Fireside: Images of the New England Home, 1760–1860* (New Haven: Yale University Press, 1994), 99–102.

16. Thomas Robbins writes in his diary for 17 December 1835: "My ink and other things were frozen hard in my chamber." Quoted in ibid., 76.

17. L#118, to Austin Dickinson, 21 April 1853, *Letters of Emily Dickinson*, 1:245. The letter is partly quoted also in Jean McClure Mudge, *Emily Dickinson and the Image of Home* (Amherst: University of Massachusetts Press, 1975), 46: on the same page, Mudge also writes that while "the Dickinsons lived there (1840–1855), the whole structure was dominated by a great central chimney, removed in later years to make a larger hall. This giant flue served kitchen, sitting room, parlor, and dining room hearths."

18. Larkin, *Reshaping of Everyday Life*, 140.

19. Nylander, *Our Own Snug Fireside*, 100. In the chapter, "Parlor-Plants and Flowers in Winter," in *Plain and Pleasant Talk about Fruits, Flowers, and Farming* (New York: Derby and Jackson, 1859), Horace Ward Beecher writes, "The thermometer should never be permitted to rise above sixty degrees or sixty-five degrees; nor at night to sink below forty degrees. Although plants will not be frost-bitten until the mercury falls to thirty-two degrees, yet the chill of a temperature below forty degrees will often be as mischievous to tender plants as frost itself. Excessive heat, particularly a dry stove heat, will destroy the leaves almost as certainly as frost" (355).

20. See Thomas J. Schlereth, *Victorian America: Transformations in Everyday Life, 1876–1915* (New York: HarperCollins, 1991), 123.

21. L#17, to Austin Dickinson, 2 November 1847, *Letters of Emily Dickinson*, 1:51.

22. Nylander, *Our Own Snug Fireside*, 79.

23. L#8, to Abiah Root, 25 September 1845, *Letters of Emily Dickinson*, 1:21.

24. Martha Dickinson Bianchi, *Emily Dickinson Face to Face* (Boston: Houghton Mifflin, 1932), 45.

25. L#34, to George Gould? February 1850, *Letters of Emily Dickinson*, 1:92.

26. Joanne Dobson, *Dickinson and the Strategies of Reticence: The Woman Writer in Nineteenth-Century America* (Bloomington: Indiana University Press, 1989), 87.

27. Alan Liu, *Wordsworth: The Sense of History* (Stanford: Stanford University Press, 1989), 49.

28. L#61, to Emily Fowler Ford, about 1851, *Letters of Emily Dickinson*, 1:154.

29. L#58, to Austin Dickinson, 17 October 1851, *Letters of Emily Dickinson*, 1:149. The eroticism may, of course, be unconscious, but the foregrounding of epistolary, poetic, and floral correspondences is very deliberate.

30. Martha Dickinson Bianchi, *The Life and Letters of Emily Dickinson* (Boston: Houghton Mifflin, 1924), 39.

31. Jack Goody, *The Culture of Flowers* (Cambridge: Cambridge University Press, 1993), 267.

32. Larkin writes that the "small minority of families—less than one in a hundred—who were able [to afford a pianoforte] . . . had acquired the ultimate 'badge of gentility' . . . the only thing that distinguishes 'decent people' from the lower and less 'distinguished' whether it was played or not." . . . "Before the advent of cheap lithographs in the 1840s, professionally produced art [by itinerant painters] was still for a relatively small minority; no more than one Massachusetts house in five had even one painting or engraving on its walls as late as the 1830s" (*Reshaping of Everyday Life*, 143, 144).

33. Mary Adéle Allen, *Around a Village Green: Sketches of Life in Amherst* (Northampton, Mass.: Kraushar Press, 1939), 67.

34. L#190, to Joseph A. Sweetser, early summer 1858, *Letters of Emily Dickinson*, 2:335.

35. Betsy Erkkila puts it this way: "Dickinson was the 'lady' and the intellectual whose leisure, freedom, and space 'to think' were made possible by the manual labor and proletarianization of others" ("Emily Dickinson and Class," *American Literary History* 4, no. 1 [spring 1992]:3).

36. It is always possible that, at some repressed level, the tools of mowing are seen as potential weapons, and that this leads unconsciously to thoughts of death.

37. Allen, *Around a Village Green*, 67.

38. The quotation is from ibid., 68. The percentages are from Clark, Christopher, *The Roots of Rural Capitalism: Western Massachusetts, 1780–1860* (Ithaca: Cornell University Press, 1990), 264–65.

39. Guy Leighton, "The Emily Dickinson Homestead," 28.

40. The quotation is attributed to Emily Fowler Ford, and is taken from Mabel Loomis Todd, ed., *Letters of Emily Dickinson* (New York: Harper, 1931), 132. Erkkila, presents the same quotation, which is where I first read it ("Emily Dickinson and Class," p. 7).

41. Bianchi, *Emily Dickinson Face to Face*, 39, 52–53.

42. The word "rose" appears sixty-nine times according to S. P. Rosenbaum, ed., in *A Concordance to the Poems of Emily Dickinson* (Ithaca: Cornell University Press, 1964), 634–35. Of these, approximately twenty-five entries are verb-forms. The plural "roses" appears a further eight times. The nearest other flower in terms of frequency is the "daisy" and "daisies": together, they appear twenty-seven times.

43. Rudy J. Favretti, and Joy Putnam Favretti, *Landscapes and Gardens for Historic Buildings: A Handbook for Reproducing and Creating Authentic Landscape Settings* (Nashville: American Association for State and Local History, 1978), 111.

44. Jay Leyda, *The Years and Hours of Emily Dickinson* (New Haven: Yale University Press, 1960), 1:10. Richard Sewall writes that one "of Emily's abiding concerns, horticulture, may have this simple obvious source"—her mother. *The Life of Emily Dickinson* (New York: Farrar, Straus and Giroux, 1974), 1:86.

45. Hooper, Lucy, ed., *The Lady's Book of Flowers and Poetry: to which are added, a Botanical Introduction, a Complete Floral Dictionary; and a Chapter on Flowers in Rooms* (New York: J. C. Riker, 1848), 248.

46. I employ the version of the poem that most closely corresponds to the one given in R. W. Franklin, *The Manuscript Books of Emily Dickinson* (Cambridge: Harvard University Press, Belknap Press, 1981), 2:836.

47. Thomas Wentworth Higginson, "A Letter to a Young Contributor," *Atlantic Essays* (Boston: James R. Osgood, 1871), 92, 91.

48. Bianchi, *Life and Letters of Emily Dickinson*, 39.

49. Wolfgang Schivelbusch, *Tastes of Paradise: A Social History of Spices, Stimulants, and Intoxicants*, trans. David Jacobson (New York: Vintage, 1993), 146.

50. My colleague at the Norwegian University of Science and Technology, Jeremy Hawthorn, points out the fascinating tension in the phrase "gift of Screws" between something that is freely transferred and something that is produced as the result of skilled and intense labor—even a kind of forced removal, like torture. Again, this points toward Dickinson's sense of herself as a craftsperson, a specialist, as it were. The message would appear to be that information cannot be extracted easily from nature by anyone—it takes skill and hard work.

51. The term is included, for example, in a glossary of botanical terms included at the rear of Peter Parley, *Cyclopedia of Botany, Including Familiar Descriptions of Trees, Shrubs and Plants; With Numerous Engravings* (Boston: Otis, Broaders and Company, 1838), 315.

52. Robert F. Fleissner, *A Rose by Another Name: A Survey of Literary Flora from Shakespeare to Eco* (West Cornwall, Conn.: Locust Hill Press, 1989), 22, 23.

53. Mrs. Almira H. Lincoln, *Familiar Lectures on Botany, Practical, Elementary and Physiological* (Hartford, Conn.: F. J. Huntington, 1836), 173; see also Richard B. Sewall "Science and the Poet: Emily Dickinson's Herbarium and 'The Clue Divine,'" *Harvard Literary Bulletin* 3, no. 1 (1992): 16–17.

54. See also Thomas H. Johnson, *The Poems of Emily Dickinson: Including Variant Readings Critically Compared with All Known Manuscripts* (Cambridge: Harvard University Press, Belknap Press, 1955), 2:719.

55. For a brief overview of Sicilian history in the nineteenth century, M. I.

Finley, Denis Mack Smith, and Christopher Duggan, *A History of Sicily* (New York: Viking Penguin, 1987), chaps. 17–20, and Denis Mack Smith, *Modern Sicily after 1713* (New York: Viking Press, 1968), chaps. 38–51.

56. L#61, to Emily Fowler Ford, about 1851, *Letters of Emily Dickinson*, 1:154.

57. Sarah Josepha Hale, *Flora's Interpreter; or the American Book of Flowers and Sentiments* (Boston: T. H. Webb and Co., 1832); Charlotte Elizabeth, *Floral Biographies; or Chapters on Flowers* (New York: M. W. Dodd, 1842); Mrs. J. Thayer, *Floral Gems, or the Songs of the Flowers* (Boston: James French, 1846); Mary Chauncey, ed., *The Floral Gift, from Nature and the Heart* (Worcester: Jonathan Grout, 1847); Lucy Hooper, ed., *The Lady's Book of Flowers and Poetry*; Miss Ildree, *The Language of Flowers* (Boston: De Vries, Ibarra and Co., 1865).

58. Laurel: Thayer, *Floral Gems*, 38; daffodil: Thayer, *Floral Gems*, 24. Hooper defines the daffodil as "Deceitful hope" (*The Lady's Book of Flowers and Poetry*, 241); lilacs: Chauncey, *The Floral Gift*, 78, Hooper also defines them as "forsaken" (*The Lady's Book of Flowers and Poetry*, 244); fuchsia: Thayer, *Floral Gems*, 112, and Chauncey, *The Floral Gift*, 48; heliotrope: Chauncey, *The Floral Gift*, 66.

59. George Frisbie Whicher, *This Was a Poet: A Critical Biography of Emily Dickinson* (1938; reprint, Ann Arbor: University of Michigan Press, 1957), 259.

60. For the purposes of a fuller textual comparison, the reader is also directed to Johnson, *Poems of Emily Dickinson*, 2:746–47, and Franklin, *Manuscript Books of Emily Dickinson*, 2:1247–48.

61. James Turner, *The Politics of Landscape: Rural Scenery and Society in English Poetry, 1630–1660* (Cambridge: Harvard University Press, 1979), 165.

62. William Empson uses this phrase in *English Pastoral Poetry* (New York: W. W. Norton, 1938), 89, to paraphrase Shakespeare's description of a flower-aristocrat. (The English version of this book was published in 1935 by Chatto and Windus as *Some Versions of Pastoral*.)

63. Elizabeth, *Floral Biographies: or Chapters on Flowers*, 175.

64. Wendy Martin, *An American Triptych: Anne Bradstreet, Emily Dickinson, Adrienne Rich* (Chapel Hill: University of North Carolina Press, 1984), 157.

65. See also Johnson's note in *Poems of Emily Dickinson*, 1:267.

66. *Ladies Manual of Art, or Profit and Pastime, A Self Teacher in All Branches of Decorative Art, Embracing Every Variety of Painting and Drawing on China, Glass, Velvet, Canvas, Paper, and Wood* (Philadelphia: American Mutual Library Association, 1887). No author given.

67. Henry Ward Beecher, *Plain and Pleasant Talk about Fruits, Flowers, and Farming*, 119.

68. The list is drawn up by looking through the index of Rosenbaum, *Concordance to the Poems of Emily Dickinson*, which includes variant readings. The list is not intended to be definitive.

69. L#195, to Dr. and Mrs. Holland, about 6 November 1858, *Letters of Emily Dickinson*, 2:341.

70. Betsy Erkkila, "Emily Dickinson and Class," 10.

71. Allen, *Around a Village Green*, 13.

72. See also Franklin, *Manuscript Books of Emily Dickinson*, 1:175.

73. Rebecca Patterson, *Emily Dickinson's Imagery* (Amherst: University of Massachusetts Press, 1979), 163.

74. See also Franklin, *Manuscript Books of Emily Dickinson*, 1:217.

75. James Guthrie, "Law, Property and Provincialism in Dickinson's Poems and Letters to Judge Otis Phillips Lord," *Emily Dickinson Journal* 5, no. 1 (1996): 36.

76. Nancy Walker, "Emily Dickinson and the Self: Humor as Identity," *Tulsa Studies in Women's Literature* 2 (1983): 65–66.

77. L#102, to Susan Dickinson, 24 February 1853, *Letters of Emily Dickinson*, 1:221.

78. Johnson's version in *Poems of Emily Dickinson*, 2:568 is the same.

79. See Franklin, *The Manuscript Books of Emily Dickinson*, 1:358. The dashes appear to be more varied than is the case in his print transcription.

80. Jeremy Hawthorn, *Cunning Passages: New Historicism, Cultural Materialism and Marxism in the Contemporary Literary Debate* (London: Arnold, 1996), 224. Much of what I say about differences between speech forms and the principle of renunciation is indebted to "Trivial Pursuits," Hawthorn's chapter on *The Turn of the Screw*.

81. The poem has many of the features that Paula Bennett identifies as masturbatory. She uses the phrase "autoerotic fantasy" in *Emily Dickinson: Woman Poet* (Iowa City: University of Iowa Press, 1990), 178.

82. Marjorie Levinson, *Keats's Life of Allegory: The Origins of a Style* (Oxford: Basil Blackwell, 1988), 27.

83. L#819, to Thomas Wentworth Higginson, late April 1883, *Letters of Emily Dickinson*, 3:773.

84. L#261, to Higginson, 25 April 1862, ibid., 2:404.

85. L#271, to Higginson, August 1862, ibid., 415.

86. Thorstein Veblen, *The Theory of the Leisure Class* (New York: Macmillan, 1899).

87. Schuyler, *Apostle of Taste*, 109.

88. L#207, to the Hollands, September 1859, *Letters of Emily Dickinson*, 2:353–54.

89. Parley, *Cyclopedia of Botany*, 105–6. The illustrations on the title pages of Parley's book demonstrate the typical belief held by nineteenth-century middle and upper-middle classes that the study of flowers was a sign of civilized taste. On one page, there is a picture of an angel surrounded by a wreath of flowers, and on the other a portrait of four children (two boys and two girls) looking at a flower: beside them is a classical vase, and in the background a balanced mixture of classical architecture and majestic trees. The values implicit in the writing of the book are most vulnerable at their point of dissemination, of course, and the book's purpose is to instill those values in the future generations represented by the pairs of boys and girls.

90. Chauncy, *Floral Gifts*, 32; Hooper, *The Lady's Book of Flowers and Poetry*, 253. The "youthful gladness" interpretation is proffered by Thayer in *Floral Gems*, p. 124.

91. Harriet Beecher Stowe, "How Shall I Learn to Write?" *Hearth and Home*, 16 Jan. 1869, 56, quoted in Richard H. Brodhead, *Cultures of Letters: Scenes of Reading and Writing in Nineteenth-Century America* (Chicago: University of Chicago Press, 1993), 114.

92. L#355, to Perez Cowan, late October 1870, *Letters of Emily Dickinson*, 2:483.

93. Empson, *English Pastoral Poetry*, 96.

94. Variants are also given by Johnson in his three-volume *Poems of Emily Dickinson*, 3:857–58. I have not seen the original manuscript.

95. Adrienne Rich, "I am in Danger–Sir–," *The Norton Anthology of American Literature*, ed. Nina Baym, 5th ed. (New York: W. W. Norton, 1998), 2:2719.

96. Empson, *English Pastoral Poetry*, 91.

97. Ann Leighton, *The Nineteenth-Century Garden* (Amherst: University of Massachusetts Press, 1987).

98. It was Sartre who said in a much quoted sentence that "Valéry is a petit bourgeois intellectual, no doubt about it. But not every petit bourgeois intellectual is Valéry" (Jean-Paul Sartre, *The Problem of Method* [London: Methuen, 1963], 56).

CHAPTER FIVE   *Letters from Home*

1. Martha Nell Smith, *Rowing in Eden: Rereading Emily Dickinson* (Austin: University of Texas Press, 1992), especially chapters 5 and 6, where Smith discusses many of the same issues. For a fuller presentation of Susan's work, and the extent of her collaboration with Emily, see Smith et al., *The Writings of Susan Dickinson* at http://jefferson.village.virginia.edu/dickinson/susan.

2. L#316, to Thomas Wentworth Higginson, early 1866, in *The Letters of Emily Dickinson*, ed. Thomas Johnson and Theodora Ward (Cambridge: Harvard University Press, Belknap Press, 1958), 2:450. In fact, Dickinson is concerned that Higginson will believe her to have been economical with the truth in claiming that she was not interested in mass publication.

3. Susan Huntington Dickinson, in Millicent Todd Bingham, *Ancestors' Brocades: The Literary Debut of Emily Dickinson and the Editing and Publication of Her Letters and Poems* (New York: Harper Brothers, 1945), 86, 115.

4. Kamilla Denman, "Emily Dickinson's Volcanic Punctuation," in *Emily Dickinson: A Collection of Critical Essays*, ed. Judith Farr (Upper Saddle River, N.J.: Prentice Hall, 1996), 191. Denman discusses the publishing history of P#1096A [J#986], "A narrow Fellow," and the altered punctuation of "You may have met Him—did you not / His notice sudden is" to the *Republican's* "You may have met him—did you not? / His notice sudden is." In 1872, Emily sent these lines to Susan, "You may have met him? Did you not / His notice sudden is," and Denman sees this gesture as showing "that the convention of print had no impact on her choice of punctuation, except to reinforce her original intentions." It seems equally clear to me, however, that the opposite is also the case: the inclusion of the question mark is a direct response to the printed version, which demon-

strated an ambiguity in the meaning, which Dickinson was unhappy about and tried to tighten.

5. Susan Dickinson, in Bingham, *Ancestors' Brocades*, 86.

6. And the unrefined were not just the general public: the penultimate line about "missing many favorites among the collection [*Poems: First Series*] which knowing your taste I wonder over" is a clear criticism of Higginson's coeditor, Mabel Loomis Todd.

7. Susan Dickinson, in Bingham, *Ancestors' Brocades*, 86. The "conflict of possession" soon resulted in the flurry of letters between William Hayes Ward, editor of *The Independent*, and Susan, Lavinia, and Mabel over Susan's attempted placement of P#187A [J#792], "Through the strait pass of suffering," in that magazine; the same issue of ownership surfaced later, in the court case over Mabel's claim to have been assigned Dickinson land as a gift by Austin (idem, 111–20). The letters should be read for themselves, and Bingham's (highly partisan) commentary either avoided or treated with caution. Susan's request that "the Martyrs" (as she titled the poem) be printed "for a money compensation" and her request that this remain "confidential as the sister [Lavinia] is quite jealous of my treasures" is suspicious only if one believes that Lavinia had the sole right to ask for money for the poems. In addition, it should be kept in mind that Susan planned to produce a volume of Dickinson's verse at her own expense—which Lavinia eventually did—and that this money for "the Martyrs" would have helped her to do that (see idem, 114–15). Though no one seems to take Lavinia seriously in all of this, her claim that Susan "[has] fine ability but lacks mental energy to complete" seems accurate at this point, though Smith points out that there were a number of reasons for the dissipation of Susan's energy, not least of which was her disabling grief at the death of Emily (*Ancestors' Brocades*, 87; *Rowing in Eden*, 213–14).

8. Susan Dickinson, in Bingham, *Ancestor's Brocades*, 118. In a footnote, Millicent Todd Bingham (Martha Dickinson Bianchi's main editorial rival at this time) adds, "I have been told by several people that at this time Sue was more interested in her daughter's literary career than in Emily's poetry" (118 n.). The remark is not borne out by the letters, which are primarily about Emily, but it would be entirely natural for the parent of a talented child to bring that talent to the attention of others, if the opportunity presented itself. In addition, Susan may have felt that the Evergreens, which displaced the Homestead as a social center in Amherst, needed its own poet to retrieve that influence.

9. Susan Dickinson, in Bingham, *Ancestors' Brocades*, 86. In *Rowing in Eden*, Smith first advanced the theory that Susan might have delayed preparing the poems for publication because she dreaded "publicity for us all." (Susan's letter is quoted from *Ancestors' Brocades*, 115; Smith refers to it on p. 214 of *Rowing*). In another letter, Susan refers to her long-term ownership of some of Dickinson's manuscript poems, many of which were "too personal and adulatory ever to be printed" (*Ancestors' Brocades*, 116). Clearly, Susan felt extremely uncomfortable about having some of the more private poems addressed to her finding their way into the public domain. Smith accepts Susan's argument that this was a personal

decision taken to protect Dickinson's privacy, but I extend her arguments slightly further in suggesting that even personal decisions may be governed by invisible class imperatives.

10. P#519A [J#441], "This is my letter to the World" is often quoted by critics as evidence that the poet's decision not to publish shows that she entrusted her work to a later audience in the belief that she would be misunderstood in her own. In fact, Dickinson seems to have underestimated her audience; after her death, some 12,000 copies of her first volume were sold, with five editions appearing between 12 November 1890 and February 1891. For a very fine and incisive reading of Dickinson, politics, and the marketplace, see Betsy Erkkila's *The Wicked Sisters: Women Poets, Literary History, and Discord* (New York: Oxford University Press, 1992). Like Erkkila, I relate Dickinson's withdrawal to an essentially conservative rejection of literature as a commodity. Unlike her, I employ Bakhtin's concept of the dialogic imagination to argue for a reengagement with the world through its languages.

11. L#397, to Susan Dickinson, autumn 1873, *Letters of Emily Dickinson*, 2:512.

12. Quoted from *The Poems of Alexander Pope* (London: Methuen, 1963), 826. William Empson's discussion of the poem can be found in his *Some Versions of Pastoral* (1935; reprint, Harmondsworth, England: Penguin, 1966), 207. I am grateful to my colleague at the University of Trondheim, Jeremy Hawthorn, for drawing my attention to this passage.

13. Margaret Dickie, *Lyric Contingencies: Emily Dickinson and Wallace Stevens* (Philadelphia: University of Pennsylvania Press, 1991), 66.

14. *The Letters of Herman Melville*, ed. Merrell R. Davis and William H. Gilman (New Haven: Yale University Press, 1960), 121.

15. There were numerous anti-Irish stories and jokes in the pages of the *Hampshire and Franklin Express*, for instance.

16. In order to restore some balance, I would suggest that it is equally possible to read the poem as a critique of an American democracy, which does not extend its voting privileges to women: "one man, one vote" means *man*, not *woman*. Thomas Docherty, writing of another subject, is also apt at this point: he writes of a democracy based "upon individualism, the result [of which] is the production of individualistic charismatic leaders, whose single choice is adopted, necessarily, by everyone: it is the democracy of 'one person, one vote'—and the leader has it." Women, however, did not have votes, and they were therefore nonpersons, or, as the poem puts it, nobodies (though not entirely voiceless ones). This is an attractive reading, not least because it demonstrates Dickinson's transforming repression and exclusion into an enabling perspective, even a preference for the exclusiveness of the speaker's position. But that perspective still relies on distinctions that are uncomfortably close to a class awareness that ascribes animal characteristics to the lower orders while retaining a discourse of the spirit for the sensitive few. See Docherty's *On Modern Authority: The Theory and Condition of Writing, 1500 to the Present Day* (Sussex, England: Harvester Press, 1987), 57.

17. Wendy Martin, *An American Triptych: Anne Bradstreet, Emily Dickinson, Adrienne Rich* (Chapel Hill: University of North Carolina Press, 1984), 89.

18. Many of Dickinson's poems identify with biblical prophets, including Moses and Jesus, who do not gain immediate social recognition or reward in their own lifetime.

19. L#238, to Susan Gilbert Dickinson, summer 1861, *Letters of Emily Dickinson*, 2:380.

20. For a complete list of these publications, see the appendix to Karen Dandurand's excellent "Dickinson and the Public," in *Dickinson and Audience*, ed. Martin Orzeck and Robert Weisbuch (Ann Arbor: University of Michigan Press, 1996), 273–74.

21. Richard Brodhead, *Cultures of Letters: Scenes of Reading and Writing in Nineteenth-Century America* (Chicago: University of Chicago Press, 1993), esp. 53.

22. L#676, to Higginson, November 1880, *Letters of Emily Dickinson*, 3:681–82.

23. L#380, to Louise Norcross, late 1872, ibid., 2:500.

24. The phrase "manuscript miscellanies" is taken from Arthur F. Marotti's "Manuscript, Print, and the Social History of the Lyric" in *The Cambridge Companion to English Poetry: Donne to Marvell*, ed. Thomas N. Corns (Cambridge: Cambridge University Press, 1993), 52–79. Marotti's discussion is primarily about seventeenth-century English (male) writers, but has potential significance for Dickinson in the sense that Marotti looks at the social implications of the manuscript production and transmission of lyric poems. His conclusions may not be applicable, but his methods are, and they inform this chapter at several junctures.

25. Marotti, "Manuscript, Print, and the Social History of the Lyric," 52.

26. See R. W. Franklin, *The Manuscript Books of Emily Dickinson* (Cambridge: Harvard University Press, Belknap Press, 1981), 1:182.

27. Aífe Murray, "Domestic Work and Poetry" (Jones Library, Amherst, Mass., 1994), 7. Murray also alludes to the description of domestic work given in Millicent Todd Bingham, *Emily Dickinson's Home: Letters of Edward Dickinson and His Family* (New York: Harper and Brothers, 1955), 113.

28. Aífe Murray, "Kitchen Table Poetics: Maid Margaret Maher and Her Poet Emily Dickinson," *Emily Dickinson Journal* 5, no. 2 (1996): 285–96.

29. In "Kitchen Table Poetics," Murray makes this point more convincingly when she says that Dickinson's periods of greatest and lowest literary productivity coincided with the presence and absence of hired help. My own argument is that Dickinson's speaker accepts that one enables the other, but that such identification is not social but metaphoric. There is no class tension in the poem because there were no such tensions in the household: the servants did their work without complaint or dissension, and Dickinson did hers. Whereas Murray offers a view of mutual respect, even of a common poetic project between Maher and Dickinson, I would suggest that the relationship between them functioned because Maher did nothing to contest her social position.

30. Dickinson would have found support for appropriating the language of labor to glorify the labor of language in her local newspaper: "*Beneath human beings to work!* Look to the artist's studio, the poet's garret, where the genius of immortality stands ready to seal her works with her uneffaceable signet, and then

you will only see industry standing by her side" (*Hampshire and Franklin Express*, Friday, 10 June 1853, p. 1).

31. Jack Larkin, *The Reshaping of Everyday Life, 1790–1840* (New York: Harper and Row, 1987), 142. Although the references to oil may appear to contradict this, the poem may be describing gaslight, which moved "prosperous American families of the 1820s and 1830s . . . farther out of nighttime darkness": such an interpretation is only feasible if one accepts that the poem is spoken by one of Dickinson's naive personae who fails to understand how a lamp can continue without a slave or that a poem can survive the death of its author.

32. Lamps were expensive to buy and the oil they burnt costly, so that social inequalities were also apparent in the nighttime illumination that families of the lower and upper classes could afford: the serf who supervised the provision of light would have relied on firelight or alternative and cheaper instruments of illumination in her own home (and such supplies would not have been inexhaustible). Imagining a lamp that could burn forever depends in the first place on having the means to buy lamps and an unending supply of oil and, therefore, to take them sufficiently for granted to be able to use them figuratively: in that sense, the poem would seem to reflect the material advantages of its author and her family. For the information on Argand, I direct the reader to Mary Ellen Chase, *The Story of Lighthouses* (New York: W. W. Norton, 1965), 112.

33. *An American Dictionary of the English Language* (1844), s. v. "dissemination."

34. Another possibility is that the poem is referring to the lamp of a lighthouse: the reference to the lens (which increases the range of projection) and to the circumference (as it sweeps around) of the light might bear this out. The light might bear this out. The light derives from one place, but what it illuminates varies.

35. Baudelaire quoted in Roger Shattuck, "Duchamps's Gamble," *New York Review of Books*, 27 March 1997, p. 27. I am grateful to David Porter for drawing this article to my attention, photocopying it for me, and discussing the status of Dickinson's manuscripts at several informal junctures.

CHAPTER SIX   *Gathering Buds*

1. Once again, I am grateful to my colleague and friend Jeremy Hawthorn, for a number of comments that helped to make this introductory passage possible. Needless to say, problems of clarity or linkage are not his responsibility. Hawthorn also suggested to me the later parallel between Dickinson and Stevie Smith.

2. Sharon Cameron writes, "If we could observe changes in the style of the poems, it might be easier to arrive at textual decisions. But, in fact, as most critics agree, there is no development in the canon of poems. The experiences recorded by these poems are insular ones, subject to endless repetition" (*Lyric Time: Dickinson and the Limits of Genre* [Baltimore: Johns Hopkins University Press, 1979], 14).

3. David Porter, *Dickinson; the Modern Idiom* (Cambridge: Harvard University Press, 1981), 267.

4. Thomas H. Johnson, ed., *The Poems of Emily Dickinson: Including Variant Readings Critically Compared with All Known Manuscripts*, 3 vols. (Cambridge: Harvard University Press, Belknap Press, 1955); and Johnson, *The Complete Poems of Emily Dickinson* (Boston: Little, Brown and Co., 1960).

5. Porter, *The Modern Idiom*, 2.

6. For another discussion of "the sheer number of poems she wrote" see Gary Lee Stonum, *The Dickinson Sublime* (Madison: University of Wisconsin Press, 1990), 5. It could justifiably be argued that leaving the texts in their unfinished state was a deliberate strategy to increase readerly participation in the construction of the text's meaning—at least at the individual level.

7. That Dickinson wanted her poems to survive her is certain: anyone who doesn't want her materials to reach others destroys them herself. But *who* she wanted to read them is another matter. Her own practice of circulating manuscripts suggests that her projected audience was fairly limited in terms of class.

8. Joyce Carol Oates, "Soul at the White Heat: The Romance of Emily Dickinson's Poetry," *Critical Inquiry* 13 (summer 1987): 806.

9. Sharon Cameron, *Choosing Not Choosing: Emily Dickinson's Fascicles* (Chicago: University of Chicago Press, 1992).

10. Martha Nell Smith, review essay on *Choosing Not Choosing*, by Sharon Cameron, *Emily Dickinson Journal* 3, no. 1 (1994): 108.

11. Martha Lindblom O'Keefe, *This Edifice: Studies in the Structure of the Fascicles of the Poetry of Emily Dickinson* (privately printed, 1986), 2. A copy of this three-volume study is in Special Collections, Jones Library, Amherst, Massachusetts. I am indebted to Dossie Kissam, a guide at the Dickinson Homestead, who first brought it to my attention.

12. Dorothy Huff Oberhaus, *Emily Dickinson's Fascicles: Method and Meaning* (University Park: Pennsylvania State University Press, 1997), 19.

13. William H. Shurr, *The Marriage of Emily Dickinson: A Study of the Fascicles* (Lexington: University Press of Kentucky, 1983). One feels nonetheless that the "child" in Dickinson's writing was in this case a traditional female metaphor for literary, not biological offspring.

14. R. W. Franklin, *The Manuscript Books of Emily Dickinson* (Cambridge: Harvard University Press, Belknap Press, 1981), 1:x.

15. Sandra M. Gilbert and Susan Gubar, *The Madwoman in the Attic: The Woman Writer and the Nineteenth-Century Literary Imagination* (New Haven: Yale University Press, 1979), 583.

16. Fernando Ferrara, "Theory and Model for the Structural Analysis of Fiction," *New Literary History* 5 (1974): 250.

17. Not all the poems are arranged chronologically or in an order corresponding to the dates they were written on. It therefore follows that some other principle might have applied, which means that the poems interact and affirm or alter the potential trajectories of each other's meaning(s). Their presentation together in fascicles affects the significance in ways that may not have been apparent or intentional at the time of their writing. Cameron, in her fine *Choosing Not*

Choosing also looks at the same packet and draws a different conclusion: it describes a narrative of sexual passion.

18. Roland Greene, *Post-Petrarchism: Origins and Innovations of the Western Lyric Sequence* (Princeton: Princeton University Press), 68–69.

19. By potentially sectarian, I mean that the imagery used in the context of a discussion of death and the existence of an afterlife might call to mind the drinking of sacramental wine during the Catholic Mass, an activity also meant to signify the promise of eternal life. Dickinson may be ridiculing this kind of literal vision. As I hope I have made clear, however, there are other ways to read the poem: either as a satire on the language of capitalism, or as a dramatization of (religious and secular) paradox—death being the path to eternity, life necessarily leading to death.

20. Gary Saul Morson and Caryl Emerson, eds., *Rethinking Bakhtin: Extensions and Challenges* (Evanston, Ill.: Northwestern University Press, 1989), 58.

21. Paul deMan, "Dialogue and Dialogism," in ibid., 105–14.

22. Bakhtin, "Discourse in the Novel,"in *The Dialogic Imagination: Four Essays*, ed. Michael Holmquist, trans. Caryl Emerson and Michael Holmquist (Austin: University of Texas Press, 1981), 298.

23. Yuri Lotman, "The Text within the Text," *PMLA* 109, no. 3 (May 1994): 378.

24. Oberhaus, *Emily Dickinson's Fascicles*; O'Keefe *This Edifice*.

25. John Gerlach, "Reading Dickinson: Bolts, Hounds, the Variorum, and Fascicle 39," *Emily Dickinson Journal* 3, no. 2 (1994): 80. Gerlach looks at the ordering of the poems in their fascicle sequence, and in different arrangements, to see how they affect our reading experience. The resulting essay is scholarly, eminently sensible, and appropriately provisional in its conclusions and recommendations.

26. George Eliot, *Middlemarch* (1871–72; reprint, Harmondsworth, England: Penguin English Library, 1969), 297. The passage is similar in many ways to this statement by Wolfgang Iser: "In the same way, two people gazing at the night sky may both be looking at the same collection of stars, but one will see the image of a plough, and the other will make out a dipper. The 'stars' in a literary text are fixed; the lines that join them are variable" (*The Implied Reader: Patterns of Communication in Prose Fiction from Bunyan to Beckett* [Baltimore: Johns Hopkins University Press, 1974], 282).

27. L#368, to Thomas Wentworth Higginson, November 1871, *The Letters of Emily Dickinson*, ed. Thomas Johnson and Theodora Ward (Cambridge: Harvard University Press, Belknap Press, 1958), 2:491–92. See also P#1604A (J#1590), "Not at Home to Callers," in Ralph W. Franklin, *The Poems of Emily Dickinson* (Cambridge: Harvard University Press, 1998), 3:1408.

28. L#381, to Higginson, late 1872, ibid., 2:500–501.

29. L#396, to Higginson, about 1873, and L#405, to Higginson, January 1874, ibid., 511–12, 517–18.

30. L#413, to Higginson, late May 1874, ibid., 525.

31. L#449, to Higginson, January 1876, ibid., 546–47.

32. R. W. Franklin, *The Manuscript Books of Emily Dickinson* (Cambridge: Harvard University Press, Belknap Press, 1981), x.

33. Dickinson Electronic Archives: http://jefferson.village.edu/dickinson. There are discussions of individual fascicles at http://jefferson.village.virginia.edu/dickinson/fascicles_index.html.

CHAPTER SEVEN *Revising the Script*

1. Martha Nell Smith, quoted in Elinor Heginbotham, "Plenary Session: Editing Dickinson," *Emily Dickinson International Bulletin* 7 (November 1995): 5.

2. Ralph Franklin, *The Editing of Emily Dickinson: A Reconsideration* (Madison: University of Wisconsin Press, 1967), and *The Manuscript Books of Emily Dickinson* (Cambridge: Harvard University Press, Belknap Press, 1981).

3. See Mary Carney, "Dickinson's Poetic Revelations: Variants as Process," *Emily Dickinson Journal* 5, no. 2 (1996): 134–35, for a fairly typical appropriation of Franklin's findings for purposes he clearly would disapprove of.

4. Susan Howe, *The Birth-Mark: Unsettling the Wilderness in American Literary History* (Hanover: Wesleyan University Press, 1993), 134.

5. David Porter, Review essay, on *New Poems of Emily Dickinson*, by William Shurr, *Emily Dickinson Journal* 4 (1995): 127. (Porter quotes from Jerome McGann, *Black Riders: The Visible Language of Modernism* [Princeton: Princeton University Press, 1993], 38.)

6. Howe, *The Birth-Mark*, 148.

7. Houghton Library, Harvard University, Ms. Am. 1118.3 (52). Subsequent references to photostats of manuscripts will use the abbreviation HL. It should be noted that I asked for, but was refused, access to the originals.

8. McGann, *Black Riders*, 28.

9. Peter Campbell, "Character Building," *London Review of Books*, 9 June 1994. Campbell emphatically denies "someone who has read the poetry of . . . Emily Dickinson only in a printed format which bears little relationship to the original manuscript [has] a necessarily imperfect understanding of [her] art" (21–22).

10. Franklin, *Editing of Emily Dickinson*, 120.

11. *The Letters of Emily Dickinson*, ed. Thomas H. Johnson and Theodora Ward (Cambridge: Harvard University Press, Belknap Press, 1958), 2:542–43. Manuscript (photostat): Galatea Collection, Ms. Am. 1093 (57), Boston Public Library. The Boston Public Library and Thomas Johnson assign different numbers for the manuscripts: in the *Letters*, the manuscript is BPL (Higg 72). Within this section, when I refer within the text to the photostat of a manuscript I will give there number of the letter in *Letters*, followed by the number of the item in the Galatea Collection (the Galatea Collection will be abbreviated as G-C).

12. I list the year in which the letters were written, how many there are for that year, and how often word separation occurs (I do not count word separation more than once in any given letter): 1875-2-2; 1876-12-6; 1877-8-5; 1878-5-0; 1879-3-1; 1880-6-1; 1881-2-1; 1882-2-0; 1883-1-1; 1884-2-0; 1885-2-2; and 1886-3-2. There are three years in which no division takes place—1878, 1882,

and 1884—as well as one, 1880, when next to none are recorded. In the early years of the correspondence, from 1862 through 1874, there are five letters where word division takes place, out of a possible twenty-one (two manuscripts were not available to me, so the figure is approximate, but fairly reliable). The numbers (as they occur in Johnson's edition) are L#261 (seventh page, lines 4 and 5 of the manuscript: "chap- / ters"); L#280 (fourth page, lines 7 and 8: "pro- / prospective"); L#319 (fourth page, lines 9 and 10: "enchant- / ment"); L#368 (fourth page, lines 2, 3, and 4: "congrat- / ulation superflu- / ous"); and L#405 (first page, lines 8 and 9, 11 and 12: "per- / mission"; "per- / haps"). Separation is therefore slightly less frequent than in later years: one in four letters rather than one in three.

13. HL, Ms. Am. 1118.3 (33).

14. McGann, *Black Riders*, 38.

15. I hope it is understood that I am not saying that she was somehow *incapable* of such an intention.

16. L#277, to Samuel Bowles, November 1862, *Letters of Emily Dickinson*, 2:419–20, the manuscript copy of which is bMs. Am. 1118.99c L277 (photostat) at the Houghton Library of Harvard University. The poem is included in L#257, in *Letters of Emily Dickinson*, 2:399–400; the manuscript copy is also at the Houghton Library: bMs. Am. 1118.99c L257 (photostat).

17. The difference between "public" and "private" variants of P#195A (J#690) is established more extensively by Carney in "Dickinson's Poetic Revelations." She asserts—rightly—that the existence of these variants "suggests Dickinson's resistance and simultaneous acquiescence to the poetic conventions of her time" (136).

18. Johnson is similarly undecided: he claims that the irregular line spacings and stanza divisions "clearly suggests a conscious experimentation" at times, while at other times they reflect "indifference" (*The Poems of Emily Dickinson* [Cambridge: Harvard University Press, Belknap Press, 1955], 1:lxiii). When Margret Sands quotes (and italicizes) only the "indifference" part of Johnson's description, she seriously, and unfairly, misrepresents this ambivalence on his part. See her otherwise excellent "Re-reading the Poems: Editing Opportunities in Variant Versions," *Emily Dickinson Journal* 5, no. 2 (1996): 141.

19. In doing so, of course, Johnson was guided by his duty as an editor to alert the reader to the presence of these poems, and his reasons are scholarly and impeccable. And although he was editing the correspondence for its own merits, the poetry was still his primary interest. The conventions of his day also insisted on such a presentation, and to expect Johnson to have behaved differently is un-realistic.

20. Ellen Louise Hart, "The Elizabeth Whitney Putnam Manuscripts and New Strategies for Editing Emily Dickinson's Letters," *Emily Dickinson Journal* 4, no. 1 (1995): 49.

21. The manuscript facsimile is no. 41 in Special Collections, Frost Library, Amherst College. The printed version is L#677 to Mrs. Edward Tuckerman, early December 1880, *Letters of Emily Dickinson*, 3:682.

22. The phrase is Jerome McGann's, from his "Emily Dickinson's Visible Language," *Emily Dickinson Journal* 2, no. 2 (1993): 50. McGann's example is a letter (L#229) to Samuel Bowles that includes P#272A (J#691), "Would you like Summer? Taste of our's." As he says, "the poem slips into the prose without any marginal signals that the textual rhythms are about to undergo a drastic shift." This is true, but it is also true that by the seventh line of the facsimile he looks at, gaps have begun to appear in the lines, corresponding (perhaps) to the end of metrical lines. The blurring of generic distinctions is accompanied by what might be construed as their continuing formal demarcation.

23. L#280, to Thomas Wentworth Higginson, February 1863, *Letters of Emily Dickinson*, 2:423. GC: Ms. Am. 1093 (17).

24. GC: Ms. Am. 1093 (19).

25. L#459 to Higginson, spring 1876, *Letters of Emily Dickinson*, 2:553–54. GC: Ms. Am 1093 (85).

26. Johnson imposes typographic conventions where Dickinson did not, of course. But I would argue that his usage is still prompted by hers.

27. Manuscript Ms. D56 (836) at Special Collections, Frost Library, Amherst College.

28. See also Johnson's version (J#1622) in *Poems of Emily Dickinson*, 3:1113.

29. At the time of this writing, this is available at http://jefferson.village.virginia.edu/dickinson/susan/tarch1.html.

30. See also the version of the manuscript reproduced in Franklin, *Manuscript Books of Emily Dickinson*, 2:1342.

31. L#381, to Higginson, late 1872; *Letters of Emily Dickinson*, 2:500. GC: Ms. Am. 1093 (43).

32. Howe, *The Birth-Mark*, 139.

33. Ibid., 150.

34. GC: Ms. Am. 1093 (37).

35. I refer again to L#381, to Higginson, *Letters of Emily Dickinson*, 2:500. GC: Ms. Am. 1093 (43).

36. Susan Dickinson, quoted in Millicent Todd Bingham, *Ancestors' Brocades: The Literary Debut of Emily Dickinson and the Editing and Publication of Her Letters and Poems* (New York: Harper Brothers, 1945), 86.

37. Since this chapter was written, this manuscript obituary has been made available on the Internet (see n. 29 above). Readers may want to "verify" my version against that one.

38. Susan Huntington Gilbert Dickinson, "Manuscript obituary notice of Emily Dickinson," HL, bMs. Am. 1118.95 (box 9), 12.

39. Franklin, *Manuscript Books of Emily Dickinson*, 1:13.

40. T. W. Higginson, and Mabel Loomis Todd, eds., *Poems of Emily Dickinson: Second Series* (Boston: Roberts Brothers, 1891), 186.

41. One of the objections to raise at this point is that Dickinson's letters and notes were almost never casual: they went through several drafts and were carefully crafted. But that does not mean that their appearance on the page mattered in any consistent way: the shift from the neat print of the early years to the

very different inscriptions of the later years could argue indifference as much as experimentation.

42. The reader will doubtless be aware that I am comparing *my* versions of Dickinson's poems and Susan's transcription, and that there may therefore be some inaccuracies. I hope the larger point I am trying to make remains acceptable, however.

43. Franklin, *Manuscript Books of Emily Dickinson*, 2:1323.

44. Susan Huntington Gilbert Dickinson, "Transcripts of Emily Dickinson's Poems," HL, bMs. Am. 1118.95 (box 12).

45. http://jefferson.village.edu/dickinson/susan/offer.html.

46. McGann, *Black Riders*, 38.

47. Martha Nell Smith, "The Poet as Cartoonist," *Comic Power in Emily Dickinson*, ed. Suzanne Juhasz, Cristanne Miller, and Martha Nell Smith (Austin: University of Texas Press, 1993), 66.

48. Jonathan Culler, "Changes in the Study of the Lyric," in *Lyric Poetry: Beyond New Criticism*, ed. Chaviva Hošek and Patricia Parker (Ithaca: Cornell University Press, 1985), 28.

CHAPTER EIGHT   *Cordoning off Dissent*

1. L#285, to Louise and Frances Norcross, 7 October 1863, *The Letters of Emily Dickinson*, ed. Thomas Johnson and Theodora Ward (Cambridge: Harvard University Press, Belknap Press, 1958), 2:427.

2. Martha Dickinson Bianchi, *Emily Dickinson Face to Face* (Boston: Houghton Mifflin, 1932), 66. Helen Campbell, *Household Economics: A Course of Lectures in the School of Economics at the University of Wisconsin* (New York: G. P. Putnam's Sons, 1898), 28.

3. See, for example, Erika Scheurer, " 'Near but Remote': Emily Dickinson's Epistolary Voice," *Emily Dickinson Journal* 4, no. 1 (1995): 86–107 (listed in the contents page as "Emily Dickinson's Dialogic Voice"), and Paul Crumbley, "Dickinson's Dashes and the Limits of Discourse," *Emily Dickinson Journal* 1, no. 2 (1992): 8–29.

4. Mikhail M. Bakhtin, "Discourse in the Novel," in *The Dialogic Imagination: Four Essays*, ed. Michael Holmquist, trans. Caryl Emerson and Michael Holquist (Austin: University of Texas Press, 1981), 285.

5. In "Dickinson's Dashes and the Limits of Discourse," Paul Crumbley makes similar points. I differ from him in emphasis: he writes that "we can understand the poems as her refusal to silence the many rebellious voices that registered clearly in her own mind despite the considerable social pressure of more orthodox opinion seeking to enforce conformity" and thus stresses the individuality of her writing, whereas I argue that Dickinson included voices other than her own, including those of conformity, in order to suggest that the self could not fashion a language that was not already permeated with other accents. Crumbley concludes that Dickinson inserts these discourses basically to record her distance

from them, which means at times that he approximates to the monologic definition of poetry that he earlier dismisses.

6. Gary Saul Morson and Caryl Emerson, *Mikhail Bakhtin: Creation of a Prosaics* (Stanford, Calif.: Stanford University Press, 1990), 320.

7. Bakhtin, "Discourse in the Novel," 291.

8. Ibid., p. 293.

9. Denise Levertov, *The Poet in the World* (New York: New Directions, 1973), 87.

10. It is possible that the poem expresses a sense of immortality as a property that time cannot rob the speaker of. (So although time is a thief who takes years and even lives away from other people, he cannot dispossess the speaker, who has "legal" evidence that she owns a soul.)

11. Gary Saul Monson and Caryl Emerson, eds., *Rethinking Bakhtin: Extensions and Challenges* (Evanston, Ill.: Northwestern University Press, 1989), 59.

12. Daniel Aaron, *The Unwritten War: American Writers and the Civil War* (London: Oxford University Press, 1973), 356. Aaron develops a point first made by Thomas W. Ford in "Emily Dickinson and the Civil War," *University of Kansas City Review* 31 (spring 1965): 199–203, where he argues that more than half of Dickinson's poems were written during this war. Other critics interested in the relation between literature and the Civil War include Shira Wolosky, *Emily Dickinson: A Voice of War* (New Haven: Yale University Press, 1984); Edmund Wilson, *Patriotic Gore* (New York: Oxford University Press, 1962), 488–91; and Ralph Marcellino, "Emily Dickinson," *College English* 7 (November 1945): 102–3.

13. Michael André Bernstein, "The Poetics of *Ressentiment*," in Monson and Emerson, *Rethinking Bakhtin*, 200; Monson and Emerson, *Mikhail Bakhtin: Creation of a Prosaics*, 320.

14. Michael F. Bernard-Donals, *Mikhail Bakhtin: Between Phenomenology and Marxism* (Cambridge: Cambridge University Press, 1994), 29.

15. Perry Anderson, "Components of the National Culture," in *Student Power: Problems, Diagnosis, Action,* ed. Alexander Cockburn and Robin Blackburn (Harmondsworth, England: Penguin, 1969), 237. Of course, Gellner is talking about Britain in "Components of the National Culture," and he distinguishes the British intelligentsia from the intelligentsia of continental Europe. But as I argue elsewhere, nineteenth-century America, and New England in particular, had a British-style intelligentsia distinguished among other things by "a lack of interest in ideas, argument, fundamentals or reform."

16. Both quotations are taken from Mary P. Ryan, *The Empire of the Mother: American Writing about Domesticity, 1830 to 1860,* Women in History, no. 2–3 (New York: Institute for Research in History and Haworth Press, 1982), 112, 104.

17. The poems are listed in Ralph W. Franklin, *The Poems of Emily Dickinson* (Cambridge: Harvard University Press, Belknap Press, 1998), 3:1531–32. The titles and numbers assigned to them by Franklin are P#2, "A Valentine" in 1852; P#11, "Nobody knows this little rose" in 1858; P#207, "I taste a liquor never brewed" in 1861; P#124, "Safe in their alabaster chambers" in 1862; P#95, "Flowers – Well if anybody"; P#122, "These are the days when birds come

back"; P#236, "Some keep the Sabbath going to church"; P#321, "Blazing in gold and quenching in purple"; and P#112 "Success is counted sweetest" in 1864. P#1096, "A narrow fellow in the grass" was published in 1866. Some of these poems were printed again in different journals: "Success is counted sweetest" appeared again in 1878. Cynthia Griffin Wolff (*Emily Dickinson* [New York: Knopf, 1986]) and Karel Dandurand ("New Dickinson Civil War Publications," *American Literature* 56 [1984]: 26–27) state that eleven poems were printed during Emily Dickinson's lifetime, but they count "Blazing in Gold and quenching in Purple" twice because it was published both in the *Springfield Republican* and in the *Drawn-Beat* in 1864. In "Dickinson and the Public," Dandurand again lists eleven poems as having being published during Dickinson's lifetime, but this time P#112 (J#67), "Success is counted sweetest," is included twice. Though it seems possible that Dickinson published more widely than has hitherto been supposed, the present state of scholarship indicates only ten poems as having appeared in her lifetime. ("Dickinson and the Public" is in *Dickinson and Audience*, ed. Martin Orzeck and Robert Weisbuch [Ann Arbor: University of Michigan Press, 1996], 273–74.)

18. The quotation is from Crumbley, "Dickinson's Dashes and the Limits of Discourse," 12.

19. Joanne Dobson, *Dickinson and the Strategies of Reticence: The Woman Writer in Nineteenth-Century America* (Bloomington: Indiana University Press, 1989), 78.

20. Ibid., 79.

21. Robert Weisbuch refers memorably to these as "non-recoverable contexts." See *Emily Dickinson's Poetry* (Chicago: University of Chicago Press, 1975).

22. Mikhail, Bakhtin, *Problems of Dostoevsky's Poetics* (Dana Point, Calif.: Ardis, 1973), (Bakhtin's italics).

23. For those who have access to only Johnson's variorum edition of the poems, note that he records "weight" as an alternative to "Heft" in line 3, and "anything" for "Any" in line 9.

24. L#656, to Louse Norcross, early September 1880, *Letters of Emily Dickinson*, 3:670.

25. Vincent Crapanzano, *Hermes' Dilemma and Hamlet's Desire: On the Epistemology of Interpretation* (Cambridge: Harvard University Press, 1992), 214. I am grateful to my colleague Jeremy Hawthorn for bringing this book to my attention.

26. *Scribner's Monthly* appeared for the first time on November 1870: Holland's remarks to Elizabeth Fowler Ford are quoted in Richard B. Sewall, *The Life of Emily Dickinson* (New York: Fararr, Straus and Giroux, 1974), 2:377.

27. Bakhtin, "Discourse in the Novel," 270.

28. Paul Crumbley, *Inflections of the Pen: Dash and Voice in Emily Dickinson* (Lexington: University Press of Kentucky, 1996), 7.

29. Dobson, *Dickinson and the Strategies of Reticence*, 79.

30. L#209, to Kate Anthon, late 1859?, *Letters of Emily Dickinson*, 2:356. The same letter includes a typically Dickinson joke about "Famine" at a time when

the effects of the Great Hunger in Ireland (during the 1840s) were still manifest-
ing themselves in the enforced immigration of hundreds of thousands of Irish to
America.

31. Michel Foucault, *Madness and Civilization: A History of Insanity in the Age of
Reason,* trans. Richard Howard (New York: Pantheon Books, 1965).

32. Richard Ohmann uses this phrase, which I have chosen for the subtitle of
this book and have included in the book's epigraph. It should be pointed out that
Ohmann uses this term in a discussion of John Updike's literary style. See *Politics
or Letters* (Middletown, Conn.: Wesleyan University Press, 1987), 101.

33. Plato, *Phaedrus and Letters VII and VIII,* trans. Walter Hamilton (London:
Penguin Books, 1973), 46.

34. James Boswell, *The Life of Samuel Johnson LL.D* (1791; reprint, London:
Hutchinson and Co., 1906), 12.

35. Ralph Waldo Emerson, "The Poet" (1841), in *Selected Essays,* ed. Larzer
Ziff (Harmondsworth, England: Penguin, 1982), 275.

36. HL, Harvard University, bMs. Am 1118.95 (box 8) My thanks to Al
Habegger for supplying the source for this quotation.

37. L#26, to Thomas Wentworth Higginson, 25 April 1862, *Letters of Emily
Dickinson,* 1:261–62.

38. Karl Marx, and Friedrich Engels, *The Communist Manifesto* (1848), quoted
in Terry Eagleton, *William Shakespeare* (Oxford: Basil Blackwell, 1986), 5.

39. Eagleton, *William Shakespeare* 13.

40. P#191A (J#300), " 'Morning' – means 'Milking' – to the Farmer" is a good
example of this. The poem is essentially a catalogue of competing definitions and
would therefore appear dialogic. But these are arranged in a reverse order of
importance, with the preferred definition placed last. It is therefore possible to
argue that the poet allows other definitions only to negate them, or to reveal
how limited they are. I prefer to chart a middle ground: there is a hierarchy of
preferences, which is as social as it is personal, but the other inclusions show
how conscious Dickinson was at all times of others views. Her poem admits the
legitimacy of those views, even as she strives to show that each is only partial. In
my own reading, Dickinson privileges the *poetic* gathering of all perspectives (and
not necessarily the one communicated by the last line), the ability to imagine
different alternatives and to grant them a degree of legitimacy.

CHAPTER NINE   *Passages of Meaning*

1. The reader is directed to Martha Nell Smith, *Rowing in Eden: Rereading
Emily Dickinson* (Austin: University of Texas Press, 1992), 180–97.

2. Ellen Louise Hart and Martha Nell Smith, "Editing Emily Dickinson: A
Report to the Society," *Emily Dickinson International Society Bulletin* 6, no. 1
(May/June 1994): 9.

3. There are a number of biographical readings of the poem, including an
excellent one in Martha Nell Smith, *Rowing in Eden,* which traces the history of

the poems's genesis in the context of the writer's relationship to Susan Dickinson. I refer to this at various stages in this chapter.

4. Johnson transcribes the poem differently, by silently "correcting" Dickinson's line arrangements. Later I will discuss whether his changes were appropriate.

5. Ralph W. Franklin, *The Poems of Emily Dickinson* (Cambridge: Harvard University Press, Belknap Press, 1998), 1:163.

6. Ibid., 160.

7. Johnson has different transcriptions of these last three poems, as well as a potted history of their reception by T. W. Higginson and, especially, by Susan Dickinson. See Thomas H. Johnson, ed., *The Poems of Emily Dickinson: Including Variant Reading Critically Compared with All Known Manuscripts* (Cambridge: Harvard University Press, Belknap Press, 1955), 1:151–55.

8. See the *Atlas of Hampshire, Mass, from Actual Surveys by and under the Direction of F. W. Beers* (New York: F. W. Beers, 1873), 48–49.

9. Celia Barbour, and Reed Davis, "Collecting Alabaster," *Martha Stewart Living*, no. 50 (June 1997): 56–62. I am grateful to Jessica Teters, assistant librarian, Special Collections, Jones Library, Amherst, for bringing this article to my attention.

10. For a more detailed discussion of these issues, see David D. Hall, "The Gravestone Image as a Puritan Cultural Code," in *Puritan Gravestone Art* (Dublin, N.H.: Boston University and The Dublin Seminar for New England Folklife, 1976), 23–32.

11. Thomas A. Zaniello, "Chips from Hawthorne's Workshop: The Icon and Cultural Studies," in *Puritan Gravestone Art*, 70.

12. Franklin, *The Poems of Emily Dickinson* 3:1270.

13. Allan I. Ludwig, "Eros and Agape: Classical and Early Christian Survivals in New England Stonecarving," *Puritan Gravestone Art*, 53.

14. Barton Levi St. Armand points out another possible source, namely "Christ's words to the ruler of the synagogue whose daughter had suddenly died: 'Weep not, she is not dead, but sleepeth' (Luke 8.52)." In *Emily Dickinson and Her Culture: The Soul's Society* (Cambridge: Cambridge University Press, 1984), 48.

15. Ibid., 48.

16. The rhyme in the poem is deliberately sporadic: as a number of scholars have pointed out, Dickinson plays off against the rigid patterns of English hymnology in general and Isaac Watts in particular. In P#124, the failure to establish a strict regime of meter and rhyme represents a formal disruption in keeping with the poem's contents. For a fairly recent discussion of these issues, see James Olney, *The Language(s) of Poetry: Walt Whitman, Emily Dickinson, Gerard Manley Hopkins* (Athens: University of Georgia Press, 1993), 27–36. Discordant music is also a feature of the carnival, of course, and it stands against the harmony of the orthodox churches. See Mikhail Bakhtin, *Rabelais and His World*, trans. Helen Iswolsky (Bloomington: Indiana University Press, 1984).

17. Indeed, any possibility of escaping upward is blocked: although satin is fragile and easy to break through, the stone roof represents an impassable bar-

rier. The sequence of these lines, where satin precedes stone, reproduces the illusions of flight and its impossibility.

18. Bakhtin, *Rabelais and His World*, 90.

19. Ibid., 141.

20. If it is accepted that the bee and birds represent the kind of bodily abandonment and general merriment often associated with the carnivaleque, then a case can be made for the breeze as representative of the mock king who often presides over these ceremonies: the castle is neither real not permanent, and the breeze too is refreshing but transient. Moreover, the carnival is associated with paganism, and the breeze, bee, and bird travesty the Christian vision of an afterlife in Heaven: they suggest the elemental forces of nature which were once connected with pagan worship. For more on the spirit of carnival, see ibid.

21. Charles Anderson identifies a related contest when he argues that "the supposed conflict between religion and science, which shook the Christian world 'at mid-century, dramatized the very real conflict between man's belief in immortality and his doubt of it." (*Emily Dickinson's Poetry: Stairway to Surprise* [New York: Holt, Rinehart and Winston, 1960], 269–70).

22. See Jane Martineau and Charles Hope eds., *The Genius of Venice, 1500–1600* (New York: Abrams, 1983), 15.

23. Frederic C. Lane, *Venice: A Maritime Republic* (Baltimore: Johns Hopkins University Press, 1973), 377.

24. Bakhtin, *Rabelais and His World*, 38.

25. Jane Donahue Eberwein, *Dickinson: Strategies of Limitation* (Amherst: University of Massachusetts Press, 1985), 132.

26. Margaret Fuller Ossoli, *At Home and Abroad, or Things and Thoughts in America and Europe*, 2d ed. (Boston: Crosby, Nichols and Company, 1856), 233.

27. Another possibility is that the poem is part of a more general wave of anti-Catholic sentiment in nineteenth-century America: this is not at all clear in the first version, but the reference in the second to the "disc of Snow" suggests the communion wafer Catholics believe to be the body of Christ. Reading the first version again with this in mind, the breeze, birds, and bee travesty specifically the doctrine of the Holy Trinity (Father, Son, and Holy Ghost), and their general gaiety mocks the supposed solemnity of the Mass, where the sacrament of Holy Communion is celebrated.

28. Anderson also points out that "the snow that obliterates the life of the year in one poem is described as 'Alabaster Wool,' and when her mother died Dickinson used the image of a snowdrift for eternity: 'She slipped from our fingers like a flake gathered by the wind, and is now part of the drift called 'the infinite'" (*Stairway of Surprise*, 272).

29. L#678, to Elizabeth Holland, early December 1880, *Letters of Emily Dickinson*, 3:683.

30. L#238 to Susan Gilbert Dickinson, summer 1861, ibid., 2:380.

31. *Poems of Emily Dickinson*, 1:152–53. Sewall has the same excerpt in *The Life of Emily Dickinson* (New York: Farrar, Straus and Giroux, 1974), 1:201.

32. Smith, *Rowing in Eden,* 191.

33. The objects probably derive from the 1860s. Of course, since Susan did not leave America until after Austin's death, it may be that they were purchased after Emily herself had died. But Emily would have been familiar with domestic fashion, if only vicariously through Susan, who was extremely knowledgeable about interior decoration.

34. Brita Lindberg-Seyersted, *The Voice of the Poet: Aspects of Style in the Poetry of Emily Dickinson* (Cambridge: Harvard University Press, 1968), 84.

35. William Empson, *Seven Types of Ambiguity* (Harmondsworth, England: Penguin Books, 1965), 225.

36. The poem was enclosed in Dickinson's first letter to Thomas Wentworth Higginson, L#260, 15 April 1862, *Letters of Emily Dickinson,* 2:403; GC: Ms. Am. 1093 (1).

37. See R. W. Franklin, *The Manuscript Books of Emily Dickinson* (Cambridge: Harvard University Press, Belknap Press, 1981), 1:92.

38. For a full overview of the printed versions, see Franklin, *Poems of Emily Dickinson,* 1:163, and Johnson, *Poems of Emily Dickinson,* 1:151–52.

39. The traditional view of the nonpublication is that it constitutes both a rejection of, and sometimes by, the patriarchal institution of print and an attempt at escaping the commercialization and regularization of literature presented typographically. This would suggest a much more radical political gesture than I am persuaded was the case, though I do not rule it out. Perhaps Dickinson, for reasons of her own, was trying to protect her reputation (or that of her family) as well: manuscript transmission would have been safer than print for a poet who, as Martha Nell Smith points out, explored aspects of sexuality and textuality to their fullest.

40. Daniel Lombardo, *Images of America: Amherst and Hadley, Massachusetts* (Dover, N.H.: Arcadia Press, 1997), 47.

41. Daniel E. Sutherland, *The Expansion of Everyday Life, 1860–1876* (New York: Harper and Row, 1989), 176.

42. The *Business and General Directory of Amherst* (Amherst: Storrs and McCloud, 1869), was the first to be printed as a book, and it lists the blacksmiths on p. 45. (An earlier directory had appeared in 1859, but was incomplete.)

43. Paul Crumbley, *Inflections of the Pen: Dash and Voice in Emily Dickinson* (Lexington: University Press of Kentucky, 1996), 4–9.

44. L#675, to Higginson, November 1880, *Letters of Emily Dickinson,* 3:681.

45. Crumbley, *Inflections of the Pen,* 8.

46. Karl Marx, *Capital* (London: Lawrence and Wishart, 1967), 1:182, quoted in Jeremy Hawthorn in *Identity and Relationship* (London: Lawrence and Wishart, 1973), 64.

47. An interesting gloss on this discussion is provided by Millicent Todd Bingham, when she writes of Lavinia's change of attitude to Millicent's mother, Mabel Loomis Todd. "To put it differently: there was no question that Emily was coming into her own. But to her sister's mind the intermediary in the process was

a menial. So long as her activities remained impersonal, all was well" (*Ancestors' Brocades: The Literary Debut of Emily Dickinson and the Editing and Publication of Her Letters and Poems* [New York: Harper Brothers, 1945]), 213.

48. This argument is pursued by Martha Lindblom O'Keefe in her privately published *This Edifice: Studies in the Structure of the Fascicles of the Poetry of Emily Dickinson* (1986).

49. Eberwein, *Dickinson: Strategies of Limitation*, 34.

50. "Emblems of the Resurrection" is reproduced in Sewall, *Life of Emily Dickinson*, 2:348.

51. The figures are given in Wai-Chee Dimock, *Empire for Liberty: Melville and the Poetics of Individualism* (Princeton: Princeton University Press, 1989), 11.

52. Laurence Urdand, ed., *The Timetables of American History* (New York: Simon and Schuster, 1996), 237.

53. Joanne Dobson, *Dickinson and the Strategies of Reticence: The Woman Writer in Nineteenth-Century America* (Bloomington: Indiana University Press, 1989), 78–98. (Dobson quotes the same letter on 85).

54. L#589, to Elizabeth Holland, early 1879, *Letters of Emily Dickinson*, 2:633.

55. I mean by this the scaffold used for hanging; the singular and plural form of the noun occurs more than three times, of course, but refers to other types of scaffolding.

56. The United Society of Believers in Christ's Second Appearing in Hancock Village "was the third of nineteen Shaker communities established between 1778 and 1836 in New England, New York, Kentucky, Ohio and Indiana. At its peak in the 1830s, 300 Shakers lived at Hancock in six groups called Families, all within a few miles of the central Church family, where the meetinghouse was located." Although utopian communities came and went, the Shakers (so-called because of the trembling and shaking which overcame them when they were affected by the Spirit) existed for over two hundred years: there is still one community today. See the brochure, "A Walking Tour of Hancock Shaker Village" (Pittsfield, Mass.: Quality Printing, 1997). For more on the Northampton Association, see Christopher Clark, *The Communitarian Moment: The Radical Challenge of the Northampton Association* (Ithaca: Cornell University Press, 1985).

57. "As she passed on in life, her sensitive nature shrank from much personal contact with the world, and more and more turned to her large wealth of individual resources for companionship" (Susan Gilbert Dickinson, "Miss Emily Dickinson of Amherst," *Springfield Daily Republican* [Tuesday, 18 May 1886]). Quoted by Smith in *Rowing in Eden*, 209.

58. Designing poetry for a very few readers who were educated, familiar with the nuances of literary form, and committed to the importance of culture might have been an elitist gesture in the nineteenth century, but looks increasingly like a liberal, and sometimes even radical, one in the twentieth.

INDEX TO DICKINSON'S POEMS

All references are to R. W. Franklin, *The Poems of Emily Dickinson*, Variorum Edition (Cambridge, Mass.: The Belknap Press of Harvard University Press, 1998). The poem number (P#) is followed by the variant chosen (A), and by the page number in the text.

GENERAL INDEX

Holland, Elizabeth, 72, 147, 165, 268, 277, 296
Holland, Joseph, 246–47
Home. *See* Architecture, nineteenth-century theories of; Dickinson, Emily, poetry of; Dickinson Homestead; Domesticity, ideology of; Domestic technology; Property, issues of
Horticulture, 146; class aspects of, 9–10, 112–15, 121
Howe, Susan, 201, 216–17

Ideology. *See* Dickinson, Emily, poetry of: class aspects of
Industrial technology, 32–36, 104
Irish, 27, 35, 59–62, 91, 97, 103, 161–63, 296

Jackson, Helen Hunt, 133, 249; *Ramona*, 109
James, Henry, 99–100, 103; *Washington Square*, 238
Jarrell, Randall, 45
Jesus, 22, 39–40, 81, 94–98, 123, 189–91, 282. *See also* Christianity
Johnson, Thomas, as editor, 93, 178–79, 194–96, 207, 213, 284–85
Jones Library, Amherst, 247, 295
Joshua, 6

Keats, John, 77–78, 88–89, 144, 159, 192, 253–54

Lane, Frederick, 274
Language, social aspects of, 4, 11–14, 228–57
Larkin, Philip, 180
Leighton, Ann, 153
Leighton, Guy, 120
Levertov, Denise, 232
Levine, Lawrence W., 89, 99–100
Levinson, Marjorie, 144
Lincoln, Almira, 124
Literature, nineteenth-century American political theories of, 89–91, 114, 122–23, 162
Liu, Alan, 118
Lombardo, Daniel, 16, 34, 41; *Images of America: Amherst and Hadley*, 286–87

Longsworth, Polly, 34, 69
Lotman, Yuri, 191
Luke, 81
Lyric poems, social function of, 170–71

McGann, Jerome, 201–2, 205, 224–25
McNeil, Helen, 53
Madness: asylums for, 62; as rhetorical position, 251–56
Maher, Margaret, 171
Mann, Horace, 239
Mannheim, Karl, 42, 109
Manuscript features: generic boundaries in, 207–12; implications behind anthologies (fascicles), 178–98; letter-shapes, 216–17; lineation, 212–16; word breaks in, 203–6
Marotti, Arthur, 170
Martin, Wendy, 163
Marvell, Andrew, 120
Marx, Karl, 290; *A Contribution to the Critique of Political Economy*, 28; *On Literature and Art*, 19–20
Marxism, 82, 101
Matthew, 81, 270
Matthews, Dick, 133
Melville, Herman, 161
Michaels, Walter Benn, 51
Miller, Cristanne, 100
Milton, John, "How Soon Hath Time" (Sonnet VII), 42, 151
M'Mahon, Bernard, *The American Gardener*, 153
"Molly Maguires," 296
Morson, Gary, 230, 236–37
Mount Vernon, 4
Mudge, Jean McClure, 53, 70
Murray, Aífe, 171

Nason, Rev. Elias, *Gazetteer of the State of Massachusetts*, 28
Native Americans, 296
New Criticism, 1, 190–91
New London, 20
New York, 34
Nichols, Thomas, 239
Norcross, Betsy Fay, 5
Norcross, Louise and Frances, 165, 228